The 60s Communes

Messianic Communities' bus at Bellows Falls, Vermont.
Photograph by Timothy Miller.

TIMOTHY MILLER

The 60s Communes

Hippies and Beyond

Syracuse University Press

The paper used in this publication meets the minimum requirements of American National Standard for Information Sciences—Permanence of Paper for Printed Library Materials, ANSI Z39.48-1984. ∞

LIBRARY OF CONGRESS CATALOGING-IN-PUBLICATION DATA
Miller, Timothy, 1944–
    The 60s communes : hippies and beyond / Timothy Miller.
        p.   cm.
    Includes bibliographical references and index.
    ISBN 0-8156-2811-0 (cloth : alk. paper)   ISBN 0-8156-0601-x (pbk.: alk. paper)
    1. Communal living—United States.   2. United States—Social conditions—
1960–1980.   I. Title.   II. Title: Sixties communes.   III. Title: Hippies and
beyond.
HQ971.M55   1999
307.77'4'0973—dc21   99-37768

Manufactured in the United States of America

For Michael, Gretchen, and Jeffrey

TIMOTHY MILLER is professor of religious studies at the University of Kansas. Among his previous publications is *The Quest for Utopia in Twentieth-Century America: 1900–1960*, the first of three volumes on communal life to be published by Syracuse University Press.

Contents

Acknowledgments

No social phenomenon as vast, open-ended, and geographically, culturally, and ideologically diverse as the 1960s-era communal tide can be adequately represented in any single volume. This book simply seeks to
provide an overview of the great siege of commune-building within a
loosely chronological and typological framework. If nothing else, the
book in its notes and bibliography will point toward useful resources for
those who would like to know more about the topic. Only the practical
realities of the world of writing and publishing kept this volume from being a thousand pages long.

The efforts of hundreds of individuals supported the 60s Communes
Project and the writing of this book, and I thank all of them most sincerely for their generous assistance. Heading the list are the former (sometimes ongoing) communitarians themselves, who provided time and
hospitality—and sometimes food and lodging as well—for interviews
about their communal experiences. Ramón Sender, the first resident at
Morning Star Ranch, deserves special credit among the interviewees for
helping me locate dozens of communal veterans (mainly in California) as
well as for extensive and generous hospitality. Those who conducted the
interviews did a heroic job; in particular, Deborah Altus, in her year of
travel for interviewing, did far more work than the job required and produced an enormous pile of tape recordings and documents with great
good energy. Other interviewers included several of my students at the
University of Kansas: Shirley Andrews, Amy Beecher Mirecki, Angela
Dilling, Lisa Doffing, Bill Jensen, Blake Jones, Aaron Ketchell, Marilyn
Klaus, Kenn Peters, Courtney Shanks, Lesley Speer, Rosalie Vaught, and
Teresa Young. Two students at Dartmouth College, Carlyn Lettan and
Erin Gaffney, also provided good field support through class projects
there. Eva Garcia and Paula Lopez-Cano contributed helpful assistance
before the project formally got under way. Benjamin Zablocki and Allen
Butcher provided helpful reflections and information during the process
as well.

Kristen Thorsen and Jack Oruch both provided useful backfiles of *Communities* magazine, the most important single periodical for primary materials in 1960s-era communal studies. Daryl Ann Dutton helped me with contacts and materials in southern California, and Lyman Tower Sargent provided a steady stream of literary references that proved most useful. Geoph Kozeny's communal database provided timely information repeatedly. J. Gordon Melton first pointed me down this line of inquiry and provided essential resources at several critical junctures. Robert Thurman helped me track down scarce material about Millbrook.

The transcription of over five hundred tapes is still in process, and many persons, most of them students at the University of Kansas, have put a good deal of welcome effort into that phase of the project. Gina Walker of the Center for Communal Studies Archives at the University of Southern Indiana has long assisted me in the quest for information, and also helped via her student staff in transcribing interviews.

The 60s Communes Project was the research backbone for this book, and I thank the National Endowment for the Humanities for its generous support of the project. I also thank Janet Crow, William Andrews, Elizabeth Granberg, Susan Pauls, and the many others at the University of Kansas (especially at the Hall Center for the Humanities, which provided a fellowship that gave me writing time and other resources) who helped initiate and operate the grant project for more than two years. Funding from the General Research Fund at the University and a sabbatical leave supported the writing of the book and are gratefully acknowledged.

A very different version of parts of chapter one (and a small bit of chapter two) were published as an article in the fall 1992 issue of *American Studies,* and part of the short item in chapter six on the Gesundheit Institute was published in the *Kaw Valley Independent* (Lawrence, Kansas) in late 1998. In winter 1992 *Syzygy: Journal of Alternative Religion and Culture* published an excerpt from what I had intended to be a book-length history of Drop City, and although the account that appears here is a different one, I am grateful to *Syzygy* for publishing my first work on the subject and helping to clarify my thinking for the account that appears here. I also thank Community Publications Cooperative and Community Service, Inc., for permission to use passages from Elaine Sundancer's *Celery Wine,* Gordon Yaswen for permission to quote extensively from his excellent memoir "Sunrise Hill Community: Post Mortem,"[1] and HarperCollins for permission to use Allen Ginsberg's poem about the Merry Pranksters at La Honda.

Gene and Jo Ann Bernofsky provided me with repeated recollections and with access to their files of Drop City art. The Bernofskys' commitment to living their values has been an ongoing inspiration. I also thank Walt Odets, who provided the use of a photograph from his extensive collection.

My colleagues in the Department of Religious Studies of the University of Kansas provided essential time and resources for my work, and my many congenial colleagues in the Communal Studies Association were helpful and enthusiastic throughout. The University of Kansas librarians provided, as usual, vitally useful help. Other libraries, including that at Big Sur, California, provided good assistance. Katherine Short, a local historian at Big Sur, helped me sort out a few obscure details. Tamara, Jesse, and Abraham have tolerated much more commune-visiting and interviewing than they ever would have chosen, and I greatly appreciate their support and patience.

The 60s Communes Project will be collecting materials of all kinds for its archives for the foreseeable future. Please feel free to contact me at the Department of Religious Studies, University of Kansas, Lawrence, KS 66045; tkansas@ukans.edu.

Introduction

Communal societies have long been an American cultural fixture, with anywhere from dozens to hundreds of them operating at any given moment since the pioneers of Plockhoy's Commonwealth and the Labadists of Bohemia Manor took to the common life in the seventeenth century.[1] Nothing in the American communal past, however, would have led any judicious observer to predict the incredible communal explosion that began during the 1960s. In a period of just a few years communal fever gripped the alienated youth of the United States—indeed, of the developed world—and thousands upon thousands of new communities were established throughout the land. The size and diversity of the new communitarianism made accurate counting of communes and of their members impossible, but the overall significance of the 1960s era (here defined as 1960 to 1975, inclusive) as a watershed in American communal history is undeniable.

Those who have seen volume one of this history will find the present tome distinctly different in approach and in content from its predecessor. American communes active between 1900 and 1960 were few enough in number to be enumerated individually, and most of those that had been very visible are discussed (at least in brief) in that previous volume. With the 1960s era, however, the subject mushrooms. We are no longer dealing with communes numbering in the low hundreds but rather with thousands—probably tens of thousands—of them, and an incredibly diverse lot at that. The best known (and certainly the subjects of the most media coverage) were the hippie communes, the countercultural encampments that thumbed their collective noses at conventional American society and were regarded both with fascination and with loathing by members of the very Establishment that they rejected. Numerically, however, the hippies probably constituted a minority presence on the 1960s communal scene, as thousands of other communes sprang up as well. Rounding out the picture were new communes founded by spiritual seekers of all sorts—Jesus freaks and other less flamboyant Christians as well as followers of dozens of Asian religious teachers—and by political radicals, artists, group-marriage pioneers, self-helpers, what today would be called yuppies, and a host of others. Given the size and complexity of it all, this volume cheerfully eschews any claim of comprehensiveness. Instead, it attempts to convey not every detail of the 1960s-era communal eruption but rather its broad outlines and prominent features, through a sampling of the contours of life and thought in some representative communes.

The Historian's Task

A generation has elapsed since the communes of the 1960s era burst onto the American scene. The topic that once attracted a veritable army of scholars and popular-media reporters now surfaces only in an occasional Sunday supplement where-are-they-now? sort of piece. At the same time, those who were involved in the great American 1960s-era communal experiment, whether still living communally or not, are more accessible than they used to be now that they are neither constantly besieged by the curious nor generally regarded as freakish social aberrations. Their memories contain prime historical data invaluable to anyone who seeks to preserve and to interpret the history of the great communal tidal wave. This book draws heavily upon those memories.

The majority of the 1960s-era communes were short-lived, but their impact on American life has been solid and ongoing as their members have gone on to other life work. As Paul and Percival Goodman once argued, communes have long had social influence beyond their own memberships and typically brief lifespans. The Goodmans were writing of an earlier communal generation, but their observations apply to the 1960s era as well:

Perhaps the very transitoriness of such intensely motivated intentional communities is part of their perfection. Disintegrating, they irradiate society with people who have been profoundly touched by the excitement of community life, who do not forget the advantages but try to realize them in new ways. People trained at defunct Black Mountain, North Carolina, now make a remarkable little village of craftsmen in Haverstraw, N. Y. (that houses some famous names in contemporary art). Perhaps these communities are like those "little magazines" and "little theaters" that do not outlive their first few performances, yet from them comes all the vitality of the next generation of everybody's literature.[2]

THE 60S COMMUNES PROJECT

As I made my first forays into the history of the 1960s-era communes, it became clear that an immense body of lore, facts, and anecdotes had not yet been made available to the public. In the late 1980s I began to track down some of the more prominent figures from the communes to see what I could learn. Some were easy to find; Stephen Gaskin, for example, still lives at the Farm community in Tennessee, which he and a caravan of fellow seekers founded in 1971. Others took a bit more sleuthing to locate, but over time it became clear that most of the 1960s-era communal veterans were not only alive and locatable but eager to see the history of their communes preserved.

In the early 1990s I began to seek funding for a project—the 60s Communes Project—that would consolidate the scattered historical fragments that existed in such abundance. Eventually the National Endowment for the Humanities agreed to support the project, and with basic funding in place my University of Kansas colleague Deborah Altus, a seasoned communal researcher, committed a year of her time to collecting information. Traveling to most of the fifty states, she interviewed well over three hundred persons who had lived in 1960s-era communes and photocopied the documents that those persons pulled out from the old boxes in their attics. I did some interviewing as well, as did several of my students at the University of Kansas and several volunteers elsewhere; by the late 1990s, we had completed about five hundred interviews and had collected several boxes of documents—correspondence, communal manifestoes, newspaper clippings, books and articles, videos and films, posters, constitutions and bylaws, and a wide variety of related miscellany. We were overwhelmed by the generosity of those who had lived the communal life, and they were gratified that we thought their experiences worthy of permanent preservation. The information that they supplied has been of central importance to this study, but it goes far beyond what can be used in a single book of this scope and will constitute a permanent archive of the 1960s-era communal experience, to be perused by historians and other writers for decades to come.

OTHER SOURCES OF INFORMATION

Many publications resulted from scholarly and media attention to the communes back when they were in the daily news, and although these accounts were terribly uneven in quality, they provide important raw material for historians. Both scholars and reporters embodied in their work a great range of points of view, from favorable to severely hostile, with a great many somewhere in the bemused middle ("I can't quite believe all this!"). A good many of these works were sensationalistic, often focusing breathlessly on the casual nudity that frequently prevailed at the countercultural communes or on the use of psychedelics and other controlled substances that was so popular among communal and noncommunal hippies alike.

However, certain of the publications by contemporary observers have had lasting value. Several of the books written at the time took the form of communal travelogues, and collectively they have preserved a slice of communal life and vitality that otherwise would not have endured. Of the many in that genre, two were especially thoughtful and are still useful today: Robert Houriet's *Getting Back Together* and Richard Fairfield's *Communes USA: A Personal Tour.* I have drawn on both works, as well as on the more recent memories of both authors, in this volume. (See the Selected Bibliography for full citations for the works mentioned here.)

Most of the early academic studies of the 1960s communes focused on specific topics such as childrearing or health issues, but a few had a breadth of interest that has allowed them to stand as useful introductions to the subject matter. The foremost work in that category is Hugh Gardner's *The Children of Prosperity,* a testing of Rosabeth Moss Kanter's theories about communal commitment mechanisms that also contains a great deal of perceptive descriptive material gathered through visits to active communities. Another useful work in that vein is Keith Melville's *Communes in the Counter Culture.* The scholarly works as a whole, however, tend to focus on relatively few of the thousands of communes that sprang up; as Benjamin Zablocki has observed, most of this scholarship was done at only twenty or so locations, the "old standby" communes that welcomed scholars. Because most social scientific scholarship uses pseudonyms, the literature *seems* to deal with a plethora of communitarian experiments—but really doesn't.[3]

A third type of on-site survey work was that of participant observers, persons with communal leanings of their own who wrote about the subject they lived and breathed. A fine example of that kind of publication is Judson Jerome's *Families of Eden,* an intriguing blend of objective observation and personal passion. Another book with similar passion in its veins is Lucy Horton's *Country Commune Cooking,* a broader work than its title implies.

Beyond the many surveys of 1960s-era communes are works on specific communes, some written by insiders, some by outside reporters or scholars. The Twin Oaks community in Virginia, for example, has been the subject of both kinds of works, including founder Kat Kinkade's *A Walden Two Experiment* and *Is It Utopia Yet?* as well as participant-observer Ingrid Komar's *Living the Dream.* The Farm community in Tennessee has published many of its founder-teacher Stephen Gaskin's works including the valuable early survey of Farm life *Hey Beatnik!* and several other titles.[4] Wavy Gravy's *The Hog Farm and Friends* remains a valuable introduction to that long-lived commune, which after three decades continues to embody the soul of hip. The similarly long-lived Renaissance Community in Massachusetts has been the subject of a full-length scholarly study, Karol Borowski's *Attempting an Alternative Society.*

Many of the 1960s communards were well educated, and they produced a variety of creative works (not necessarily about their own communities) that help us to understand the period from which they emerged. The epicenter of such writing was Packer Corner Farm in Guilford, Vermont, better known to the world as Total Loss Farm, whose remarkable assemblage of writers evoked the communal imagination of their time in lyrical prose and poetry. Raymond Mungo's *Total Loss Farm* was the most widely circulated of their creations, but several other works—including the anthology *Home Comfort,* to which most of the members contributed—are important as well. Probably the most widely distributed of all such works was Alicia Bay Laurel's *Living on the Earth,* a surprise bestseller that perfectly captured the whimsical communal spirit of Wheeler's Ranch in California, where the author lived before she joined the literati at Packer Corner. These books and many more like them depict the mind and mentality of the 1960s communes more clearly than does any academic study.

The participants in the alternative culture of the era had their own independent publishing venue, the underground press that was manifested in hundreds of independent local newspapers in the late 1960s. Those papers tracked the coming of the communes with great interest, and some of them—including the *San Francisco Oracle* and the *East Village Other*—published useful accounts of innovative communes from coast to coast. Those accounts have been drawn on here repeatedly.

Many scholarly works on specific communal topics have been published, mainly in the 1970s, and provide useful information for the historian. As examples, a study of communal childrearing by Bennett Berger and his associates produced several reports and articles, and David Smith (the founder of the Haight-Ashbury Free Medical Clinic) headed up several studies of communal health and disease.[5] Perhaps most prominently, Rosabeth Moss Kanter's *Commitment and Community*—an analysis of commitment mechanisms in both historical and 1960s-era communes—has become (despite some controversy about Kanter's definition of success and failure) a standard work in communal studies.

Finally, the general popular press watched the development of the communes with breathless interest and published hundreds of accounts of the unexpected development of this new way of living. Locating all of that material (or even a representative sample of it) is far from easy, but where they can be recovered such accounts provide first-hand—if often jaundiced—insight into communal life.

TOWARD A COMMUNAL CENSUS

How many communes existed during the 1960s era? Thousands, probably tens of thousands. How many people lived in them, at least briefly? Probably hundreds of thousands, conceivably a million. Could you please be more precise? No, I can't.

The plain fact is that no one has a better idea than that of just how widespread communal living was in those days. Of the many observers who visited and tried to track communal America, dozens made estimates of the size of the communal outpouring, but in all but a few cases those estimates were simply wild guesses, utterly without foundation, or quotations of the wild guesses of others. And even the judicious estimates could be far off the mark.

The most frequent guesses as to the number of communes were in the low thousands. An article in the *New York Times* in late 1970 threw out the figure of nearly 2,000 communes in America, and that number was widely quoted as authoritative—often modified, without justification, to "*more than 2,000.*" But the article offers not a hint of how the number was arrived at, and it appears to have been simply a guess. Benjamin Zablocki, writing at about the same time, offered another widely-cited figure of about 1,000 rural communes and twice that many urban ones, but again the basis of the estimate (if any) was not provided. Herbert A. Otto cited only an unnamed "source at the National Institute of Health" as the basis for his count of 3,000 urban communes in 1971. Earlier, in 1969, *Newsweek* had thrown out a smaller guess—10,000 hippies in "more than 500" communes.[6]

Other authors provided estimates of local communal populations much higher than any of those given just above. William J. Speers, a newspaper reporter writing in 1971, calculated that 100 to 200 communes existed in his city of Philadelphia alone. In the same year another observer reported that members of the Christian World Liberation Front, a leading Jesus movement organization, counted over 200 Jesus communes in California alone, a number supported by pins stuck in a wall map. Also in 1971, Mark Perlgut surveyed his immediate neighborhood in Brooklyn and noted "several" communes close by, with at least four on one specific street, leading him to conclude that New York City alone probably had as many as 1,000 communal houses. A scholar writing in the mid-1970s found estimates of 200 to 800 communes in Berkeley and 200 in Vermont in 1972.[7] And so the numbers go. Even if some of these estimates are not solidly founded, they generally would point toward a count of American communes well up in the thousands.

The scholars who have examined the matter in a bit more depth tend to go toward larger numbers as well. Hugh Gardner, writing in 1978, figured on the basis of a good deal of travel and research that 5,000 to 10,000 communes could be found in rural America and more in the cities. Although he conceded that one's definition of "commune" would greatly affect any estimate, he nevertheless concluded that it was likely that the great 1960s-era wave of communes had involved over a million participants at one point or another. Patrick Conover, also a judicious scholar whose guess was rooted in a good deal of communal research, in 1975 came up with numbers in Gardner's ballpark: 50,000 communes, with 750,000 members.[8]

The most careful of all the commune-counters was Judson Jerome, who took the earlier estimates, evaluated them, and then added several sensible interpolations of his own. Noting that over 2,500 colleges operate in the United States and estimating that an average of ten communes might be presumed to have been operating in the general environs of the typical campus at the height of the commune boom—and then adding in an estimate of some tens of thousands of urban communes, not including "creedal" religious ones—Jerome concluded that perhaps a quarter million persons had lived in noncreedal urban communes. Figuring, plausibly, that creedal communal populations would equal noncreedal numbers, Jerome estimates that half a million urban communards were on the scene. Relying on evidence of rural commune concentrations and populations sifted from extensive travel and visitation, he estimated that the United States probably hosted at least one commune per hundred square miles of countryside—or 30,000 rural communes. Adding his numbers together, Jerome concluded that perhaps three-quarters of a million persons lived in tens of thousands of communes in the early 1970s.[9]

My own (less systematic) conclusion supports Jerome's math. I have identified over 1,000 specific communes, yet interviewees in the 60s Communes Project almost invariably knew of more communes that the interviewers had never heard of. Also, a great many communes were not named and thus do not appear on most lists of specific communes (including my own list at the end of this volume). Thus a conclusion that the communes numbered several thousand, probably some tens of thousands, seems reasonable, and if the common observation that communes typically had a membership of perhaps twenty to fifty persons is correct,[10] a communal population of several hundreds of thousands would be a good guess. Moreover, many of the 1960s-era communes were short-lived, so an inclusive count would be much larger than the number active at any given moment. Similarly, membership turnover was often high, and thus many more persons were involved in communal living than a one-time census would have indicated. In its largest dimensions the wave of communal living that swept the country constituted an enormous social movement.

Communes Examined in This Volume

This volume, in its attempt to capture the overall dimensions and meaning of the 1960s-era communal scene, inevitably deals with different communes at greatly different levels of depth. A few experiments in community that either became unusually well known or were especially vivid examples of what the movement was all about are presented here in some detail. Others are touched on more briefly, still others are only mentioned, and a great many are not mentioned at all.

Some communes received a great deal of publicity at their height, and insofar as they came to represent the larger communal movement in the public mind, it seems sensible to give them relatively substantial treatment here. Others were less famous, but for one reason or another were important shapers of the communes movement and deserve credit for the role they played; on those grounds Drop City, Morning Star Ranch, the Farm, and several other communes will get more attention here than other communes. On the other hand, some big and influential communal groups that would logically deserve a fair amount of space in this volume are not dealt with in depth here simply because not much information about them seems to have survived. The Morehouse communes in the San Francisco Bay area and elsewhere, for example, were said to have numbered in the dozens and their residents well up in the hundreds, but little information about them surfaces in any of our standard sources. We could not locate a single former Morehouse member to interview for the 60s Communes Project. In other cases information may be abundant but of dubious reliability; some of the coverage of communes in the underground press was far from objective, and some visiting reporters and scholars conveyed distorted pictures of what they were observing (indeed, in some cases they were deliberately hoodwinked).

More than a few communes actively kept the outside world at bay. A Boston-based commune frequently (but unofficially) called the Lyman Family after its founder Mel Lyman received an intensely negative burst of publicity in a two-part feature story in *Rolling Stone* in 1971 and 1972 and subsequently shunned most outside contact, remaining little known ever since despite its ongoing successful existence.[11] Another long-lived commune, the Finders of Washington, D.C., seems to delight in not giving out information (or at least accurate information) about itself and is similarly veiled in mystery—this despite one former member's characterization of it as having "absolutely crazy people living there, and also these wonderfully brilliant people, this wonderful mix of souls."[12] I chose not to expend a great deal of energy plowing difficult ground when so much material on other communes was available for the asking.

Definitions

Neither scholars of communal societies nor members of them have achieved any kind of consensus on exactly how the term "communal" should be defined—on which groups qualify for that label and which do not. It is generally agreed that residentially-based groups whose members pool most or all of their assets and income and share a belief system or at least a commitment to important core concepts—the Hutterites or the Twin Oaks community, for example—qualify. Beyond that, however, definitions diverge. What is a commune? Which group might more properly be called a "cooperative," or a "collective," or simply an "interest group"? Do owners of units of a condominium qualify as communards? Are fraternity and sorority houses intentional communities? Should the urban crashpads so abundant during the 1960s era really be counted as the communes that they often considered themselves to be? Should an intermittent community qualify—as in the case of the Rainbow Family, in which (for all but a small mobile core group) living together only occurs during one week-long campout a year? Can you be communal without a single permanent location, as in the case of the Hoedad groups that spent most of the year on the road in communal tree-planting projects? Does a commune come into being when an existing town—Canyon, California, for example—is largely taken over by longhairs who institute many cooperative economic and social activities and who consider themselves an intentional community? The communard who called herself Elaine Sundancer spoke to such ambiguities in *Celery Wine,* her autobiographical work on a 1960s-era community in Oregon:

> Each commune is different. There are communes that live on brown rice, and communes that have big gardens, and communes that buy white bread and frozen vegetables at the grocery store. There are communes with no schedule whatsoever (and no clocks); there is at least one commune where the entire day is divided into sections by bells, and each person states, at a planning meeting at 7 A.M. each morning, what work he intends to do that day. There are communes centered around a particular piece of land, like us, or travelling communes like the Hog Farm, or communes centered around a music trip or a political trip, like many of the city communes.
>
> This diversity raises certain questions. A piece of land that's simply thrown open to anyone who wants to live there, or a place where each family lives entirely in its own house but the land is owned jointly: shall we call these places "communes" or not? Communes differ greatly.[13]

No matter what definition one eventually adopts, gray areas will exist around its edges; however, for the sake of clarity, some definition must be used. Volume one of this work sets out a relatively open, multipart definition of intentional community, which will be recapitulated (in abbreviated form) here and will guide this volume as well. To be included in this survey a community must have the following features:

1. *A sense of common purpose and of separation from the dominant society.* Common purpose can be located in an exclusive religious ideology, or it

can simply be a desire to get together with other like-minded folks and to live communally. A rejection of (or at least separation from) the dominant society is involved in that sense of purpose; some dissatisfaction with the way things as a whole are going is fundamental fuel for communitarianism. A living situation in which a common residence is only incidental to the lives of the group's members does not qualify.

2. *Some form and level of self-denial, of voluntary suppression of individual choice in favor of the good of the group.* Communitarianism is predicated upon some degree of downplaying individualism and pursuing the common good.

3. *Geographic proximity.* Members of the community must live "together"—all in one dormitory, or in rooms in one or more common buildings, or in separate houses on commonly owned ground, or even in separately owned houses on clustered small landholdings. Somehow a geographic closeness and a clear spatial focus must be involved.

4. *Personal interaction.* Those living closely together cannot simply be neighbors who commute to jobs and who shut their doors when they return home. Intentional communities always have a good bit of gemeinschaft about them; their members have regular, personal interaction at a level deeper than that of, say, a street in suburbia.

5. *Economic sharing.* The range of options here is enormous. Some groups have total community of goods, but most modern communities have allowed a fair degree of personal property ownership. Thus, the threshold for this study is low; as long as there is *some* mingling of finances (as in sharing expenses) or of property ownership, the standard is considered met.

6. *Real existence.* To a very large degree, the world of utopian communities is a world of dreams—including a good many that never reach any kind of actuality. Many a would-be founder of a commune has written a tract, issued a prospectus, mailed letters to inquirers, published a utopian novel, given a speech, or otherwise proclaimed in good faith that some commune or other is in the works. The communities surveyed here, however, are only those that managed to get off the drawing board and into real existence (at least as far as I could determine), even if their populations were small, their lifespans short, or both.

7. *Critical mass.* Although I hesitate to establish a rigid size threshold here, I am not regarding a family (nuclear or extended), or a single person interested in having others move in, or a pair of roommates as a commu-

nity, even if those involved are magnanimous, community-minded souls. Generally it seems reasonable that an intentional community should include at least five individuals, some of whom must be unrelated by biology or by exclusive intimate relationship. In many cases, of course, the size of a group was not recorded, so some smaller ones may crop up in this work.

A final definitional note: no generally accepted system of terms describing communalism exists. What to one author is "communal" may be to another "cooperative" or "collective." I here use such terms as "commune," "community," "enclave," and "colony" interchangeably.

Diversity and the Necessity of Categorization

The communes of the 1960s era were so diverse that nearly any attempt to generalize about them is preordained to failure. The only generalization that comes close to holding is that the communal population tended to be young, white, and of middle-class background—but of course there were countless exceptions to this rule. The communes were diverse in religious commitments, or lack of them; they were diverse in setting, many being located in cities but some of the most colorful and innovative in rural locales; they were architecturally diverse, with structures ranging from large urban buildings to tepees in the hinterlands.

A great many communes were specifically religious, but they fell along a broad spectrum of tradition and belief. Christian communes have been around for centuries, and many of them were present during the 1960s era. Within that larger genre a specifically new type of commune appeared with the rise of the Jesus movement, an offshoot of hippiedom whose participants affected some hippie accoutrements (such as funky clothing, hip slang, rock music, and a disdain for majoritarian social institutions—including churches) but added to it all a conservative Protestant theology. Indeed, so many of them erupted that the Jesus communes may have been, in terms of sheer numbers of communes and of members, the largest identifiable communal type during the 1960s era. A great many of the religious communes of the time were based in religions other than Christianity, however. A few were Jewish. Many more were based in various Asian religions, a result of the great arousal of interest in such religions that accompanied the easing of immigration laws in 1965 and the consequent arrival in America of many Asian religious teachers. The communal Hare Krishna movement blossomed from about 1967 onward, even as dozens of communal yoga retreats and other Hindu-oriented sites were being established. Several types of Buddhists—Zen and Tibetan among them—built monasteries and other communal centers. Adherents to movements with Islamic or Middle Eastern roots—notably Sufis and Gurdjieff students—built communes as well. Moreover, outside the major traditions were the independent spiritual teachers who built an imaginative array of communities that included the Farm, Love Israel, the One World Family, Padanaram, and dozens of others.

If thousands of communes were religious in orientation, however, thousands more, urban and rural, were secular—at least in the sense of not being entirely devoted to a specific religious path, whatever the religious interests of individual members may have been. Many communes were centered on some political commitment, often leftist politics; others, less stridently perhaps, sought to work for social change in ways that ranged from running homeless shelters to helping persons secure socially responsible employment. Some were explicitly opposed to political activism, often finding meaning in psychedelics rather than in agitation. Several opened their premises to all without restriction, taking in anyone who walked through the gate. Others were rural and remote, often striving for agricultural self-sufficiency and not too friendly to the waves of visitors that inevitably showed up. Dozens, at least, of communes arose with the emergence of public advocacy of rights for homosexuals, creating communal havens on the basis of sexual orientation; radical heterosexuals, on the other hand, also thumbed their noses at prevailing social mores by creating several group marriage communes. Environmentalism was everywhere in the communes movement, and some communities were specifically devoted to becoming environmental demonstration projects, pointing the world toward a future of lessening the human race's adverse ecological impact on the planet. Some communes focused on the arts, as in the case of the Grateful Dead, who lived communally while the band played the music that energized the young and hip. Several communes devoted themselves to medicine, therapy, or personal growth. And some changed focus in midcourse, moving, say, from a specific mission toward pluralism or vice versa; the Church of the Five Star Ranch, for example, was founded south of Taos in 1967 as a center for Christian teaching but after functioning quietly for a time evolved into a secular hippie commune and eventually found itself inundated with so many visitors—and its life so dominated by parties and drugs—that the founders moved out and the commune degenerated into a low-life crashpad, collapsing not too long thereafter. More than a few communes, typically in urban areas, did not have artistic, social-reform, or other mission-oriented emphases so much as simply adopted the economical communal form in order to provide their members with affordable as well as congenial housing. The variation was endless, mind-boggling.

No system of categorization can possibly do justice to the thousands of communes that dotted the America of the 1960s era. However, a historical survey has to proceed in some kind of logical fashion—even when its subject does not readily lend itself to easy systematization—and so some way of dividing up the communal ranks is necessary. In this book, I have tried to preserve some sense of the diversity of it all by keeping the categorization scheme simple. The larger framework is chronological, tracing the development of communes in the United States from 1960 onward. The prolific period from 1967 to 1975 is broken down into three very broad subcategories, each receiving chapter-length attention: the countercultural hippie communes, mainly rural, that attracted so much attention at the time (even though they were numerically probably the least common type); the religious communes of all varieties; and the secular communes, predominantly urban, that usually embodied some kind of political or social-reform or service agenda.

The world of the 60s communes was fabulously heterogeneous. It could be visionary and inspiring; it could be depressing. For better or worse it was a colorful and eccentric episode in American culture that well deserves recording. This volume is a modest contribution to the preservation of a unique slice of American history.

The 60s Communes

Set and Setting
The Roots of the 1960s-Era Communes

The communes of the 1960s era stood firmly in the American communal tradition. To be sure, several observers have noted that many hippies and others of their generation were not consciously interested in history, seeing themselves as new people creating a whole new social order independent of the past, and have hypothesized that the 1960s communes had sources entirely apart from the dynamics that led to such earlier communal movements as those of the Shakers, the Hutterites, and the Oneida Perfectionists. In this view, Robert Houriet—generally one of the more perceptive contemporary observers of the 1960s-era communes—wrote: "At the outset, [the 1960s communal movement] was the gut reaction of a generation. Hippie groups living a few country miles apart were unaware of each other's existence and equally unaware of the other utopian experiments in American history. They thought theirs were unique and unprecedented."[1] However, although a sense of newness and of discontinuity with the past did indeed characterize the 1960s outlook (particularly among the counterculture), the people of the new generation emerged from a historical context as surely as any other generation ever did; the communes, like the rest of the cultural milieu, had sources in history as well as in contemporary culture. Some individual communards may have been doing something entirely new, but more than a few had important connections to the American communal past.

Many of the reporters and scholars who studied communes during the 1960s accepted the notion of ahistoricity, locating the origins of the communes entirely in the social conditions of the time. Focusing primarily on the counterculture rather than on the other types of communes (which in fact outnumbered the hippie settlements), these observers interpreted the 1960s communes as products of the decay of urban hippie life in Haight-Ashbury, the East Village, and other enclaves. The hip urban centers, so the thesis ran, were joyous centers of peace and love and expanded consciousness only briefly (if at all), soon devolving into cesspools of hard drugs, street crime, and official repression of dissident lifestyles. The hippies at that point fled for the friendly precincts of the countryside, where they built communes as new places for working out the hip vision. Voila! An entirely new social institution!

Examples of this explanation of the origins of 1960s-era (and especially hippie) communalism abound both in popular and in scholarly writings. Maren Lockwood Carden, for example, writing in 1976, says matter-of-factly that the hippies' "first communes were created within the urban areas in which they already lived" and that beginning in 1966 "and especially during 1967 and 1968, such community-oriented hippies left the city." Helen Constas and Kenneth Westhues purport to trace the history of the counterculture "from its charismatic beginnings in the old urban bohemias to its current locale in rural communes," concluding that "communes signify the routinization of hippiedom."[2]

Actually, however, the new communes began to appear before there was a clearly recognizable overall hippie culture, much less a decaying one. Catalyzed by shifts in American culture in the late 1950s and early 1960s, the new generation of communes was not initially a product of hippiedom but rather a crucible that played a major role in shaping and defining hip culture. In other words, the urban hippies did not create the first 1960s-era communes; it would be closer to the truth to say that the earliest communes helped create the hippies. Although communes were indeed founded by hippies who fled the cities, they were johnnies-come-lately to the 1960s communal scene.

To argue that the communes of the 1960s (or even just the hippie communes) were completely without historical rootedness ultimately requires that one believe the preposterous: that of the thousands or even millions of persons who lived communally, none had any knowledge of the American communal past. On the contrary, even though a great many new communards were surely without much historical knowledge about their undertaking, surprisingly many more did have such knowledge. The Diggers, for example—the communal shock troops of the early hip era—consciously named themselves after an important countercultural movement of an earlier century. The 1960s world was salted with old beatniks who understood that the venerable tradition of bohemianism embraced communities (if not always residential communes) of creative souls. The pages of the *Modern Utopian,* the trade journal of the 1960s communes, were liberally dosed with material on communes from earlier ages. Art Downing, describing his life in the 1960s commune popularly known as Kaliflower, recalled that he and his compatriots studied the nineteenth-century classic *The History of American Socialisms* by John Humphrey Noyes, founder and leader of the Oneida Community, and consciously tried to imitate Oneida in several of their communal practices, including a form of group marriage.[3] And more than few communards of the 1960s personally embodied important links to the communal and cooperative past. Before examining some of those links specifically, however, we will take a brief look at the larger context out of which the distinctive cultures of the 1960s emerged.

The Cultural Roots of the Cultural Revolution

The huge social upheaval that we generally refer to as "the sixties" was rooted in cultural developments that began to take shape over a century earlier and that were clearly taking on the distinctive contours of what would become known as 1960s culture by the mid-1950s.[4] Laurence Veysey has identified "a counter-cultural tradition, inherited from the mid-nineteenth century, burgeoning somewhat after 1900, remaining alive on the fringes, and then leaping into a new prominence after 1965."[5] He roots that tradition in antebellum reformism (including the Transcendentalist uprising) and in the rise of anarchism and mysticism in the second half of the nineteenth century, further tracing its development through the rise of nudism, alternative healing practices, pacifism, interest in Asian and occult religions, back-to-the-land romanticism, and Depression-era socialism, as well as the ongoing presence of intentional communities.

In the 1950s that countercultural milieu started down the slippery slope that would give us the 1960s. The most important harbinger of what was to come was the emergence of the beat generation as the 1950s incarnation of the long Western tradition of bohemianism. The beats were an alienated crowd, skeptical of the pursuit of money, of traditional family life, of the American way of life itself.[6] Allen Ginsberg's "Howl," first read publicly in 1955 and published in 1956 following an obscenity suit, heralded the change of direction that the alternative culture was taking. It was a new blast of poetic wind, a stunning challenge to the formal, academic style that dominated American poetry and that even the earlier beat poets had been unable to dislodge. Other beat authors, notably Jack Kerouac and William S. Burroughs, soon began to find serious followings as well. At the same time, new and daring entertainment began to emerge; Lenny Bruce, to name one prominent performer, devastated nightclub audiences with a new type of standup comedy, a savage assault on American icons with shocking swear words never previously heard outside of private conversation.

New magazines were also pushing at the cultural boundaries. In 1958 Paul Krassner founded *The Realist,* a little newsprint journal that engaged in uninhibited social criticism and displayed freewheeling graphics—outrageous content for its time. In the early 1960s Krassner was marketing, through his magazine, such artifacts as the "Mother Poster," which consisted of the words "Fuck Communism" done up in a stars-and-stripes motif. He reached the peak of his iconoclastic renown in 1967, when he published a satire on the assassination of John F. Kennedy that included a scene in which Jacqueline Kennedy witnessed Lyndon Johnson "literally fucking my husband in the throat" (i.e., the fatal wound) just before being sworn in as president. Another new periodical, this one begun in 1962, was *Fuck You: A Magazine of the Arts,* put out in a mimeographed and stapled format by Ed Sanders, who had hitchhiked from Kansas City to New York in 1958. In his first issue Sanders issued a manifesto announcing that the magazine was "dedicated to pacifism, unilateral disarmament, national defense thru nonviolent resistance, multilateral indiscriminate apertural conjugation, anarchism, world federalism, civil disobedience, obstructers and submarine boarders, and all those groped by J. Edgar Hoover in the silent halls of congress." Much of the magazine's content consisted of experimental poetry and the works of leading beat literati, but Sanders also ran polemics and sexually explicit graphics; advocating the legalization of psychedelic drugs, he asked: "Why should a bunch of psychologists hog all the highs?" Sanders, like Ginsberg, would be a key figure in constructing the bridge from beat to hip. In 1964 he opened the Peace Eye bookstore in the East Village, where a good deal of hip culture was incubated, and later in the 1960s and 1970s he would gain prominence as leader of one of the farthest-out hip musical groups, the Fugs, and as a historian of the Charles Manson family.[7]

The beats, more than any other identifiable grouping, pointed alternative culture in new directions that would soon be embraced on a much wider scale. Murray Bookchin, the anarchist whose career as a public dissenter bridged beat and hip, found specific beat origins for environmental concern, the psychedelic experience, communes, the health food revolution, hip art forms, and other cultural innovations associated with the 1960s. Not every innovative idea was without antecedents.[8]

Meanwhile, other new cultural arrivals abetted the beat critique of the status quo. The seemingly innocuous *Mad* magazine, for example, which started out as a comic book, became a satirical bimonthly that had a powerful impact on children just forming their views of the world, lampooning venerable social icons and irreverently questioning authority right and left. Its contribution to the changing social milieu was no accident; as its longtime editor, Al Feldstein, said in 1996, "When Charles Wilson (Eisenhower's secretary of defense) said 'What is good for GM is good for America,' we were saying 'Well, maybe not.' *Mad* was my chance to orient young people to the reality of the world—'They are lying to you.'"[9]

The list goes on: Television exposed Americans to an unprecedented range of cultures and visual images. Science fiction introduced the young to ecological issues, cultural relativity, and the ambiguities of progress;[10] indeed, one science fiction novel alone, Robert Heinlein's *Stranger in a Strange Land,* so entranced many sixties communards with its jabs at predominant social mores—especially monogamy and monotheism—that it became virtual scripture in several communes, such as Sunrise Hill in Massachusetts. New contraceptives and treatments of sexually transmitted diseases opened the door to relatively hassle-free casual sex, and a few social radicals actually began to advocate nudity and freewheeling sexuality openly. The new rock music of Chuck Berry and Elvis Presley was, compared to its immediate predecessors, primitive and sexual. Post–World War II prosperity put cash into the hands of the nonproductive young, changing their way of thinking about the relationship of work and wealth. Higher education mushroomed—with the unexpected result that a great portion of a generation was isolated from its elders, ghettoized, and given a chance to try new experiments in living.[11] In their heyday in the 1950s, liberal religious bodies (in contrast to their strait-laced predecessors) advocated loving social action and critical thinking about matters both temporal and spiritual. Even the Catholic Church was in the early stages of a modernization process that would culminate with the far-ranging reforms of the Second Vatican Council. Moreover, religions from beyond the Christian and Jewish mainstream began to creep into American culture; Zen, for example, had begun to enlarge its slender American presence as contact with Japan was expanded in the wake of World War II and as a new generation of writer-seekers, notably Alan Watts, presented the venerable tradition to English-speaking readers.[12]

The racial climate was changing as well, on campus and off. The civil rights movement, whose beginnings coincided with the rise to prominence of the beats in the mid-1950s, brought to the fore a new politics of moral passion and a new appreciation for blackness. Black radicals (notably Malcolm X) would soon emerge as cultural heroes among alienated white youth. Marijuana, that great component of the 1960s cultural upheaval, would pass from black musicians into the countercultural milieu. As Norman Mailer wrote in 1957, "the source of Hip is the Negro."[13] Civil rights—followed by antiwar political protest—would become a central, defining feature of the 1960s.

And, crucially, psychedelics, those vital shapers of the whole 1960s cultural revolution, were just beginning to show up in the 1950s. As we will see in the next chapter, the new mind-opening substances played central roles in two of the earliest 1960s communal scenes, Millbrook and the Merry Pranksters. Whatever else may be said about LSD, mescaline, psilocybin, and other related chemicals (including the milder marijuana), their use tends to break down social and intellectual conditioning and to raise in the user both a feeling of having new insights and a sense of the inadequacy of the old order. The fact that they are illegal to possess or to use creates a communal bond among those willing to take risks for the exploration of consciousness. Thus the psychedelics were powerful contributors not only to the development of an alternative culture but specifically to the formation of communes. As communard Stephen Diamond wrote, "People got stoned and they woke up."[14]

In sum, not everything—perhaps even not much—that happened in the 1960s era was *de novo*. Bennett Berger's observation on rural countercultural communes characterizes the 1960s generally: the period embodied a "complex mix of traditions, synthesized in fresh ways."[15]

But *Why* Communes?

The historical and cultural events, forces, personalities, and movements mentioned above help us understand the cultural upheaval of the 1960s, but they do not completely explain the huge wave of communal living that surged along with all the rest. After all, activists could have fought political battles, consciousness explorers could have sailed the psychedelic seas, and poets could have declaimed without living communally. Here the American communal past adds crucial tiles to the cultural mosaic in the form of the many specific individuals who embodied the transmission of the communal impulse to a new generation.

1960S THEMES LONG BEFORE THE 1960S

Much of what the public at large (and sometimes the communards themselves) regarded as new and sometimes shocking about 1960s communal life was not new at all, but merely a recapitulation of themes that had long danced across the American communal stage. The youth of the 1960s were not the first American communitarians to be infected with back-to-the-land romanticism; in fact that theme has been a major American communal staple. A concern for good diet and natural foods can be traced back at least as far as Fruitlands, the Massachusetts Transcendentalist commune presided over by A. Bronson Alcott from 1843 to 1845. (Indeed, had Fruitlands been founded 125 years later it would surely have been pigeonholed as a hippie commune, with its crowded housing, dedication to pacifism, idiosyncratic clothing, full economic communism, vegetarianism, high idealism, and eschewal of creature comforts.) The passion for order, for spiritual development, and for closely regulated personal behavior (including sexual behavior) that was common in the religious communes of the 1960s era was reminiscent of the Shaker colonies and of many other disciplined religious communities that reach back as far as the eighteenth century. The yearning for personal growth and fulfillment rather than for conventional social achievement that characterized the 1960s outlook reflects a central force in many historic American communes—the Spirit Fruit Society, for example.[16] Private ownership of land was rejected by several earlier communal leaders, including Peter Armstrong, who in the 1860s deeded the land of his Pennsylvania adventist community, Celestia, to God.[17] Anarchistic communes—embracing voluntary but noncoercive cooperation and rejection of the prevailing government and culture—dotted the communal landscape of the nineteenth and early twentieth centuries. Altruistic sharing and charismatic leadership are not recent communal inventions. Nor was it novel that communes sometimes attracted loafers and deadbeats; the Shakers, for example, had a chronic problem with "Winter Shakers," persons who would arrive in the fall proclaiming their interest in joining only to leave in the spring after being nicely sheltered through the winter. Such an enumeration of prefigurations of the 1960s could be extended at great length.

THE ENDURING COMMUNAL PRESENCE

It is also important to realize that earlier American communitarianism had not ground to a halt when the new generation of communes appeared so visibly on the scene. Dozens, perhaps hundreds, of intentional communities founded before 1960 were still alive when a new generation started building its experimental communities, and there was often a good deal of interaction between the newer and older communal streams. A steady stream of young idealists, for example, sought out Koinonia Farm, the interracial commune in south Georgia founded in 1942 by Clarence Jordan, whose program of building houses for the poor led to Habitat for Humanity—an organization that as we enter the twenty-first century continues to build and to rehabilitate houses for low-income persons around the world.[18] Dozens of other examples of transgenerational communal interaction could be cited; many of the communitarian groups founded prior to 1960 that are discussed in volume one of this work figured into later communal events as well.

Several of the older communities, in fact, were so compatible with the newcomers that they were virtually taken over by them, becoming indistinguishable from their newer communal siblings. East-West House in San Francisco and Quarry Hill in Vermont, for example, accommodated the new communal ethos readily. Zion's Order, a commune rooted in the Latter Day Saints tradition in southern Missouri, absorbed some of the many communal inquirers who dropped in to visit. In other cases the contact was more casual, but still formative. A few of the new communal seekers sought out the one surviving Shaker village open to new members (at Sabbathday Lake, Maine), wanting to know more about the longest-lived communal tradition in the United States. Although the highly structured Shaker life appealed to few of them and none joined as permanent members (a few stayed for a time as organic farming interns), there was some convivial interaction between the mainly aged Shakers and the young visitors, and the Shakers helped to give direction to one organized group of visitors who went on to found the Starcross Monastery in Annapolis, California.[19] Asaiah Bates, a longtime member of the WKFL Fountain of the World commune (which operated in California and Alaska for three or four decades beginning in the late 1940s), reported that when the 1960s communal surge arrived, a steady stream of commune-seekers visited the Fountain to consider joining.[20]

HEATHCOTE CENTER

A case of special significance here is that of the School of Living and its Heathcote Center intentional community in Maryland. Founded by Ralph Borsodi in 1936, the School of Living promoted cooperative clusters of homesteads that would seek self-sufficiency through a combination of mutual aid and individual initiative. (Borsodi's projects are discussed in more detail in volume one of this work.) Borsodi eventually resigned from personal leadership of the project, but his work was taken up by Mildred Loomis, who started a new School of Living at her family's Lane's End Homestead near Brookville, Ohio. At Lane's End, she and her family elevated self-sufficiency to a high art, producing virtually all of their own food and living the good life with very little money. In the late 1940s Loomis began to develop what became something of a continuing-education program for rural self-sufficiency, with classes and demonstration projects carrying on the work of Borsodi and other Depression-era Decentralists, whose goal was nothing less than the overthrow of modern industrial society. A major new building was erected to house Lane's End's growing array of activities, and Loomis's thoughts turned increasingly toward developing a full-scale intentional community.

At the beginning of 1965 the School of Living acquired a thirty-seven-acre plot with five buildings, including a large old stone mill, in rural Maryland. A series of work parties effected the renovation of the mill into a group residence, and by 1966 the programs of the School of Living were operating from their new home, known as Heathcote Center. At the same time, of course, a new generation of potential communards was beginning to seek alternatives to the sterile middle-class ways of living in which they had grown up. Heathcote was within reasonably easy reach of several major East Coast population centers; more importantly, Mildred Loomis was remarkably open to the new generation of seekers who saw in Heathcote the seeds of something worthwhile, and soon the old mill was both a communal home and a conference center.[21] The physical facilities were spartan and the population rode a roller coaster, but Heathcote in effect became one of the first hippie communes. Several of the residents hand-built their own inexpensive little dwellings to achieve a level of privacy not available in the mill building. Members paid their thirty-dollars-per-month assessments for food and other expenses in a variety of ways, often through odd-job work in the neighborhood that they located through a classified ad run periodically in the local paper: "Odd jobs by odd people. Heathcote Labor Pool."[22] Heathcote's educational mission also led to the establishment of other communes, as seekers came to Heathcote conferences and left determined to pursue the communal vision elsewhere. Some of that activity will be detailed in the next chapter.

To be sure, Heathcote was not without its shortcomings. Population turnover was considerable, and sometimes there were so few residents that it hardly deserved to be called a community. Loomis, for all her rapport with those a generation or more younger than she, was not completely comfortable with the unstructured hippie life and had trouble understanding that some of those who lived there did not want to study the ideas of the venerated Ralph Borsodi. One account by a visitor in winter (Heathcote's slow season) depicts the community as a collection of dreary persons living in squalor, in their sexual behavior as hypocritical as any of the suburbanites that they despised, claiming to be monogamous but actually having many furtive affairs.[23] Many twists and turns have ensued, but Heathcote is alive and well as of this writing, over thirty years after its founding and more than a dozen after the death of its matriarch, Loomis, in 1986. It played a critical role in shaping the communal scene of the 1960s.

The Predisposed: New Communards with Old Communal Ties

One of the strongest arguments for connectedness between communal generations lies in individual 1960s communards. In a remarkable number of cases, those who lived communally—and especially those who had founding and leadership roles in the communes—had communitarianism, or things related to it, in their backgrounds. Many of the interviewees in the 60s Communes Project were asked if they had personal predisposing factors in their backgrounds that might have pointed them toward communal living. That is, had they had contacts with communes founded before the great 1960s communal tide? Did they have parents or other older relatives who had lived communally? Did they have relatives who engaged in other forms of organized cooperation? Did relatives or others important to their formation in some way support the common good and question the American ideal of me-first individualism? At a minimum, did they come from politically and socially progressive families that taught concern for others and questioned prevailing social values? Did their interest in community have discernible roots beyond their own 1960s experience?

Yes, came the answer in a great many cases. Rachelle Linner, who was at various times a Catholic Worker and a member of the Community for Creative Nonviolence, came from a generally progressive family; one of her cousins was a radical activist, and an aunt had supported the Abraham Lincoln Brigade in the Spanish Civil War. Cat Yronwode, who founded the Garden of Joy Blues and lived at several other communes as well, grew up in what she characterized as a bohemian left-wing environment; her mother, Lilo Glozer, had been involved in intentional communities, at one time having had some association with Ralph Borsodi of the School of Living. Tolstoy Farm, until a disastrous fire, had a communal library that included works by Borsodi and other earlier utopians, partly because founder Huw Williams had grown up in a Christian socialist family familiar with such thinkers. Verandah Porche of Packer Corner grew up in a family of Trotskyites and union organizers. John Neumeister, who lived at Footbridge Farm in Oregon and was active in radical politics, grew up near Antioch College in Yellow Springs, Ohio, and often went with his parents to programs at that community-minded school—which was once headed by prominent communal-living advocate Arthur Morgan. (Yellow Springs is the home of Community Service, Inc., the original Fellowship of Intentional Communities, and the Vale community; thus, Antioch has one of the nation's more substantial communal archives.) Judson and Marty Jerome, founders of Downhill Farm, came into contact with the communal ideal when they enrolled their handicapped daughter in a Camphill school in Pennsylvania, part of an educational network that has been serving persons with special needs in communal settings in Europe and North America since the 1930s. (Jud Jerome went on to become a scholar of 1960s-era communes.) Daniel Wright, founder of Padanaram, was raised in a strongly community-minded Brethren church near Des

Moines. Richard Kallweit, one of the earliest members of Drop City and the person who lived there longer than any other, had parents who had lived in the Jewish farm colonies of southern New Jersey. Peter Rabbit, another Drop City Dropper, had attended the communal Black Mountain College a decade previously. Robert Houriet, whose personal interest in the communes led to one of the most insightful contemporary books on the subject, went to Tivoli (a Catholic Worker farm in New York state) to meet Dorothy Day in his quest to find the roots of what was going on. Vivian Gotters, an early resident of Morning Star Ranch in California, grew up in cooperative housing in Queens and had socialists in her family; of communal living she said, "It's in my blood."

And on and on. Dozens of the interviewees were red diaper babies—that is, their parents or other close relatives had been Communists or Communist sympathizers, usually in the 1930s. Lou Gottlieb, the founder of Morning Star Ranch, had himself been a Communist some years before he opened his land to a wave of community-seekers. Richard Marley, who lived communally at East-West House and then with the Diggers before becoming the principal founder of Black Bear Ranch, was a red diaper baby who became a party member himself as a young adult.

The communal predisposition of Ramón Sender, the first resident at Morning Star and a veteran communard at several locations, was remarkably broad. Born in Spain, he came to the United States at age four; his father, a famous writer who espoused anarchism and later (briefly) Communism, had been influenced by the anarchist communes of Catalonia during the Spanish Civil War. At age sixteen Sender met a great-granddaughter of John Humphrey Noyes, whose Oneida Community was one of the most notable American communes of the nineteenth century. With her he visited Oneida, where her grandparents were living in the Mansion House, the huge unitary dwelling of the community where her grandfather had been born a stirpicult—a product of a communal planned breeding experiment. After getting married the Senders enthusiastically set out to find a community in which to settle. In 1957 they visited the Bruderhof, then relatively recently established in New York state; Sender, although initially enthusiastic, did not endure beyond a trial period, but his wife remained there permanently.[24] Thus it is not entirely coincidental that Sender was the first person to live at Morning Star Ranch, or that he later lived at Wheeler's Ranch, or that he visited many other communities and still keeps up communal historiography and contacts with old communal friends today. Like Vivian Gotters, he has community in his blood.

Some 1960s-era communitarians were so interested in what had gone before that they immersed themselves in the cooperative tradition. John Curl, an early member of Drop City, went on to publish seminal historical works on cooperation and communitarianism.[25] Early East Wind members built what remains one of the more important library collections on the history of intentional community and cooperation. One bit of historical connectedness is embodied in the building names at Twin Oaks, the egalitarian commune founded in 1967 in Virginia. The original farmhouse was called Llano, after the Llano del Rio colony that operated in Texas and Louisiana from 1914 to 1937; later structures were called, among other things, Oneida, Harmony, Modern Times, Kaweah, Degania, and Tachai—all earlier communes in the United States and abroad. Twin Oakers have not been ignorant of the communal line in which they stand.

That is not to say that all of the new communitarians embodied or sought out links with the American communal past. Al Andersen, an active pre-1960s communitarian, in 1996 could not recall from his days of close association with young 1960s activists that anyone asked his advice on commune-building.[26] Much of what the 1960s communards did *was*, from their point of view at least, all new. But communal predisposition among a great many of their number was too pervasive to ignore and points to a greater continuity of the communal tradition than many have presumed to be the case.

Getting Together

The fact that some 1960s communards had some predisposition to cooperation and other progressive values does not by itself, of course, explain why so many young Americans joined the great surge of community-building. The social circumstances of the day certainly had a great deal to do with community formation, and once the migration into communes got off the ground, it became so perfectly a part of the zeitgeist that its own momentum propelled it rapidly forward.

Even though many of the communards (especially rural ones) came to disavow overt activism, the political climate of the 1960s and the daily realities of the activist lifestyle initially had a great deal to do with making community such an attractive life option. Marty Jezer's account of his own somewhat unintentional slide into communal living—while he was working for bare subsistence wages at the radical *Win* magazine in New York in 1967—evokes an experience shared by thousands:

Our poverty led us to share our meager resources, something we had only dabbled in before. It strikes me now how weird we were about money. In college, I had a friend named Marty Mitchell, who I turned on to jazz and who then became my constant companion. Mitchell never had any money, so whenever I wanted to go somewhere with him, we'd have to go through a standard routine.

"Hey, Mitch, Ornette's at The Five Spot, want to go?"

(Fingering his empty billfold) "I can't afford it."

"How much do you need?"

"Oh, maybe a couple of bucks for the minimum and a bite to eat later."

"I'll lend you the money and you can pay me when you have it."

Of course, we both understood that he would never "have it." But Mitchell would open a little notebook, just the same, and record the loan in his list of debts. By graduation he owed me and his other friends hundreds of dollars. We never expected him to pay and he never intended to. Yet we kept the ritual going and he maintained an accurate list of his debts. In point of fact, we were functioning communally, but none of us were aware of the concept. . . .

We took to opening our houses to the many movement people who always seemed to be passing through New York. Some stayed and so shared whatever apartment, food, bed, clothes that were available. We stopped being guests at each other's houses and no longer felt the need to entertain or be entertaining. Kitchens became liberated territory. Women still did most of the cleaning and the cooking (that would become an issue later), but we stopped thinking of our little apartments as *ours*. . . . There were four or five apartments scattered throughout the city where I could spend time, eat, sleep, and feel at home.

Slowly, we were becoming a family. We weren't aware of the process, one step suggested a next step and circumstances dictated the direction. . . . The world seemed to be coming apart all around us; yet in the growing hippie subculture we were experiencing an unprecedented ecstatic high. Our world, at least, was getting better all the time, and, if nothing else, we had our friends, which seemed more than enough. "With our love, we could save the world," we felt, "if they only knew" and, by God, we were more than ready to share in the good news. [We became a] family, and with thousands of other small families scattered across the nation, one big spaced-out tribe.[27]

From that kind of situation it was not hard to jump into more specifically defined communal living, as Jezer and a dozen or two of his friends did when they bought a farm in Vermont in the summer of 1968.

What in God's name had I gotten into? Here I'd invested every cent I had in a farm which we knew nothing about, with some crazy people who I hardly knew. . . . But that feeling didn't last for long. Our lives, by then, had become structured on faith. If I couldn't trust my brother, who could I trust? The farm had to work out because I couldn't think of what I'd do next if it didn't.[28]

One, Two, Three, Many Communes

Once it got well started, about 1968, the communal stream became a torrent as the alienated young banded together in thousands of places, likely and unlikely, urban and rural. Media publicity had a good deal to do with it. The early coverage of the new-generation communes tended to be in specialized publications and in the underground press, which by 1968 was thriving in hundreds of American cities and towns. Soon, however, the colorful communes were featured in all the mass print media—daily newspapers, *Time* and *Newsweek* and *Life,* rural weeklies, and just about every other venue. Reporters and readers alike were fascinated with and often outraged by these strange-looking eccentrics who had suddenly taken up residence in their midst. In the smaller papers the coverage was often hostile, but more often the reportorial attitude was one of bemusement—"Here's what's going on up there on Backwater Road, I can hardly believe it either, but look at this!" Sensationalism, then as now, was the order of the day for any self-respecting news outlet; so much of the coverage focused on nudity and drug use, real or rumored—and thus helped to feed the local hostility toward communes that broke out so often. As Hugh Gardner observed, "Reporters (and to a lesser extent sociologists) were considered second only to the police as bearers of the plague."[29]

The avalanche of publicity, unsurprisingly, brought new legions of seekers swarming into communes—and often overwhelming them. One of the notable slick-magazine features was a cover story entitled "The Commune Comes to America" in the July 18, 1969, issue of *Life,* consisting mainly of exquisite color photos of a rural forty-one-member hippie clan, sometimes nude, sometimes wearing bells and beads and buckskins and granny dresses, living in tepees and bathing in the creek. The story carefully avoided naming the commune or locating it anywhere other than "somewhere in the woods," but word quickly circulated that it was actually the Family of the Mystic Arts, a rural Oregon commune, and hippies by the hundreds swarmed to and over the idyllic locale, undoubtedly hastening its decline. Such a scenario was repeated less dramatically wherever press coverage surfaced.

The mass-media coverage was supplemented by sympathetic reporting in specialized publications that were eagerly read by persons intrigued by the communes. The *Modern Utopian,* founded by Richard Fairfield while he was a student at the Unitarian theological school at Tufts University in 1966, became the flagship of the genre, featuring news coverage of as many communes as possible, interviews with key communal figures, and other coverage of interest to alternative-minded people. A variety of short-lived newsletters supplemented Fairfield's work; in the San Francisco Bay area, for example, an intercommunal periodical called *Kaliflower* was distributed to hundreds of communal houses and other places, fueling the great interest of the young in new lifestyles. Coverage in the underground press continued apace, of course. And eventually the communes movement was producing books of its own, books that in some cases got wide circulation and introduced a great many young persons to the idealized delights of intentional community. The foremost of that genre was *Living on the Earth*, a hand-lettered and whimsically illustrated paean to dropout life by Alicia Bay Laurel, written while she was living at Wheeler's Ranch, an open-land community in California. Originally published by a small press called Bookworks in Berkeley, the book was picked up by Random House and—in the wake of a surge of publicity that included three major notices in the *New York Times* in the space of six days, among them a glowing review by Raymond Mungo in the *Times Book Review*—found an enormous nationwide audience.[30] Laurel, who had resolved to live in carefree hippie poverty, gave away most of the profuse royalties that stemmed from her successful authorship.

Thus did the word spread. By the late 1960s the United States was well into the greatest epoch of commune-building in its history.

2

The New Communes Emerge

1960–1965

The first stirrings of the new communalism of the 1960s came early in the decade. Even though it was not until 1965—with the establishment of Drop City in southern Colorado—that the new genre of the hippie commune became fully formed, the first few years of the decade saw incremental developments in communal life that in retrospect can be seen to have anticipated and shaped what was to come soon afterwards. Notable new experiments in community developed on both coasts that offered a new vision of how life could be lived.

The Merry Pranksters

A communal (or at least semicommunal) scene decidedly unlike most of what had gone before evolved on the peninsula south of San Francisco throughout the early 1960s with the Merry Pranksters of Ken Kesey. In 1958, having been awarded a Woodrow Wilson Fellowship to attend the graduate writing program at Stanford, Kesey and his wife Faye moved from Oregon to Palo Alto. While Kesey honed his skills as a novelist, the couple lived in a congenial literary world of cheap little houses on Perry Lane in Palo Alto's bohemian neighborhood. In 1959 Kesey volunteered to be a subject in controlled experiments with psychoactive drugs, including the major psychedelics (LSD, psilocybin, mescaline), and soon the remarkable new substances found their way to Perry Lane. The psychedelics had a powerful effect on local social life, and although nothing that amounted to a commune developed on Perry Lane, the freewheeling, convivial social and literary atmosphere embraced a camaraderie unlike anything mainstream America had ever seen. Tom Wolfe described the scene:

> All sorts of people began gathering around Perry Lane. Quite an . . . *underground* sensation it was, in Hip California. Kesey, Cassady, Larry McMurtry; two young writers, Ed McClanahan and Bob Stone; Chloe Scott the dancer, Roy Seburn the artist, Carl Lehmann-Haupt, Vic Lovell . . . and Richard Alpert himself . . . all sorts of people were in and out of there all the time, because they had heard about it, like the local beats—that term was still used—a bunch of kids from a pad called the Chateau, a wild-haired kid named Jerry Garcia and the Cadaverous Cowboy, Page Browning. Everybody was attracted by the strange high times they had heard about . . . The Lane's fabled Venison Chili, a Kesey dish made of venison stew laced with LSD, which you could consume and then go sprawl on the mattress in the fork of the great oak in the middle of the Lane at night and play pinball with the light show in the sky . . . Perry Lane.
>
> And many puzzled souls looking in . . . At first they were captivated. The Lane was too good to be true. It was Walden Pond, only without any Thoreau misanthropes around. Instead, a community of intelligent, very open, out-front people—out front was a term everybody was using—out-front people who cared deeply for one another, and *shared* . . . in incredible ways, even, and were embarked on some kind of . . . *well*, adventure in living. Christ, you could see them trying to put their finger on it and . . . then . . . gradually figuring out there was something here they weren't *in on* . . .[1]

It all came to an end in July 1963, when a developer bought most of Perry Lane and prepared to tear down the inexpensive dwellings there to make way for fancier houses. Kesey took the money that was rolling in from his smash-hit first novel *One Flew Over the Cuckoo's Nest* and bought a small house over the mountains in rural La Honda. The new place was relatively isolated, and quickly quite a few of the Perry Lane crowd showed up and began to camp out in the woods at the new scene, creating an instant, if unintentional, community. Speakers on top of the house belted out music at full volume. LSD, still legal, was plentiful. The La Honda encampment precipitated the Merry Pranksters, whose legendary role in the formation of the new hip culture was cemented by their fabled LSD-fueled bus trip to New York and back during the summer of 1964. The bus, a wildly painted 1939 International Harvester modified to be lived in, sported a destination sign that read "Furthur."[2]

A potentially pivotal moment in the history of early 1960s communal life almost occurred during the trip when the Pranksters drove up to the Millbrook, New York, mansion where Timothy Leary and company had recently established the country's other notable communal psychedelic scene. The first meeting between the two principal prophets of psychedelia—Kesey full-tilt raucous, Leary a mystic and scholar—could have been momentous, but Leary, sick with the flu, in the throes of a brand-new romance, and just coming down from (or perhaps in the middle of) an intense LSD trip, refused to go downstairs and meet the visitors, granting only a quick visit to Kesey and his longtime sidekick Ken Babbs.[3] "I didn't know history was being made, a meeting of the acid tribes," Leary later said. "I was preoccupied with other things."[4] The Pranksters, both mystified and miffed at the rebuff, drove off.

Back in La Honda after the trip, the scene intensified. The crowd kept growing as word of the strange doings and stories about the bus trip spread. People who were tuned into the flow hung on, living in tents or coming and going regularly. Carolyn Adams Garcia, who met Jerry Garcia there and later was married to him, remembered her accommodations as primitive: "Six boards nailed together with a tarp over the top, and that was a bedroom. There was a treehouse, and some old outbuildings that were converted into sleep areas, and then there were vehicles as living areas." Members of a San Francisco band, the Warlocks—soon to be known as the Grateful Dead—were there a lot. A bit later Hunter Thompson introduced Kesey to the Hell's Angels, who with the help of LSD fit into the scene far better than anyone could have imagined. Allen Ginsberg, who was present at the first encounter of Angels and Pranksters, observed "the blast of loudspeakers . . . a little weed in the bathroom . . . one muscular smooth skinned man sweating dancing for hours . . . and 4 police cars parked outside the gate."[5]

The twists and turns of the Merry Pranksters in those years are far too complicated to chronicle here, what with Acid Tests, huge LSD parties in San Francisco, and two marijuana arrests that would push Kesey into becoming a fugitive from justice in Mexico and the United States and, apprehended and finally convicted, a prisoner on a work farm for five months. When he got out, in late 1967, he went back to Oregon with his family and settled on his brother's farm outside Springfield. Gradually some of the Merry Pranksters migrated to the area, and for a time some of them lived in what began to be the next Prankster commune. Carolyn

Garcia, by then living with the Grateful Dead in San Francisco but a frequent visitor to the Springfield scene, recalled that "it was really communal at that time," with as many as sixty persons living at the farm, in buses and other vehicles and in the barn. Her brother, Gordon Adams, called it "a pretty jazzy, busy scene, almost like an urban enclave in a farm situation."[6] Times had changed, however, and Kesey tired of it all. He had lived more or less communally for five or six years, by his reckoning, and was becoming put off at what he started calling the "Communal Lie": "It was just a lie in terms of our existence. We were all lying to each other, and saying that what we were doin' was righteous when we didn't really feel it." Longtime Prankster Ken Babbs took busloads of the Pranksters and hangers-on—sixty-odd of them in all—to the Woodstock festival in August 1969, with instructions from Kesey not to return,[7] and Kesey soon winnowed the remaining crowd down to just his own extended family. That family remains there today; some of the old Pranksters and other friends live nearby.

More New Communities Coalesce

The Merry Pranksters certainly helped to engender new ways of looking at lifestyle issues, but they were hardly alone in their social experimentation. Several other communities established before 1965 in widely scattered locations also helped to point toward the communal future.

GORDA MOUNTAIN

Open land—land on which anyone could settle for a season or, theoretically, a lifetime—eventually became a philosophy on which hundreds of 1960s-era communes were based. The first of them (at least as far as we know) was Gorda Mountain, outside the hole-in-the-road town of Gorda, near Big Sur, California. In 1962 Amelia Newell, who owned an art gallery at Gorda, opened her land to anyone who wanted to stay there, and by mid-decade it had become known on the West Coast countercultural grapevine as a center for drug trading and a convenient stopping-off place and crashpad for people making the run between Los Angeles and San Francisco. The population, most of it not very permanent, grew slowly until the commune movement as a whole caught fire; at its peak, during the summer of 1967, it rose as high as two hundred or so. Newell, it was said, provided bulk foods for them all.[8]

Only two published accounts deal with Gorda at a length of more than a few lines. Rasa Gustaitis, on an excursion from a stay at the nearby Esalen Institute (a well-known human growth/human potential center and itself a place that had some communal features), visited Gorda Mountain to attend a wedding. A long walk in over a terrible road brought Gustaitis through territory dotted with odd structures and gardens—and persons; a community bathtub had been rendered useless, as had all sanitary arrangements, by local antagonists who had cut off the community's water supply. She located and interviewed a white-haired woman who must have been Newell:

> I go over to talk with her and she tells me she's the landlady in this place. She had read some letters in the papers that criticized the beatniks, she says, so she invited any beats who wanted a place to stay on Big Sur to settle in Gorda. They didn't take her up on the invitation, she says, but the hippies did. For a while this was a lovely community but now a lot of people are gone and it's more transient. There's been too much harassment by the health department, the police and neighbors. She'd like to see it turn into a quiet community of artists but this is how things are now, as I see them. What can anyone do when the waterline keeps getting cut?

In all, Gustaitis painted a rather bleak scene with affectless people, and the wedding never did take place that day.[9]

Lewis Yablonsky, visiting Gorda at about the same time that Gustaitis did, wrote an even grimmer take, depicting people dwelling in tents and caves and on mountain ledges as well as in the more-than-decrepit main stone house, a population dominated by ex-convicts and derelicts who threatened and stole from each other like the small-time hoodlums they apparently were. When Yablonsky finally left late in the evening, he feared being mugged on his way back down the two-mile path to his car.[10] Gorda Mountain seems, all in all, not to have received much good press. The 60s Communes Project was unable to locate anyone who had lived there, and Newell, the matriarch of the land, died some time ago.

Gorda Mountain's neighbors apparently did not care for the place any more than did the visitors who wrote about it. Newell reportedly left for a time under threat of being involuntarily confined for her alleged insanity. The proprietor of the local gas station wore a revolver and refused to serve anyone from the community. The severed water line was the work of a neighbor who reportedly wanted health officials to condemn the place for not having proper plumbing.[11]

The local harassment and internal weaknesses of Gorda Mountain finally took their toll. It was closed for good in 1968.

THE HIMALAYAN ACADEMY

The anarchic Gorda Mountain was not the only new-style commune to be created in 1962. At about the time that Amelia Newell was opening her land, Master Subramuniya was establishing his own disciplined communal yoga center, the Himalayan Academy.

Subramuniya grew up in the Lake Tahoe area as Bob Hanson. In the 1940s he traveled to Ceylon to study yoga and was initiated into Hinduism by a Tamil guru. Following his return to the United States he established his own religious organization in 1957, opening what was first called the Krishna Temple and later the Christian Yoga Church. For a time Subramuniya focused on the interface between Christian mysticism and the Hindu tradition, but over time the movement became more specifically Hindu.[12] His earliest followers tended to be older women of the sort that had also been a major constituency for such earlier Indian teachers as Vivekananda and Yogananda, but in the mid-1960s the older members were rapidly displaced by young countercultural spiritual seekers.[13]

Subramuniya taught his earliest American followers in San Francisco, where a very few lived communally, but soon he acquired rural retreat centers as well. In 1962 he bought an old brewery building in Virginia City, Nevada, where the first major Himalayan Academy community was established. With great effort the building was restored and transformed into in impressive edifice in which a rigorous spiritual life was developed. Monks and nuns—primarily the former at first—lived in contemplative community under vows of celibacy and poverty, which they believed essential to spiritual advancement. The group also established a commercial printing operation, the Ponderosa Press, which produced yoga instructional publications and helped to finance the movement by printing (among other things) commercial materials for several casinos.[14] In the early years in Nevada the monks wore flowing robes and shaved their heads, but after enduring a fair amount of hostility from their Virginia City neighbors they toned down their distinctive appearance—after all, what mattered was within, not without—and in due course became well accepted locally.

In 1967 Subramuniya and several followers traveled the world seeking a new location for their headquarters and finally settled on the Hawaiian island of Kauai, where the movement remains centered today and is constructing a traditional South Indian temple on the fifty-one-acre monastery site. Other centers operate in other parts of the world as well. In the meantime, the Himalayan Academy has become a major communications nexus for the Hindus of the world; in 1979 Subramuniya founded the periodical *Hinduism Today*, which has become a leading English-language purveyor of news and feature stories of interest to Indians abroad.[15] Thus, this pioneering American communal religion has become perhaps more influential in the world Asian community than any other movement of its kind.

TOLSTOY FARM

A major step toward the new communalism that would become so prominent in the later 1960s was taken in 1963, when Huw "Piper" Williams established Tolstoy Farm on some of his family's farmland near Davenport, thirty-odd miles west of Spokane, Washington. Tolstoy became the second 1960s-era open land community, after Gorda—but unlike its predecessor it has survived.

Williams was a peace activist in the early 1960s, and that commitment started him on the road to Tolstoy. A major focus of peace activity in the quiet early 1960s was protesting Polaris submarines, those stealthy underwater launching pads for the missiles that would, if the button was pushed, rain nuclear destruction on the Soviet Union; protest actions involved not only demonstrating with signs and chants but, frequently, crossing military security lines and boarding submarines. The New England Committee for Nonviolent Action (CNVA) spearheaded these protest activities and began to use Robert and Marjorie Swann's forty-acre farm near Voluntown, Connecticut, as a training center and base for the work. Activists lived communally at the farm between protest actions (and in some cases between jail terms for their civil disobedience), growing food, producing literature, organizing workshops, and doing all the other things involved in running an ongoing social protest organization. Beatings, arson, and vandalism at the hands of a few of CNVA's more undisciplined antagonists were also part of life at the farm.[16]

Huw Williams encountered the CNVA farm in 1962, and he became inspired to start a West Coast counterpart. He had read a good deal of Tolstoy and Gandhi and was determined to implement their principles (as he saw them) with "a simple living kind of alternative Christian lifestyle, cooperation, self-reliance."[17] After he got back to Washington in 1962 he moved onto his grandparents' farm, and he soon managed to purchase land nearby. In the spring of 1963 he invited friends from the peace movement, including several who had been active in the Catholic Worker, to join him and to "attempt to live in a way that would not require violent acts, being in the military, courts, jail, or police."[18] Early on the ten or so founding members adopted as the sole rule of the community the principle that no one could be forced to leave, so that "[w]e would have to work out our differences in the right way." With no rules restricting sexual activity or drug use and with wide-open membership, Tolstoy Farm lurched closer to hip than anything that had gone before.

Many were attracted to Tolstoy—Robert Houriet says that there were fifty the first summer[19]—and the community focused mainly on living at a near-subsistence level. With a cash flow of less than one hundred dollars per month, Williams recalled, "[w]e were pretty poor, trying to grow our own food, build our own shelter, use old tools and equipment. It occupied us and challenged us." After some shifts and land acquisition, benefactions from Williams's parents, and a purchase subsidized by a sympathetic friend and paid off by donations from residents, Tolstoy Farm by 1965 ended up consisting of two separate parcels of land, one of 120 acres in a large canyon and another of 80 acres two miles to the north. An existing farmhouse, known as Hart House after the family that had previously lived there, became the communal center. A diverse crowd took up residence there, especially as hippie interest in communes boomed in 1966 and 1967. Anarchy was taken seriously as a guiding principle; as a result, the members who wanted to grow marijuana did so, bringing two major busts down on the whole farm in 1966 and 1972, and unrestricted sexual behavior led to a good deal of jealousy and even a suicide. Decision making was by consensus and, given the diverse and strong personalities present, was excruciatingly difficult. But life went on. Members pooled money for food and land payments, putting it as they had it into envelopes tacked up on the wall.

More than a few of the newcomers—whose numbers included runaways and mental patients—created problems for the longer-term residents. In the spring of 1968 Hart House burned to the ground as a result of a fire probably set by a teenage girl whom Williams described as "kind of off balance." Many of the earlier settlers had already built simple homes elsewhere on the two pieces of land and were not entirely sad to see the chaotic Hart House scene come to an end.

After the fire the community consisted of scattered private households, although cooperative features—a collective pottery studio, a cooperative irrigation system, various collective child-care setups—endured, and at one point many of the residents formed a group-within-the-group that instituted total economic sharing. That experiment lasted about two and a half years before breaking up primarily due to problems of personal relations, including sexual jealousy.[20] Population estimates vary widely, but it appears that at its late-sixties peak the community had perhaps 80 to 100 more or less permanent residents, and perhaps 150 to 200 during the summer. For some years a healthy contingent of children attended the cooperative, loosely structured alternative school, taught by Williams and housed in an unusual eighteen-sided dome-topped building built over several years by Tolstoy volunteers. Residents also participated in a number of cooperative work projects and cottage industries. In 1970 a journalist wrote of a community of "serious, straightforward people who, with calculated bluntness, say they are dropouts, social misfits, unable or unwilling to cope with the world 'outside.'"[21]

Life was never easy at Tolstoy Farm; many contemporary newspaper accounts of life there commented on the farm's run-down physical plant. "Dotted with shacks and makeshift abodes, it is reminiscent of a Hooverville of the 1930s," one reporter wrote. But the residents had a sense that those who had learned to live outside of the dominant culture's technological support systems would be the better off for it when, as many believed, the time would come when world crisis might remove such systems. Rico Reed, who lived at Tolstoy from the mid-1960s until the mid-1990s, gradually developed an extensive photovoltaic power supply for his house and shop and a wood-fired hot water system. There was also unquestioned freedom. As one young female resident proclaimed, "I like it here because I can stand nude on my front porch and yell, fuck! Also, I think I like it here because I'm fat, and there aren't many mirrors around. Clothes don't matter, and people don't judge you by your appearance like they do out there."[22]

Eventually, however, the hard life at the farm took its toll on the residents. Huw Williams endured many ups and downs, but eventually bailed out himself. "Things got wild and different," he later said. By then he was married with two children, and his wife became determined to leave Tolstoy; they ended up moving to another tract of Williams family land. Williams, however, has never given up his communitarian vision; since leaving Tolstoy he has gathered another community, the Earth Cyclers, on land owned by his parents twenty-five miles from Tolstoy. In 1990 the new community consisted of nine persons living simply and carrying out organic farming and forestry projects. In that year Tolstoy reported a population of 27 adults and 22 children, the members living independently as families but still retaining some sense of community.[23] The old school building, although not in the best of repair, is now a communal library; in the early 1990s the residents were having potluck meals every Sunday and keeping a cooperative milk cow. In the fall of 1990 residents built a communal sweat lodge. For many years an all-night Corn Dance has been held at the first full moon in May, and other full moons are often celebrated ritually as well. At the end of the 1990s, Tolstoy Farm very much survives; things have changed and not changed in a third of a century.

MILLBROOK

Just as the Merry Pranksters reached full steam at the Kesey place in La Honda, the nation's other notable communal psychedelic vanguard began to take shape in the upstate New York town of Millbrook. Timothy Leary, a respected academic psychologist, was introduced to magic mushrooms in Mexico in August 1960, and upon his return to Harvard University (where he was an adjunct faculty member) he instituted a psilocybin research project. A young professor, Richard Alpert (later to be known as Ram Dass), became interested in the work, as did various other faculty members and students, many of whom became subjects in ongoing experiments in the use of various psychedelics. By 1962 a controversy was raging at Harvard over the whole affair, and the following spring Alpert, who had further undermined his position by becoming involved in an unwise gay romantic relationship, was fired from his tenure-track position. Leary, although he had already told Harvard that he was resigning, was symbolically fired as well.

In the meantime Leary, Alpert, their graduate student Ralph Metzner, and several others had formed the International Foundation for Internal Freedom (IFIF), which quickly attracted a dues-paying membership in the thousands. IFIF soon became communal as core members took up residence in "colonies for transcendental living," as they put it, in, sequentially, two old houses in Newton, Massachusetts. Their life there anticipated the hippie communalism that would soon descend on the Western world:

Sometimes a dozen stereos were going at the same time, Hindu *ragas* flowing out of one room to merge, in the hall, with Tibetan bells and Thelonious Monk. The cumulative din drove the neighbors crazy, as did the sight of bare-chested young men practicing yoga in the yard. "They all wear a beatnik uniform—tight pants and jerseys, no shoes or stockings," complained one neighbor, who compared the Leary-Alpert house to a weekend motel. "One young man in his twenties is letting his blond hair grow down to his shoulders; every time I look at him I want to vomit." Then you had the decor. . . . The kitchen was filled with Rohrschach's [*sic*] inkblots and the rest sported collages that daily grew more bizarre. The one in the living room consisted of nudes clipped from magazines, with a single solitary bra pinned to it.[24]

Small wonder that Leary and Alpert's relations with staid Harvard were severed that spring. They launched a bold plan to establish a new psychedelic exploration center in Zihuatanejo, Mexico, but once the Mexican government sized up the situation the IFIFers were given five days to leave the country. Other problems ensued, but just when all looked bleak, Peggy Hitchcock, who had become an active IFIF member, happened to remember that her twin brothers, Tommy and Billy, had recently purchased an estate in Millbrook, New York, two hours north of New York City. The Hitchcocks were grandchildren of the founder of Gulf Oil and niece/nephews of financier Andrew Mellon, and they had a *lot* of money.

It's safe to say that no 1960s commune was handed better real estate on which to carry out its experiment. The estate at Millbrook consisted of several thousand acres, over half a dozen houses, several other buildings—and a grand sixty-four-room mansion that the Hitchcock family hadn't figured out what to do with. The mansion needed restoration, but it was entirely liveable and—with its gargantuan fireplace, gingerbread ornamentation, parquet floors, Persian carpets, crystal chandeliers, and other grand embellishments—more than luxurious in its dotage. As Jay Stevens has observed, the estate was both ashram and research institute, populated by spiritual seekers and psychologists, as well as "a school, a commune, and a house party of unparalleled dimensions."[25] Leary and other true believers in the company were sure that it would be the center from which human consciousness would be permanently changed, transformed, elevated. They moved in in August 1963, under the aegis of their new corporate entity, the Castalia Foundation.[26]

A core group of between twenty-five and thirty people were at the center of Millbrook, including Leary's family (his new wife Nena and his children Susan and Jack). Several academics and graduate students, mainly from the Boston area, moved in. So did a number of seekers of spiritual insight, including several (under the leadership of Bill Haines) who lived in a separate building known as "the ashram" and later moved to Benson, Arizona, to start the Sri Ram Ashrama; adherents of Leary's League for Spiritual Discovery, which had a center in New York City as well as the one at Millbrook; and eventually Art Kleps, a psychologist who moved into the gatehouse below the mansion and founded the psychedelic Neo-American Church.[27] Among other things Millbrook was a grand intellectual community; the professors who moved in brought their personal libraries with them, combining them into a fine research library, and they published a serious scholarly journal, the *Psychedelic Review*. Of course visitors were abundant, and included, during the first year or two, Allen Ginsberg, Alan Watts, Paul Krassner, and Charlie Mingus, among many others.[28]

Seriousness of purpose guided Millbrook through the bulk of its existence. Unlike the Merry Pranksters, who took lots of LSD casually and had roaring parties, the Castalians took their psychedelics under controlled, even somber conditions, with guides and carefully controlled physical environments. They also had a clear sense of group endeavor, undertaking study projects (spending a month reading Aldous Huxley or Gurdjieff, for example) and coming together for group LSD sessions. The creation of art in a variety of forms was constant, with projects ranging from the production of some of the earliest psychedelic light shows to painting all kinds of images—mandalas, Tantric symbols, images of Asian deities—on the house, inside and out.

The mundane realities of daily life seemed not to be a major problem. Some effort was made to split up chores, to assign duties on a rotating basis; lunch and dinner cooking were regularly handled in that fashion, for example, and essential tasks managed to get done fairly smoothly, although much of the time the less attractive work—cleaning and dishwashing—was neglected, often rendering the place a mess. As for paying the bills, some of the residents had enough money to help meet the basic needs of the group. In addition, seminars and LSD sessions—LSD was still legal during Millbrook's first few years—were run for paying guests, and they found a steady market among upscale New Yorkers. The outflow of money, however, was much greater than income, and over time bankruptcy loomed. For many members life remained easy; after all, no one had to work outside the estate, which was cozily insulated behind its wall, and life went on with a grand sense of adventure and exploration of the inner world. But by the fall of 1965 some disintegration was setting in.[29]

The goings-on at the Hitchcock estate naturally attracted the curiosity of the local community, and before too long agitation to do something about what was presumed to be a cesspool of drugs and vice began to surface. The legal situation changed when LSD and its psychedelic relatives were banned by federal and state law, and in any event marijuana and other proscribed substances and activities were consistently present. Leary took his first hard fall in December 1965, when he and his daughter were arrested for crossing the Mexican border with a small amount of marijuana, a crime for which Leary was sentenced to thirty years in prison. Then, on the night of April 16, 1966, one G. Gordon Liddy, a Dutchess County prosecutor, kicked in the front door and raided the place. (Yes, it was the same G. Gordon Liddy who would go on to prominence in the Nixon White House as one of the leak-fixing plumbers and masterminds of the Watergate burglary, and who ironically ended up many years later on the public lecture circuit teamed with Leary.) Liddy neglected to read the accused their rights, and thus the case was thrown out of court, but the heat was on. Liddy's minions set up roadblocks and thoroughly searched everyone who came to or went from the estate.[30] That pressure, as much as anything, led to the dissolution of it all. After a year of internal frictions and external pressure Billy Hitchcock decided to close the scene down. Millbrook was essentially terminated in 1967, and the last hangers-on were given final notice to leave the estate the following spring.[31]

By then, however, America was becoming well populated with psychedelic communes, and the communal search for high experience and expanded consciousness had many chapters yet to be written.

TRANS-LOVE ENERGIES

While psychedelic pioneers and others on both coasts were paving the way for the post-1965 wave of communes, another group was similarly anticipating the near future in the Midwest. John Sinclair was the figure around whom a good deal of long-lived communal energy evolved in Detroit and Ann Arbor, Michigan. In 1964 he and several others started the Detroit Artists' Workshop and rented a house that would provide living space for two members and performance and meeting space for all. That quickly led to the Artists' Workshop Cooperative Housing Project, which became increasingly communal over time. In a 1996 interview, Sinclair described the scene:

We went into communal living because it was economical, financially, spiritually, and productively. In those days it was difficult to even play your music without being hassled. But if we had all the same people in the house, all musicians or poets or people involved creatively with one another, we wouldn't bother the other tenants. Then we had control, mentally, of the whole space. And also because we were all marijuana users, we wouldn't have alien elements in our building who would turn us in. So that's how we started.[32]

Eventually the artists got pressured out of Detroit ("It was the police and the marijuana issue and the weirdness issue," Sinclair says) and moved to Ann Arbor. There the cultural workers, by now calling their group "Trans-Love Energies," reestablished their communal setup, which encompassed two rock bands (including the nationally prominent MC5) and lots of grassroots publishing activity—magazines, broadsides—much of it produced on a mimeograph. By the early 1970s they had two huge former fraternity houses plus a carriage house filled with an interracial crowd of musicians, poets, and activists. "We were very energetic and productive," Sinclair recalled. "We were organized around cultural work, which is the best kind of work." In Ann Arbor the thirty-five or so workers had a recording studio and a massive sound system, managed bands, played music, ran an underground newspaper and the Rainbow Press, and were active in all the radical political activities of the day. It all went on frenetically until about 1974, when things began to crumble. "The Movement was dying, Nixon was expelled from office, they finally ended the war, they wiped out the Black Panther Party," Sinclair lamented. They closed up shop in Ann Arbor and a group of seven moved back to Detroit to continue the communal life on a smaller scale until the end of the decade, when the last of them moved into private homes.

OTHER COMMUNITIES ACTIVE IN THE EARLY 1960S

Tracking down small and often short-lived or publicity-shy communities in out-of-the-way places is difficult business. Undoubtedly a good many of them dotted the first half of the 1960s, but their traces are often as elusive as those of transuranic elements. Here are four whose existences seem well enough attested but for whom documentation is scanty, to say the least.

Cedar Grove. A Baha'i commune founded in New Mexico in about 1960, Cedar Grove is mentioned several times by Rosabeth Moss Kanter in *Commitment and Community;* it does not show up in the major lists and directories of 1960s-era communes, although it apparently survived a decade or longer. From Kanter we learn that the community embraced a

Shaker-like belief that work was spiritually important, ran a free school, and operated a public cafe. One would surmise that Cedar Grove generally eschewed publicity, and did so more successfully than did many other shy communes.[33]

The Society for the Preservation of Early American Standards. Said to have been founded in 1961, this group was located outside Oxford, New York. In 1970 it was reported to have thirteen members. The Society was a back-to-the-land movement that discouraged visitors but was apparently open enough to accept new members after a trial period of residence. It appears in a few communal directories, but never with more than a sentence or two of basic description.[34]

The Amity Experimental Community. This little-noticed community coalesced in Seattle, perhaps as early as 1959, but moved and published at least one newsletter (in October 1963) from a base at Littleton, Colorado. The newsletter describes a communal economic plan that suggests that the community had at least eight members, four of them employed full time, and a communal home, Amity House. A dictionary entry on the community describes it as a group marriage and says it closed in 1964. Further information, however, seems to be nonexistent.[35]

Ananda Ashram. Founded in 1964 by Dr. Ramamurti Mishra, Ananda Ashram of Monroe, New York, survives today as one of the oldest communal centers grounded in an Asian religion in the United States. It appears in several directories of communities, but clearly does not go out of its way to seek visitors, new members, or publicity. Ananda announced its membership as full (at twenty) in the 1995 *Communities Directory,* although students of yoga were welcome to enroll in its classes and retreats. Ananda is one of hundreds of small but vital communal religious centers that quietly go about the business of spiritual development and personal growth.[36]

Entering a New Communal Era: Drop City

American communal history turned a major corner on May 3, 1965, when three persons recently out of college purchased six acres of scraggly goat pasture outside Trinidad, Colorado, and proclaimed the establishment of Drop City. Drop City brought together most of the themes that had been developing in other recent communities—anarchy, pacifism, sexual freedom, rural isolation, interest in drugs, art—and wrapped them flamboyantly into a commune not quite like any that had gone before. Drop City thus represents the point at which a new type of commune-building had definitively arrived. It was defiantly outrageous, proclaiming itself a whole new civilization, its members rejecting paid employment and creating wildly original funky architecture. It pioneered what soon became a widespread hippie love of integrated arts, creating multimedia extravaganzas, using color profusely, employing trash as source material, blending art with everything else in life. It gave its inhabitants new names, rejected all kinds of social conventions, and became a pilgrimage site for those seeking new cultural horizons. For all of those reasons it deserves a relatively detailed chronicle here.

Drop City's founders were Gene Bernofsky and Jo Ann Bernofsky, husband and wife, and Clark Richert, who had met as students at the University of Kansas at Lawrence in the early 1960s. At one point Jo Ann spent several months in San Francisco, and Gene, needing a place to live, moved with Richert and a friend into a loft overlooking the main drag of downtown Lawrence. There "drop art" emerged. In its earliest form, drop art involved the painting of rocks that were then dropped over the edge of the roof onto the sidewalk below. In a fashion that Richert compared to the television show *Candid Camera,* the drop artists stayed on the roof and watched the responses of passersby to the mysterious missiles from heaven. So "droppings" was a literal description of what the art was doing; the term also referred, as Gene recalled, to "droppings, those things that birds leave when they fly over. That's kind of the way we thought of it."[37]

Gradually the droppings took on more elaborate forms. Across the street was the city's main hotel, and one morning the Droppers cooked up a complete breakfast (bacon, eggs, orange juice, toast, even grapes), arranged it in a full place setting on the sidewalk in front of the hotel, and then stood back to watch the reactions of passersby. "We were kind of hoping someone would eat it," Richert said, "but most people who passed by just walked around it, trying not to get close to us." There were many other droppings; the idea was to bring conceptual art out of the artificial environment of a gallery or museum and into the real world.

In 1964 the Bernofskys left for Africa, grandly envisioning founding their own new civilization in an isolated place. But they didn't get past Morocco, instead returning home to set up their civilization where, as Gene said, "we wouldn't have a problem with language and good, solid capitalistic goods were available instantaneously everywhere." They met up with Richert, now in graduate school in Colorado, and as they all shared their visions of new civilizations and enclaves of the arts they began to sketch out a collaboration. They would build A-frames, make art, and—crucially—not pay rent.

In the spring of 1965 Gene and Clark began driving around Colorado from Richert's home base in Boulder, looking for land to buy with Gene's $500 to $600 life savings. Near the New Mexico border, in the hamlet of El Moro, outside Trinidad, they found a farmer nearing retirement who wanted to sell six acres of goat pasture next to his house for $500. They negotiated the price down to $450 and bought it on May 3, 1965. The Bernofskys moved there immediately; Richert waited until school was over, finishing his master's degree in fine arts, and joined them in the summer.

The vision at that point was glorious, even cosmic: an entirely new civilization, one not built on any existing pattern. As Jo Ann Bernofsky said,

"We knew that we wanted to do something outrageous and we knew we wanted to do it with other people, because it was more exciting to be with a group than to be just one or two or three people. There was this kind of heady arrogance—talk about arrogance!—that we could just do something so outrageous and so far out, that we could pull it off even though none of us had many resources. . . . It was full of vitality, and it was extremely exciting and wonderful. You had the sense that anything was possible, that the potential was unlimited."

BUILDING DROP CITY

At first the Bernofskys simply lived in their car and then in a tent on the land, but soon they decided that they needed a building. In April, shortly before they bought the land, Richert—along with Richard Kallweit and Burt Wadman, who would also shortly become Droppers—had attended a lecture by Buckminster Fuller in Boulder and come away inspired to build geodesic domes. It was hard and creative work. The Droppers set in foundation piles—old telephone poles. They went to a lumber yard and carried away the waste mill ends, the pieces of two-by-fours too short or defective to sell. Once the frame was in place a covering was devised using tar paper, wire, bottle caps, and stucco. It was all incredibly labor-intensive; the Droppers punched two holes in each bottle cap and threaded the caps together with wire making a sort of skeletal fabric for both the inside and outside of the dome. At least the bottle caps were free; the bars in Trinidad were amused at the newcomers who wanted all the used bottle caps they could get, and supplied the raw materials in abundance. There were some false starts, but eventually somehow the bottle caps and wire and stucco coating all hung together, and Drop City was on its way. Two more domes soon followed.

By the time the third dome was ready for an exterior skin, New Mexico–based Steve Baer had arrived on the scene with the revolutionary idea of chopping tops from cars in junkyards and using the metal panels as sheet metal roofing. Baer startled junkyard owners by walking in and offering them a nickel or a dime for car tops; he and the Droppers would take big double-bladed axes and cut the tops out of cars, load them into a truck, drive them to his shop on the outskirts of Albuquerque, shape and form them into dome panels, and then truck them back to Drop City for installation. Together Baer and the Droppers built large, visionary, incredible "zomes," as Baer called his variation of geodesic design, which became the signature architecture of Drop City.[38]

POVERTY AND LIFE

By the prevailing standards of a relentlessly acquisitive society, Drop City was always an economic disaster area. The Bernofskys and Richert had exhausted their resources buying the land and a water meter. To visitors the place often seemed engulfed in poverty, but the Droppers considered poverty a state of mind. As Richert put it, "We were not in a state of poverty mentally, and no one ever went hungry. We owned our land, our buildings, owed no rent, were free of employment, free to create. I felt freer at Drop City than at any other time in my life, and I just can't see that as poverty." The Droppers philosophically opposed employment for pay. As Gene said,

It's important to be employed; work is important, but we felt that to be gainfully employed was a sucking of the soul and that a part of one of the purposes of the new civilization was to be employed, but not to be gainfully employed, so that each individual would be their own master and we idealistically believed that if we were true to that principle, that if we did nongainful work that the cosmic forces would take note of this and would supply us with the necessities of survival.

Scrounging played a role in providing both food and building materials. For a time the principal economic benefactor of the community was the Trinidad Safeway store. One day some Droppers went to the store's manager and asked for food being thrown out. The manager, like many other Trinidadians fairly sympathetic to the down-and-out Droppers, for a time gave them outdated milk, moldy-on-the-outside-but-good-on-the-inside cheese, and the like. Poor soil and aridity made gardening at Drop City unproductive, so Safeway's refuse became a basic link in the food chain.

Scrounging for the material used in building the domes was truly creative. Short pieces of scrap lumber, which were free or very cheap, worked well in domes. Scrap piles and dumps were combed for supplies. At one point the Droppers disassembled bridges on abandoned railroad lines.

The occasional unsolicited donation was a glorious windfall. Gene Bernofsky marveled, "If a check came in for twenty or thirty dollars we felt, BOY! this is great, we've got twenty or thirty dollars, we're gonna make this last; this is going to be great. You know, we're SOLID. And when we felt we were financially stable for a couple of weeks it was as if all of time stretched before us." The Droppers report one special bit of funding at a tight moment: a gift from Buckminster Fuller. They sent Fuller pictures of the domes and encouraged him to visit; he never did get there, but he proclaimed Drop City the winner of the 1966 Dymaxion Award for "poetically economic architecture" and sent a check for five hundred dollars.

EQUALITY

The Droppers were all equal in their poverty. The economy was thoroughly communal. Those joining who had money available contributed it (it never seemed to be much) to the common kitty. Everything else was shared, too. As Jo Ann Bernofsky recalled, "We had this one place where everybody put all their clothes, so theoretically you could wear anything that fit you. Our money was all jointly shared. Cars were shared." Decision making was also shared. When the population reached a dozen or so, Jo Ann noted, "we would sit down in the big dome together and talk—and unless everybody agreed on something, it wouldn't happen. And basically not a whole lot of decisions were made. There was a real strong feeling that anarchy was a good thing, and that everyone should do what they wanted." From the beginning the Droppers were resolutely opposed to having leaders in name or in fact.

NEIGHBORS

One problem that plagued Drop City significantly less than it did many other communes was relations with other residents of the area.

Many of the locals regarded them as crazy, perhaps, but in perennially de-
pressed southern Colorado eking out a marginal living was not at all unusual. Jo Ann, reflecting on the years when she lived there, put it this way:
"People in town thought we were nuts, but interesting nuts. They
thought we were fun. There was no problem with the neighbors. The only
way you could get out of that community was to join the army, or go to
Pueblo; otherwise you were just locked in there. So the kids about our age
were real intrigued by what we were doing. And the adults just thought it
was strange."

CREATIVITY

Art was always a major preoccupation of the Droppers. Some of it
served, intentionally or not, to confuse and astound anyone who would
drive by. The art was amazing, perhaps bewildering, in its variety. There
were large statues and small ones, assemblages of all kinds, found items
painted and mounted, imaginatively painted furniture, and garments, especially strange, colorful hats. There were sculptures of rocket ships and
scarecrows, and many more that were not representational. Some were
puzzling conceptual pieces—a box mounted on a post; a duffel bag hanging from an old floor lamp.

The most renowned artwork created at Drop City, at least in the opinion of the original Droppers, was the Ultimate Painting, a large circular
geometric painting that was rotated under a strobe light—with galvaniz-
ing effect, by all accounts. The Droppers invested a great deal of labor in
the Ultimate Painting and were enormously proud of it; they periodically
offered it for sale at $50,000 or more. There were no buyers, alas, and
eventually it disappeared. An ongoing artwork, perhaps the largest project
of all, was Gene Bernofsky's filming. His interest in cinematography pre-
dated Drop City, and his 16mm camera was there from the very beginning. He documented all of the construction and all of the hordes of
visitors streaming through to the tune of over 20,000 feet of film, although most of it, like the Ultimate Painting, has long since disappeared.

Another artistic project was the creation of *The Being Bag*, a hand-
made black-and-white comic book and a very early example of what
would become an important genre in hippie culture, the underground
comic book. "We wanted the writing to be mysterious and revolutionary
and avant garde," Gene Bernofsky recalled, "and we wanted the illustra-
tions to be the same way. We wanted to put it on heavy bond beautiful pa-

per." Dropper Charlie DiJulio assembled silk screens, and he and other Droppers hand-printed two hundred copies of their fourteen-page revolutionary periodical. They were sure that the comics would sell like hotcakes, providing Drop City with an honest income based on its members' artistic vision. However, it was ahead of its time; only a handful were sold. The first issue of *The Being Bag* was also the last.

Whimsical artistry was even reflected in the Dropper names that every resident soon acquired. Richert recalled that when the very first reporter to visit Drop City (in 1965) asked Gene Bernofsky what his name was, "he just said 'Curly Benson' off the top of his head. Then I said I was Clard Svensen to rhyme with Benson, and then Richard [Kallweit] said he was Larry Lard, to rhyme with Clard. Peggy Kagel said she was Miss Oleomargarine, something superior to lard. So everyone had a Dropper name after that."

The creativity of Drop City was not limited to the artworks. Alternative energy, for example, was pursued there before many Americans had even heard such a phrase. By about 1966 at least one dome was equipped with a solar heat collector. Some of the alternative energy devices were works of art in themselves: one reflective solar collector, for example, was made with an array of automobile mirrors positioned along pieces of pipe—all scrounged materials, of course.

THE OPEN DOOR

Drop City never closed its doors to wayfarers. In the early, relatively stable years, the Droppers were able to cope with the occasional problem visitor, and for the most part they enjoyed meeting artists and writers interested in their iconoclastic new avant-garde commune. As Gene Bernofsky put it, "We wanted to be able to take care of people, society's rejects, and help them. We believed, perhaps insouciantly, that we could do so. During our two years there we provided confidence and hope to *many* hurt people." Furthermore, he said, "We believed in the essential goodness of the cosmic forces, that people who believed in violence and robbing, stealing, shtuping somebody else's old lady, beating on their children, hunting rabbits, strangling coyotes, and shooting birds out of the air" would not have anything to do with Drop City. In the long run, however, the policy caused problems. The "UFO marine" who lived off the community bank account was more than a mooch; Richert recalled that "he carried a gun and threatened people with it—a loaded gun. Everyone was afraid to ask him to leave because he would have just pulled out his gun and said, 'Sorry, I'm not leaving.'" When the FBI came looking for the offender the Droppers were relieved.

TRANSITION

Drop City prospered for its first three or four years. By the first summer a fairly stable group of Droppers had developed, along with a number of transients. Clark Richert reckons the number of core Droppers at twelve to fourteen. Gene believed that after about a year the Droppers were "melding as a group," that "we were starting really to form up as an organism." But by 1970 the commune was badly off track; by 1973 it was closed. Somehow the dream was derailed.

Some of the older Droppers blame the long decline on the assiduous cultivation of publicity for Drop City by Peter Rabbit, who had arrived in 1966. The commune soon gained national attention: the *Time* cover story for July 7, 1967, was a feature on "Youth: The Hippies," and Drop City was described and illustrated with a color photograph. That summer also witnessed the Joy Festival, conceived and promoted by Peter Rabbit, which featured rock and roll music and a display of Dropper art, along with (in Richert's words) "all kinds of drum music and bell ringing, jingling and jangling, chanting." One person's joy is another's disaster, however, and the Joy Festival marked the end of the Bernofskys' road. As Gene said, the Joy Festival, "coupled with the arrival of *Time* magazine symbolized the end of a place and the way we had envisioned it would go. We figured that the powers of evil had finally won out. The powers of media had won out. They were going to suck us. Too much, too early, and it was the end."

Richert generally was happier with the direction Drop City was taking than were the Bernofskys. When he left in 1968, a year after the Bernofskys had gone, it wasn't out of disgust: since settling at Drop City he had married one of the local young frequent visitors there, and his wife, Susie, was now pregnant. They decided that they needed to improve her diet, get an income, and at least for the time being drop back into the real world. Richert thought he might return, but never did. Peter Rabbit left later in 1968, not long after the departure of the Richerts, to become a cofounder of the Libre community.[39]

Despite the departure of the founders, good times still remained for Drop City. Life went on with no great changes for another year or so, save for a fairly steady turnover of personnel. Visitors continued to stream through; among the celebrities Peter Rabbit lists as having visited were Bob Dylan, Timothy Leary, Billy Hitchcock, Richard Alpert, Jim Morrison, and Peter Fonda.[40] One of the major domes went up in 1968 and provided housing for the many visitors.

At some point the open-door policy was abandoned, and visitors were discouraged. A note in a directory of communes in the Fall 1969 issue of *Modern Utopian* rather curtly announced that "New members must meet specific criteria."[41] The community was declining and changing; after 1969 or 1970 Drop City ceased to resemble much of anything the founders had envisioned or participated in. By late 1969 only one Dropper who had been there in the first year—Larry Lard (Richard Kallweit)—was still present,[42] and he would leave within a few months as the downhill slide accelerated. Drop City about this time saw its first death, a suicide. Reporters and writers continued to visit, and their depiction of life there is fairly consistently grim. Hugh Gardner reported it this way:

The entire commune of forty (give or take a few) people and its constant stream of visitors somehow got by on food stamps and a sporadic income that seldom exceeded $100 a month. If one was simply marking time and interested in having fun, Drop City in 1970 was a very economical way to do it. But fun came at a certain price. The kitchen was filthy, and there was no soap because money was short. Hepatitis had recently swept through the commune, and still no one was motivated enough to see that soap was made available. Sleeping quarters were seriously overcrowded. The outhouse was filled to overflowing, and there was no lime to sterilize it. In 1970 Drop City had become, if it was not from the first, a laboratory dedicated to a totally minimal existence.[43]

And things were to get yet worse. Clark Richert visited occasionally, and he characterized the residents as "motorcycle and speed freaks"; on one of his last visits he found the occupants to consist of a motorcycle gang living in squalor (putrid outhouses, infestations of insects). Jo Ann Bernofsky was equally glum: "It reminded me of a New York City subway station, kind of, in its qualities—kind of dragged out. Too many people had walked through. Nobody had done the dishes for a long time. It was just like there was none of the nurturing going on. It was just like it was all sucked dry."

The final dissolution of Drop City as a communal residence came in early 1973, when the last desperate residents moved out. A few old Droppers dropped back by, locked and nailed shut some buildings, and posted "Keep Out" signs all around. In about 1978 the land was sold to a neighbor. Without maintenance the domes began to crumble, although most survived for a few years.

The Bernofskys left Drop City sadly. Gene, especially, believes that the wonderful dream of a new civilization turned out disastrously. Jo Ann is not quite as downbeat as Gene; her feelings are ambivalent, a mix of fond memories and regrets that things didn't turn out quite as she and Gene had hoped. Clark Richert, on the other hand, continues to treasure his Dropper memories: "I always saw it as the best thing that ever happened to me in my life. I don't regard it as a failure at all. The energy of those times was intense. I think most people, or many people, feel that way about the period. There was something very special about it. We really felt that we were right on the forefront of existence, that we were going to change everything, or at least participate in a total change of everything." In that regard Drop City was part of the larger energy of the counterculture. Richert again: "Ideas were in the air, and they were hatching all over the place. There was a sense of creativity and being on the cutting edge. That was the feeling of the times. So what I'm talking about that I associate with Drop City was felt by people all over the world."

3

Communes Begin to Spread

1965–1967

Drop City marked the beginning of what would be for a year or two a trickle and after that a flood of communes throughout the United States. The majority of the early communal activity took place in three general locations: California, especially the northern part of the state; northern New Mexico; and the Northeast, from New England down to Virginia.

California: The Hog Farm and Friends

Although most of the California communes that stirred the public imagination ran northward from Santa Cruz, the one that was probably the first of them all was hundreds of miles to the south, in the greater Los Angeles area. The Hog Farm emerged from the imaginations of Hugh Romney and friends in 1965, about the time Drop City was getting started; after 1969, when the Hog Farmers ran a "Please Force" that oversaw feeding and medicating the multitudes at the Woodstock rock festival, it became one of the most famous hip communes of all.

Romney was involved in comedy and the theatre in New York and then California in the late 1950s and early 1960s, hanging out with Merry Pranksters and other protohippies; by 1965 he was, among other things, teaching improvisation to brain-damaged children and to young actors at Columbia Pictures.[1] Suddenly he and a small group of friends were offered an inviting deal—the free use of a farmhouse and thirty-odd acres in Sunland, California, on a mountain overlooking the San Fernando Valley, in return for tending the owner's swine and paying the nominal taxes on the place. Their communal name followed their new function, and the Hog Farm was born. Over the first year of life on the mountain new Hog Farmers found their way to the offbeat encampment, and a durable hip institution began to take shape as an array of geodesic domes, tents, and miscellaneous vehicles provided the built environment for a free-form community. Life was the stuff of countercultural legend: the Hog Farmers carried slop for the hogs up the hill on their backs when the dirt road was impassable, lived on brown rice and discarded overripe produce, kept a community clothing stash in an abandoned Buick, and indulged themselves in plenty of play and psychedelics. Crowds would come out for the happenings and celebrations that took place every Sunday afternoon. Fortunately for the Hog Farmers, one ominous visiting party exuded bad vibes and was asked to leave; Charles Manson and his "girls" were among the few ever resolutely kicked off the Hog Farm.[2] Manson (who had not yet achieved infamy as an orchestrator of ritual killings) aside, the neighbors were predictably worried about it all: they blocked the convenient access road to the Hog Farm, forcing the Farmers to clear and use an old Forest Service road, and in 1967 the local newspaper rumbled that local residents "wonder if these people might be a Red Trojan horse in their midst."[3]

Wanderlust soon affected the Farmers, and by 1967 they had acquired some old buses and began to take to the road, running light shows and other support functions at rock concerts and entertaining the multitudes of onlookers they attracted. At about the same time they also acquired what they expected to become a permanent base, a tract of some twelve acres in Llano, New Mexico. By 1969 they had enough of a history as a group to be plausible support troops at Woodstock, where they were hired to run a free kitchen and to tend to medical needs—especially drug-related freakouts. By all accounts they performed a horrendously difficult task splendidly, and Romney, both at the festival and onstage in the movie version that followed, became a nationally familiar figure.[4] Shortly after Woodstock they were offered another similar gig at a Texas music festival, at which B. B. King anointed Romney with the name that he has worn ever since: Wavy Gravy.

The Hog Farmers eventually wended their way back to New Mexico, only to find that their new fame had preceded them. As Wavy later recalled, "Hundreds and hundreds of people had loaded their stuff up and hopped into cars" and shown up to join the party.[5] At dinnertime hundreds would line up to be fed, and even the resourceful Hog Farmers were not willing or able to meet that challenge on an ongoing basis.[6] After sorting their way through that chaotic scene the Hog Farmers hopped back on their buses and went to Texas for their festival job there. The New Mexico Hog Farm has remained in existence, largely independent of the larger group that resettled in California.

Many of the Hog Farmers, including Wavy, purchased a house in Berkeley in 1976, and then in 1979 they moved into a house on Henry Street that has been the main center ever since. In 1982 they purchased the first tract of land for Black Oak Ranch, their retreat at Laytonville, California, that now encompasses several hundred acres; both Berkeley and Black Oak thus serve as stable main Hog Farm habitats at this writing. Black Oak Ranch has become the scene of a major annual party—"Pignic"—each Labor Day weekend, the proceeds of which make the mortgage payments on the property, and as of the late 1990s—despite some local opposition reminiscent of that the rock festivals faced in the 1960s—it was a solidly popular event, drawing crowds in the thousands.[7]

Wavy and the Hog Farm continue largely to live up to their standard early description of themselves: "The Hog Farm is an expanded family, a mobile hallucination, an army of clowns . . . we are 50 people on a perpetual trip, citizens of earth."[8] Wavy personally runs Camp Winnarainbow at Black Oak Ranch for most of each summer, providing what is widely acclaimed as a fine alternative summer camp for children, with activities ranging from classes in clowning to watersliding into a lake. An adult camp is held as well. The group does serious charitable work with the Seva Foundation, which (among other things) fights blindness in third-world countries. Wavy has continued to poke fun at the political process with election-year tours promoting Nobody for President, and he has reached perhaps his greatest post-Woodstock renown by having a flavor of Ben and Jerry's ice cream named after him, the royalties from which support the Camp Winnarainbow scholarship fund. The Hog Farm, one of the oldest surviving 1960s communes, is alive and well at the dawn of the twenty-first century.

The Diggers

At the same time as the Hog Farm was reaching its peak in southern California in 1966, a new communally-oriented group was taking shape in

San Francisco. The Diggers, named after a seventeenth-century English movement of defenders of the commons against royal usurpation, were collectively a key catalyst for the great mushrooming of hip culture. Diggers were a lot of things at once: a theatrical troupe, a service organization, a band of outlaws, and an urban commune, or more properly several—perhaps as many as thirty-five—scattered communal houses. They emerged in large part from the San Francisco Mime Troupe, which in the early 1960s combined avant-garde theater and art with radical politics. By the fall of 1966 the Diggers, fighting the supremacy of money in society, were practicing "garbage yoga," taking society's leftovers and distributing them in the form of dishing up free food daily in the Panhandle extension of Golden Gate Park, running free stores in which "customers" could take and leave items at will, and living communally in several houses that became notable Haight-Ashbury community centers. Much of the food was gathered by Digger women who charmed vendors out of their leftovers at the local farmers' market; they were so successful that one of them later recalled, "We had so much food that we were using squash for doorstops."[9] Reflecting on Digger life from the vantage point of the early 1980s, Judy Berg recalled:

> We put together a credo, which was "Do your own thing"—no restraints, no rules—and "Everything is free." That provided so much open space that anything could happen, and often did. . . . What we did we called "life acting," where you act out your fantasies, you act out the best way you would like things to be. It was essentially an Anarchist Life Theater.[10]

Sympathetic physicians began to offer free medical care at a free store, a project that soon grew into the Haight-Ashbury Free Medical Clinic.[11] Digger-like groups began to spring up in other cities. Digger thinking had a huge influence on the emerging counterculture, and the antimoney, communitarian Digger way had a powerful impact on those who would found communes, both in the city and in the countryside.

The Crashpads

The Digger commitment to the free life inspired countless other similar activities, and one of the results of it all was the emergence of thousands of crashpads, places where at least in theory anyone could drop in for a day or a month. At its worst the crashpad had no organization at all but was simply some kind of indoor space in which anyone could stay, and except for having a high concentration of persons staying there they could hardly be regarded as intentionally communal. Crashpads did, however, represent a step toward serious communal living. Allen Cohen has observed that they were "not quite communes, but we started to develop the idea of communal living by living together in that sort of association. We learned skills of intimacy and we got used to sharing and being concerned about each other."[12] As Jay Stevens described the scene,

Your first night in the Haight was usually spent in one of the many communal crashpads, sandwiched together with a dozen friendly strangers. Your inhibitions and frequently your virginity were the first things to go, followed by your clothes and your old values—a progressive shedding that was hastened along by your first acid trip. Within days your past life in Des Moines or Dallas or wherever was as remote as the school outings you took as an adolescent.[13]

Some surveying the scene saw mainly infectious diseases (including hepatitis and gonorrhea), chaotic childrearing and resultant high pediatric disease rates, and other disasters.[14] But not all of the urban crashpads were disgusting; some functioned quite well, with organized meals and assigned sleeping places, and several amounted to full-blown social service agencies. The most famous of the latter was Galahad's pad on East 11th Street in New York City's East Village. Galahad, originally Ronald Johnson from Kansas City, took over an abandoned tenement building and its ten or so run-down apartments and typically had twenty to thirty mostly teenaged crashers staying there on any given day. He imposed rules, at least in theory—no drugs on the premises, and no hitting on underage girls. By middle-class standards it was squalid, but for a time it all worked remarkably well and Galahad's generosity was widely admired in the straight world as well as among the hip.[15] It crumbled, however, after his pal Groovy (James Hutchinson)—who had helped him get it all going— was brutally murdered in October 1967, in one of the insane crimes that had a lot to do with bringing to an end the age of hip.

Similarly, in California, Sylvia Anderson—who would go on to live at Wheeler's Ranch, Ananda Village, and the Farm (Tennessee)—opened up her Haight-Ashbury apartment to crashers when she found herself unable to turn down people who needed a place to stay and found it a positive experience:

Suddenly my apartment became a crash pad. That was my first real experience with communal living although it wasn't totally communal because I was paying the rent and buying the food and doing all the housework. But at least it was living with a bunch of people. Finally I went to the country for a week and left all the crashers/extended family in my household. I came back to find they had taken care of everything themselves; they had gone out and manifested the money and done the housecleaning and had a real community going. I created a vacuum and it was filled by the kids that were living there and that was a good teaching for me.[16]

An unusual twist on crashing came in 1968 with the establishment of the Family in Bronx Park in New York. A crowd ranging from twenty to forty persons, mainly in their upper teenage years, took over a quiet corner of the park and built odd little shelters. Park officials seemed to look the other way for a time, and the little band worked merrily at improving its buildings, even winterizing them. A cruising police officer, however, eventually saw a fire (contained in a brazier), and the violation of the no-open-fires rule in the park brought it all down. The Family's shelters were flattened, and the shelter of a hermit who had long been living quietly nearby was destroyed as well.[17]

Free Land in Sonoma County:
Morning Star Ranch and Wheeler's Ranch

While the Diggers were transforming the Haight-Ashbury, new cultural currents were also beginning to run an hour-and-a-half's drive north, a few miles west of Sebastopol. In the spring of 1966 Ramón Sender moved onto a 31.7-acre tract of land that would become the most storied of all the hip communes of its era, Morning Star Ranch. The story of Morning Star, however, properly begins with that of its owner (at least until he donated the land to God), Lou Gottlieb. Gottlieb, a talented musician and scholar,[18] was the bass player and irrepressible humorist for the Limeliters, a trio that rode the folk-music boom of the late 1950s and early 1960s to considerable fame and fortune (the latter mainly from a Coca-Cola commercial and some prime-time television work). By 1963, however, the stress of life on the road, a harrowing plane crash, an introduction to LSD, and unsettling health problems had left Gottlieb looking at new life options. "When an illness is undiagnosable it's a thirst for the divine," he told one interviewer. "If you're grooving with the environment, you don't need a doctor."[19] He decided to seek his environmental groove.

In the meantime, Gottlieb had purchased land in Sonoma County, a beautiful tract with second-growth redwood trees, two houses, the remains of a once-extensive chicken farm, and a producing apple orchard.

He initially had the notion of dividing it into seven lots for upscale homes, but his musical career and family and other obligations kept him from taking any action—or even visiting the land very often.

Living in San Francisco, Gottlieb took a job as music critic for the *San Francisco Chronicle*. The job lasted only a few weeks, but during that short span he met several persons who were on the cutting edge of the changing music and cultural scene—Ramón Sender, Stewart Brand, Ben Jacopetti, and Bill Graham, among others. In March 1966 Gottlieb and some of his new friends drove up to the land to spend a day, and the following month Sender and his girlfriend, Gina Stillman, asked Lou if they could spend their Easter vacation week there. Gottlieb said sure, and with that the land at Morning Star was opened. Stillman left at the end of the week to return to her teaching job, thereafter visiting only on weekends, but Sender became the land's first permanent resident.

Within a few weeks Ben Jacopetti and his wife Rain moved up as well. Gottlieb joined them in June, having had the old egg storage shed remodeled to house him and his grand piano. Gradually others began to show up, and the nucleus of the community took shape. One day someone found some old bills made out to "Morning Star Ranch" in a closet, and that former name—which stemmed from an earlier owner's dedication of the land to the Virgin Mary—was quickly revived. Most of the members were active spiritual seekers in those days, Sender doing the sun yoga in which he had become interested from his reading of Aurobindo, Ben Jacopetti sitting Zen. Together they read a wide variety of spiritual texts— the works of John Humphrey Noyes, Ouspensky, Lama Govinda—often out loud. They did yoga and meditated and examined their chakras. When three of them went to a community conference in Santa Cruz that fall, they represented Morning Star, a small religious ashram.[20]

Through most of that first summer the Morning Star seekers numbered only a handful. In November, their chronicle records, the first seven young persons arrived from the Haight-Ashbury.[21] A steady stream followed thereafter, until the deluge hit in the summer of 1967—the Summer of Love. As Gottlieb (in 1996) explained the sequence of events,

From time to time people would come by and eventually, in early '67, Digger Ed and a guy named Calvino de Felippies and others from the Diggers came by and said, "Well, we're expecting two million freaked out teenagers and these people gotta have something to eat; is it okay if we send somebody up to take care of the orchard so we could have the apples?" I said all right. Next thing I know, the Dig-

ger store in Haight-Ashbury, I am told, had a sign in it that said visit the Digger
farm with instructions on how to get to Morning Star Ranch and that was the beginning of the deluge. So, by July 1967, there were frequently evenings when we
had three hundred for dinner.[22]

It didn't take long for the growing crowd of residents and visitors to
be noticed by the local public officials. One resident who arrived early in
1967, a sixteen-year-old girl, went to the local hospital with a yeast infec-
tion, and hospital officials—horrified about such a medical problem in
such a young girl—notified the police. On April 1 the inevitable drug raid
occurred. No illegal substances were found, because the residents had
been warned of the raid, and in any event (as Gottlieb put it) "[t]here was
rarely any sacrament on the place because when it arrived, it was con-
sumed."[23] But encounters with law-enforcement and public health officials
would become a major feature of the Morning Star life.

Among many other things, Morning Star with its resolute lack of rules
became a haven for nudity, to the consternation (and fascination) of the
neighbors. Reporters, naturally, made the presence of nudity prominent
in their stories, and—in a fashion reminiscent of the Doukhobors, the
Russian-Canadian separatists who disrobed to protest the state's exercise
of its authority over them—unclothed women were always the first to
greet the public officials who arrived to try to shut the ranch down. Some
Morning Star stalwarts went so far as to make it a point to disrobe upon
arrival and get dressed again only when they left to go into town. Sandi
Stein, one of the young teenagers who was drawn to Morning Star, sometimes kept her clothes stashed near the gate, since they weren't needed
anywhere else. Pam Read was photographed nude for the *Time* cover story on the hippies of July 7, 1967; as she later wrote, "My parents couldn't
brag that their daughter was in a national magazine because she was stark
raving naked."[24]

As one might surmise, Morning Star saw a lot of sexual activity. Some
residents were coupled, but a great many were single and right at the heart
of the sexual revolution that was just then climaxing. One woman who
lived at Morning Star for some time recalled in 1996:

I was very young, and sexually active. Part of the deal was that, clearly, when I
went to Morning Star, I was supposed to have sex with everyone. There was kind
of an underlying assumption of free love. Morning Star had a myth that there was
a "phantom fucker." If you were alone at Morning Star—anybody, a man, a
woman—somebody would come in the night and console you, and have sex with

you. I'll tell you, it was pretty interesting to wake up in the night and find somebody in your sleeping bag with you. It was just kind of an assumed thing that everybody wanted to have sex with everybody else. Whether this is the downside or the upside or the in-between side, I don't know. But it was part of the deal.[25]

Nudity, psychedelics, and sex notwithstanding, the focus of Morning Star remained largely spiritual in its early years. Many of the residents continued their practice of yoga, and reading the works of great spiritual masters (particularly Asian) was standard Morning Star fare. Some of those who showed up from early 1967 on were practicing Christians, and their practice blended right into the spiritual stream. As time went by and the renown of Morning Star increased, various spiritual leaders visited the Ranch. One of the first, in April 1967, was Swami A. C. Bhaktivedanta, known to his followers as Prabhupada, the founder of the International Society for Krishna Consciousness, who gave a talk, oversaw the chanting of the Hare Krishna mantra—and made six converts on the spot, several of whom became leaders in ISKCON. Gottlieb drily noted in his autobiography that two of them "came back to Morning Star after they had become celibate and tried to proselytize, but the girls all gathered around them in the nude and they decided that their principles would be less severely tested elsewhere."[26]

The Asian spiritual quest peaked late in 1968 when Gottlieb joined some friends on a trip to India. There Gottlieb met up with several other visiting Californians—including Don McCoy, by then the patron of the Olompali Ranch commune near Novato, California—who introduced him to their newly-discovered guru, a beggar named Ciranjiva Roy. In a matter of minutes Gottlieb believed that he had met the "Lord Shiva in human form" and became his disciple. Eventually, Gottlieb was able to sponsor "Father" (as Ciranjiva liked to be known) to the United States, and with great fanfare he arrived at Morning Star. His Shivite practice embraced the use of marijuana and any other consciousness-affecting substance—Gottlieb wrote that "he was offered every kind of mind bender in the world, and I never saw him turn anything down"—and that of course endeared him to the psychedelic pilgrims of Morning Star.[27] They were a bit disconcerted, however, when he tried cheap American fortified wine and pronounced it spiritually as useful as hashish or anything else—and, because it was cheaper, actually preferable. Not only were they convinced that alcohol was an inferior drug, but a group of drinkers had settled into a corner of the Ranch that became known as Wino Flats, and with their fighting, aggressive shaking down of visitors, and thievery had become a big headache for everyone else.

Ciranjiva may have meshed with Morning Star's interest in alteration of consciousness, but the lack of creature comforts there decidedly did not appeal to him, and within a week he was ready to move on. As Don Mc-Coy recalled, "Father said, 'I didn't come to America to eat brown rice and take off clothes. I want steak! I want steak!'"[28] He asked for an apartment in San Francisco, which his devotees duly provided for him. Although his association with Gottlieb, McCoy, and many other rural communards continued, he founded his own communal movement, Siva Kalpa, and developed his own new following—at the core of which were eight "goddesses," or plural wives for the master, who bore him some twenty-two children. For the several years until his death in 1981 Ciranjiva was venerated by his followers as a profound spiritual teacher.[29] Those less captivated by his message had a decidedly different opinion of him: he was mainly interested in endless sex and drugs, and it all became tiresome.

Hostility from neighbors and public officials increased right along with the population of Morning Star. The deadbeats of Wino Flats and occasional visiting gun-toting motorcycle gangs were particular nuisances, and the nudity and substance use of the hippies were continually offensive to the public sensibilities of most of the people of Sonoma County. A sympathetic visitor, C. P. Herrick, undertook an "ecological study" of Morning Star in 1968 and found serious overcrowding and deterioration in the few available buildings, some two dozen impromptu structures that were not "close enough to code that they could be legalized without major reconstruction," and many tents. The two toilets on the property were overwhelmed (Gottlieb at one point sank a good deal of money into a community bathhouse, but it failed to pass inspection); thus the residents were forced to eliminate in the woods and often "did not adequately bury their feces and paper." A less sympathetic visitor, sociologist Lewis Yablonsky, titled his chapter on the Ranch "The Morningstar Bummer" and related tales of rape and other violence, concluding that "apparently the chaotic violent scene we were viewing was the normal condition at Morningstar." Gottlieb was unmoved by the critics of disorder: "I've changed my attitude about litter and garbage considerably. A parade ground is neat as a pin: 'All right, men, let's field strip this place, let's get this place policed up. . . .' That's death! . . . I'm not sure but that the whole world has to become a compost heap, because we've just about done mother in."[30] Once Gottlieb went so far as to say that because he equated God with a pantheistic respect for nature, "shitting in the garden" was nothing less than the constitutionally protected free exercise of religion.[31]

In July 1967, Gottlieb was arrested and charged with running an "organized camp" in violation of state sanitation regulations. "If they find any evidence of organization here, I wish they would show it to me," he deadpanned, but he pleaded no contest and was given time to comply with the rules.[32] County officials pressed on, in mid-September obtaining a court order for him to close the property. After several further skirmishes the county arrested twenty residents in January 1968 for living on the property in violation of the court order. More arrests and fines followed throughout the year. Then, in May 1969, Gottlieb dropped an unanticipated bomb on the county—he deeded the land to God, volunteering to continue to pay the taxes for the deity. A judge, however, ruled that "whatever the nature of the Divine, God is neither a person, natural or artificial, in existence at time of conveyance and capable of taking title."[33] Other responses to Gottlieb's move were oddly supportive: in an act as poetic as any of Gottlieb's, one Betty Penrose of Phoenix sued the deity for $100,000, claiming that she had suffered a major loss by an act of God when lightning had struck her house in 1960, and God now had assets that could presumably be sold for her benefit. The defendant, however, could not be located for legal service. Not to be outdone, a prisoner at San Quentin who claimed to be God announced that the land was now his.[34]

The county finally took decisive action by bulldozing the many odd structures—idiosyncratic houses and shacks by the dozens—that dotted Morning Star. In fact the bulldozers would eventually level the property four times; after each razing some of the stalwart defenders of the Morning Star faith doggedly rebuilt their rude shelters and continued to defy the authorities by living on at the Ranch. Some continued there until 1973; but by then everyone was tired. Many had fled to friendlier open-land precincts nearby, or as far away as New Mexico. The Morning Star property finally became uninhabited; God's land was at peace.

THE GOSPEL OF OPEN LAND

Lou Gottlieb was not the inventor of the concepts of open land—land access to which is denied no one, as he put it—or of deeding one's land to God, but he was certainly an eloquent spokesman for those points of view.[35] Open land became his passion during the battle of Morning Star, and he persuaded other landowners similarly to give access to all. Until his death in 1996 he expounded the concept at every opportunity.

The reason Morning Star Ranch was a "beacon" and its main historic significance, in my opinion, is that it constituted the first attempt to live on "land-access-to-which-is denied-no-one"—the legal form of which is "waqf"—Arabic for divine ownership of immovable property. It was an attempt to solve the principal problem of communal organization, namely, who stays and who's gotta go, by letting the land choose its inhabitants thereby forming a tribe. The day may arrive when transferring the ownership of small remote portions of Public Land to God will provide appropriate tribal sanctuary for some of the desperate, technologically unemployable, inner city inhabitants—a constructive alternative to incendiary rioting.[36]

The Morning Star houses were rented when Gottlieb bought the land, and he continued to collect rent for a time; he had not yet concluded (as he later would) that "[c]ollecting rent is lower than whale shit which, as you all know, is at the bottom of the ocean." His first step toward enlightenment apparently came during the first days of Morning Star settlement in the spring of 1966, when Bruce Bailey asked what it might cost him to rent a small shed there to use as a film cutting studio. Gottlieb responded, "Oh, $40 a month," whereupon the dog standing beside them bared her teeth at him.[37] When the large crowds began showing up in 1967 another lesson was driven home:

We had a meeting. It was decided that Nevada, Gypsy, TW and Crazy Annie had to go. They were too much. Out of the question. They could not stay. Gypsy, for example, had the habit of pulling his knife in grocery stores. . . .

When their car pulled into the area next to my studio, I went out to confront them. All [of them] were in the car. I said, "That's it! We've decided you have to leave." Well, they took it in good grace except that Nevada said, "Hey, it'll take me about a week to get my stuff together—to find another place to stay." The next day Gypsy came to me and said, "I'm beggin' you, I gotta stay here." And I said, "No, no, I can't, you know." I was very firm.

Then I began to get into serious physical trouble. I had the worst "yin fit" I've ever had in my life. I had a headache I could have entered in the World's Fair, cold sweats, mild nausea and uncontrollable weeping, all of which summarized in my mind that God's will was for me to stop doing that. That was the last time I ever asked anyone to leave Morning Star.[38]

Actually, he did—albeit involuntarily—ask people to leave again later that year. The most vocal hostile neighbor had sought a permanent injunction to close Morning Star, and a sheriff's deputy told Gottlieb that the only way he could avoid it was to order everyone to leave and then to make a citizen's arrest for trespassing of any who remained. So he went around the gathered throng announcing that each was under arrest, and then they were hauled off to jail. The world-class headache returned.

From that point on Gottlieb evicted no one, and he paid dearly for his convictions in steep fines levied by the Sonoma County court. His attachment to open land became if anything more devout and sweeping in its analysis:

Remember, open land has a terrifying connotation: free rent. That upsets not only the running dogs of imperialism, but a vast number of petit bourgeoisie who are renting a garage apartment, or the mother-in-law facility or something. I'm talking about some of my best friends, dear hearts who may feel a little self conscious collecting rents, but no great guilt about the landlord role which may be the core of the wrong relationship to the earth's surface. . . . We are talking about the fons et origo of an ecological mistake that could render the planet uninhabitable by homo sapiens—in legal terms "fee simple" which conveys to the title holder "absolute dominion over the land."[39]

In short, as ur–Morning Star resident Ramón Sender summarized Gottlieb's position, "Free rent strikes at the heart of the beast."[40] And, as Gottlieb contended for the rest of his life, opening some pieces of land might just help solve chronic social problems such as homelessness. If we were to open just eight widely scattered eighty-acre tracts in California, then "we are inviting the participation of the creative faculty of the universe in human affairs in a way that's never been done before. I'm saying put God into the real estate business."[41]

WHEELER'S RANCH

The heat at Morning Star did eventually disperse its residents, and one outlet was Bill Wheeler's ranch a few miles to the west. Wheeler had used his inheritance from a sewing-machine fortune to purchase a good bit of land—the main ranch has 360 acres—in 1965 and happened, as any neighbor would, upon the Morning Star scene. Lou Gottlieb, ever the apostle of open land, made Wheeler a convert.

After the mass arrest in early 1968 for living on the land in violation of a court order, many at Morning Star searched for a new place to settle. Bill Wheeler's land was an obvious solution to the problem. When asked by a Morning Star resident (at the time Gottlieb's girlfriend) who called herself Near-Vana to open his land, Wheeler replied that he had never closed it. As he later recalled,

I was deeply sensitive to the fact that I had more land than I needed. I began to feel it was my duty to share it. The Morning Star family was being hassled and arrested daily. It was a heartbreaking drama. They desperately needed a home. . . . What I would like to say essentially about opening the Ridge is that it was a real leap of faith, a real leap into the darkness, or the light—or whatever you want to call it. And it was an incredible, very revolutionary thing. One of the reasons why I opened the Ridge was because I wanted a place in history.[42]

Larry Read was the first Morning Star refugee to appear at Wheeler's that spring. Once he had chosen an isolated campsite at the bottom of a canyon he brought his wife Pam and son Adam Siddhartha over from Morning Star, and after that others came streaming in. Little shelters soon dotted Wheeler's Ranch. Hoping to avoid the situations that had focused so much controversy on Morning Star, Bill Wheeler—in his role as benevolent and benign leader—proclaimed a few basic rules that were obeyed to some extent: no open fires during the dry season; no dogs (they would wreak havoc on the neighbors' sheep, not to mention the community itself); bury your feces. Of the last rule, one resident explained: "When one's bowels began to move, one took a shovel in hand and a brief walk in the fresh country air to select the perfect spot for a donation to Mother Earth. . . . I chose to have a different view from my toilet every day."[43]

The expansiveness of the hundreds of acres punctuated by deep canyons spared Wheeler's the population density that gave Morning Star ongoing problems. Although the population at its peak exceeded two hundred, anyone could find a place to build a simple shelter well removed from the rest. Those who so chose could work on common projects, especially the large community garden that produced a good deal of the community's scarce food. Bill Wheeler bought a cow, and then another, for a community milk supply that provided a basic level of protein that otherwise probably would have been missing.[44] Chickens ran loose, and anyone who found an egg could eat it. Generally the scattered residents fended for themselves, but food was often shared, both informally and at common meals—especially the weekly Sunday feast. Other communal events flourished: parties, sweat baths, and psychedelic occasions. Those who wanted to grow a bit of marijuana could usually find a remote place to do so. Many who published accounts of their visits found Wheeler's the quietest, most easygoing commune around.[45] Visiting journalist Sara Davidson observed that at Wheeler's "the days mulled together and no one wore watches."[46] Nudity was as common at Wheeler's as it had been at Morning Star, but Wheeler's did not have immediate neighbors to be offended by it. In fact the community was far removed from just about any casual observation, down a miles-long, excruciatingly potholed and muddy driveway.

On the other hand, what was going on at Wheeler's could not exactly be kept secret. The driveway crossed over a neighbor's land, and the neighbor took an intense dislike to the new scene. Later a court injunction would close access, forcing those who would go in or out to walk by another route some eight miles long, through an adjoining property that Bill Wheeler had quietly purchased as a safety valve. And the remoteness of the property did not keep out all the riffraff; several of the "Impossibles" from Morning Star, as they were generally known, migrated up the Coleman Valley Road to the new mecca of open land, causing huge headaches for Bill and Gay Wheeler and everyone else—sometimes even shooting their guns off randomly. Over time these problem cases would abet the Ranch's difficulties.[47]

The first skirmishes with authority came when federal agents came onto the land looking for draft evaders. Periodic drug busts, predictably, also punctuated the commune's legal history. Before too long the Sonoma County authorities sought, as they had at Morning Star, to shut down this new haven of unrestrained and decidedly unconventional behaviors. In late April 1969, the county building inspector showed up with a warrant to make an inspection of the structures, which he did at great length. In July the district attorney asked for the local court to order the destruction of all of the impromptu dwellings on the land. Wheeler hired a lawyer and fought the county for a long time, at one point even filing a suit alleging that Sonoma County was violating the community's civil rights. In 1970 Wheeler tried a variation of Gottlieb's deeding of his land to God, giving the property to a new religious body, the Ahimsa Church.[48]

Eventually, however, it became clear that he could spend all his money and still lose. Even the volunteer assistance from a major San Francisco law firm that suddenly materialized just when Bill Wheeler had reached the end of his rope with his previous attorney could not stave off the inevitable. Once it became clear that the bulldozers were at hand, in May 1973 people began to dismantle their little structures in the hope that they somehow might be able to reuse the lumber. Before they could finish, the bulldozers did indeed appear—just as they had at Morning Star. After witnessing a day of destruction, Wheeler resolved not to let his adversaries have the satisfaction of completing their job—an expensive one that would be billed to him, no less—by spending several more days bulldozing the fifty remaining homes. With a friend he set out to beat them to the punch:

Rod poured some gas in a corner, threw a match, and the house was a roaring inferno. Flames licked up through the fog, burning a hole through to the clear, night sky. Hypnotized, we watched with a strange pleasure, a morbid fascination. In a flash of nature's energies, a house disappeared in just five minutes.

All that night we went from house to house reenacting the same ritual. We began competing for the right to light the match, turning into insane pyromaniacs. Purification. God power. . . . At dawn we torched the last house on the Knoll. We had burned all fifty. Stumbling home, I met Rod, who was standing by his burning cabin. "Let it all go," he said. "Wanna roast some marshmallows?"[49]

Wheeler threw in the towel. He rebuilt his own house to minimal code, even going so far as to install a septic tank. At this writing he remains at the Ranch, with a landmate or two but no big crowd. He has pursued the career as an artist that was diverted by all the controversy over open land, selling creative paintings for good money. Life and land continue.

Communal Rumblings in the East

Across the continent from Morning Star and Wheeler's Ranch, communes developed independently of but in chronological synchronicity with their western counterparts. Two main wellsprings contributed to the early eastern communes: the behaviorism of B. F. Skinner and the revival of old communitarian enthusiasm at the School of Living's new Heathcote Center. Several communes emerged from those energy sources in 1965 and 1966, after which the floodgates opened as they did elsewhere in the country.

THE WALDEN TWO EXPERIMENTS:
THE ROAD TO TWIN OAKS

In 1948 the psychologist B. F. Skinner published a book that would have a greater impact on 1960s-era communalism than any other: *Walden Two*. Skinner's novel follows a classic formula for literary utopias: a visitor happens into an ideal intentional community and describes what he sees in glowing terms—in this case a community that uses the relatively new social science of behaviorism to provide its members, living in a near-paradise, with lives of agreeable work, abundant leisure, and intellectual stimulation. Members build their own low-cost, efficient buildings; they can choose which jobs to perform, with compensation in work-credits reflecting the desirability of the work; planners and managers steer the community's life and work for the benefit of all. At first the novel attracted little attention, but in the 1960s it developed a wide following. Skinner's vision was an attractive one, and it had a seeming practicality about it—to many readers it seemed to be a plausible blueprint for a satisfying way of life. Thus, a good many persons caught up in the Skinnerian vision decided to enact it, just as readers of earlier utopian novels had tried to enact those works.[50]

The first of the Walden Two communities was Walden House, a seven-bedroom edifice in a run-down neighborhood in Washington, D.C., which opened in 1965 as a cooperative in which everyone paid an equal share of the costs and did equal housework and maintenance.[51] The scanty reports on it are mostly negative: it was dogged with financial problems, its policy of open membership attracted some residents generally regarded as undesirable, and it saw conflicts over its social direction, as in the case of whether to embrace open sexual relationships.[52] Cofounder Kat Kinkade, a true believer in *Walden Two,* pronounced Walden House "a dismal failure in every way."[53] But it did start the Walden Two ball rolling.

In August 1966 several of those infatuated with Skinner's book held a conference at a center appropriately named Waldenwoods near Ann Arbor, Michigan, to pursue again the idea of building a community. Although the conferees never came up with a workable communal plan, and the gung-ho contingent who wanted to get a Walden Two community going right away thought the whole event far too academic and abstract, the conference did serve as a meeting point for the Walden House group (now looking to leave the city) and other grassroots enthusiasts. One man at the conference happened to have an inheritance that he hoped to dedicate to some socially productive cause, and by early 1967 the group that would found Twin Oaks was looking for land.

The search came to fruition in April, and in June the first handful of members moved in. Using the money of its generous benefactor the group had purchased a run-down 123-acre tobacco farm (later expanded several times over) near Louisa, Virginia; it had a house and some outbuildings and tobacco and other crops. The new communards named the community Twin Oaks after a double oak tree on the premises, and they began to put together a modified version of the form of government outlined in *Walden Two.* Later that summer they began to make rope hammocks for sale, and by fall they began work on an urgently needed second building.

Twin Oaks certainly had a learning curve. In its first two or three years it suffered from incompatibility among the members, differences over economic and social goals and activities, illness, and assorted other impediments to real progress. But through it all the community built more buildings, learned about agriculture, and developed industries. Although one could hardly say that the path of Twin Oaks was thereafter ever upward and unobstructed, the community over time did grow—eventually reaching around one hundred members—and became financially comfortable, if never wealthy. The hammock business expanded and eventually Twin Oaks became the prime contractor for hammocks and related products for Pier One stores. That business has become the financial backbone of the community, so successful that production has been farmed out to other intentional communities in times of peak demand. Several other businesses, ranging from tofu-making to book-indexing, have also provided support. In the early years some members commuted to outside jobs to make ends meet, but the on-site industries eventually became remunerative enough to meet all the community's modest needs.

The Skinnerian system on which Twin Oaks was founded has been officially abandoned, although some important features of it (such as planner-manager government and labor credits) are still in place. Work, after some early experience with shirkers, came to be required, but schedules and tasks were made as flexible as possible: one could work more hours on some days and have others off, choose to work at relatively congenial times of day, and select preferred jobs or even refuse to do certain particularly distasteful ones. Initially the problem of work that no one wanted to do was handled in purely Skinnerian behavioral terms: increase the pay (in labor credits) that that job will command. But fine-tuning that system proved to be a nightmare, and it was largely rejected in favor of equal hourly credit—with everyone required to wash a fair share of the dishes.[54]

Freedom, though, has always been taken seriously. One is almost entirely free to set one's own schedule, working in the middle of the night if one so prefers. Nudity, although sometimes restricted when visitors are present, has always been accepted as perfectly within the realm of personal choice. One's sexual activity is strictly one's own business, as long as it doesn't upset community life, and by the standards of the larger society Twin Oaks has been unusually tolerant of a goodly variety of sexual behaviors.[55] As a result of this kind of openness Twin Oaks has attracted a fairly diverse lot of residents.

One early Twin Oaks precept that has been adhered to with remarkable tenacity has been financial equality. Few communities have for so long had such a fully common purse. From its early days Twin Oaks committed itself to egalitarianism and has adhered to that vision steadfastly.

Everyone's basic needs—food, housing, clothing, medical care, a bit of recreation—are provided by the community as a whole. All members get an equal, small discretionary allowance—in 1994 all of $50 per month; from that come expenditures for personal phone calls, tobacco, candy, alcohol, and other such nonessentials. Members are not required to donate their assets to the community upon joining, but with certain exceptions (as in the case of taking a vacation) one cannot use that money while a member. Everyone agrees upon joining that while in residence co will spend only cos personal allowance.[56] (On "co" and "cos," read on.)

Equality also extends quite seriously to race and gender. Like most communes Twin Oaks throughout its history has been mainly white, but it has sought and eagerly received nonwhite members. And it has been unusually serious about gender equality, making no distinction between male and female in work assignments or anything else (save for the occasional setting aside of women-only space). This commitment to equality has been underscored by a linguistic innovation: rather than use the cumbersome "he or she" formulation to maintain gender neutrality in language, Twin Oaks uses "co" to communicate the same concept. When a person joins Twin Oaks, co gives up gender privilege, and co also gives up cos financial advantages or disadvantages over other members. The commitment to equality has also led to a certain androgyny at the commune, where men can wear skirts if they choose and women can adopt male or androgynous names as well as work at traditionally male jobs. After studying Twin Oaks (and its Missouri offshoot East Wind, which shares its parent community's egalitarianism), anthropologist Jon Wagner concluded: "These communities may be among the most nonsexist social systems in human history."[57]

Twin Oaks has been a formidable survivor among the 1960s communes, and the inspiration for several later communities (which will be discussed below).[58] Few have embodied the spirit of the 1960s era so long or so well.

EARLY COMMUNAL STIRRINGS IN THE NORTHEAST: SUNRISE HILL AND COLD MOUNTAIN

Not long after the Walden Two movement got under way, unrelated envisionings of community led to the establishment of the first post-1965 communes in the Northeast. The first of them, Sunrise Hill in Massachusetts, met an early demise but had a successor, Cold Mountain Farm in

New York state; these two exemplars anticipated what became a host of other communes in New England and the rest of the Northeast over the next few years.

It all began at Heathcote, in Maryland, that crucial bridge between the communal generations. By early 1966, a year after the commune's founding, enough communal energy was in the air that Heathcote announced that it would hold a conference on intentional community that June. The conference was, by all accounts, a transformational, revelatory experience. The enthusiasm in the air by the end of the conference was akin to that of a church camp or revival or music festival—so powerful that many felt their lives permanently changed by it. Gordon Yaswen's account of the conference evokes the spirit it engendered:

For so many of the people involved in that ten-day experience, it became a crucial milestone in their lives. There developed—at that conference—such a feeling: of camaraderie and kinship, of the reunion of a long-dispersed Family, and of common membership in a newly-evolving breed of human being; as few could have predicted and for which none could have come prepared. Electricity seemed to go snapping through the air between the souls there assembled, and a peace-bringing sense of fulfillment and Hope seemed to hover outside of each heart, awaiting entrance. And in addition to the feelings of bond and friendship, there was a sense of hope and faith in the futures of all of us: a sense that this was . . . the Beginning of Something. And it was.

The culmination of the conference came upon its last night. A huge campfire was kindled, and beer and wine were available freely. As darkness drew over the dell, a spontaneous music of voice and percussion—wordless and tuneless—began emanating from the assemblage. As more time passed the music went on, and grew until it seemed to fill the very night sky above, and spill out over the dell's rims to drift off across the countryside. . . . In me, it aroused the belief that I was witnessing the evidence of a turn-point in a societal evolutionary cycle that was about 5000 years long. It seemed to me that night—that Man was upon the verge of a new Primitive Age, and that this group (at Heathcote) was among the vanguard of the descent into that new era. After this music had gone on for quite a while, many of its participants broke into a wild and spontaneous dancing, interspersed with embracings and "heapings" of exhausted bodies comfortably atop one another. It was plain by now that we had something on our hands that was decidedly not programmed, and it was anyone's guess as to where it was headed. Something awfully powerful was working its will among us, and the night soon was swept into a frenzied and ecstatic blur.[59]

Yaswen and about twenty others similarly swept up in euphoric communal passion immediately began to plan their own commune. One of those twenty, Bryce Ford, owned a house with land near Conway, Massachusetts, which he offered for the use of the group. Inspired further by Robert Heinlein's science fiction novel *Stranger in a Strange Land*—in which members of a communal "nest" become "water brothers" who share not only possessions but bodies and minds—the pioneers moved to the forty-acre tract in July 1966 and began their bold experiment.[60] The first (and only) summer was idyllic. Yaswen again:

We thrived upon a daily diet of working out-of-doors, interspersed with icy plunges into our delicious pond. We ate ravenously of the fresh greens, vegetables, chickens, and goat milk which were produced on our farm, combined with cheap but wholesome natural foods bought elsewhere. . . . We held many meetings, and (at least in the beginning) these could be quite exciting, for in them we plotted out and grappled with the problems of Utopia itself, and spoke often and heatedly of all that we would do in our future together, and of how immensely important were the consequences of those doings. . . . The whole phenomenon of the Community was giddying to us all. . . . Here was finally a solid footing to our Revolution of life-ways, a place where we could actually begin to build that Civilization we had dreamt about so long.[61]

For all the exhilaration of the first few months, however, Sunrise Hill was not to have a long or even a very happy life. When fall approached members began to realize that they needed more housing than they had in order to make it through the winter, but an attempt to build a large second building never got very far along. As time went by it became ever more painfully clear that the community had no adequate financial base. Work became drudgery, and interpersonal conflicts flared. By Christmas only five adults and four children remained at Sunrise Hill, and in February the last few left, signing the land back over to its original owner. The experiment that had begun with such gusto was ignominiously finished.

Idealism is not so easily destroyed, however. Four of Sunrise Hill's veterans regrouped and moved on to join a new commune called Cold Mountain Farm near Hobart, New York. Cold Mountain emerged from a group of friends who lived near each other, sometimes sharing apartments, on New York's Lower East Side. They were, as the group's historian Joyce Gardner put it, "political activists of the old and new left, artists, communitarians, pacifists, students, poets, vegetarians, Reichians, technicians. We called ourselves anarchists, because it was the only name that seemed to fit us all."[62] They, like the Sunrise Hill founders, attended the entrancing School of Living conference in 1966 and in fact would have moved to Sunrise Hill had it been big enough to hold them all. So they bided their time until a run-down 450-acre farm, complete with a big old house, suddenly was made available to them. They moved in in the very early spring of 1967, just as Sunrise Hill was breaking up.

The Cold Mountain group was not fixated on rural isolation; its members had headed for the country in large part to further their political goals, especially by supplying free food to their activist friends in the city. But that turned out not to be such an easy task. Despite some timely help from neighboring farmers, agriculture conducted by city folks wasn't terribly productive. A problem family arrived with children with whom the rest had trouble dealing. The casual nudity that the Mountaineers so thoroughly enjoyed had to stop when they learned that they had attracted voyeurs, and with word spreading in the area that these new neighbors were nothing less than dreaded hippies, a precipitous decline in local acceptance put a cloud over everything. Life in the big house became unbearable, at least to some, who moved out into their own self-built structures. An article in the *East Village Other,* New York's underground newspaper, induced a wave of unneeded visitors. In short, the enthusiasm that fueled the early months of communal life played out, just as it had at Sunrise Hill.

And then the real problems began. A devastating hepatitis epidemic laid the whole commune low. That sparked a visit from the local health inspector, who demanded impossibly expensive (and, to the Cold Mountain regulars, undesirable) improvements such as electricity, refrigeration, and an indoor toilet. It didn't take long for things to go to rack and ruin. Residents moved out and scattered.

As had been the case with Sunrise Hill, however, there was a partial regrouping. By the following summer, 1968, several of the former Cold Mountain residents joined Bryn Athyn, a commune in Vermont that had been founded shortly after Cold Mountain in the summer of 1967. Bryn Athyn was a bit more stable than some of the other early communes in the Northeast because of its wealthy patron, Woody Ransom, who after his marriage broke up opened his farm to those who were surging to the country. The atmosphere there was rather eclectic; at one time it would be a training ground for New Left revolutionaries, while at many others it would be primarily a scene of free love and psychedelia. It all survived fairly happily until the end of 1969, when—amid a hepatitis epidemic—Ransom threw everyone out and announced the formation of a new, disciplined commune called Rockbottom Farm. The old Bryn Athyn crowd lived briefly in a donated house in nearby Lyme, New Hampshire, before dispersing. Rockbottom Farm went on to relative communal longevity, surviving as a no-nonsense collective of serious rural workers for several years thereafter.[63]

New Mexico Beckons

New Mexico became a great magnet for communitarians toward the end of the 1960s, a symbol of the entire rural countercultural impulse. Just why it happened there remains something of a mystery; New Mexico has beautiful scenery and ancient Indian cultures, but it is also a land of harsh climate, of poverty, and in the late 1960s of a populace much indignant at the arrival of hippies in its midst—so much so that there was more anti-hippie violence in New Mexico than anywhere else in the nation. In any event, a good many hippies did migrate there. The bulk of commune-building in New Mexico took place after 1967 (and will be discussed in the next chapter), but the first stirrings were felt earlier.

One part of the early communal energy amounted to a spinoff effect from Drop City, as those utterly inexpensive funky domes surged through the counterculture's collective imagination. One reason domes were as popular as they were in New Mexico had to do with the presence of Steve Baer, the dome-design genius who had refined the early Drop City domes into remarkable "zomes"; Baer lived near Albuquerque, and he readily helped other dome-builders build their (and his) vision, especially in the Placitas area just a few miles from his home. The first communal enclave at Placitas was Drop South, a self-proclaimed daughter commune of the great original a few hours' drive away and one at which at least two of the earliest Droppers from Trinidad would eventually live. Over two or three years several other fairly informal communities grew up in the area as well—the Domes, the Lower Farm, Sun Farm, Towapa, and one simply called Placitas. Each of them led a mainly quiet existence and some endured for many years. The exception was the Lower Farm, a cluster of adobe buildings that acquired a fair reputation around the New Mexico counterculture as being an unusually lowly, down-and-out place; indeed, in 1970 two resident junkies were killed, and the self-anointed leader of the Lower Farm—who had just had a minor dispute with the victims—disappeared.[64] Not much was heard of the Lower Farm thereafter, but several other Placitas-area communes lived on less dramatically.

The center of communal energy in New Mexico eventually moved to the Taos area. The first notable commune there was New Buffalo, founded in 1967 by a group of newly arrived New Mexicans who were fascinated with Indian culture and who hoped to become involved in a peyote church. One of them, Rick Klein, had money from an inheritance and agreed to use it to buy the group land for a commune, whereupon they located a hundred acres north of Taos. They moved in in June and immediately set to building adobe buildings. The main building had a large oval meeting room with an eponymous buffalo head mounted on the wall, an adjoining kitchen, and two wings of bedrooms stringing out rather on the pattern of a motel. Scattered tepees dotted a good deal of the rest of the property. The name was consciously chosen because the new tribe wanted their commune to be what the buffalo had been to the Indians, provider of everything to its people.

New Buffalo would have a lot of twists and turns in its history but despite heavy turnover would survive with some communal elements for nearly three decades. Right away it became popular, soon finding itself inundated with up to fifty residents—far more than the twenty-five or so it might have handled well. On the other hand, new people were needed steadily, because turnover was high. A year after the founding only four or five of the original twenty or twenty-five pioneers remained.

New Buffalo made a serious attempt to support itself agriculturally. Some of the residents worked hard at farming and building, as one member noted to a visiting reporter around 1970: "Like, we all make bricks whether we want to or not. Maybe making adobe bricks isn't your own thing, but you *make* it your own thing if you live here."[65] But the climate of northern New Mexico is severe, and a commune with a lot of visitors and crashers would not tend to get its work done very efficiently under the best of circumstances. Self-sufficiency was complicated and hard, as cofounder Max Finstein said in an interview in 1968:

Well, if you're burning wood and building with some wood, you have to use some kind of vehicle to bring the wood down and then you're hung on a gasoline economy. You've got to go 40 or 50 miles to get gas. You can't just carry it on your back. Throw the tractor away and use horses, but that requires a whole adjustment in your thinking. I especially don't know how you do it in the face of this landscape. If you're going to carry all your wood by horse and wagon, it means you've got to go away for a few days.

It's hard to get a man to go out and grow a field of corn or something, which he knows is just barely enough to keep him alive, when he can go to the Safeway. I mean, why go hunt a bear, take chances with your life, when you can just go to the Safeway and get some hamburgers? And at a place like The Buffalo you have to work things out in terms of: do enough people agree to do this?[66]

New Buffalo went on for years, with too many people most summers and just a few in the wintertime. In the 1980s it dwindled to one family, whose lifestyle and hostility kept others away. By the end of the decade, however, Rick Klein, who had always lived in the area and kept his interest in New Buffalo alive, managed (with his wife Terry) to evict the problem family and to reclaim the buildings and grounds. After some major refurbishment they opened a bed and breakfast in what was by then a historic hippie site. However, by the late 1990s that episode closed and the Kleins put the property up for sale.

The Spirit of the Times

Something must have been in the air, or in the water, in the mid-1960s: even as independent clusters of communes were emerging in California, on the East coast, and in Colorado and New Mexico, other communal groups were quietly doing the same thing in a good many other places, largely unaware of each other. In Parsons, Kansas, the Ahimsa Community was founded in 1965 and survived for several years; it reportedly had a stable population of eight adults by 1969, by which time it was not seeking new members and admitting visitors only on weekends.[67] Communal houses were stirring up the cultural scene in Austin, Texas, by 1965.[68] Late that year a group of protohippies rented a big house in Newport, Oregon, and started a commune that they soon named the Zoo.[69] And in 1966 a group of Bostonians that had coalesced around Mel Lyman began to live communally at Fort Hill in the Roxbury ghetto. The Lyman Family, as it became known, rose to public prominence through its involvement with the *Avatar,* a Boston underground paper, which printed a series of Lyman's rather grand metaphysical pronouncements.[70] Soon the Lymans expanded their presence from Boston to Los Angeles, New York City, and an isolated farm in Kansas, supporting themselves with a successful construction and remodeling business and farming operations. They withdrew from the spotlight in the early 1970s after receiving unfavorable publicity that accused the group of abusive behavior and serious drug and weapons violations; nevertheless, at the end of the 1990s, the family—including many long-time members—survives, with a reported one hundred or so members in the several locations.[71] Mel Lyman is said to have died in 1978.

By 1967 the alternative communities were very much on the scene. But much more was still to come, as the next few years saw wave upon wave of new communes inundate the country.

4

Out of the Haight and Back to the Land
Countercultural Communes after the Summer of Love

The latter months of 1967 through the first few years of the 1970s saw a frenzy of commune-founding that dwarfed what had gone before. Indeed, so pronounced and visible was the communitarian surge that many observers mistakenly date the beginning of the new communalism to that period. What is not mistaken is that a great rise in communal activity did take place, most colorfully perhaps in rural locations but also in the cities.

Why did it happen? Ultimately one cannot say why communes became enormously popular in the late 1960s any more than one can definitively say why the cultural revolution we generally refer to as "the sixties" happened at all. Although certain lines of historical events can be tracked, the "why" is inevitably subjective. Disgust with the direction that American culture had taken—especially with the worship of the almighty dollar—had something to do with it. Psychedelics had something to do with it. The war in Vietnam had something to do with it. Philip Slater argued as long ago as 1970 that American culture had "deeply and uniquely frustrated" three basic human desires—for community, for engagement, and for dependence—and that the sixties represented an attempt to overcome that long-felt but little-articulated frustration and to meet those basic drives of the human spirit.[1] His argument contributes importantly to explaining the wave of commune-building, but finally one can only say that an extraordinary zeitgeist materialized in the late 1960s and that the communes were a part of that much larger fabric.

Specific events in each of the three years before 1970 also contributed to the move toward communes. In the months after the Summer of Love (1967), the Haight-Ashbury district of San Francisco—the principal urban center of hip—took a steep downward turn. Extravagant media publicity about the Haight that summer lured huge waves of young newcomers, most of them homeless and jobless refugees from straight society and some of them not right in the mind, who swamped the district. Social services were overwhelmed; the crime rate rose sharply; the euphoric and relatively harmless psychedelics gave way to speed, heroin, and other less benign drugs. When the Diggers proclaimed the death of hip in the fall of 1967, they seemed to know what they were talking about. Within a period of just a few months the scene became unhappy enough that large numbers of urban hippies were receptive to the call of the countryside. A similar scenario played itself out in the East Village in New York and in other urban hip enclaves around the country.

The following year, 1968, was the year of political confrontation—most notably the siege of Chicago, when the Democratic National Convention encountered legions of young antiwar protesters who engaged in heated, violent confrontations with the Chicago police that thoroughly overshadowed the deliberations in the assembly hall. But politics turned sour. The despised Lyndon Johnson was replaced as president by Richard Nixon. The most radical of the political protesters, the Weathermen and other similar groups, turned violent in their frustration at it all, in many cases going into hiding and in any event alienating most of their predominantly nonviolent constituency. Confrontations on college campuses rarely resulted in useful victories for radical students. Politics seemed like a dead end, and for the disillusioned the rural communes suddenly loomed as an inviting alternative.

On a more positive note, the summer of 1969 was the summer of Woodstock, the music festival that quickly took on mythic stature to the young American romantics. Three days of rock and roll and sex and dope and peace and love and rain and mud became forever enshrined as heaven on earth. After the crowd of several hundred thousand had overwhelmed the festival's support services, sharing what one had—whether a sandwich or a hit of acid—became the order of the day. Money became irrelevant. The crowd was far too big to be policed, but antisocial behavior was rare. Ecstasy pervaded the festival; as one young woman present was reported to have said, "It was like balling for the first time. Once you've done it, you want to do it again and again, because it's so *great*."[2] The presence of the Hog Farm commune from New Mexico, which had been hired as a "Please Force" to provide food, emergency medicine, and crisis intervention, was inspiring: here was a working commune that seemed to manifest a better future. Woodstock directly inspired several communes founded soon afterwards (Earth People's Park in far northern Vermont is one example) and undoubtedly helped to steer thousands of seekers in a communal direction.

The thousands of communes that were founded from the autumn of 1967 through the mid-1970s defy any kind of counting or even comprehension. This chapter and the next two provide only a sampling, not a comprehensive inventory, of the communes that flourished during that period. In an attempt to provide some kind of sorting-out of the diverse communes, I have divided them into three groups: back-to-the-land countercultural communes; religious and spiritual communities; and secular, mainly urban, intentional communities devoted to social change or, in a few cases, simply to a pleasant life. Those categories are certainly imperfect and fuzzy, and many communes could fit in more than one. The Farm, for example, is here categorized as spiritual, because it did have an important spiritual core and was led by a spiritual teacher, Stephen Gaskin; but it also was (and still is) thoroughly countercultural in style and a classic embodiment of back-to-the-land idealism. Such ambiguities are inescapable in an exercise of this kind.

Forging ahead boldly, in these three chapters we will sample individual communes that embody some of the diversity of the larger phenomenon of commune-building. Those dealt with in these pages will represent geographical diversity, with some attention given to the prominent locations where the communal presence received a good deal of national attention; they will represent ideological diversity; and they will represent diversity of lifestyles and patterns of organization.

The Northwest

If the communes of the 1960s era could be counted accurately, the largest number of them would probably turn out to have been in the area from San Francisco northward to the Canadian border and from the Pacific inland perhaps a hundred miles. The relatively mild Northwest climate provided a congenial place to settle in communes that often lacked modern amenities, and the epicenter of the countercultural population was there as well. Three communes in northern California and one in Oregon represent some of the diversity of the countercultural communes of that time.

OLOMPALI RANCH

Olompali Ranch in its communal life embraced the extremes of the communal experience. It was wealthy, and then it was poor; it had both secular and spiritual foci; it had great joys and great tragedies; it had a lovely rural location but was close to San Francisco. It had wonderfully good times and terribly bad times.

The property, outside Novato, California, featured a huge house built in stages in the nineteenth and early twentieth centuries. In 1948 the University of San Francisco purchased the property as a retreat center, adding a swimming pool and other amenities.[3] In 1966 and 1967 it served as the communal rural retreat for the Grateful Dead rock band and friends, but its most notable communal phase commenced later in 1967 when Don McCoy rented the house and asked his circle of close friends to move in.

McCoy was a classic 1960s figure who had money and wanted to disperse it rather than sit on it. He had a substantial inheritance, and he and his brother had also done well operating a heliport and owning and renting out houseboats in Sausalito. In the summer of 1967 a circle of friends with whom he had become involved started spending a great deal of time together, so much that they hated to part company at the end of the day. McCoy began looking for a large place where they could live together, and at the end of 1967 rented the very large house and 690 acres of land at Olompali. More friends joined the original twenty-six, and soon they were all known as the Chosen Family—because, as Sheila U.S.A. put it, "God chose us to be family with each other, and also, we chose each other for family."[4] They lived very comfortably from McCoy's checkbook. Just about anything people asked for, they received; McCoy paid all the bills and bought his friends motorcycles, horses, light show equipment, and any number of other things. He gave one member $7,000 to pay off her old bills. The Chosen Family lived a very happy life, by all accounts—no one had to work, and nude socializing around the swimming pool and ubiquitous marijuana-smoking occupied a good deal of everyone's day. Even a nun who had happened onto the group got in the spirit of things, moved in, and doffed her habit.[5] The Grateful Dead got along famously with the new residents and continued to visit, playing there several times. Members did not just engage in self-indulgence, however; they had equipment for a commercial-sized baking operation (supplied by the Diggers of San Francisco, those tireless purveyors of free food) and with it baked hundreds of loaves of bread twice a week for the San Francisco communes. Nineteen sixty-eight was a grand year at Olompali.

But the good year was followed by a bad one. Don McCoy had become friends with Lou Gottlieb of Morning Star Ranch and became intrigued with Gottlieb's devotion to open land. Morning Star was in the throes of its conflicts with the authorities in Sonoma County, and some of its residents were leaving to avoid further arrests and evictions; although quite a few of them went to Wheeler's Ranch, some went elsewhere—including Olompali, where McCoy welcomed them. The rest of the Chosen Family, however, was not so taken with all the new company camping in their woods. Morning Star had a diverse crowd, some of them definitely not culturally congenial with the high-living Olompalians. As Vivian Gotters, one of those who made the trek from Morning Star to Olompali, put it, "We were persona non grata in a lot of places. We were too crazy."[6] In a 1996 interview, Noelle Barton of the Chosen Family described the conflict graphically:

So now come those things out of God knows where, who are camping and pissing here. I've already gone to visit Morning Star, and gone through one of my walks in the woods and stepped in people shit, which is worse than dog shit. And I said, "No, we're not having this at our ranch." So now we start dividing. Some say, "We are all one, let everybody come live with us," and then some of us say, "Yeah, but who's footing the bill here, and who's eating the food, and who's going to do the work, and who are these people anyway? Get out of my living room, get off my couch, no, don't use my hairbrush." And so there was division.[7]

Distaste for the new campers disrupted Olompali's routines; among other things, swimming pool maintenance stopped and the pool fell into foul unusability. Disaster struck more seriously when Don McCoy's family, arguing that he was squandering his children's future, imposed a conservatorship on him that stopped the money flow. Suddenly the cooks were reduced to taking up collections for food, and the rent wasn't getting paid. Additionally, given the easy availability of marijuana around the house and grounds a bust was inevitable, and it came not once but twice, eight days apart.

As if not enough had happened, the house suffered a bad fire in February when the antiquated electrical wiring suffered one overload too many. Barton recalled that fateful night:

We came home one night stoned on acid from doing a light show at Longshore-man's Hall. All of a sudden there were sirens behind us. So we busted up the free-way; we thought we would get to our house and lose them. So as we drove up you could look up and see the mansion, and it was like an Edgar Allen Poe movie, with the flames leaping out the window. And we're stoned, so it's like, "This isn't really happening." In the meantime, the police chief had had a heart attack on his way to fight the fire, and landed in the ditch. Now, all the fire trucks had arrived, and they can't do anything until they have their fire chief there. So the mansion is being gut-ted, and we're all standing out there, stoned, watching everything we know going up in flames! I mean, my father got double-cremated.

Other buildings remained, and for several months the dwindling number of commune members soldiered on, trying to make Olompali a working commune, with a heavy emphasis on its alternative school. But in June 1969, the decisive disaster hit: two little girls were riding their tricycles un-supervised around the half-empty swimming pool—and fell in and drowned. Plenty of bad press ensued, the residents were evicted, and dur-ing the summer Olompali faded into history.

The full catalog of disasters at Olompali is longer than what has been told above. Some of the residents later decided that the place had proba-bly always had an evil spirit; and indeed, there are troubling stories that date back to Indian days. But the residents have gone on to other things, and like many former 60s communards most have warm memories of good times that tend to eclipse the downside.

BLACK BEAR RANCH

Many of the 1960s communards sought seclusion for their communi-tarianism, and none succeeded more fully at finding it than those who founded Black Bear Ranch, not only located several hours' drive from any major city over miles of poor roads but also surrounded by national forest land and thus ten miles from the nearest neighbors. That isolation served one founding purpose of the commune well: for the political revolution-aries who wanted a secluded location for weapons training and generally keeping out of sight of the authorities, Black Bear filled the bill just about perfectly. But that original goal was soon submerged under a wave of communitarian idealists less resolutely fixated on such political ends. Ac-cording to Richard Marley, a principal founder,

The original group weren't thinking of a commune; they were thinking of a mountain fortress in the spirit of Che Guevara, where city activists would be able to come up, hide out, practice riflery and pistol shooting, have hand grenade practice, whatever. My plan was to have half a dozen people come up, spend that first winter, prepare the place, get it ready for the revolutionary activists to come up, but what actually happened was that about a hundred people came up from Haight Street all at once, and just occupied everything. I remember saying, I can either just turn around and leave, or I can give in and stay, just go with it, and I stayed.[8]

The eighty-acre Black Bear property was a ghost town that had once boasted the richest gold mine in the area. In the 1860s hundreds of miners—many of them Chinese—had worked the lode, and the boomtown of Black Bear had dozens of buildings and even a post office. When the mine played out, however, the population disappeared, and by 1968 the property was for sale for $22,500. Several members of the informal collective behind the purchase raised a good down payment, and eventually the balance was paid off. Many years later Marley, in whose name the land had been held, signed it over to the Black Bear Family Trust, an act that should ensure that the Ranch is community land for a long time to come.

Initially facilities were tight; as many as sixty persons slept on wall-to-wall mattresses in the not-gigantic main house. Personal habits and sexual activities were soon known to all. Gradually those who planned on staying built their own cabins, but the main house remained an active community center and the locus of most meals. One historical account records some of the social experiments that were conducted: the (temporary) total abolition of private property, in which even all clothing was shared; the adoption of a rule that no one could sleep with the same person for more than two consecutive nights to avert "coupling." When parents feared for the safety of their children in this land of bears, cougars, and lynx, "timers were set, and once every hour the coffee-klatching and the bitching were suspended, and everyone ran outside to do laps around the house, screaming at the tops of their lungs to frighten away potential predators."[9]

Given Black Bear's isolation, its members were more self-reliant than most. The community could be snowed in for a month or two at a time in the winter, so preparedness was essential. The residents gathered prodigious amounts of firewood, made a major food run for bulk staples every fall, slaughtered animals for food, and built a small hydroelectric system. The Ranch kept a goodly stock of medical supplies on hand and managed to treat illnesses ranging from hepatitis and staph infections to gonorrhea

as well as to deliver a good many babies and to do its own veterinary medical work. The members ran their own sawmill, maintained their own
chainsaws and vehicles, and schooled their own children. They disdained
welfare—partly because they didn't want social workers or anyone else
snooping around—and for two or three years managed to support themselves on whatever odd bits of income came their way. One of the biggest
cash expenses was the $25 monthly mortgage payment, which in the early
years was sometimes paid by sympathetic dope dealers in the Bay area. By
the third year residents hit upon a fitting part-time employment opportunity: they fought forest fires. That seasonal work produced enough cash to
meet basic needs, including the big annual food run.[10]

Black Bear Ranch was remarkable among the 1960s communes for its
forthright self-sufficient lifestyle as well as for its longevity. Most of the
founders have long since departed, but at the end of the 1990s a second
generation is thriving and appears likely to keep the tradition alive for
years to come.

TABLE MOUNTAIN RANCH

Table Mountain Ranch represents a sort of middle path between the
luxury and hedonism of Olompali and the extreme seclusion of Black Bear
Ranch. It was secluded, but only two miles from a paved road. It did not
have electricity (or, until much later, a telephone), but it did have refriger-
ators and a stove that ran on bottled gas and hot and cold running water.
It was founded as a result of the same kind of forces as was Black Bear—
the decline of the Haight-Ashbury scene and the welling up of rural and
communal idealism; in fact, Table Mountain and Black Bear had a special
affinity for each other and thought of themselves as sibling communes.

Table Mountain was located in Mendocino County, California, in redwood country. The funding for the purchase of the house and 120 acres of
land was the essence of simplicity: two prosperous hip sympathizers
plunked down $50,000 for it and put out the word that some of those get-
ting burned out on the Haight could live there. Fifteen or twenty persons,
initially, took them up on their generous offer. The large farmhouse on the
property served as a community meeting place as well as kitchen and din-
ing room; as residents had the means and desire they constructed their
own little homes nearby. As was the case at so many communes, they lived
a simple and mostly satisfying lifestyle on very little money, with a minimum of modern technology.

One important focus at Table Mountain Ranch was education. Like many communards of the 1960s era the people of Table Mountain wanted to steer their children away from decadent mainstream American values and recognized that private schooling was essential to that goal. The school for the Ranch children eventually became stable enough to accept other nearby children, and finally it became a full-scale alternative school complete through high school. The school promoted practical as well as academic learning and let the children have some say in their own education. It came to be much admired by the many hip persons who lived in the surrounding area and eventually had as many outsiders as Ranch residents in its student body.

Table Mountain had no religious creed, although several of its members were serious spiritual seekers. One sociologist who studied the commune found "no charisma, no missionary zealotry" but "more [ideas] than you can shake a stick at," including

peace, freedom, love, spontaneity, spiritual questing (through drugs and otherwise), nature, survival, health, equality, intimacy, brotherhood-sisterhood (the latter later—and very important), the do-it-yourself therapies (from Eastern yogic practices to Esalen westernisms, and involving a great deal of talk about "consciousness," "spaces," and "working through" hang-ups), and living with as few possessions as were useful or necessary, rather than with as many as one could be induced to want.[11]

But was there one core value? When asked that by the same scholar-guest, one member replied: "Yes, wash your own dish."[12]

For a decade or more after Table Mountain's founding the population tended to go slowly downward, but more recently an infusion of second-generation members has lifted the place from near-oblivion to pretty much what it had been years earlier.[13] Earlier members still retain a good deal of affection for the Ranch and some of them visit fairly frequently. At this writing Table Mountain, like Black Bear, seems likely to continue for a long time to come.

ALPHA FARM

In 1971, four people in Philadelphia discovered a strong bond of agreement among them—an agreement that went beyond words. They shared a powerful spiritual "leading"—indeed, a compulsion—to embrace like-minded people in intentional community and to have faith in the spirit they felt. They realized that the social and political activism in which they were engaged needed to be relinquished, and something drastically different and really quite simple needed to take its place. They wrote in a prospectus, "The renewal of the social order, we now see, must begin with ourselves. We seek to change our basic assumptions and patterns of daily living; to accomplish this we must alter our patterns of thought. We must live ourselves into the future we seek."[14]

Thus begins Alpha Farm's own descriptive brochure. In 1972 the Philadelphians, having settled on Oregon as the best place for carrying out their dream, purchased 280 spectacularly beautiful acres with a house and barn in the coast range west of Eugene and began to build a small but durable community that ever since has averaged about fifteen to twenty members. As was the case at Morning Star Ranch, the name was discovered by accident after the group had moved in: the farm had been named Alpha early in the twentieth century, and the living room of the farmhouse (now the main community facility) had served as the local post office, which used "Alpha" as a postmark. Life was hard at first for the thirteen original settlers, but gradually they developed businesses and agriculture and have become comfortable, if not wildly prosperous. Although Alpha Farm is nonsectarian, the Quaker roots of some of its founders are discernible in its commitment to egalitarianism, nonviolence, consensus decision making, and simple living. Cofounder Caroline Estes, in fact, from her work at Alpha and her lifetime as a Quaker has become a leading authority on making consensus decision making work and for years has conducted workshops on the process at innumerable conferences. She travels to other intentional communities frequently to help them get their own processes working.

Alpha is located deep in the countryside, and as Estes said, "We didn't want to be known as the strange people up the road, but there was no way anyone was going to come meet us here." Thus from the beginning the Alpha settlers sought to get to know their neighbors. Desperate for cash income shortly after they arrived, the group collectively signed up to carry a rural mail route, which worked out splendidly on all sides: the money from the job was a Godsend, and by delivering the mail to every household for miles around the communards soon became quite familiar to their neighbors—and the usual rumors of orgiastic revelries, dope dens, and so forth were relatively short-lived. Six months later they became even more interactive with the larger community when they opened a bookstore and cafe in Mapleton, the biggest town in the area, some fourteen miles from the farm. The books in the store tend to focus on progressive political and social topics, and the cafe sells grainburgers as well as more middle-American fare, but gradually the newcomers and the old guard meshed well. In the early days one logger, asked if he wanted sprouts on his sandwich, exploded, "Sprouts? Alfalfa sprouts? I feed alfalfa to my horses." Since then local diners have made the avocado and tomato sandwich with sprouts the most popular item on the menu.[15]

Although Alpha has remained relatively small, from the beginning it attracted like-minded people who settled nearby. Today most of the homes for at least a mile or two around are occupied by alternative-culture people who see Alpha as their social and cultural center. (That status is buttressed by large parties that Alpha hosts several times a year on major holidays.) One commitment shared by the residents of Alpha and its neighbors is environmentalism. In the Pacific Northwest this concern has led to several conflicts with other interests over logging and herbicide-spraying, especially; as a result of the cooperation of the Alphans and their neighbors, those impacts have been reduced—the local crews no longer spray weeds along the road that serves Alpha and its near neighbors, for example, and every plan to log in the vicinity meets with strong opposition. As a result the local environment is less compromised than it is in other nearby areas. Alpha Farm is alive and well at century's end, continuing to embody the 1960s values and spirit on which it was founded.

THE LARGER NORTHWEST SCENE

Olompali, Black Bear, Table Mountain, and Alpha Farm to some degree exemplify some of the diversity of communitarianism in the Northwest, but of course can hardly be regarded as definitive representatives of what was a tremendously diverse larger communal movement. A more complete account might chronicle the Family of the Mystic Arts (the Oregon commune featured in *Life* in July 1969 and subsequently swamped by young visitors),[16] the Family of the Three Lights (in Skagit County, Washington), Four Winds Farm (near Hood River, Oregon), or Mu Farm (near Yoncalla, Oregon), all of which have stories worth telling. Several other Northwest communes, those focused on religion or social change, will be covered in the following two chapters. No part of the United States had a stronger communal presence in the 1960s era than did the Northwest.

The Southwest

The culture of the American Southwest has long been shaped by three layers of ethnicity: Native American, Hispanic, and Anglo. The arrival of the migrant hippies in the late 1960s added a new layer, and the newcomers were often not well received, especially by the Hispanics. Thus, the Southwest—especially New Mexico and southern Colorado—became not only a countercultural communal mecca of mythic proportions but also the locus of the largest cultural conflict the communes movement saw anywhere.

THE TAOS SCENE

The romantic epicenter of countercultural communes in the Southwest was Taos County. Taos had the romance of a surviving, working Native American culture, complete with one of the nation's oldest communes in Taos Pueblo. It had a literary and artistic heritage, artists and writers from D. H. Lawrence to Georgia O'Keeffe having worked there for decades. It remained a small town and had wide open spaces in every direction. Land was still fairly cheap, largely because agriculture was difficult in the arid climate.

The new communes arrived in the Taos area in 1967 or before. The Hog Farm was one of the first on the scene, but its largely mobile and California-oriented existence kept its role in the overall communal presence smaller than it might have been. The commune that set the pattern in New Mexico was New Buffalo, established in 1967 north of Taos at Arroyo Hondo (and discussed in the previous chapter). Soon thereafter dozens of communes were flourishing within a radius of twenty-five miles or so around Taos.

One individual played a particularly important role in putting Taos on the communal map. Shortly before the hippies arrived, Michael Duncan used his inheritance to purchase some 750 acres of land atop a mesa just a few miles from New Buffalo. Soon Lou Gottlieb, traveling through the area, was introduced to Duncan and preached his passionate gospel of open land—land access to which is denied no one—to the young heir. New open land was needed, he remonstrated, because the harassment of those who lived at Morning Star and Wheeler's Ranch appeared destined to continue indefinitely, and the peaceful California free-land hippies needed someplace to go. Duncan had local models to look to as well— Rick Klein, for example, had bought $50,000 worth of land and given it to the New Buffalo communards—and finally agreed to take in the refugees. The migrants from Morning Star arrived in New Mexico early in 1969 and named their renewed attempt at open-land community Morning

Star East. A few months later another communal veteran, Max Finstein, a cofounder of New Buffalo who had become convinced that fascists were about to take over the United States and wipe out the nation's leftists, organized a second commune on Duncan's land. It was called the Reality Construction Company and was populated with radicals drawn to Finstein's apocalyptic vision, most of them from New York and San Francisco. Both Morning Star East and Reality, just a few hundred yards apart, constructed adobe buildings as their headquarters and lived quite primitively (neither had electricity, running water, or even a reliable on-site water supply), but beyond that they were not very much alike. In fact at one point the differences were punctuated with gunfire; originally the two groups had agreed to farm jointly, but when the rather laid-back Morning Star contingent helped itself to some common corn one summer after failing to do its fair share of planting that year, the pickers were greeted with hot lead over their heads.[17]

Morning Star East nominally had no bosses and no rules, but somehow certain basic work seemed to get done. A visitor described his day there thus:

We awoke at about 8:00, *schlepped* out into the glaring morning sunlight, and walked over to the partially constructed communal kitchen, where several women were preparing a breakfast of oatmeal and rank coffee for anyone who wanted to come. When the meal was ready, a large bell was rung and about 20 people in various stages of undress stumbled out of huts, teepees and pueblo rooms and ambled zombie-like across the mesa. . . .

By 9:00 I was in the fields with a traveling companion, a shovel and a wheelbarrow full of shit. . . . There were about 15 people and one sway-backed nag in the fields that morning, plowing, shoveling shit, seeding, irrigating, weeding. . . . By noon the temperature had reached 90 degrees, and most of the laborers had stripped off some or all of their clothing. What in all the world is more beautiful than a dark, bare-breasted girl pulling weeds from a field of sprouting peas? . . .

A young couple had driven up the switchback road and asked to crash for the night. They'd brought with them a gallon of Red Mountain's famous Burgundy and a lid of grass. Needless to say, they were welcomed with open arms and salivating smiles. The rest of the afternoon was spent in the covered kiva—a round structure, built underground in descending oval tiers. About 15 people gathered to drink wine, smoke weed and rap about the work schedule, while a gentle rain pattered overhead.[18]

Morning Star East, like its California namesake, attracted many would-be communards with its open-land policy. Its peak population was close to one hundred, even though life was hard there with the cold winters (temperatures often dropped far below zero, and firewood was as far as thirty miles away), the difficult access over a poor road, and the necessity of hauling in all domestic water. People built pleasant, modest little houses. Peyote meetings, often led by local Indians, were held regularly. For a year or two the community had good group consciousness. But gradually centrifugal force overbalanced the center and the commune deteriorated.[19]

Reality Construction Company, by contrast, was grim and disciplined, discriminating in its acceptance of new members and willing to expel those who didn't fit. It maintained a population of around twenty-five for much of its existence. Unwanted visitors—and most were unwanted— were met at the gate by a rifle-toting guard, often one of the two militant black males who dominated the commune. Despite its hostile attitude, its material accomplishments were not notably more than Morning Star East's—but then the goal was not to prosper materially but rather to prepare a redoubt for the coming armed struggle. In any event, Michael Duncan, never any too happy with what was transpiring on his land, decided to close it all down in 1972. Reality presented him with no problem: when cold weather arrived that fall, its last members left. At Morning Star East a few hangers-on pleaded desperately to stay, but Duncan foreclosed that option by partially demolishing the main buildings of both communes.[20] Today only ruins remain of the twin experiments.

The lifespans of Morning Star and Reality, which both operated from 1969 to 1972, were similar to those of many of the other Taos-area communes. Of those many others the most stable was the Lama Foundation, which is still going (and which will be discussed in chapter 5). Somewhat shorter-lived were Lorien and Lila, like Morning Star East and Reality separate but adjacent entities supported by a prosperous patron. In this case the patron, Charles Lonsdale, did multiple good deeds in Taos and Questa, a few miles north, founding an organic grocery store, a free clinic, and a countercultural newspaper. North of Questa he purchased some six hundred acres of land on which to start an intentional community, where he began to build a home and allowed others to settle as visitors on openland principles. That agglomeration was Lorien, never fully organized and eventually destroyed when, in Lonsdale's absence in early 1970, quarreling factions got into a gun battle that resulted in multiple arrests and hospitalizations.[21] Lonsdale then turned his attentions to Lila, a mile away, which had recently been started separately as a closed, disciplined community that banned alcohol and drugs and focused on yoga (rather like the nearby Lama). A little semicircle of shoddy cabins was quickly built to house the new communards, and plans were laid for building a much better adobe structure to replace the temporary hovels.[22] Communal life went forward, with required labor and religious activities. But within two years it had all come to an end. The final blow was financial: Lonsdale required that each member come up with $500 per year to meet the $10,000 annual land payment, and most of them drifted away. In 1972 Lonsdale subdivided the land and sold it as lots—a few of them to Lila members who were now on their own.[23]

Most of the other communes started in the Taos area after 1967 were little documented or short-lived. The Church of the Five Star Ranch, the Furry Freak Brothers, the Kingdom of Heaven, and many others were for the most part communal comets, flaring brightly but briefly and—given the hostility toward communes for which Taos was famous and which will be discussed in more detail in chapter 9—sometimes witnessing tragedy.[24]

COLORADO: LIBRE AND ITS NEIGHBORS

Not far north of Taos, in southern Colorado, grew up another district of communes, many of them in Huerfano County—a bit to the north and west of the pioneer Drop City. Several of them are still in quiet operation, and one, Libre, has become the communal flagship of the area. Libre in several ways represents a refinement of Drop City: like its predecessor, Libre embodied a good dose of anarchy, an interest in unconventional architecture, a devotion to the arts, and a general skepticism about the direction in which mainstream American culture was heading. Unlike Drop City, however, Libre limited its membership (and visitors) and erected its buildings out of sight of each other.

Dean and Linda Fleming moved to southern Colorado in 1967. Dean had established himself as a successful artist in New York, cofounding an artists' co-op and helping open Park Place (the first gallery in Soho), but he felt mystically drawn to the mountains and trees of the Rockies. So he and Linda headed for Colorado, by chance settling near Trinidad and inevitably soon encountering the Droppers. Drop City, with its focus on art and its exciting, chaotic daily life, enchanted them. They soon became friends with Peter Rabbit, the most visible of the Droppers, who was tiring of the frenetic Drop City scene; together they envisioned a quiet community of artists, one that would screen its members. As Dean Fleming later commented,

From my observation the one single factor leading to the destruction of Drop City was the heavenly ideal of the wide open door. No one was turned away and soon the most capable were driven out by pure criminals and misfits that had no place else to hide. Libre took most of its clues for a survivable community from Drop City and the very first was to *not* have a completely open door policy.[25]

The plan had one impediment: the would-be founders were impoverished. Rabbit, however, had heard that Rick Klein, who had funded the purchase of New Buffalo, was still in the process of giving away his inheritance. So off they went to inquire, and at their first meeting Klein, liking what he was hearing, volunteered to buy land for the new community. After some searching they located 360 acres for sale for $12,600. Klein came up with the money as promised, and Libre was born.

One early rule at Libre was that each member or family had to have its house site approved by the whole community. The earliest structures were inspired by Drop City; the Flemings built a forty-foot dome, and Rabbit, enlisting the advice of crack dome designer Steve Baer, built a fantastic "zome." Even more unconventional structures were built thereafter. Some were made of stacked railroad ties; one builder came into a cheap supply of one-inch lumber and built a large two-story home with nary a two-by-four. An energy-conscious pioneer observed that a huge boulder on a south-facing hillside got warmed by the sun every day and, wanting to cash in on the daily free heat, built a house around that boulder—which only had the effect of cutting off the sunlight from the rock, turning the boulder from always hot to always cold and rendering the house impossible to heat.

Libre quite deliberately never built any central facility, any common building where crashers might land. As one member wrote, "Each member upon acceptance by the council would build their own house and be responsible for their own food and finances. No more dressing from the communal closet and no more giant pots of inedible lentils."[26] In their separate dwellings the people of Libre—typically numbering twenty to thirty—pursued their arts, including painting, sculpture, writing, pottery, jewelrymaking, and music. Unlike some of their communal cousins in New Mexico a few miles to the south, they rarely ventured very actively into radical politics, although their sympathies lay generally in that direction. Libre had a major bust for marijuana cultivation in 1979 (which sent one member, thereafter expelled, to prison) and an early battle or two with neighbors over water and road access, but mostly it has coexisted with the rest of the valley in peace.

And thus has Libre life continued since 1968. Although new members have joined from time to time and a few have left, the population may well hold the American record for stability, with many early members still on the scene. Most still do not hold full-time jobs, supplementing their art income with a variety of sideline endeavors and above all living quite cheaply. *Libre* means "free" in Spanish, and the free individuals who live on common ground on the side of Greenhorn Mountain are living exactly as they have chosen to.

Since the arrival of the Libre settlers at least a dozen other communes have been founded in the general vicinity, some of which survive today. In 1969 a group of young artists, many of whom had been classmates at Beverly Hills High School and some of them children of blacklisted Hollywood writers and producers, arrived to start the Red Rockers commune east of Libre in Red Rock Canyon. There the following spring they built a single building—a sixty-foot dome, the biggest one in the countercultural communal world. In that dome the entire group, with around thirty members, lived and worked virtually without personal privacy. Red Rocks was the site of a great many theatrical, musical, and literary events; when the communards departed they left behind their dome, which the larger countercultural community continued to use as a theater for years afterwards.

Across the valley settled AAA, the Anonymous Artists of America, a commune initially centered on a popular rock music group and still in operation (sans band) today. Ortiviz Farm was created soon thereafter; located on good farmland—something most of the other communes in the area did not enjoy—it became a major source of produce and dairy products for the surrounding countercultural population. Later Archuletaville was established in some decrepit farm buildings tucked under a rock cliff, and the Medical Opera arrived from California, living communally and providing health care to a region much in need of it. The Huerfano communities made few headlines, but together they have provided a durable testimony to the communal spirit.[27]

The Northeast

Given its population, the northeastern part of the country was bound to have a goodly contingent of communes. Hundreds existed in New

York City alone, and they popped up with regularity in small towns as well as in the cities. The most widely noted of them tended to be in New England, whose old farms and rural mystique seemed just the place for those burned out on city life to settle. Among the New England communes the Brotherhood of the Spirit (later known as the Renaissance Community) in northwestern Massachusetts was probably the largest and certainly one of the best known and longest lived. Also achieving prominence were Packer Corner Farm (better known as Total Loss Farm) and related communities in southern Vermont and northern Massachusetts.

BROTHERHOOD OF THE SPIRIT/
RENAISSANCE COMMUNITY

The inspiration for the Brotherhood of the Spirit came directly from the Summer of Love. Michael Metelica, who later changed his name to Michael Rapunzel, journeyed to the Haight-Ashbury at the age of sixteen and returned to his hometown of Leyden, Massachusetts, not knowing what to do next. Soon he built a treehouse to live in while he pondered his future and the visions he had had from childhood, and before long several friends wanted to join him there. The treehouse quickly had half a dozen occupants. Neighbors burned down the treehouse, so Metelica and friends built a cabin. Moving several times to increasingly larger quarters, by the fall of 1969 the group had rented a summer-camp dormitory at Heath, Massachusetts. Soon eighty persons were overwhelming that primitive structure. For all of the physical privation that the community endured, however, the spiritual bond that was developing was strong. The members did odd jobs to support themselves and spent a great deal of time meditating and talking. By early 1970 they were calling themselves the Brotherhood of the Spirit (the group had several names over the years, finally in 1974 settling on the Renaissance Community). Soon they were strong enough financially to buy an inn and restaurant with a small tract of land in Warwick, Massachusetts, and to build a large dormitory next door to it. The members were, as an early Brotherhood publication put it, "people who wanted more than anything else to understand and experience something beyond the obvious day to day routine of earning a living (8 hrs.), having or trying to have a good time (8 hrs., or more if they could do that at work), sleeping the remaining 8 and on Sundays resting up from it all."[28] Despite the fact that Metelica credited much of his enlightenment to LSD taken during his California sojourn, the group for several years banned drugs, alcohol, and promiscuous sex (i.e., sex other than within a committed relationship).[29]

The community's esoteric spirituality has evolved over time. While he was still a teenager Metelica met Elwood Babbitt, a locally prominent trance medium who became an influential spiritual adviser to the group and whose messages—said to be from entities ranging from Krishna to Sam Clemens—confirmed the group in its belief that its fundamental task was nothing less than saving the world. Babbitt convinced Metelica that the latter's visionary experiences, which had long puzzled him, were real and that it was his destiny to found a spiritual movement.[30] Babbitt also introduced Metelica and his followers to the venerable esoteric Christian treatise *The Aquarian Gospel of Jesus the Christ,* which the community adopted as a basic spiritual text.[31] From such bases and with regular teaching sessions by Metelica and Babbitt, the group developed its own distinctive New Age spiritual life, bonding the members even further. The community had little overt ritual, but it had frequent meditation sessions and members spent a good deal of time exploring their past lives; Metelica, for example, had been the apostle Peter and Robert E. Lee.[32] They also worked hard, growing much of their own food and building buildings for their burgeoning community.

In the early 1970s word of the dynamic community in Massachusetts spread throughout the Northeast, and a steady stream of young seekers came to check it all out. Membership grew rapidly, probably peaking at over three hundred in the mid-1970s and staying fairly steady a bit below that figure for several years thereafter.[33] To house and provide income for its large population the community bought properties in several towns in the area and started several businesses, one of the most successful and prominent of them the Renaissance Greeting Cards Company, later sold to members who departed from the community.

In 1975 the community reversed its movement toward decentralization when it purchased eighty acres in the town of Gill and began to plan the 2001 Center, which was projected as a spiritually-based ecovillage. Development of that project proceeded for several years; by the early 1990s it had seven large houses plus several common buildings, a food co-op, and a large organic garden. The community built solar and wind power systems and operated three construction-oriented businesses, which employed several members.[34]

By the 1990s, however, the community had changed. In the 1980s the strictures against drugs and alcohol had virtually vanished, and rumors of drug dealing and guns within the community became widespread.[35] Metelica gradually came to be seen as a liability rather than a leader, and in 1987 he was ousted following an accusation that he stole $60,000 from the group's treasury to buy cocaine, a charge he denied.[36] But finally the situation settled down, and what remains is essentially a land-trust community, with a good deal of cooperation but privately owned homes and independent incomes.

THE COMMUNAL LITERATI: PACKER CORNER, MONTAGUE, AND FRIENDS

One cluster of communes in northern Massachusetts and southern Vermont rose to unusual prominence because of the literary abilities of their members. Both Packer Corner Farm and Montague Farm had best-selling authors in their numbers, which certainly helped their finances but also gave them more publicity than they really wanted.

Packer Corner is best known to the rest of the world as Total Loss Farm, a name invented by Raymond Mungo and the title of his romantic book about communal life.[37] Mungo, Marty Jezer, Marshall Bloom, and several others came together as staffers at Liberation News Service (LNS), the chief supplier of news on the Left and on the new alternative culture to the underground papers of the late 1960s. Even then they were all tiring of the circumstances of their cause-driven lives. The New Left, the Movement, was splintering into any number of chaotic and uncoordinated fragments, which tended to obviate any hope of achieving the new society of which the romantic young revolutionaries had dreamed. A deep split in the LNS itself—between those that Mungo termed the "Vulgar Marxists" and the less intense, more idealistic cultural revolutionaries of his own faction, the "Virtuous Caucus"—led the latter to stage a daylight raid on the LNS offices, packing up most of the equipment and mailing lists and heading north. A huge fracas ensued, naturally, and two separate operations called themselves LNS for a time; then, as the rural life enveloped the Virtuous Caucus, in early 1969 their part of the action quietly dissipated. What was left was to lead the hip communal life in Vermont.[38]

The refugees settled into their new home in July 1968, having pooled all their meager resources—"Marty's life savings from a former life of editing encyclopedias and his Bar Mitzvah bonds, Peter's purse, and Raymond's indefatigable finagling, and change from the couch"—to make their down payment on the $26,000 property in Guilford, Vermont.[39] As proper countercultural anarchists they never adopted any structures but rather became a family by living as one. The financial scene was as unstructured as anything else:

Our records are chaotic. We have no treasurer and have never bothered keeping books to detail income and expenses. Money is spent as it comes in. Sporadically. Sometimes we've got thousands of dollars in our checking account. Other times you can't even find loose change under the cushions of the couch. The checkbook is accessible to all and we trust each other not to make unnecessary expenditures. But what's an unnecessary expenditure? We tend not to get petty about the outflow of petty cash. Anarchy isn't completely successful, however. Some of us are more reluctant to dip into the common checking account than others. But we're learning gradually that there is no need to be shy. Money's never caused much of a problem. People earn whatever they can, some earn nothing at all, and that's OK, too. People who earn money usually take out pocket money before depositing their checks into the common account. That's OK. Anyone who goes out and makes a wage deserves a hamboogie or two on the sly.[40]

With expenses of less than $1,000 per person per year—a typical communal financial situation—they managed to survive on various odd bits of income, the largest fraction of which came from their books. Ray Mungo's *Famous Long Ago* and *Total Loss Farm* both sold handsomely, and Alicia Bay Laurel, joining the Packer Corner crew a bit later, brought with her the lingering royalty income from her smash bestseller *Living on the Earth,* written and published while she had lived at Wheeler's Ranch. Several other books also contributed bits of income, and in cooperation with other communes in the area, the group published and sold locally an occasional periodical called the *Green Mountain Post.*[41] Like many other communards they grew much of their own food (including animals), cut their own firewood, and generally simplified their lives to the point that having very much money didn't matter.

Given the prominence of some of the founders of Packer Corner, not to mention the fact that young hippies everywhere were just then fanning out to hunt down country communal homes, it was not surprising that the DRV—Democratic Republic of (or Revolution in) Vermont, as the farm styled itself briefly—was overrun with uninvited guests.[42] After some soul-searching the members asked most of the visitors to leave, and the commune settled down to a core population of about thirteen.

Most of the original Packer settlers are long since gone (although some live nearby), but the community itself is quite alive and well; a report in 1996 counted eight residents—including two who were raised there, left for a time, and have now returned. The residents mostly work at outside jobs, emphasizing self-sufficiency less than did the founding generation, and have become pillars of the larger Guilford community.[43]

A few miles south of Packer Corner, in Massachusetts, was Montague Farm, also noted for its literary output, in this case notably Stephen Diamond's *What the Trees Said.*[44] Diamond—like Mungo, Jezer, and Bloom of Packer Corner—had been involved in Liberation News Service and shared with the others the sentiment that the time had come to abandon the city and to seek friendlier, more laid-back precincts. Montague was purchased shortly before Packer was, and in fact was a staging area where the LNS founders who liberated the office equipment and press stopped and did battle with the irate New York faction (who had tracked them down) before finally landing on their own farm. "Our two farms are like sisters. Two clumps of people of the same *karass,* relatives of the same family," Diamond wrote.[45] Like Packer, Montague Farm has quietly lived out its history for years afterwards.

A complete survey of New England communes, or even those within a hundred miles of Packer Corner and Montague, could easily be a book of its own. Mayday Farm, founded in 1970 in southern Vermont, was a mixture of political radicals and psychedelic dropouts housed in a 200-year-old house on 250 acres provided by a generous owner in return for the residents' making the house habitable. Red Clover was probably the most intensely politically radical of the Vermont communes; subsidized by a wealthy countercultural benefactor, its members originally saw themselves as creating a rural redoubt for the coming revolution but ended up building an alternative infrastructure, including an organic restaurant and an alternative school. Johnson's Pasture, with open-door membership and no electricity, plumbing, or telephone, was considered by its peers the down-and-out commune of southern Vermont—an image cemented in 1970 when a faulty stovepipe torched the main communal dwelling, killing four persons sleeping inside. The Pasture thereafter gradually drifted into oblivion. At the other extreme, Tree Frog Farm, thanks to another wealthy hippie benefactor, had everything from kitchen appliances to bulldozers, although it soon lost its communal spirit and all its members except the owner. No commune was typical.[46]

We Are Everywhere

The largest concentrations of communes between 1968 and 1975 were, insofar as we may rely on imprecise statistics, in the regions covered just above—the Northwest, Southwest, and Northeast. In the central states and the Southeast the numbers of communes may have been smaller, or perhaps they just received less publicity. It is clear, in any event, that communes, while not perfectly evenly distributed, were found in every part of the land (as the appendix to this volume demonstrates). Virginia, for example, was home to several spiritual and egalitarian communities (some of which will be discussed below), plus many others such as Shannon Farm, a land-trust community with clustered housing and collective businesses that was founded in 1974 and is thriving at this writing.[47] Tennessee became the home of the Farm (discussed in the next chapter) and of several other communities, including Dunmire Hollow, founded in 1974 by a dozen or two communitarians who had begun living together in the university community of Champaign-Urbana, Illinois, searched the country for affordable land in an agreeable climate, and have pursued largely self-sufficient living and thrived quietly ever since.[48] Stories like theirs could be told hundreds of times over.

THE FEDERATION OF EGALITARIAN COMMUNITIES

One network of communities founded primarily in the early 1970s deserves special mention for its ongoing embodiment of the best of 1960s-era values. As discussed in the previous chapter, the Twin Oaks community from its founding in 1967 prized equality and nonviolence; it is staunchly opposed to racism and sexism, operates under conditions in which members are economically equal, and strives to live in harmony with its natural environment. Over a period of several years other communities were founded on similar principles and soon banded together into the Federation of Egalitarian Communities (FEC). Federation communities hold all property in common, meet the basic needs of members, are governed by egalitarian principals, support human dignity, are dedicated to environmental protection, and are committed to open communication among members and nonviolence in all situations. The organization supports member communities in a variety of ways, such as a health care fund that helps communities meet large medical expenses.[49]

Two FEC communities are direct descendants of Twin Oaks. East

Wind, whose members moved to 160 acres in the Ozarks at Tecumseh, Missouri, in 1974, was organized by Kat Kinkade, a cofounder of Twin Oaks who moved to the new community for several years. East Wind grew slowly but steadily to seventy-five or so members in the 1990s, at the same time building several buildings, including one that houses a nut butter business (the East Wind brand can be found at health food stores nationwide) and another that is used for hammock-making, a joint venture with Twin Oaks. Acorn, the other descendant, is much more recent in origin, having been founded in 1993 just a few miles from the parent Twin Oaks community.

Sandhill Farm, founded on 135 acres near Rutledge, Missouri, in 1974, has always been deliberately small, with around ten members. Characterizing itself as a "family of friends," Sandhill is one of the most genuinely agricultural of the back-to-the-land communities, making most of its living from sorghum molasses, livestock, honey, and other products. Other FEC communities (Tekiah, in Check, Virginia, and Veiled Cliffs, in Scottown, Ohio) have been founded since 1975, and a few active prior to 1975 (Appletree, at Cottage Grove, Oregon, and Dandelion, located near Kingston, Ontario) have since folded or reorganized. Several other communities have associate member ("Communities-in-Dialogue") status.[50]

OTHER FEDERATIONS

Other federations of communities have served geographic or ideological constituencies in a manner similar to that of the FEC. The Earth Communities Network, for example, served to connect the environmentally-oriented communities of the Pacific Northwest (Oregon, Washington, and British Columbia) in the 1970s. Across the continent, the Intercommunities of Virginia, which appears to have first become active around 1973, has long fostered cooperation, labor sharing, and social life among the many communities that have settled in Virginia since Twin Oaks blazed the path. One of its early projects was the rehabilitation of an old bus, known as Big Red, that member communities could use for group transportation.[51]

A Cast of Thousands

Any survey of the countercultural communes of the 1960s era is bound to be woefully incomplete, and anyone with knowledge of the subject would undoubtedly argue with my choices for examination here. The communes described above have tended to be the more prominent and longer-lived ones, and given that thousands of the communes—the vast majority, undoubtedly—were short-lived and not very prominent, this selection may be seriously unrepresentative. The reader who is interested in examining many more communal venues can pursue them easily by consulting the references provided in this chapter. The larger point here is that the countercultural 1960s communes were diverse in every way, and each of them in its own peculiar way made its strokes on the American canvas.

5

Searching for a Common Center
Religious and Spiritual Communes

The American 1960s were a time of cultural innovation and experimentation, and religion was as lively a center of the action as any. Asian teachers were streaming into the United States as never before, the esoteric ancient-wisdom religions were getting a new round of inquirers, and unanticipated conservative Protestants in hippie garb surprised just about everyone.

It should be acknowledged at the outset that the subject of this chapter, religious and spiritual groups, is difficult to delineate. A great swath of 1960s counterculturists considered their lives and works spiritual in nature. A sort of vague introspection, often a kind of nature mysticism and often held to be beyond description in words, characterized huge numbers of hippies. A great many of those who took LSD and its analogues felt that their psychedelic experiences were spiritual in nature, and that opening set many off on extended spiritual quests. (If the psychedelic sacrament, which helped one to strip away external crap and get to the essence of what the universe was all about, pointed toward spiritual experience, who could not take that road?) This chapter examines the kind of commune in which spirituality was explicit and structured, usually led by one or more spiritual teachers who guided the whole community (at least in theory) down a discernible common spiritual path.

The new communalists of the 1960s era did not, of course, invent the spiritual commune; several of those operating between 1900 and 1960 (examined in the predecessor to this volume) were very much alive and well when the new spiritual seekers burst on the scene. The Catholic Worker, that dynamic movement of social activists whose piety was matched only by their radicalism, saw quite an influx of new communitarians into the various Worker houses and farms around the country. The two Koinonia communities, one in Maryland and the other in Georgia, both had many 1960s-era inquirers show up. In the former case, Koinonia, Maryland, ended up changing its focus considerably, moving from a previous concern with world missions to the broader social and cultural issues that tended to dominate the 1960s debate. In Georgia, Koinonia Farm's radical commitment to racial equality meshed well with the concerns of young race-relations activists whose sensibilities had been honed by the civil rights movement, and a good many of them spent longer or shorter periods of time there. Some of the grand old communal movements of the nineteenth century, such as the Amana Colonies and the Shakers, were mere shadows of their former communal selves, but even they were touched by the cultural ferment of the 1960s era in various ways. (The House of David, whose male members with their beards and long hair had always looked like hippies, probably would have been a natural magnet for the 1960s crowd, but they were already aging and remote from the cultural revolution.) In short, the venerable tradition of religious communitarianism received a shot in the arm in the 1960s and early 1970s.

The Jesus Movement Communes

One 1960s-era spiritual phenomenon that no one saw coming was the Jesus movement, populated by "Jesus freaks" or "Jesus people," evangelical Protestants who adopted hippie styles of clothing, graphic expression, and language. Some Jesus freaks ("freak" was a common hippie self-descriptor) were young committed Christians who were drawn to the romantic world of the counterculture; by adopting its outward trappings they could live the life vicariously without descending into the forbidden realm of sex, drugs, and radical leftist politics. Others were former full-tilt hippies who for one reason or another—drug freakouts or sexually transmitted diseases, for example—had decided to modify their lifestyles, but only partially. Robert Ellwood, in his early book on the Jesus movement, demonstrates that there was great continuity between the secular hippies and their Christian compatriots: a desire to get high (on dope or on spiritual experience), a negative reaction to modern technological culture, and a sense of being on a cultural cutting edge were common to both types.[1] Just as the secular hippies criticized majoritarian society for its moral shortcomings and repressive ways, the Jesus freaks criticized the religious establishment as stuffy, sometimes racist, too much concerned with right doctrine and too little interested in pursuing authentic religious experience.

As with 1960s-era communes generally, we will never have anything resembling an accurate count of Jesus communes or of their members. Hiley H. Ward, in a contemporary book-length ethnography of the Jesus communes, provided in passing a count of around eight hundred of them but offered no explanation of the figure and in fact acknowledged that the communes were hard to track down.[2] It seems plausible to believe that several thousand of them existed at one time or another. Most of those that can be documented were urban; rural retreats seem to have been rarer for the Christian communards than they were for their secular hippie counterparts, perhaps because preaching the gospel was easiest to do when one lived in a large population center. California probably had the largest numbers of Jesus communes, but they were found just about everywhere.

The Jesus movement began to take shape in the late 1960s, with early stirrings in 1968 and major publicity by 1970; the requisite *Time* cover that certified the new Jesus activity as a Significant Social Movement came on June 21, 1971. Suddenly the United States was witnessing a colorful wave of seeming hippies being baptized in the ocean, preaching on the streets, publishing alternative papers with psychedelic-style graphics—and living in communes. Most of the communes as a matter of policy banned all drugs (often including alcohol) and nonmarital sex, although, of course, the spirit of social experimentation that permeated the culture of the young in those days could hardly be excluded entirely.[3] Like their secular hippie counterparts, the Jesus freaks tended to live cheaply, often eschewing paid jobs in favor of street missionary work. Also like the secular communards they often had generous benefactors who purchased communal houses for them and sometimes paid the bills—Christian businessmen, typically, who saw the Jesus movement as a hopeful sign amid the general drift of the young toward seemingly undisciplined indulgence in hedonistic diversions.

Many of the Jesus communes were locally organized and operated, sometimes in conjunction with a local church; the booming Calvary Chapel of Orange County, California, for example, one of the first evangelical churches to welcome longhairs with open arms, sponsored several communes. Many had short lives. Some, however, proved durable (many still existing through the 1990s) and several evolved into major independent networks of communities.

THE SHILOH MOVEMENT

The largest of the Jesus-movement communal networks was the Shiloh Youth Revival Centers, which in less than a decade founded more than 175 local communal houses. It all began in 1968 when John Higgins converted to Christianity and began converting others and inviting them into his home. Soon they together rented a larger house in Costa Mesa, California, called the House of Miracles. The following April about thirty of these new Christians traveled to Eugene, Oregon, where they lived simply, preaching the gospel at every opportunity and attracting many new members. Soon they were able to buy a ninety-acre tract outside Eugene that became Shiloh's central commune, which could house over one hundred. Shiloh expanded rapidly across the country, opening Shiloh Houses and taking believers into refuges where they could wait for the Second Coming (which they believed imminent). As Shiloh's last administrator, Joe Peterson, has written, "Shiloh members created a nearly self-sufficient, coast-to-coast empire. They owned farms, fishing boats, canneries, construction companies, auto-mechanic shops, a tree planting and logging company, their own credit union, a medical clinic, their own twin-engine plane, and much more. . . . Many business endeavors were tried. Some failed, but others were very successful."[4]

The glory days lasted for about a decade. Looking back, some former members can see that problems were welling up in Shiloh early on. Leadership was authoritarian. As in many other Jesus communes, women's roles were sharply restricted—at a time when women's options were expanding rapidly in the outside world. The emotional "high" of loving Jesus was sometimes hard to maintain in the face of long hours of hard work and poor living conditions.[5] Crucially, the business administration of the community with all its holdings and assets was not good. Thus in 1978 and 1979 Shiloh would shrink from one thousand members to a handful. Although the remnant pursued several strategies for saving the land at Eugene, ultimately the real estate was seized by the Internal Revenue Service for unpaid taxes and interest. By 1989, the largest communal network to come out of the Jesus movement was no more.[6]

THE CHILDREN OF GOD

The most controversial of the many Jesus movement communes began to take shape in greater Los Angeles in 1968, when David Berg—son of an itinerant revivalist and himself a pastor in the Christian and Missionary Alliance denomination—began working with teenagers in a coffeehouse setting in Huntington Beach, California.[7] In 1969 Berg and a band of one hundred or so young adherents began to travel the country, preparing for the end of the world, which they believed to be at hand. Often dressed in sackcloth and ashes, carrying long staffs and Bibles, they made a striking sight—and began to engender controversy. Calling themselves the Children of God, the early followers were a thoroughgoing doom-and-gloom group, with an elaborate picture of terrible millennial events about to happen and a belief that the United States, populated as it was by sinners in the hands of an angry God, was on the verge of devastation. In 1970 the group, now numbering nearly two hundred, settled down on a ranch in Texas and in an old skid row mission building in Los Angeles.[8] As a matter of policy the Children did not work at outside jobs, relying instead on donations and windfalls and often living in less than luxurious conditions. Parents of some of Berg's young adherents began to believe that their children were being abused and in the early 1970s formed the first of the modern anticult organizations, eventually known as Free the Children of God, or FREECOG.[9]

Trying to avoid both controversy and millennial disaster, most of the Children left the United States and worked for several years in other countries around the world, reportedly experiencing explosive growth in the process: Berg counted 2,348 members in 134 colonies in 41 countries in October 1972.[10] Berg himself relocated to England, but he stayed in touch with his scattered minions with "Mo letters," illustrated pamphlets of teachings and instructions. Early in this diaspora the Children did most of their proselytizing by "litnessing," selling or giving away Mo letters on public places. In 1976, however, the movement inaugurated its most sensational and controversial practice, "flirty fishing"—sending women out to have sex with men outside the movement in an attempt to convert them. After all, if God loves all persons, could not that love be expressed sexually? The practice was later discontinued, but not before the movement had experienced a rash of pregnancies, sexually transmitted diseases, and internal disruption of the Children's communal homes (many of the women doing the "fishing" were already married mothers).

In the early 1990s the Children, long virtually out of sight in the United States, began quietly returning and opening communal houses again under the movement's new name, the Family. A new generation has emerged as the original members' children have married and had children of their own. Shorn of some of its more controversial practices, but with its missionary zeal intact, the Family today is an evolved 1960s-era Jesus commune that has survived.[11]

THE ALAMO CHRISTIAN FOUNDATION

Susan Horn, raised in a small town in Arkansas, and Tony Alamo, a Jew from Montana whose birth name was Bernie Hoffman, both had had rough childhoods and multiple divorces when they met in 1966. Alamo had just been converted to Christianity and the couple, living in Los Angeles and both interested in show business, soon started an independent ministry that prospered with the rise of the Jesus movement. Its first communal explorations came at a private home soon after the founding of the Alamo Christian Foundation.[12] As the numbers of believers grew the movement bought land in Saugus, fifty miles north of Los Angeles, where communal life had room to grow, although living conditions were decidedly less than luxurious and outside critics began to allege that members were being abused. In 1977 the Alamos decided to move the entire operation to western Arkansas, where a main campus was built outside Susan's home town of Dyer. Over several years the movement established many businesses, including a restaurant with live entertainment (Dolly Parton and Tammy Wynette were among the many stars who performed there), farms, a truck line, a concrete company, a grocery store, and many others. Controversy and court proceedings did not abate, however, as allegations of illegal and abusive behavior continued to circulate.

A major burst of publicity came in 1982, when Susan died of cancer. Tony refused to bury her body, instead instituting a prayer vigil to bring her back to life. Only two years later did Tony relent and allow the body to be entombed. Alamo's problems continued; he was charged with a number of criminal and civil offenses and began a series of unsuccessful marriages. He also aroused a storm of controversy for his vicious attacks on the Catholic Church, proclaiming, for example, that the Vatican is "the world's largest cult and that narcotics, prostitution, pornography, booze and black market—every filthy thing—can be traced right back to the Vatican and her government agencies."[13] Eventually the situation came to a climax in 1990 and 1991 when the Internal Revenue Service seized and sold millions of dollars' worth of Alamo Foundation property to help satisfy various judgments; finally, in 1994, Tony Alamo was convicted on federal tax charges. Even with their leader in prison, some members continued to support the cause, and in 1999, with Alamo's release from custody at hand, appeared ready to reignite the movement.[14]

THE MESSIANIC COMMUNITIES (TWELVE TRIBES)

In 1972 Elbert and Marsha Spriggs opened a Christian coffeehouse in Chattanooga, Tennessee, that immediately attracted a large following of young converts who formed the nucleus of what has become a network of closely related Christian intentional communities called the Messianic Communities. Soon new converts began moving into the Spriggs home, and the project quickly grew to include five houses and a business, a health-food cafe. As the group grew it experienced increasing conflicts with Chattanooga residents over such matters as racially integrated communal housing, and soon the members decided to relocate. In 1978 they moved from Chattanooga to Island Pond, in northern Vermont, and from there the movement has expanded to a present total of more than fifteen communities in five countries. Like many communities founded in the ferment of the Jesus movement, the Messianic Communities are strongly millennial and separate themselves to a fair degree from the outside world, schooling their own children, adhering to specific dress and appearance standards, and even having their own religious terminology based on their transliteration of biblical texts (Jesus, for example, is known as Yahshua). They have developed their own businesses, including restaurants in several cities.

The Messianic Communities have been the subject of a good deal of controversy, most notably over their strict disciplining—critics call it abuse—of their children.[15] In the meantime, the movement has continued to attract new members to the various communities and in 1994 had a membership estimated at 1,000 to 1,500, approximately half of them children.[16] Imitating early Christianity, the communities have many Jewish practices—a festive Friday/Saturday Sabbath, for example, and a practice of giving members new Hebrew names. They are firmly patriarchal, with a precept of submission of wives to husbands and with male leadership, although in nonspiritual matters several women do have positions of authority.

JESUS PEOPLE USA

One of the largest single-site communes in the United States is the headquarters of Jesus People USA in Chicago, with around 450 members plus other residents. JPUSA, as the group calls itself for short, had its beginnings about 1972 in Milwaukee in a fundamentalist youth ministry. By 1974 the JPUSA members had settled permanently in Chicago and were beginning to acquire property and businesses. Eventually the group managed to buy a decrepit hotel not far from Lake Michigan, a building large enough to accommodate the many members and also to house low-income retired persons on the upper floors. From that base they have operated extensive programs of evangelism and service as well as the several businesses that provide their financial underpinnings. The group's service program includes a soup kitchen for the neighborhood, a homeless shelter, a job training program, a jail chaplaincy, a transitional housing facility, and a crisis pregnancy center. JPUSA supports itself and its programs through a series of industries including a moving company, a recording studio, a t-shirt business, and several construction- and maintenance-related businesses.[17]

JPUSA continues to subscribe to the principle of simplicity of lifestyle and operates at a per-capita income level that under other circumstances would be defined as poverty. All money is held in common and dispensed rather parsimoniously as needs arise. As member Jon Trott declares, "We've made the Pascalian wager, we've wagered on life in Christ, and we've bet everything on it. We didn't hold anything back. We've laid our entire lives on the line and said, 'We believe this! This much!' That's the part I think is the radical call."[18]

SOJOURNERS COMMUNITY

Some of the energy of the Jesus movement of the early 1970s welled up on college campuses, and in at least one case that college enthusiasm led to the creation of a community that still survives today. What is now the Sojourners Community grew from a group of students at Trinity Evangelical Divinity School who wanted to deepen their orthodox Protestant faith and to apply it to the social crisis that they saw around them. They began publishing a newspaper that embodied their commitment to faith and radical social action, the *Post American,* in the fall of 1971. The following summer members organized an intentional community in Rogers Park, Illinois, a Chicago suburb, but it disintegrated in 1974. Reevaluating their options, the surviving community-minded remnant decided to tackle urban problems and national politics by moving to Washington, D.C. Settling in the inner-city neighborhood of Columbia Heights and pooling their assets and incomes, they gradually established a network of social outreach programs and set up households in several nearby buildings.[19]

The community is best known to the public beyond its own neighborhood for its magazine, *Sojourners,* the successor to the *Post American,* and for the writing and speaking of founding member Jim Wallis.[20] The combination of firm evangelical Protestantism and radical politics has aroused a good deal of criticism from evangelicals whose social priorities run in markedly different directions. The Sojourners social critique is virtually identical to that of most other evangelicals on such matters as sexual conduct (to be restricted to heterosexual marriage) and abortion (condemned) but sharply different in condemning militarism, corporate excesses, and exploitation of third-world peoples. The Sojourners advocate economic justice, expanded services for the poor, and other such positions seen by most evangelicals as part of the "liberal" agenda. Unfazed by their critics, however, they continue their work with determined dedication.

OTHER COMMUNES FROM THE JESUS MOVEMENT

Most other communes that emerged from the Jesus movement were less publicized and shorter-lived than those described above, but their overall impact on the 1960s-era movement toward communal living and on the larger culture was often substantial. Frequently they were locally controversial, usually because they simply seemed unconventional. Zion's Inn in San Rafael, California, reached out to the larger community by operating a refuge for troubled young women.[21] The Belly of the Whale in Princeton, Illinois, combined Christianity with environmental activism.[22] The Christ Brotherhood of Eugene, Oregon, did serious biblical scholarship and ran a homeless shelter—but ended up seeing its leader imprisoned for sex offenses involving underage girls.[23]

As is the case for 1960s-era communes generally, the great majority of the Jesus communities are no longer operating. Some communards dedicated to lives of poverty and service just burned out after living so simply for many years. Some communities—including pacifist groups that did not share the dominant political outlook of the Reagan years—were hounded to exhaustion by the Internal Revenue Service in the 1980s.[24] But other Christian communities have been founded all the while, and some of the veteran communities remain quite alive and well. The Jesus movement as such has come and gone; Christian community is very much with us.

Other Christian Communes

Not all of the Christian communes founded in the 1960s era were products of the Jesus movement; other Christian groups were also active in founding and perpetuating communities during those socially tumultuous years. The Plow Creek Fellowship, for example, an intentional community related to the older Reba Place Fellowship of Evanston, Illinois, was established in 1971 in Tiskilwa, Illinois, and has carried on an important Mennonite witness ever since.[25] Several L'Arche communities, rooted in Catholicism and dedicated to serving persons with developmental disabilities, were founded in the early 1970s on the pattern of the French original (whose influence has spread worldwide).[26] The Christ of the Hills Monastery in San Antonio sought to recreate traditional monasticism apart from the official structures of the Russian Orthodox Church, on whose principles it is founded.[27] The Church of the Redeemer in Houston was a declining Episcopal parish until it turned charismatic and communal in 1965 under a dynamic new rector, Graham Pulkingham, growing to embrace hundreds of members in dozens of communal households and becoming a model that many other new-generation Christian communities have emulated.[28] Most of these and many other Christian communities have been studied at some length; to give them all their proper due here would require a volume in itself.

PEOPLES TEMPLE

One other 1960s-era experiment in Christian community—one that went more ghastly wrong than any other in American history—does merit mention here. The suicide/murder of over nine hundred persons in Jonestown, Guyana, remains beyond our comprehension or explanation, but the historical pathway to that terrible end is a matter of public record:

for several years in the 1970s the Peoples Temple—officially a local congregation of the Disciples of Christ, a major Protestant denomination—was one of the largest Christian communities of them all.

Jim Jones began his public life as a preacher in Indiana, leading a migration of many of his followers to Ukiah, California, in 1965. In the early 1970s the Peoples Temple, known to Californians principally for its thorough racial integration and for its extensive social service programs, began to develop a commune for those of its members who chose to live together. Eventually the church had at least nineteen and perhaps as many as seventy communal homes in San Francisco, many of them populated by elderly persons who made substantial financial donations and were promised care for life. Members were supporting in heroic fashion a cause in which they deeply believed.

For a variety of reasons far too complex to be quickly summarized here, the Peoples Temple began to develop its ultimate commune, Jonestown, in 1974. On November 18, 1978, at the conclusion of a visit by Congressman Leo Ryan, who had traveled to Jonestown to investigate allegations that persons were being mistreated and held against their will, the sweeping suicide/murder episode was enacted. For the world of intentional community the ongoing tragedy was that after the incident all communitarian enclaves, especially those that subscribed to unorthodox doctrines or had strong leaders, were suspected of being Jonestowns-in-waiting. Even at the end of the 1990s, a commune gone terribly wrong continues to bring considerable grief to communards whose only error is believing in human cooperation.[29]

The East Comes West: Asian-Based Religious Communes

After the repeal of the Asian Exclusion Act in 1965, larger numbers of Asian spiritual teachers than ever before became able to spread their messages in person in the United States. At the same time some Westerners visited Asian spiritual teachers and congregations and returned to found their own Asian-based spiritual communities. As a result the country experienced a great flowering of "cults," as the unfamiliar religions were often derogatorily and unfairly stigmatized, many of which opened communes. Typically not all members of a given movement joined one of its communes, at least permanently; householders went about their lives in private dwellings, while monks and nuns with special dedication populated the ashrams and other communes. In a few cases, though, communalism became normative for a whole movement.

Communal Asian movements numbered in the hundreds, if not thousands, and thus were far more extensive than the following survey can comprehend. The directories of American Buddhist organizations typically list hundreds of centers, many of which were founded during the period we are examining and are to some extent communal, and the other Asian traditions have similarly proliferated.[30] Those discussed below are primarily the oldest, largest, and most prominent religious communities, representing a much larger constituency.

Communal Religions from India

Indian teachers were present in the United States as early as the 1890s; the early Vedanta swamis from the Ramakrishna Mission set up several ashrams, or communes, among their followers early in the twentieth century, and another Indian, Paramahansa Yogananda, probably had an even greater impact than did the Vedantists. The first Indian-based teacher to espouse communal living for his followers after 1965, however, came from a different part of India than his predecessors and did not preach the expansive universalist religion that the Vedantists and Yogananda had. His movement was strict, and it became one of the most controversial new religions to appear in the American 1960s.

THE INTERNATIONAL SOCIETY FOR
KRISHNA CONSCIOUSNESS

In India in the 1920s and 1930s, A. C. Bhaktivedanta Swami Prabhupada (as he came to be known to his disciples)[31] became active in a wing of Hinduism known as Caitanya Vaishnavism, which stressed *bhakti* (devotional service to God).[32] Having been instructed by his own spiritual master to spread his message in the West, Bhaktivedanta traveled to the United States in 1965 at the age of 69. The communal phase of the International Society for Krishna Consciousness (ISKCON) started rather informally as Keith Ham, an early disciple, became Bhaktivedanta's cook and housekeeper in the master's very modest apartment on Second Avenue in New York.[33] As more devotees joined the movement they acquired bigger quarters, and before long they were expanding to other cities as well.

ISKCON's initial constituency was largely among the hippie drop-outs, typically persons whose spiritual explorations had begun with LSD. As we have seen, Bhaktivedanta even visited Morning Star Ranch—a place certainly not known for its asceticism—and left with several new disciples.[34] The new believers abandoned the material search for bliss in favor of seeking transcendence through spiritual discipline. Life in the ISKCON temples was rigorous, to say the least: members had to arise very early in the morning (typically around 4 A.M.), do hours of chanting every day, take lessons in the *Bhagavad Gita,* and perform a variety of services for the temple and the larger movement—including *kirtan,* the street preaching, chanting, dancing, and bookselling for which they became well known. Members also had to observe strict self-denial in their personal lives, especially in complying with what were called the four regulative principles: avoidance of eating meat, including fish and eggs; avoidance of gambling; avoidance of intoxicants, including psychedelics and tobacco; and avoidance of illicit sex, defined as any sex not undertaken for procreative purposes within marriage (and that only under such sharply limited conditions that ISKCON was virtually a celibate movement, at least in theory).

Of all the dozens of ISKCON communal locations the best-known came to be New Vrindaban in West Virginia, the first of several Krishna-conscious rural communes. Keith Ham, who had taken the spiritual name Kirtanananda, led a small group of devotees to an isolated farm. Soon they decided to build a suitable house for their spiritual master to occupy when he visited, and they commenced to erect Prabhupada's Palace, as it was quite properly called—an opulent building truly fit for royalty and not like anything ever seen in the West Virginia hills. It became a major tourist attraction, and the commune prospered from visitors who came by the busload to tour the palace and to patronize the New Vrindaban restaurants and shops. At the height of it all the community even erected time-share condominiums for those who wanted to take their vacations there every year. Bhaktivedanta, incidentally, had died before he could ever stay in his palace.

ISKCON had a terrible time surviving the death of Bhaktivedanta in 1977. Sensational allegations of misdeeds and crimes swirled around several of its temples, and New Vrindaban in particular went through one of the most intense scandals to hit communal America. The community was accused of harboring drug dealers and of engaging in violent behavior.

Kirtanananda was battered and gravely injured by a disaffected former member. A murder on the premises brought a state and federal investigation, and Kirtanananda was eventually convicted on charges related to the criminal activity there and was incarcerated. In 1987 he and the New Vrindaban community were expelled from ISKCON.[35] However, with Kirtanananda absent New Vrindaban has calmed down and in the 1990s moved back into the ISKCON orbit. ISKCON itself seems to have weathered its crises; several temples still operate as small communes, and a few rural agricultural communes survive as well. A notable Asian-based religious communal movement seems to have stepped back from the brink.[36]

ANANDA WORLD BROTHERHOOD VILLAGE

Paramahansa Yogananda, as charming and personable as he was spiritually adept, attracted a substantial following soon after arriving in the United States in 1920. His *Autobiography of a Yogi* may well be the best-selling Asian religious work of all time in the West, and his organization, the Self-Realization Fellowship (SRF), is now one of the largest Asian-oriented religious associations in the West.[37] According to his disciple Donald Walters, who took the spiritual name Swami Kriyananda, Yogananda had long had visions of establishing a network of spiritual communities in America.[38] The vision was not to be enacted during his lifetime, but in due course Walters, who joined the SRF in 1948, would pick up the ball. Walters was expelled from the organization in 1962 for alleged schismatic tendencies, but on his own he continued to teach Indian philosophy and yoga, and in 1967 located land suitable for his long-desired meditation retreat. In 1969 work began in California on the cooperative community called Ananda Village.[39]

The building of Ananda was at first slow and pitfallen. Chronic shortages of funds led to recurrent financial crises, and in the early days the place was overrun with young dropouts who wanted to live in community but did not want to do the hard work that it would take to build that community. The most devastating setback was a fire that swept through the land in July 1976, searing 450 acres and destroying 21 of the 22 homes then at Ananda—all uninsured—and leaving more than fifty residents homeless. Several families left after losing their homes, but the rest managed to regroup and, with a good deal of outside volunteer help, to reconstruct their community.[40]

Crises aside, over time the community prospered. Members built homes in secluded locations. The community established its own schools and small businesses. The retreat center, now called The Expanding Light, grew steadily, offering an extensive and virtually nonstop program of personal retreats, yoga classes, and workshops and courses on a wide variety of Indian and New Age topics. Steady growth in population took hold; after a decade the land had 87 permanent residents,[41] and by 1992 the number had jumped to 356—with even more in about half a dozen satellite communities, including one in Italy.[42] In the late 1990s, however, legal problems clouded Ananda's previously sunny horizon. The community successfully (but at considerable expense) defended itself against a suit brought by the Self-Realization Fellowship, which claimed that Ananda had violated its copyright ownership of the image and works of Yogananda, but in 1998 a jury assessed Walters and Ananda over a million dollars in damages on fraud charges related to allegations of sexual battery made by a former Ananda member. Although the community claimed that it had been unfairly stigmatized by being labeled a "cult" and hoped to appeal, the judgment and legal bills pushed Ananda close to bankruptcy.[43]

Life at Ananda, as one observer noted, "is an individual and collective effort to get closer to God."[44] Walters resigned as head of the community following his loss in the fraud/sexual battery suit, but he continues to be honored and to play a de facto leadership role. The spiritual discipline of the community involves private morning prayer at home plus a period of silence and meditation at noon. In the evening members meditate and study spiritual texts. Ananda members subscribe to a code of conduct that emphasizes cooperation, self-improvement, and right livelihood and lifestyle; in its earlier, looser days Ananda tolerated alcohol and marijuana, but the agreements that govern community life now forbid both—and dogs, for that matter.[45] Thus has a spiritual community from the late 1960s survived and prospered.[46]

SIKH COMMUNITIES

The groups discussed just above are all rooted in the diverse Indian group of traditions generally known as Hinduism. However, India's world-leading religious heterogeneity includes a number of other religions not within the Hindu fold: Islam, Sikhism, Jainism, several smaller ones, and many Christian denominations that have been established as the result of American and European missionary activity. In particular, Sikhism and a Sikh offshoot known as Radhasoami inspired several groups that opened American communes during the 1960s era. The most visible of them were the Healthy-Happy-Holy Organization of Yogi Bhajan and the Divine Light Mission of Guru Maharaj Ji.

The Healthy-Happy-Holy Organization. Sikhism, which has been influenced by Hinduism, Islam, and other religions, was begun about five hundred years ago in the Punjab (which straddles the border of India and Pakistan) and stresses the repetition of the name of God as its prime devotional practice. Yogi Bhajan came from the Punjab to America in 1969 with the intent of spreading Sikhism among non-Indian Americans. His Healthy-Happy-Holy Organization, or 3HO, which combines traditional Sikh teachings with Kundalini yoga and also shows some Radhasoami influence,[47] has established several American communes. In 1969 a new follower in New Mexico offered the guru a twelve-acre site south of Santa Fe, and Maharaj Ashram soon established a rigorous spiritual discipline and reached a membership of fifty. Maharaj disbanded two years later, but quickly another ashram was established farther north, near Española, which is still in operation.[48] Over the years the heavily communal 3HO has opened over one hundred ashrams around the country, many of which support themselves with food-related businesses, including specialty food production, vegetarian restaurants, and health food stores. The daily spiritual practice central to ashram life includes the repetition of a mantra and Kundalini yoga practice, which combines traditional yoga postures with breathing exercises and is said to prepare one to sit and meditate on the holy name of God.[49]

The Divine Light Mission. "Orthodox" Sikhism teaches that truth was imparted by a series of living gurus, the tenth of whom was the last, dying in 1708. The Radhasoami movement, which arose in the nineteenth century, claimed that in fact living gurus were ongoing; at the end of the twentieth century, several dozen Radhasoami groups operate under as many active gurus. Radhasoami teaching stresses the importance of the guru-disciple relationship and of special yoga practices that lead to direct communion with God (known as Naam, or the Word). Among other things, it is said that religious experience involves sound and light: one can learn to say or sing divine sounds, hear divine words and music, and see divine light.

The largest Radhasoami group in America was the Divine Light Mission, to whose leadership Maharaj Ji ascended when he was eight, upon the death of his father. He visited the West in 1971 when he was thirteen and soon attracted thousands of followers. As early as 1973 the movement was reported to be active in fifty-five countries, and the headquarters in Denver had a staff of 125.[50] The movement soon had a large communal component, as practitioners moved into the ashrams that were established in many localities. There they conducted businesses to support themselves and practiced the movement's distinctive spiritual exercises that led the believer to experience divine sounds, sights, and tastes. Premies, as members were called,[51] flocked to see Maharaj Ji in his far-flung personal appearances whenever possible. Ashram residents were pledged to poverty, chastity, and vegetarianism; they followed a rigorous daily schedule of meditation, satsang (spiritual instruction), and work. Less strict were Premie Centers that operated informally in many locations for several years.

During the 1980s Maharaj Ji began a slow dissolution of the Divine Light Mission, including the ashrams. Eventually he stepped down as a Perfect Master and became simply Maharaji, a lecturer on spiritual topics. In that capacity he retains some of his former following, but the communal dimension of his movement is gone.[52]

THE LARGER INDIAN PRESENCE IN AMERICA

As is the case with all categories of communes described in this volume, many more communal groups rooted in Indian traditions are or were active than can be characterized here. Ananda Marga, for example, has had a fairly strong American presence dating back to 1969. Founded in India in 1955 by Prabhat Ranjan Sarkar, it claimed thousands of members and over one hundred centers, some of them communal, in the United States by 1973.[53] The movement has been known for its political and social activism as well as for its spiritual side, and because of the zeal of its members it has been accused to being a violent terrorist organization, a charge members deny.[54] Amrit Desai, the founder of another organization, Kripalu Yoga, was teaching yoga in the United States even before Ananda Marga arrived; Desai opened a spiritual community at Sumneytown, Pennsylvania, in 1972, later expanding to other locations including a former Jesuit seminary in Lenox, Massachusetts. Although Desai recently departed following a sex scandal, both of those locations still function as intentional communities for yoga practitioners as well as retreat centers for members of the larger noncommunal Kripalu Yoga organization and for the general public.[55] The Himalayan Institute was founded at Honesdale, Pennsylvania, in 1971 under the leadership of Swami Rama, who had recently achieved considerable attention by volunteering as a subject in scientifically controlled experiments that tested and measured the remarkable physical feats, such as stopping and restarting one's heart at will, that some swamis have been able to achieve.[56] Yet another Indian tradition with a vibrant communal presence is Siddha Yoga, which began to open ashrams following the second American tour of its late guru, Swami Muktananda Paramahamsa, in 1974. With its American headquarters in a large ashram at South Fallsburg, New York, Siddha Yoga has prospered but also has been the focus of considerable controversy centering on posthumous revelations of sexual and other abuse of disciples by Muktananda and on the authoritarianism of Muktananda's eventual successor, Chidvilasananda, also known as Gurumayi.[57] Furthermore, Indian communal religiosity has become even stronger since 1975, as many more groups have opened major centers.

Probably the largest Indian-based communal presence in America, overall, is found in the many local ashrams and yoga centers that operate quietly in hundreds or thousands of places around the country. Most of those that are residentially communal have at most a few dozen members (and often only a handful), but together they have long been important components of the larger religious communal scene. The J'Ananda community of Elk, California, the Raja-Yoga Math and Retreat of Deming, Washington, the Rochester (New York) Ashram, and a host of others have all been repositories of the Indian communal spirit in America.

Buddhist Communities

Buddhism was first present in America in isolated pockets of Chinese and other Asian immigrant populations and for decades was separated from the larger society by language, culture, and prejudice against Asians. Gradually, however, Buddhism has been embraced by a wider constituency, and since the small beginnings made by Dwight Goddard in the 1930s (discussed in the predecessor to this volume) has developed a number of communal centers as well. In the 1960s era most of those communes were loosely within two broad Buddhist schools of thought, Zen and Tibetan.

ZEN COMMUNITIES

The first American Zen centers were opened in the 1920s in California and in New York. Although their constituency was modest, they had an impact larger than the numbers of their adherents would suggest because of their interaction with several beat poets and writers in the 1940s and 1950s—notably Allen Ginsberg and Gary Snyder, each of whom retained a lifelong interest in Buddhism after being introduced to Zen at the First Zen Institute of America in New York. In the 1950s the previously low profile of Zen in America was raised considerably by the appearance of several popular books on the subject by Alan Watts and Daisetz T. Suzuki.[58] Amid that wave of new interest several Zen centers were opened in cities and rural locations, some of them wholly or partly communal.

San Francisco Zen Center. In 1959 Shunryu Suzuki arrived from Japan to become chief priest at the Zen temple in San Francisco. He soon attracted a non-Asian American following; in the early 1960s the Caucasian Zennists started their own San Francisco Zen Center within the Japanese temple, and in 1969 they acquired a separate facility for their work, which from the beginning had a residential community of teacher and students (numbering as many as seventy) as well as many more nonresidential members. Suzuki moved with the Americans to the new Zen Center and remained their teacher until his death in 1971, and the center has been a principal hub of American Zen ever since.[59] Richard Baker, Suzuki's successor, led the community through more than a decade of growth and prosperity, but he resigned late in 1983 under fire for misuse of authority, money, sex, and power. The following year he moved to Santa Fe and started a new Zen community, the Dharma Sangha, and later moved again to Colorado, where he started the Crestone Mountain Zen Center. The San Francisco Zen Center spent years afterwards struggling to rebuild itself.[60]

Retreat centers in the mountains have long been integral to Zen in Asia, and the San Francisco Zen Center from its early days sought to obtain such a facility. In 1966 the dream came to fruition with the purchase of the Tassajara Zen Mountain Center, a former hot-springs resort located in a suitably remote valley in the Big Sur area. Many in the community spend as long as several years there in intensive Zen training.[61] Tassajara grows a good deal of its own food and has become well known for its cooking, especially through two best-selling books that emerged from its kitchen, *The Tassajara Bread Book* and *Tassajara Cooking.*[62] As a retreat center it attracts large numbers of visitors willing to pay dearly for cabins that have few modern amenities but are unparalleled for tranquility.[63] Over the years the San Francisco Zen Center has opened several other satellite facilities, some of them with related residential communities attached. The most notable of them is Green Gulch Farm, purchased in 1972 to be a working farm and monastery in Marin County, north of San Francisco. Green Gulch has typically had twenty-five to thirty resident members and a steady stream of visitors, especially on weekends.[64] Its several facilities make the San Francisco Zen Center the largest communal center of Zen, and probably of Buddhism, in the United States.

Zen Center of Los Angeles. Like their counterparts in San Francisco, the first non-Asian American Zennists in Los Angeles began to practice in an established Japanese temple and then moved out on their own, establishing their first center—which included residential quarters for their first teacher, Taizan Maezumi, and several of the students—in a rented house in 1967 and soon thereafter moving into quarters they purchased. Gradually the Zen Center of Los Angeles (ZCLA) expanded to occupy most of a city block, and around 150 of the several hundred members lived there by the early 1980s.[65] ZCLA is rigorous in its practice—several hours of zazen a day, plus periodic full-time intensives; it also carries on a wide range of businesses and educational programs. In 1980 the community bought land for a rural retreat (reminiscent of Tassajara) that, like the urban center, provided a rigorous program of Zen training. Like more than one other American Zen center, however, ZCLA had a leadership crisis in the 1980s when Maezumi's alcoholism and affairs with female students became known. (Maezumi, like Richard Baker, was married.) The teacher accepted a program of therapy and reestablished his authority, although as in San Francisco the ZCLA went through a wrenching period of readjustment in response to the crisis.[66] Maezumi died in 1995 at age 64.

Kwan Um Zen School. The San Francisco and Los Angeles Zen Centers are both in the Soto school, a Japanese version of Zen (Taizan Maezumi of Los Angeles also had training in Rinzai, the other principal Japanese Zen school). By contrast, the Kwan Um Zen School is in the Chogye Zen tradition, whose roots are in Korea. Seung Sahn, Kwan Um's spiritual master, came to the United States in 1972 and established a temple in Providence, Rhode Island, which became the headquarters of a movement that was established in several American cities and college towns. The Providence temple grew and established a residential community in the outlying town of Cumberland, to which the headquarters was eventually transferred. Centers now exist in several countries, including Korea; some of them are or have been communal at various times in their past.[67]

Like its counterparts in San Francisco and Los Angeles, the Kwan Um organization has had to struggle with disclosures of controversial sexual conduct on the part of its leader; Seung Sahn was generally understood by his followers to be a celibate monk, and the revelation that he had had affairs with female students caused some members to leave the movement. The organization's vitality was less impaired, however, than had been the case in California.[68]

Other Zen communities. Several other Zen communities were founded during the 1960s era, some of them still in operation, some not. One of the better known of them is the Zen Center of Rochester (New York), founded in 1966 by Philip Kapleau—the noted American Zen teacher who wrote the early and influential *The Three Pillars of Zen*[69]—not long after he had returned from Japan after spending thirteen years there studying and practicing Zen. Kapleau was particularly known (and sometimes criticized) for his efforts to present Zen in a Western context rather than requiring students to wear Asian clothing, chant in Japanese, and so forth.[70] Several alumni of the Rochester Zen Center have gone on to found Zen centers of their own. Another well-established Zen community is the Order of Buddhist Contemplatives at Shasta Abbey, California, which was founded in 1970 as a training center for priests (male and female) as well as for others who attend shorter-term programs. On the other hand, some of the communal centers have not survived. The Maui Zendo, for example, on its eponymous Hawaiian island—founded by Robert and Anne Aitken in 1969 as a branch of their Honolulu-based Koko-an Zendo—was designed to serve 1960s-era spiritual seekers and quickly became "a kind of mission to the psychedelic Bohemia," Robert Aitken said.[71] Most flower children were not long interested in the rigors of Zen, however; although the Aitkens left most lifestyle decisions (diet, sexuality, use of psychedelics) to the individual, they did enforce a rigid daily schedule of zazen and work. Turnover was high, and in the mid-1970s the ranks of the committed practitioners dwindled. In the 1980s the Maui Zendo was closed. The Aitkens returned to Honolulu to pursue new Zen projects there.[72]

TIBETAN BUDDHIST COMMUNITIES

Although several branches of Buddhism besides Zen were active in the United States in the 1960s era, the only other one to institute communal living on a major scale was Tibetan. Two notable Tibetan teachers established spiritual communities, made up mainly of non-Asian Americans, in the early 1970s.

Chogyam Trungpa. When the Chinese swept through Tibet in 1959, several of the country's religious leaders narrowly escaped, fleeing for their lives. Among them was Chogyam Trungpa, a former Tibetan abbot who continued teaching in exile, in the process acquiring some American disciples.[73] These disciples soon informally established what would become their movement's chief communal center, originally called Tail of the Tiger (later Karme-Choling), in Barnet, Vermont. Trungpa himself arrived in the United States in 1970, settling in Boulder, Colorado, where he established several interrelated spiritual and educational organizations now collectively known as Shambhala International. A group of hippie Trungpa disciples known as the Pygmies soon developed a second spiritual community, the Rocky Mountain Dharma Center (now the Rocky Mountain Shambhala Center) in northern Colorado, which started as a free-form commune but evolved into a serious meditation center.[74] Several smaller urban and rural communities eventually appeared as well.

Trungpa was not your average Asian guru. Although he demanded extensive spiritual practice and study, including sitting and walking meditation and months-long intensive spiritual retreats, he rejected asceticism as a norm for one's personal life. Trungpa ate meat, smoked cigarettes, drank alcohol prodigiously, and presided over raucous parties. He was not sexually abstinent; he had given up his position as celibate guru and had married before he arrived in the United States, and he openly maintained affairs with several female students. His detractors have told disheartening stories of humiliation and abuse of disciples and other persons out of his favor, sometimes in situations aggravated by his binge drinking.[75] His unrestrained lifestyle probably contributed to his early death in 1987. More problems were to come as Trungpa's designated successor, ösel Tendzin (an American originally named Thomas Rich), developed AIDS but remained sexually active and did not inform his sexual partners of his illness. However, upon Tendzin's death in 1989 the leadership passed to Trungpa's oldest son, Sawang ösel Rangdrol Mukpo, and leadership has been stabilized. All of the major communal centers and many of the smaller ones have survived through the 1990s.[76]

Tarthang Tulku. Like Trungpa, Tarthang Tulku left Tibet just ahead of the Chinese invasion, and after living as a refugee in India arrived in the United States in 1968, settling in Berkeley, California, and founding the Nyingma Institute. In 1971 he and his students purchased and renovated an old fraternity house, which they named Padma Ling ("Lotus Ground"), to house a meditation center and to provide a communal resi-

dence for Nyingma members. The Institute's headquarters, at another location in Berkeley, also provided collective living space for members.
Tarthang Tulku did not bend nearly as far as did Trungpa to accommodate
himself to secular Western culture (although he, like Trungpa, abandoned
celibacy); in his monastery not only did students learn the various kinds of
meditation and prostrations used in Tibetan Buddhism, but they held rituals according to the Tibetan calendar and chanted in Tibetan.

In 1975 the Nyingma Institute purchased nine hundred acres north of
Jenner, California, to house Odiyan, or the Nyingma Country Center, to
accommodate a wide variety of activities, including meditation, study, the
arts, and a self-sufficient farming community. By 1996, according to a
news report in the Buddhist journal *Tricycle,* Odiyan—built as a replica of
Samye, Tibet's first Buddhist monastery—had expanded to 1,100 acres
containing "more than 1,750 stupas, 6 major temples, 108 meditation sites,
1,242 electric prayer wheels, 108,000 statues of Padmasambhava [who
brought Buddhism to Tibet], and 800 prayer flags," all built at a cost of
over $10 million.[77] Thus has Tarthang built up a network of communities
and other spiritual institutions.

AN INDEPENDENT ASIAN COMMUNAL MOVEMENT: THE UNIFICATION CHURCH

In parts of Asia (as in America) an important element in the overall religious mosaic has been the appearance of "new religions"—movements
that, typically, syncretically build new religious organizations on various
mixtures of old and new themes. One such new religion has been the Unification Church of the Rev. Sun Myung Moon of Korea. Moon's religion
combines Christianity, traditional Korean shamanism, bits of Taoism and
Confucianism, and his own purported revelations: in 1936, when he was
16, he claimed to have received the key revelation that he was to complete
the unfinished task of Jesus in restoring the Kingdom of God to earth. In
1959 Moon sent his first emissaries to the United States.[78]

The movement made few converts until the 1970s, but until well into
the 1980s those who did convert chose a communal lifestyle. Typically a
local congregation—often with fewer than half a dozen members—would
buy or rent a house and live communally, pooling finances and living in
close quarters, although with strict separation of the sexes. (In Unifica-
tionist thought, which saw the family as the pivotal institution in restoring the Kingdom, premarital sex was the worst of all sins.) In the 1970s

and early 1980s the energy of the young devotees—and the fervent opposition that the movement aroused in some of their parents—made Unificationism among the most visible of the country's new religions. By the mid-1980s, however, many members, having served their movement as celibates for several years, finally entered the highest church "blessing," marriage, in several well-publicized mass weddings. Many members thus moved into private family life. A maturing religious organization has moved through its mainly communal stage into a life that features a mixed domestic economy.

A Sufi Community: The Abode of the Message

Sufism is often described as the mystical branch of Islam, although contemporary Sufism in the West can hardly be contained in such a category. By the twelfth century several Sufi orders were taking shape, each under a spiritual master (called a *shaykh* or *pir*) and each with its own rituals and other practices.[79] Several of these independent orders have developed followings in America. Hazrat Inayat Khan, the first visiting pir, established the Sufi Order in the West in 1910. Under the leadership of his son, Pir Vilayat Khan, the Sufi Order in 1975 purchased land in upstate New York on which to establish an intentional community called the Abode of the Message. The land chosen had been part of the Mount Lebanon Shaker village—the longtime headquarters of the Shaker movement, which had been abandoned as the Shakers shrank in numbers—and was chosen over more economical property elsewhere out of a sense that this religious community was called to resettle hallowed Shaker ground.[80] Gradually the new settlers established small businesses, gardens, a school for their children, and remote retreat huts in addition to their housing in the old Shaker dwellings. They started the experiment with a substantially common economy, although over time they moved to a formula that let people keep part of the money they earned. As spiritual communities go the Abode was not demanding in its religious life, and in fact admitted to residence non-Sufis who were otherwise compatible with the group. But the basics were there, with group prayers three times a day, frequent study classes and seminars, and the distinctive Sufi Universal Worship every Sunday.[81] The community has continued to exist through the 1990s essentially in the spirit in which it was founded.[82]

The Abode is not the only intentional community established by Sufis.

Many of them, often small and informal, have operated in several of the Sufi orders, and many Sufis have joined other communities compatible with their spiritual interests, such as the Lama Foundation (where the 1960s-era teacher "Sufi Sam" Lewis is buried). Certain other movements with a more distant relationship to Sufism also have established communities; for example, students of the work of G. I. Gurdjieff, the Sufi-influenced explorer of human consciousness, founded Two Rivers Farm, a community near Aurora, Oregon, in 1974, by way of heeding Gurdjieff's injunction that persons should incorporate their values in their daily lives.[83] A complete list of Sufi and related communities would be lengthy.

Jews for Community: The Havurah Movement

Judaism has long had a special sense of community, and within the larger tradition close-knit groups of believers—the Hasidim, for example—live in close community (although rarely communally, in the sense in which the term is used in this volume). In the 1950s and early 1960s some Jews, typically younger ones, saw Judaism as having become overly cold and formal, characterized by large synagogues that concerned themselves with proper rituals and nice facilities but not with maintaining the warmth and intimacy of true Jewish community.[84] Their initial response was to build their own close fellowship groups (*havurot* in the plural; *havurah* is singular), independent of established synagogues. Among other things, most havurot abolished sexual distinctions in Jewish practice, and they tended to favor left-wing politics.

The first havurah commune was Havurat Shalom, established in Somerville, Massachusetts, in 1968. By 1970 it had thirty-eight members (some of them nonresident), all supporting their communal house and studying the Jewish tradition—and, in good 1960s fashion, rejecting the hoary Jewish establishment as irrelevant to modern life. Havurat Shalom members affected long hair, hippie clothing, and perhaps use of psychedelics.[85] Weekly Sabbath services were distinctly unorthodox, with occasional periods of Quakerish silent meditation and regular singing and dancing.[86] One immensely popular intellectual product may be said to have come out of Havurat Shalom: *The Jewish Catalog,* which was compiled by Havurat Shalom alumni (and which contains a section describing existing havurot and giving instructions for founding new ones).[87] Although fully communal living lasted only a relatively short time, Havurat

Shalom has remained vital as a close-knit Jewish fellowship group, and the lives of its dozens of members are still closely intertwined. Havurat Shalom also inspired several other groups, including the New York Havurah, the Fabrangen Community in Washington, D.C., and the House of Love and Prayer in San Francisco, although their levels of communitarianism varied.[88] It also inspired similar organizations that sprang up near college campuses—*batim* (houses), 1960s-era communes dedicated to the study and promotion of Judaism.[89] By the mid-1970s there were probably several dozen of them in college communities.[90] There also may have been a few other communal havurot populated by nonstudents, as in the reported case in which several Jewish families purchased an old bank building in Jersey City, which they planned to turn into thirteen condominiums that would operate as a havurah.[91]

Many synagogues responded to the havurah fever by forming noncommunal havurah groups among their members. In any event, the havurah keystones—first enunciated in the 1950s and early 1960s—of close community, sexual equality, spontaneity, and skepticism about entrenched tradition made them the prime Jewish contribution to the communal 1960s era.

The Lama Foundation

The Lama Foundation defies ready categorization. Founded in 1967, it is a religious retreat center as well as an intentional community whose members usually do not plan to stay for life. Inherently a place of elevated spirituality as well as topography, Lama sits at 8000 feet in breathtaking New Mexico mountain country twenty miles north of Taos. Named after a nearby village site (not Tibetan priests), Lama was founded by Steve Durkee and others as a place for working on physical, emotional, and mental health and growth that would espouse no "single way or doctrine, or set of beliefs."[92] In its early years it became in the popular countercultural mind the unofficial headquarters of spiritual teacher Ram Dass (the former Richard Alpert, once an associate of Timothy Leary); it also became well known for the book *Be Here Now,* published in 1971 by Ram Dass and others, which has sold a reported half million copies and has become a countercultural Bible.[93]

Lama's early residents built a central dome complex, a kitchen, and other necessary buildings in a common core area, and individual residences and retreat huts are scattered throughout the property. In the early years the community kept a common daily schedule of work, spiritual practice, community meals, and, often, special evening programs. Life over the years became less centralized, but an active conference schedule remains at the heart of Lama's ongoing mission.

Lama met its greatest challenge in early May 1996, when a wildfire swept through the community, destroying hundreds of acres of forest and some two dozen buildings.[94] Remarkably, the central dome complex and two kitchen buildings were spared, and with a good deal of help from its far-flung network of friends and former residents Lama quickly got on the road to rebuilding. Some residents decided to leave permanently, however, having lost both their homes and the beauty of the forest. Lama will never be quite the same again, but it seems destined to survive.

The Farm

If one had to perform the impossible task of picking the one commune that most perfectly epitomized the spirit of the communal 1960s era, the Farm would be a leading candidate. Established near Summertown, Tennessee, in 1971, the Farm was conceived in the Haight-Ashbury, powered by the highest hippie ideals, and dedicated to ego-denying communal equality. It was rooted in prototypical hippie spirituality and religiosity, espousing a unique faith that drew from the deepest insights of all the world's major religious traditions and trying diligently to put its ideals into practice. It was steeped in rural idealism and for over a decade tried to achieve agricultural self-sufficiency. It had a charismatic leader who was a veritable archetype of the hippie philosopher. It took in and cared for thousands of down-and-outers who showed up at the gate. Members took vows of voluntary poverty and dedicated themselves to helping the poor of the third world.[95] They were dedicated environmentalists and pioneers in the use of solar and other alternative energy. They also unabashedly used marijuana and natural psychedelics and regarded getting high as an essential implement in their spiritual toolbox. Their favorite music was rock and roll, and they had their own touring rock band, recording studio, and FM radio station. They delivered thousands of babies for free, operated their own schools, and put a great deal of effort into raising their many children with high ideals and good values.

The large group of hippies who would settle the Farm first came together in San Francisco in the late 1960s. Stephen Gaskin, the Farm's founder and spiritual teacher, was a faculty member at San Francisco State College in the late 1960s whose classes about the cultural upheaval then in progress outgrew the campus and moved to successively larger locations, finally ending up in a large rock and roll auditorium called the Family Dog. By 1969 thousands were attending Monday Night Class, which always began with group meditation and then saw long discussions of an incredible array of spiritual and secular topics. As Stephen (as he was always called) described it,

We met and we talked and we argued and we hassled about enlightenment and about truth and what standards about that stuff is really about. The way it worked was open door—anybody could come in, like in the dharma combat trips in the old Zen stories, where any wandering monk could come in and ask embarrassing questions. Monday Night Class was like a forum that met for four years in San Francisco—a meeting that was dedicated to Spirit and religion.[96]

Stephen frequently said that he was teaching nothing new but was simply recasting ancient, universally accepted truths in modern language and glossing them with stories drawn from the world's religions. He taught the law of karma: you reap what you sow. He taught the Golden Rule. He taught the essential Oneness of all beings and that every person has a higher self plugged into that great Oneness. He taught honesty and straight talking in all dealings with others. He taught the value of meditation, which he defined as "learning to be quiet and shut your head off long enough to hear what else is going on."[97] Describing his way of synthesizing the great truths of the ages, Stephen compared the world's spiritual teachings to a deck of old-fashioned computer punch cards (envelope-sized cards that contained data in the form of holes punched through them). All he was doing, he said, was picking up that pack of cards and holding it up to the light; where the light came through, where all the religions had punched their holes in the same places, were the universal truths.[98]

In 1970 Stephen announced that he would take an extended speaking tour, and hundreds of his fellow seekers wanted to go along. Thus when Stephen rolled out of San Francisco it was with an entourage of dozens of buses, vans, and other vehicles modified to provide living quarters—a collective home on the road for the vagabonds. The members of the Caravan, as the fleet became known, decided to settle in rural America, and in 1971 they found a home in southern Tennessee on a tract that now encompasses about two thousand acres.[99] The population grew steadily from a few hundred to a peak of about 1,500 in the early 1980s.

Stephen's advocacy of psychedelic enlightenment was forthright. As he summarized the Farm's outlook, "We believe that if a vegetable and an animal want to get together and can be heavier together than either one of them alone, it shouldn't be anybody else's business."[100] Local officials who at the outset were none too enamored of their new neighbors soon located marijuana growing on the Farm, and on August 31 of the first Farm summer, 1971, they staged a raid and arrested Stephen and three others, all of whom spent a year in the Tennessee penitentiary. The Farm weathered its teacher's absence surprisingly well, however, with others stepping forward to assume major leadership roles.[101] Only once did the police again appear uninvited: in July 1980, a police helicopter, acting on a tip from a disgruntled ex-member, detected what looked like marijuana plants growing in a watermelon field. A forty-car police raiding party showed up that night and identified the heinous plants as—ragweed! Ragweed Day, July 11, is now the Farm's major annual homecoming event.

Especially in their early days the Farm members lived under more primitive conditions than did even most other communards. They got lessons in low-tech living from Amish neighbors, and sometimes referred to themselves as "Technicolor Amish."[102] For years great numbers lived in tents and in the many school buses that had been parked permanently on the land, and in the early days laundry was hauled to the creek and washed by being beaten against the rocks there.[103] Strong environmental convictions plus a spiritual respect for animal life meant that the Farm practiced veganism, avoiding not only meat but eggs, milk products, honey, leather, and anything else of animal origin. Soon after arriving in Tennessee they began planting soybeans and figuring out ways to use them creatively— this at a time when few American had heard of tofu or soy milk. Not only did the people of the Farm eat prodigious quantities of soybeans, they also made the bean one of their basic commercial enterprises, developing a variety of retail grocery products from it; probably the best-known was Ice Bean, the first commercially available soybean ice cream product. Farm Foods and the Farm's dozens of cookbooks went on to play a major role in the emergence of vegetarian foods in the American diet.

Respect for life also extended to condemnation of abortion, which coupled with a disdain for artificial birth control (many at the Farm practiced a natural birth control related to the rhythm method)[104] and a sexy population mainly of prime childbearing age meant that births became frequent on the Farm. Soon doctors, nurses, and especially midwives—led by Ina May Gaskin—were delivering hundreds of babies a year at the Farm clinic—not only of Farm mothers, but also soon the babies of other women in the area and eventually from around the country. In its opposition to abortion the Farm made a remarkable offer: "Hey Ladies! Don't have an abortion, come to the Farm and we'll deliver your baby and take care of it, and if you ever decide you want it back, you can have it."[105] The offer was as good as it sounded: a pregnant woman could go to the Farm, receive prenatal care, have her baby delivered, and then stay at the Farm with the child, take the child and leave, or leave the child behind with a Farm family and return later at any time (if she so chose) to reclaim her offspring—all at no charge. Not surprisingly, a lot of women found the offer irresistible.[106]

The members of the Farm always saw their mission as nothing less than saving the planet, and they spread both their words and their work far and wide. In 1974 the Farm chartered a charitable organization called Plenty—soon dubbed "the Hippie Peace Corps" by observers[107]—that would do relief and development work. Some of Plenty's efforts were local and unheralded, often involving helping needy neighbors with building repairs and the like. Larger projects were also soon undertaken, as when Plenty sent a busload of Farmers to help repair tornado damage in nearby northern Alabama. The first major foreign project came in 1976, when a bad earthquake occurred in Guatemala; the Farm and Plenty sent carpenters and other workers to help with the rebuilding, and from that they branched out to perform a variety of rural development projects there. The Farm teams and the Guatemalans hit it off well; they had a lot in common, after all, because the Farm's living conditions were not terribly unlike those of third world countries. A Farm–Latin America connection remains intact today, with ongoing visits in both directions and Farm mail-order operations selling Central American clothing and other products produced by worker collectives.[108] Later Plenty's work expanded to several other countries and within the United States as well. Probably the best-publicized of the organization's domestic activities was the free Plenty Ambulance service in the South Bronx, which quickly established a shorter response time than the expensive public ambulances and branched off into several other local service projects.[109]

One of the lasting legacies of the 1960s era is concern for the state of the environment, and the Farm has translated its ecological concerns into actions in many and diverse ways. Albert Bates, a lawyer who moved to the Farm shortly after it opened, established the Natural Rights Center, a public-interest law firm that filed lawsuits on behalf of victims of exposure to nuclear radiation, fought Army Corps of Engineers plans to control wild rivers and fill wetlands, conducted and published basic research on global warming,[110] and attempted virtually to shut down the entire nuclear power and weapons industry.[111] The Farm has also long been active in developing environmentally sound technology, doing extensive passive solar construction, building wind-power systems, and manufacturing practical electric cars.[112] It built its own original telephone system ("Beatnik Bell") and, as a part of its ongoing campaign against radiation hazards, manufactured Geiger counters.

At its center, however, the Farm remained a spiritual community. Sunday morning was a time of worship, with group meditation and talks by Stephen.[113] Weddings—despite some early experiments in multipartner arrangements, the Farm always supported conventional marriage and families—were conducted at the close of the Sunday services.[114]

For several years it all went well, at least outwardly. Hundreds, and eventually well over a thousand, idealistic hippies lived simply and built one of the most remarkable alternative societies the United States has ever seen. In the 1970s the Farm even founded several satellite Farms in its earnest attempt to change the world. But problems simmered and finally boiled over. After years of relative hardship, some members began to want material comforts that often seemed just out of reach—little luxuries such as good shoes for their children. Stephen, although he disclaimed leadership in nonspiritual parts of Farm life, inevitably was enormously influential, and no adequately functional management structure was ever established.[115] Plenty and other generous projects tended to give away money and labor that the Farm didn't have to spare. A medical crisis or two—as when a member fell out of a tree and ran up a quick $40,000 hospital bill—devastated a commune that didn't carry health insurance. Crucially, a disastrous national agricultural recession in the late 1970s and early 1980s hit the Farm as hard as it did the rest of rural America. The community found itself over a million dollars in debt, and in 1983 it voted to address the difficult situation by decollectivizing the Farm and charging monthly dues to members—who thus would have to have some kind of income, be it from a Farm business or an outside job. The impoverished

Farm could not support everyone then resident, and the surrounding towns and countryside were a classic sink of rural poverty. Jobs were hard to come by, and members left in droves. By 1986 the population had dropped by over a thousand from its peak, to under four hundred; by 1994 it stood at about 225.[116]

In recent years, however, the situation has become stable, and the worst of the crisis appears to be over. Several small businesses operate successfully, selling products ranging from tie-dyed clothing to specialty vegetarian food products and various kinds of services. And since the changeover a new commune within the larger community has appeared. The Second Foundation was begun by around forty Farm members who refused to give up their commitment to commonality and simple living and have thus reestablished a common purse, albeit one in which individual families retain some discretionary income.[117]

Two new ventures in community further characterize the spirit of the Farm in the 1990s. At the beginning of the decade Stephen created a foundation to purchase one hundred acres of land adjacent to the Farm and began developing it as a communal retirement home for aging hippies. He named the new eldercommune Rocinante, after Don Quixote's horse. As Stephen has described his motivation for the project,

The idea on Rocinante is that I'm not trying to build a nursing home where I hire a staff and some old people come and get waited on. I'm trying to organize some old people into an environment where they can delay having to have professional help for as long as possible or, maybe, put it off forever by dint of having good friends that work closely together and help each other out.[118]

Rocinante also aims to let its residents die naturally and with dignity rather than having their days artificially prolonged. Some small cabins have been built already, and plans have been laid for a clinic, wheelchair-accessible gardens, and paved paths for powered wheelchairs and utility carts. Where will old hippies finally end up? Some of them, clearly, at Rocinante.[119]

The second project created to help carry the Farm into the next century is the Ecovillage Training Center, described by Albert Bates as "a whole-systems immersion experience of ecovillage living with classroom instruction as well as access to information, tools, and resources,"[120] on which construction began in 1994. Designed as a model for sustainable development, the center provides for thousands of visitors each year working examples of permaculture and organic gardening; strawbale, cob, geodesic, and other alternative building styles; biological waste treatment and constructed wetlands; solar power generation; hybrid vehicles; and passive solar heating and cooling.[121]

Other Independent Spiritual Communities

Stephen Gaskin was far from the only independent spiritual leader to head up a 1960s-era commune. Indeed, dozens of communes were started by leaders whose messages ranged from warnings of impending doom to contact with extraterrestrials to relatively conventional wisdom from various world religions. Just two of them are briefly sampled here.

THE LOVE ISRAEL FAMILY

Paul Erdman was a television salesman who got swept up in the social ferment of the late 1960s, moved to Haight-Ashbury, and began having religious experiences that taught him the oneness of all of humanity and the necessity of loving God. As he later recalled, "I came back to realizing love is the answer, and that's one thing I realized in San Francisco, truly. That love is the answer, that we are all one person, just different faces, and different parts, and different talents, and that it was time to come together."[122] He soon took the name Love Israel, both to announce that "love is real" and to indicate that the community that he founded saw itself as the continuation of the biblical Israel. In 1968 Love rented a small house on Queen Anne Hill in Seattle and gradually attracted a circle of fellow seekers. Several of them moved into Love's home, and as the clan grew they rented and purchased more houses nearby, eventually occupying fourteen of them. All members took the last name Israel, and Love gave them new first names as well—Honesty, Serious, Devotion, Understanding. They dressed in biblical robes and sandals. They also did good works, among them operating an inn that provided free meals and temporary lodging and beautifully maintaining public parks in the area. The community's membership approached four hundred in the early 1980s.

But the good fortunes were soon to change. Internal struggles and challenges posed by hostile ex-members began to take a heavy toll. A large exodus of members occurred in 1983. Even Love, accused of extravagant living and assorted incidents of misconduct, departed with his companion Honesty Israel to work as a mortgage banker in Los Angeles, although they returned to the community two years later. Compelled to pay a claim to an ex-member who sued to recover his substantial donations, the community sold the urban properties, declared bankruptcy, and regrouped—now only about fifty strong—at its 280-acre ranch at Arlington, about fifty miles north of Seattle. As Serious Israel, a longtime Family leader, observed, "We were left with basically a lot of debt and a very debilitated work force."[123] But the remaining members have worked at recovering, reaching eighty to one hundred members in the mid-1990s and building a cluster of over a dozen homes, several of them yurts, in which community members live in family units. Several businesses and specialized farming operations have been created, and the Israel Family now markets such products as flower salads and garlic. As is the case with many communities, conservative behavioral patterns have overtaken youthful exuberance: experimentation with multiple sexual partners has generally yielded to monogamy, and nudity, once common, is now rare.[124]

Whatever the community's achievements, problems remain, especially in regard to zoning and building issues. Many of the Family's homes were built without building permits and not to building code standards, although the Family has recently been seeking classification as an "urban village" in order to consolidate its communal status.[125] However the land use issues are resolved, the Love Israel Family seems destined to endure for the foreseeable future.[126] Maybe forever, in fact: Love and his associates have never renounced their early claim that they are eternal and will not die.

PADANARAM SETTLEMENT

Daniel Wright was an independent minister who had a visionary experience that led him to establish a spiritual intentional community on a particular piece of land near Williams, Indiana, in 1966. Leading a group of twelve, he purchased the beautiful wooded valley and they began to build a remarkable village, dominated by several heavy-timbered multistory log buildings that look as though they could house the two hundred Padanaram residents with plenty of room to spare.

Padanaram has always had a common purse and has supported itself largely through its own industries, chief among which are logging and sawmilling. It also has extensive organic farming activities, producing food (including livestock) primarily for the community's own consumption. Padanaram has a strong work ethic, one that is incorporated into the education and training of its many children.[127]

Daniel Wright's philosophy, "Kingdomism," is a dispensational system that sees a new age at hand. Soon the decadent existing political system will fade; in the meantime, including the present, small utopian settlements will start building the basis for the Kingdom, establishing the pattern the rest of the world will soon follow.

Although in its spiritual inclusivity and millennial vision Padanaram has a good deal in common with several New Age communities, and with its environmental commitments reflects other parts of the 1960s-era outlook, it remains a traditional community in other ways, especially in maintaining relatively conventional gender roles.[128] Padanaram has had a stable membership, retaining large numbers of its maturing youth and attracting a steady stream of converts by word of mouth, and in the mid-1990s opened a satellite community of about a dozen members in southwestern Arizona.

OTHER SPIRITUAL COMMUNES

A great many religious and spiritual communities dotted the 1960s-era landscape, devoted to a wide variety of beliefs and practices. The One World Family of the Messiah's World Crusade, for example, composed of the followers of Allen Michael the Cosmic Messiah (more mundanely, Allen Noonan), claimed to be in regular contact with spaceships that would save them from the doom that was in store for the rest of humanity. The commune, which typically had a few dozen members, was economically based on the One World Family Natural Foods Restaurant in Berkeley and other health food restaurants, which served food inspired by the Galactic Beings of the UFOs. It was founded in 1968, although Noonan claimed that his call to Messiahhood came in 1947 and that he had been building his movement ever since. At this writing it continues, now based in Santa Rosa, California, where the Messiah lives with a small band of faithful followers and continues, tirelessly, to preach his message half a century after he received his original revelation.[129]

One of the newly visible religions of the 1960s era was ritual Satanism, in most of its incarnations a sort of hedonistic and indulgent critique of staid orthodox religion more than any real threat to prevailing social values. One Satanist group that had a communal phase was The Process—The Church of the Final Judgment, founded by Robert de Grimston More in 1966. The initial commune was in Xtul, Mexico, but for several years members lived communally while they preached their rather gloomy message in the United States as well. Satan in this case was only one of four gods—the others were Lucifer, Jehovah, and Christ—and in some of its literature the church portrayed itself as celebrating "the union of Christ and Satan." As de Grimston wrote, "Through Love Christ and Satan have destroyed their enmity and come together for the End. Christ to Judge, Satan to execute the Judgement."[130] In the early days members wore black robes and symbolic jewelry that often combined Christian and Satanic motifs.[131] By 1974, however, de Grimston's followers had chosen the other deities over Satan and reorganized without the founder, forming a conservative Christian church now known as the Foundation Faith of God.[132]

Other unconventional religions also had communal expressions; some of them, such as the Stelle Community, were rooted in movements that originated prior to 1960 (and thus were discussed in the predecessor to this volume). Religious community flourished in the 1960s era just as it has for over three centuries in American life.

6

Secular Visionaries
Communes for Social Reform and the Good Life

Religious conviction has historically been a mighty motivator of activists who would make the world better, but not all reformers have founded their social-improvement programs on religious bases. In the 1960s era as throughout American communal history, many communes had no focus that could be properly identified as religious—but they did want to change things. Often that meant they envisioned nothing less than the re-making of society as a whole, an undertaking for which the commune would be a demonstration project and launching pad; in a few cases the goals were more modest, entailing more limited social reforms or simply seeing collective living as an efficient way to improve their own material lives. But even then the commune typically embodied a lighthouse ethic: not only are we living this way for our own benefit, but we want the world to see what we're doing so that people everywhere will come to un-derstand the wisdom of the common life.

The secular communes, especially the ones with strong social reform agendas, represent perhaps the most important link between the commu-nal generation of the 1960s era and that just before it—the communes of the 1940s and 1950s. What many 1960s-era secular communes were doing was not unlike what the Fellowship of Intentional Communities groups had been doing just a few years earlier. For those who think the world could stand a good deal of material improvement, communal living often seems a feasible vehicle for achieving great goals.

Reformers and Radicals

Many of the secular communes had left-leaning social and political agendas, ranging from liberal to hard-radical. The handful surveyed here—only a small fraction of the total—demonstrate something of the range of ideology and focus of the groups seeking major social change.

MOVEMENT FOR A NEW SOCIETY/
PHILADELPHIA LIFE CENTER

Centered in Philadelphia and populated to a fair degree by Quakers—whose credentials as advocates of progressive social change are impeccable—the Movement for a New Society (MNS) pursued a broad agenda of combatting the social evils of the day, doing so in part by founding a network of intentional communities. Beginning in about 1970 the MNS evolved out of an earlier social-change organization called A Quaker Action Group, as members sought to expand both their numbers and the scope of their concerns. As a member described the organization in 1976,

MNS members sometimes debate whether to use such phrases as *decentralized socialism* or *communitarian anarchism* to describe our vision of the society we would like to see. If you like such terms, fine; if you don't, it doesn't matter, because it's not the terms but the society we're working toward and the strategy we use that make the difference. We believe in taking charge of our own lives and starting to *live the revolution now,* creating new institutions alongside the old, developing new forms of human relationships.[1]

Within the larger MNS were several communal subgroups, most prominently the Life Center, which at its peak (around 1980) was comprised of over twenty communal houses in a declining West Philadelphia neighborhood (and still survives in a few scattered locations). Houses had somewhat different foci (including feminism, children, religion, and neighborhood organizing), and thus MNS members had an option rare among 1960s-era communes: if a member didn't quite fit in a given house, she or he could move to another with a different emphasis within the overall program of social change activism for which MNS stood. Most houses did not pool members' incomes, but group living kept costs low so that members could work part-time, pay their shares of the expenses, and have plenty of time left for social change work.

Although the bulk of the MNS presence was in Philadelphia, the movement did have social-change action groups and sometimes residences in several other places, including Minneapolis, Ann Arbor, Madison, Denver, Eugene, Seattle, and Durango, Colorado.[2] The social action collectives—not necessarily congruent with the residential ones—addressed issues ranging from local to international in location and scale, from neighborhood food distribution to nuclear power and world militarism. As one member wrote, "The communities set forth by MNS . . . do not see themselves so much as utopian models, but rather as a school for a future life of sharing and working together towards a world of peace and justice."[3] And in such a fashion several MNS houses continue to function at century's end.[4]

COMMUNITY FOR CREATIVE NONVIOLENCE

In Washington, D.C., a leading communal embodiment of the drive for social change was the Community for Creative Nonviolence (CCNV), which in some ways resembled the Catholic Worker (indeed, many of its members were Catholics) but did not have the Worker's explicit religious commitments. The CCNV, formed in 1970 by students and recent graduates of George Washington University, opened its first communal house with six residents in early 1971 and from that base performed a variety of service and activist functions. Initially the focus was on antiwar activism, with members organizing and participating in various demonstrations, some of which involved civil disobedience. By 1972, however, the community, broadening its focus, had opened a soup kitchen just a few blocks from the White House. The next year saw the opening of Hospitality House, which became known not only as a homeless shelter but as a center for activism on behalf of the homeless. A free medical clinic was eventually added as well.[5]

CCNV was most in the public spotlight for a few years after 1974, when a new member, Mitch Snyder—who had a long record of arrests for political causes—achieved a mountain of publicity when he undertook extended fasts to call attention to the plight of the homeless. In 1984—on the eve of Ronald Reagan's election to the presidency—his fifty-one-day hunger strike led to victory when the federal government turned an unused building over to the District of Columbia government for use as a shelter. A second strike in 1986 made the point that the federal government had not provided money to make the building usable, and that too was successful when an emaciated Snyder got the news that $5 million had been designated for the rehabilitation project.[6] Snyder's end came by suicide when he was despondent over setbacks in the cause of the homeless as well as a romantic breakup.[7] At that point the shelter he had created was running well, and some sixty volunteers were helping CCNV keep it going.[8]

RADICAL RESISTANCE COMMUNES

The unpopularity of the war in Vietnam led directly to the organization of a number of communes. One of the earliest began to take shape in 1966, when David Harris (the radical president of the student body at Stanford University) and a few friends began to organize for draft resistance and started a commune as a residential organizing center. That commune, which had around a dozen members, only lasted a year or so, but its legacy was the spread of draft card burnings and other frontal attacks on the military draft throughout the Bay area and eventually around the country.[9]

Several communes were located near the Canadian border and helped draft resisters and evaders and military deserters slip into Canada. Even now specific information on them can be hard to come by, because those who were there remain reticent to talk about the illegal activity that they were involved in. Some centers of such activity are fairly well known, however. For example, in northern Washington state in the early 1970s, the Marblemount Outlaws commune was a major staging area on a sort of underground railroad for West Coast resisters and deserters, who from there would be walked to communes in British Columbia that received the illegal immigrants. One former resident recalls walking the refugees "thirty-seven or thirty-eight miles up through the primordial forest on the Lightning Trail, which ended at a golf course at Hope, B.C."[10] Similar border crossings were undertaken from Earth People's Park, an open-land community in far northern Vermont.

Communes in remote areas also had their share of political refugees. Not only deserters and draft resisters but also persons fleeing prosecution for criminal radical acts found the isolated communes good refuges. The Weather Underground, many of whose fugitive members escaped capture for years, sojourned in several such places. Some secluded communes resisted harboring radicals or their accoutrements—Libre, for example, said no thanks when visiting radicals announced that caves on the property would be ideal for weapons caches—but in many cases the fluidity of the scene was such that persons came and went without disclosing much about their backgrounds, or even their real names. Black Bear Ranch of northern California, one of the most remote of all communes, "did a lot of harboring fugitives," one of its founders said. "We were one of the links on the railroad to Canada for draft resisters."[11] However, at the time most of those living there probably never knew just who was who. As longtime Black Bear resident Kenoli Oleari commented, "A lot of the underground people disappeared into an underground that was made up of Black Bear Ranch [and other communes]. I think we sheltered a lot of these people without having any idea we were sheltering them."[12]

MOVE

Many communes of the 1960s era espoused a back-to-nature philosophy, but none did it with quite the flair of MOVE, which began to take shape in Philadelphia in the early 1970s. Vincent Leaphart, a native Philadelphian, lived in a bohemian university neighborhood on the west side of the city and gradually developed a "naturalist" philosophy that respected all life, even to the point of refusing to control insect and rodent pests. In 1973 he and several associates moved into a house on North Thirty-third Street; they eventually took the name MOVE, which is not an acronym but was chosen simply to express vitality. Leaphart about that time began to call himself John Africa, and soon all the others were using the same surname. Something of the group's social critique may be gathered from an undated manifesto:

The purpose of John Africa's revolution is to show people how corrupt, rotten, criminally enslaving this system is, show people through John Africa's teaching, the truth, that this system is the cause of all their problems (alcoholism, drug addiction, unemployment, wife abuse, child pornography, every problem in the world) and to set the example of revolution for people to follow when they realize how they've been oppressed, repressed, duped, tricked by this system, this government and see the need to rid themselves of this cancerous system as MOVE does.[13]

The MOVE lifestyle shocked most observers, even in the freewheeling early 1970s. Members, most of them African Americans, did not bathe with soap or cut or wash their hair. They dressed in blue denim. They generally avoided meat and ate great quantities of raw garlic and other raw fruits and vegetables. The women had many babies, which they delivered without professional assistance, biting off and eating their umbilical cords and licking the babies clean. MOVE had a large throng of unvaccinated pets and its premises were infested with cockroaches, termites, and rats. They set up loudspeakers in their yard over which they often read, at high volume, day and night, from John Africa's teachings. They denounced anyone who challenged them with vitriolic, obscene harangues. MOVE members were arrested frequently, typically on charges of obscenity or loitering, and their trials often turned into circuses as members refused to observe the canons of courtroom decorum. In August 1978, the police raided the MOVE house, and gunfire from within the house killed an officer. Eleven MOVE members were arrested for murder and later convicted after predictably raucous trials. Their filthy house was bulldozed.

But MOVE, even with several members incarcerated, resumed its life in the movement's well-established style in another house. More years of "natural" living and vituperative confrontations followed. The climactic confrontation took place on May 13, 1985, when the Philadelphia police dropped an explosive device onto the house from a helicopter. The resulting fire not only burned the MOVE house but also most of its city block, some sixty homes. Eleven MOVE members, including John Africa, were killed in the fire and in associated battles with police, but others survived; they have reportedly lived communally since, but have kept their collective profile low.[14]

VOCATIONS FOR SOCIAL CHANGE

One dominant theme of the 1960s cultural upheaval was the pursuit of lasting systemic change for a society that seemed to have lost its moral compass. One group that embodied a commitment to helping people make their lives count for change was Vocations for Social Change, a communal organization that published a monthly periodical with that title from a house at Hayward, California, and later from two houses at nearby Canyon—itself a town that due to outside pressures melded into what was virtually an intentional community.

Vocations for Social Change (VSC) coalesced in the late 1960s, reaching a membership of ten in 1968. Its stated goal was to function as an impartial clearinghouse for information about jobs with employers that "are aimed at changing institutions in the direction of humanitarian goals." Soon after the first publication of the magazine in June 1968, the periodical was running hundreds of job listings every month and the VSC office was providing job-seekers and employers with information on each other. As an intentional community VSC was crowded and certainly not affluent, but members had the satisfaction of doing real grassroots social change work.[15]

Group Marriage Communes

One of the most frontal challenges that the 1960s era made to the American status quo was in the area of sexual conduct. The norm in Western culture from time immemorial had been heterosex within marriage, and although that standard had never been perfectly or universally observed, it certainly functioned as the consensus principle about which those who did not observe it generally kept silence. The 1960s era suddenly brought a wholesale challenge to the old sexual verities, proclaiming that free persons should be at liberty to express themselves sexually just as they chose. It was with a great deal of shock and misgiving that many Americans of the old school watched the young cultural revolutionaries advocating sex before marriage, sex outside of marriage, sex with multiple partners, homosexual contact, and generally the freedom to do anything that felt good.

Large numbers of the 1960s-era communes witnessed and encouraged the new open sexuality. Many of the secular communes—and some religious ones—rejected sexual exclusivity and promoted (or at least easily tolerated) multilateral and serial relationships. A few went further, making group marriages central to what the commune was all about. Several of them got substantial publicity, although in fact the group marriage communes were few in number (indeed, scholars who tried to study them had a good deal of trouble locating them) and with a few exceptions were short-lived.[16]

KERISTA

As early as 1956 John Presmont began to claim that he was hearing voices directing him to establish a new kind of communal religious movement, and taking the new name Brother Jud (for "Justice under Democracy") he established Kerista in the early 1960s. The early Keristans, who were noticed by journalists in New York by 1965, were uninhibited practicing existentialists, especially noted for their practice of wide-open free love but also pioneering in their smoking of marijuana and proclaiming an unabashed pursuit of hedonism. The Keristans were among the earliest exponents of anything goes, the first of the "Do It!" people.[17]

In 1971 Jud met Eve Furchgott, and together they launched the first lasting, communal Kerista in San Francisco. The centerpiece of Kerista was a group marriage system its practitioners called "polyfidelity"—strict faithfulness within a group of lovers. Each family subgrouping (in Kerista called a B-FIC, for Best Friend Identity Cluster) had a sleeping schedule so that every member slept with each member of the opposite sex in rotation. Keristans proclaimed that they had overcome jealousy, and they had marathon sessions of what they termed Gestalt-O-Rama to work through personal hangups and conflicts.[18]

Kerista had children around from time to time when new members brought offspring with them, but the movement was largely made up of childless young adults who eventually decided to make nonreproduction a matter of policy and had all male members get vasectomies. When the AIDS epidemic arose the community quickly devised ways of deflecting what could have been a devastating scourge, requiring new members to undergo extended abstinence, for example. It all worked; Kerista never had problems with AIDS or other unwanted byproducts of its unorthodox sexual system.[19]

Kerista boomed in the 1970s and 1980s, never reaching more than a few dozen members at a time but thriving for several years on its successful computer business. Keristan computer buffs had become early Macintosh zealots, and they rode the early tide of personal computer sales and training with great good fortune. The phenomenon of Kerista came to a grinding halt late in 1991, however, when founder Jud was expelled from his B-FIC and shortly thereafter left the commune entirely, retaining possession of the name and receiving a cash settlement for his decades of contributions to the group. Since then he has tried to reconstitute Kerista, but without great success. Several other Keristans eventually moved to Hawaii and continue to live communally there, in mid-1994 numbering about half a dozen and supporting themselves by specialty gardening for nearby hotels and by doing computer and other work in which they had so much experience in San Francisco.

THE HARRAD COMMUNITIES

Robert Rimmer's *The Harrad Experiment* and *Proposition 31* were bestselling novels that became road maps to several groups of 1960s-era sexual pioneers.[20] *Harrad* tells the story of an experimental college in which students are encouraged to expand their sexual horizons with jealousy-free multilateral relationships; *Proposition 31* makes a case for group marriage. The books were widely read by counterculturists who were fascinated with the sexual revolution in which they found themselves, and in several cases devotees tried to enact the novels in real life.

The best known of the experiments was probably Harrad West in Berkeley, which grew out of a discussion group on intentional communities and alternative sexuality that had been started by Richard Fairfield (editor of the *Modern Utopian,* a grassroots periodical that chronicled and championed communes and sexual freedom). Organized in 1969 in a large Berkeley house, Harrad announced: "Our basic idea . . . is that perhaps six, eight, or even a dozen or more adults can form 'marriage' relationships with each other as means of attaining far more than monogamous marriage can offer. . . . All adult members of Harrad West are considered married to all other adult members of the opposite sex."[21]

At the outset Harrad West had about half a dozen adult members, plus three children; thereafter members came and went. It survived into the early 1970s before members went their respective individual and paired ways.[22] A number of other Harrad communities had even shorter lifespans.

THE FAMILY (TAOS)

What was apparently the largest of the group marriage communes was located near the hip communal bastion of Taos. The Family had about fifty members—sometimes more—who lived together packed tightly into a small house and a school bus. As Richard Fairfield wrote after a visit, "Crowded? A key to their success was having to deal with impossible situations. They deliberately chose the crowdedness. It required them to be *together.*"[23]

The core group had come together in Berkeley about 1967 and soon resolved to move, first to Arizona and then on to Taos. To raise a bankroll, according to Family lore, one member took a small sum to Reno and turned it into $14,000 at the tables. Once in Taos they rented a two-bedroom adobe house a few miles from town and set up their home in which the members called each other "Lord" and "Lady"—Lord Byron (the leader, and one of several black members), Lady Jane, Lord Buckley. At night everyone slept in multiperson, multitiered beds or on mattresses on the floor, and the sexual activity in ever-changing pairings could hardly have been anything but public.[24]

Seeing a need for services to the hippies who were descending on Taos in droves, the Family prevailed upon a wealthy local counterculturist—one of the young heirs who played such vital roles in sponsoring communes—to underwrite a natural-foods general store, a free medical clinic, an alternative newspaper called the *Fountain of Light,* and a sort of hippie switchboard, the Taos Community Information Center. The group also ran an alternative school. Those enterprises never produced much income, however. Family members soon decided to make a film about the Taos communes and invested a great deal of additional money in it—but by all accounts the film was disastrously bad and the Family never could recoup its investment. The film was "a wet towel, aimless and wandering from pointless to pointless so that even though they were *in* it they were yawning," as visitor Elia Katz observed.[25]

Family life lasted for about two years in Taos.[26] It must have been at least initially appealing; Richard Fairfield told of being reluctant to leave when it was time to go, and Elia Katz was so taken with the scene that he "joined" for a short time—although not to the extent of giving the group all his money, as true membership would have required.[27] Eventually, however, Family members must have tired either of Taos or of their own incredibly close quarters. The community was reported to have moved collectively to Detroit, and nothing seems to have been heard of it thereafter.[28]

OTHER GROUP MARRIAGE COMMUNES

Some communes were committed to something like group marriage without espousing that terminology. Greenfeel, a commune of about half a dozen members that operated near Barre, Vermont, for a year or two around 1969, expressed its outlook thus: "We are not a nudist colony (although we go naked sometimes when it's warm). We're not a sexual freedom league (although we frequently feel sexually free). We [seek] to have sex spontaneously, in ways that our instincts, experiences, and sensitivities tell us are the most natural, healthy ways of acting and feeling."[29] Similarly CRO Farm, near Veneta, Oregon, beginning in 1966 sought to create a "total immersion community"; some of its members were group-marriage advocates, although the community had a diversity of sexual styles, including monogamy, among its thirty or so adult members.[30] And others changed direction sharply after experimenting with alternative forms of marriage: Talsalsan, for example, founded in 1968 in southern Oregon and derived from the discussions on community and alternative sexuality that Richard Fairfield had convened in Berkeley, started out as an open-marriage commune but got caught up in a Pentecostal revival that swept the area in 1971. Some of its members turned one of its houses into what was in effect a Jesus-movement service commune, and then the whole setup collapsed in the face of the culture clash that ensued.[31]

Gay and Lesbian Communes

One of the elements of the 1960s cultural awakening was the emergence of gay and lesbian sexuality from millennia in the closet. Demanding the same rights to sexual expression that heterosexuals have always had, the gay-rights pioneers found some of their best allies among the if-it-feels-good-do-it counterculturists. Among the communes acceptance of homosexuality was mixed; some of the religious communes condemned homosexuality as always wrong, and even some of the rule-free secular communes found same-sex attraction if not intrinsically wrong at least not within their own orbits. A good many communes did accept homosexuality, but given the prevailing heterosexuality of the populations they housed, gays and lesbians sometimes did not fit in well. In any event, before long homosexual communes (usually separate ones for men and women, although combined ones in a few cases) were a part of the 1960s-era communal landscape.

The lesbian communes made the larger, earlier mark, with most gay male settlements coming after 1975. Oregon seems to have had the largest concentration of lesbian communes and to have kept that distinction since. As always, however, any enumeration of the groups in question is bound to be woefully incomplete, in part because enclaves of homosexuals often aroused great public opposition and therefore needed to maintain low profiles. The appendix to this volume lists about ten documented lesbian communes in existence by 1975; certainly there were many more than that.

WOMANSHARE FEMINIST WOMEN'S LAND

One lesbian commune has been more public than most, even going so far as to publish a book about itself. WomanShare was founded when three close lesbian friends purchased twenty-three acres with two houses in southern Oregon in 1974. Others joined them soon thereafter, although the permanent resident population has not usually been larger than four or five. From the beginning WomanShare was designated women's land—a feminist retreat center and territory generally closed to males. The members worked hard to be as self-sufficient as they could and specifically set out to master such traditionally male tasks as car repair and chainsaw operation. Over the years they have developed cordial social and working relationships with their straight neighbors. As one member has written, "We are not blatant about our lesbianism in the outside world. We live in conservative southern Oregon and with considerable justification feel we have to protect ourselves from downright hostility. On the other hand, if asked about our sexual identities, we do not hide. We hope people from the outside community will ask only when they are ready to know."[32] Issues of sexual orientation aside, WomanShare has had a life much like that of any other commune, with scheduled chores to be done, interpersonal issues to be dealt with, and financial obligations to be met. Other lesbian communes—with names like Cabbage Lane, Dragonwagon, and Rootworks—also emerged from the 1960s-era wave of commune-building, and some of them also survive today. In the meantime many gay male communes have appeared as well. At century's end, sexual orientation serves as the organizing principle for dozens of communes—another piece of evidence that the 1960s era has had a lasting impact on American culture.

Environmental Communes

As stated repeatedly above, generalization about communes is well-nigh impossible, beyond matters of definition: they involve people who choose to live together, but otherwise no single characteristic marks all communes. One matter, however, probably comes closer than any other to being a communal universal: concern for the environment. Beyond differences about sexual orientation, financial arrangements, religion, land use, and a thousand other matters, it is safe to say that the great majority of twentieth-century American communes have exhibited some degree of environmentalism. Organic gardening was widely practiced in the 1960s-era communes long before it received widespread national attention. Large numbers of 1960s communards believed that by living with others they could lower their demands on the earth's resources. Communes were notable centers of innovations in alternative energy, installing solar, wind, and hydro power facilities, utilizing passive solar architecture, and taking steps to minimize their dependence on petroleum. Some communities sent large numbers of their members to participate in environmental protests and demonstrations. In several cases concern for the preservation of the natural order was the commune's central focus.

ARCOSANTI

The most visionary of the explicitly environmentalist communities has been under construction in the Arizona desert since 1970. Arcosanti embodies the dream of Paolo Soleri, who first went to Arizona in 1947 to study with Frank Lloyd Wright at Taliesin West and remained to pursue his own architectural and environmental aspirations. He calls his concept "arcology"—architecture and ecology as one integrated process.[33] Arcosanti is ultimately to be an environmental town of 5,000, with all necessary facilities for the residents designed to be as environmentally sensitive as possible, with solar heat, no automobiles, and no suburban sprawl.

The buildings of Arcosanti are far from complete at this writing; Soleri has chosen to build slowly, without government or other outside support that might compromise his vision. A resident community of fifty to seventy-five works daily not only at building the new city but also at manufacturing products (ranging from bronze bells to bakery goods) to sell to support the project and its workers, at guiding the many tourists whose fees also help finance construction, and at maintaining the existing structures. The architecture at Arcosanti is fantastic, unlike anything the unprepared visitor would expect, and if and when the project is finished it will be one of the world's architectural marvels.[34] However, its excruciatingly slow progress shows no strong signs of accelerating dramatically.[35]

CERRO GORDO

Most projects promoting communal, sustainable living—now often called ecovillages—have been rather more architecturally modest than Arcosanti. They have tended not to envision huge urban structures but rather clustered houses built with low environmental impact in mind. A prominent example is Cerro Gordo, begun outside Cottage Grove, Oregon, in 1973. Bounded largely by national forest, most of the 1,158 acres of Cerro Gordo are to be preserved in their natural state, with several clusters of homes and businesses for a population that could reach a maximum of over 2,000. Automobiles are banished to a parking lot on the edge of the property.

Several buildings have been built at Cerro Gordo, but progress has been slowed by seemingly endless problems. As many other intentional communities have discovered, zoning regulations usually do not address ecovillage development, so Cerro Gordo has spent a good deal of energy trying—and waiting—to secure legal approval for its plans under Oregon's stringent land-use laws. Similarly, lending institutions tend to be skeptical about unconventional building projects, and Cerro Gordo ran into early problems trying to finance nonfreestanding homes in a rural area. Delays and forced revisions in the imaginative overall plan and allegations of financial shenanigans among community leaders disillusioned some supporters, some of whom have filed suit against Cerro Gordo's organizers for real estate fraud and breach of contract.[36] For all of that, some progress has continued and the true believers at Cerro Gordo continue to work toward their dream of combining community, environmental protection, and the good life.[37]

Other ecovillage projects were also started in the 1960s era, and many more have been inaugurated since that time.[38] Some see a major part of the future of intentional community to lie at its nexus with environmentalism, and ecovillages sit exactly there.

Communities of Art and Culture

The arts played important roles in communal life in the 1960s era. Almost every commune had working artists among its membership, and hundreds, if not thousands, could properly be regarded as having taken art as their central communal focus. Many of the 1960s rock bands lived communally; a great many communes had artist members whose income helped finance the venture. Several of the communes discussed earlier in this volume were importantly focused on the arts (see the sections on Trans-Love Energies, Drop City, and Libre, for example), and art has continued to fuel many communities since those early ones were founded. Communes grounded in the arts were nothing new; a notable group of them flourished with the arts and crafts movement of the turn-of-the-century era,[39] and others had come and gone since, as in the case of Almanac House, the Greenwich Village communal home of the Almanac Singers (whose numbers at various times included Woody Guthrie, Pete Seeger, Lee Hays, and Bess and Alan Lomax), whose rent was paid by hootenannies, informal concerts in the house for which a thirty-five cent admission was charged.[40] But never before had so many communal artistic enclaves emerged as during the 1960s era.

The 1960s cultural revolution had to do with sex and dope and rock and roll and communes, and all of those energies came together in many communes of artistic endeavor, most notably in San Francisco, where the Jefferson Airplane, Big Brother and the Holding Company, the archetypal hip band the Grateful Dead, and many others lived communally. The Dead commune in the band's early years was right in the heart of the Haight-Ashbury in a rambling old Victorian mansion at 710 Ashbury Street, with (at first) a rural retreat at Olompali Ranch north of San Francisco.[41] The Dead's introduction to community had come at La Honda, California, where Jerry Garcia and other band members were part of the Merry Pranksters scene around 1964. At the new commune they shared expenses and the proceeds from band gigs. Carolyn Adams, a Prankster who married Jerry Garcia, helped to keep it running:

Fifteen bucks a week, everybody had to kick in. It was per person, I don't care if it was you and your girlfriend and you never eat, you have to pay the fifteen bucks, because there's toilet paper, there's electricity, and I was the collector and cook. We had a hilarious time. It was like a made up family. I just remembered how warm and comforting and nurturing and pleasant the times were that we had there.

The communal aspect lived on with our business dealings with each other. The paychecks got cut pretty similar to each other whether you were driving a truck or were a musician. It was like a lifetime commitment, 24 hours a day. You had to be completely, totally committed to this thing. The music held everything together. It was so compelling, so powerful, so dramatic, we cared about it so intensely that nothing could wedge us apart for a second.[42]

The intense scene on Ashbury Street lasted from 1966 until band members began gradually to move to private quarters in 1968 and 1969, but for the rest of its life the Grateful Dead scene was heavily communal, both for the band (which had little turnover in personnel) and for the prime audience, the Deadheads who followed the band from concert to concert as something of a neotribal rolling community.

Bands elsewhere similarly lived and worked and played together. Music was a powerful maker of 1960s culture. John Sinclair, who lived in the Trans-Love Energies communes (which had two rock bands among their members), saw music as fueling a communal future:

We are moving towards a conscious community of artists and lovers who live together, work together, share all things—smoke dope together, dance and fuck together, and spread the word together every way we can—through our dress, our freedom of movement, our music and dance, our economy, our human social forms, through our every breath on this planet.[43]

THE ROCHESTER FOLK ART GUILD

A rather more restrained approach to an arts-focused community marked the creation of the Rochester Folk Art Guild in 1967. The community came together initially as a group studying the teachings of G. I. Gurdjieff under Louise March, one of the master's students. Work in the arts began for self-exploration, but soon many were doing craft work full-time. Once the group was able to buy its 318-acre communal farm a dozen moved in to create art—pottery, wood, fabrics, iron, glass—in like-minded company. By 1984, when the Guild had reached a resident membership of forty-five adults and a dozen children, visitors were able to report: "The Rochester Folk Art Guild is a fine example of a community where people make very little money, yet their quality of life, both materially and spiritually, is very high."[44] Crafts income is supplemented by sales of farm products, especially grapes. Members are not paid; their basic needs are met (including many medical needs, thanks to the donated services of two member physicians), and occasionally they take small outside jobs for extra cash.

PROJECTS ONE, TWO, AND ARTAUD

Some communities functioned as spaces where independent artists could pursue their muses economically and in compatible surroundings. In San Francisco three such communities were housed in warehouses. Project One and Project Artaud were both founded in 1971 and had within their walls personal living space, artistic studios, free schools, food coops, computer centers, and other facilities and amenities. Project Two, founded in 1972, had similar endeavors plus a bit of light industry (e.g., a print shop). In each case the participating artists paid a very modest rent for the space. Government was informal, with, usually, monthly meetings and boards of directors to oversee basic operations. Project One was huge, with an estimated 650 residents at its peak in the mid-1970s; Project Artaud had about 125 residents by 1976. Life there could be intense: one Project One resident noted, "We're all so involved here we forget to go out."[45]

and the wide range of artistic and other activities, the prevalent sexual openness and experimentation, and the essentially public toilet and shower facilities all contributed to the countercultural and communal atmosphere of Project One's huge building.[46] Despite (or perhaps because of) that intensity, turnover tended to be high, but all three projects—intentional communities of an unusual type—were great creative centers.[47]

Living Together for the Good Life: The Urban Middle-Class Communes

Not all of the secular communes pursued social or artistic visions. Some who observed the commune mania of the early 1970s recognized the financial advantages inherent to communal living and realized that one's material life could be enhanced considerably if one lived with the right group of persons.[48] The duplication of houses, tools, appliances, and other paraphernalia of life would be rendered unnecessary when all shared and shared alike, and the resulting economies could lead to some nice luxuries in life—better food, good entertainment, perhaps a pool table or a swimming pool. Alternatively, those not desiring luxury could live comfortably on much less than they could alone, and communal living meant an opportunity to escape full-time employment without sacrificing one's standard of living.[49] With no higher goal than comfortable living in mind, thousands of persons got together to form middle-class communes. Numbers of such communes, as always, are elusive, but they were clearly high: Rosabeth Moss Kanter in 1974 found more than two hundred urban communal houses in the Boston area alone.[50] A *New York Times* reporter began to suspect that something big was afoot when he encountered four urban communes on a single street in Brooklyn, and upon further counting concluded that New York City probably had nearly one thousand such enclaves.[51] So powerful did the appeal of the communal life become to urbanites that by the end of the decade a how-to book on the subject had been published.[52] Many of the urban communal homes were small, with under a dozen residents, and they were often short-lived,[53] but in sheer numbers they were probably the largest single component of 1960s-era communitarianism.[54]

Some of the urban communes were resolutely middle-class. One with eight adults and three children in a New York suburb made a point of telling a reporter that they harbored no drugs, radical politics, or religious fanaticism. Members were restoring a large, deteriorating old house and all the adults were employed in outside jobs; in fact they said that their bid to be listed in a directory of communes was turned down for their having a housekeeper, operating six cars, and "not owning a single goat."[55] Other communes were task-oriented, as in the case of one comprised of medical professionals and medical students at the University of California Medical Center in San Francisco.[56] Still others were countercultural or were centers of radical politics.[57] The range of purposes and styles was great.[58]

Communes for Health, Healing, and Personal Growth

Many communes of the 1960s era were founded specifically to improve the lives of their members. The particular foci in this general category were diverse, encompassing physical health, mental health, self-improvement, drug rehabilitation, and other such personal needs of members.

SYNANON

Probably the largest and longest-lived of the wholeness-oriented communities was Synanon, which for several years ran an extensive network of communal centers housing a membership in the thousands, mainly on the West Coast. The movement's charismatic founder/leader was Charles Dederich, who started Synanon as a drug addiction and alcoholism rehabilitation program in 1958. Dederich's approach to ending addiction was hard and blunt—cold turkey, without drugs or other crutches, but with all the moral support one might need, day or night. Eventually smoking was banned as well. The only way the concept would work was in some kind of communal format, so from its early days Synanon was residential. For about a decade it was populated exclusively by addicts, and at that point it could have properly been regarded as a specialized treatment program more than an intentional community. In the late 1960s, however, nonaddicts began to move in, and Synanon diversified (even though specialized features necessary for a treatment program, such as specific regulations for the behavior of new members, were left in place). Synanon soon developed businesses (preeminently an advertising specialties business) that enabled the organization to be self-sufficient economically. The community also charged a nonrefundable entrance fee, at least for those who had money.

The heart of the Synanon experience was the "game," Synanon's term for a sort of encounter group in which members criticized each other and vented negative feelings. The game was played several times a week and took on many roles in the community—group therapy, entertainment, government, and bull session. A session usually included seven to fifteen persons, always seated in a circle, and the only rule was that players could not use or threaten physical violence. Otherwise you were free to express yourself at will. The game usually lasted two to four hours and was supplemented by other exercises designed to promote communication and to educate members on a variety of topics. Experiments of various sorts popped up frequently, as in the case of a wave of marriages arranged by a matchmaker, some of which became so fulfilling as to outlast the community itself, and an episode in 1977 in which all male members got vasectomies.

Synanon had a full range of communal facilities, including private schools, communal kitchens, and dormitories. The communal centers spread from Santa Monica to many locations throughout California and beyond. Problems finally brought it all to an end in the early 1990s, however. In the late 1970s some Synanon members put a rattlesnake in the mailbox of an attorney opposing the group, setting off a wave of bad publicity. The organization was accused of illegal behavior ranging from kidnapping to ownership of illegal weapons. In the early 1990s the community—already shrinking drastically—lost its tax-exempt status and was assessed enormous back taxes that put it into bankruptcy. The residences were closed, and Synanon was no more.[59]

GESUNDHEIT

Patch Adams had a growing realization in medical school that his medical practice would not be conventional. Resigning from his medical residency at Georgetown University Hospital soon after his graduation from medical school in 1971, he and some friends moved into a house in Arlington, Virginia, where they lived and practiced medicine communally. There they developed a radical approach to medical practice: they never charged patients for their services or accepted payment from insurance companies; they refused to carry malpractice insurance; they emphasized rapport with patients and preventive medicine over conventional therapies; they sometimes worked cooperatively with healers other than allopathic physicians, such as chiropractors and homeopaths. They also took up clowning—both for fun and as a way of communicating with the children who were their most frequent patients. Moving from one setting to another and finally purchasing a 310-acre tract in West Virginia, the fifteen to twenty members of what eventually was called the Gesundheit Institute dealt not with illnesses so much as with whole people.

At the end of the 1990s the Gesundheit story is still unfolding. Over the years members have raised a good deal of money toward their ultimate goal of building a forty-bed free hospital. However, the enormous expense of everything medical has so far kept the project from completion, although the release of the major feature movie *Patch Adams* may generate new support. A dedicated corps of volunteers slowly works to improve the site in West Virginia, while Adams and others live in the Washington, D.C., area, where they do some limited medical practice and work to raise the huge sums of money necessary to make the dream come true. They also travel frequently, especially to Russia, where they entertain and heal at pediatric hospitals. They are determined to see their dream come true—or at least have a rollicking good time trying.[60]

THE MOREHOUSES

For a multilocation communal network that reportedly had many hundreds of members at its peak, the Morehouse (or More House, meaning people should live more fully and abundantly) communities have been remarkably little documented. Maitland Zane, writing in 1970, counted seven Morehouses in California and Hawaii, each with around a dozen "responsible hedonists" living quite comfortably.[61] A Chicago reporter, writing in 1974, found many more than did Zane—over a hundred of them scattered around the United States.[62] Laurence Veysey, a judicious scholar, counted about twenty locations with three hundred members.[63] In the world of communes they represented something of a fringe phenomenon; the group houses were business propositions at least as much as they were intentional communities. Residents paid a fee (usually $200 per month) for basic living expenses, including meals, and in addition were required to work, gratis, to rehabilitate the houses that were initially decrepit. The idea—or at least the pitch—was that everyone would live very comfortably on relatively little money, and given the inherent economy of communal living, things indeed tended to work out that way.

The Morehouses were founded in 1967 by Victor Baranco, a former football player, who proclaimed life an opportunity for fun and entertainment, not sacrifice. The business of Baranco's organization, the Institute of Human Abilities, was to offer (for a fee) human-potential seminars on such topics as "Basic Sensuality," "Basic Communication," and "Jealousy, Money and Possession." Those interested in pursuing the concept further could move into one of the houses, most of which were in the San Francisco Bay area.[64] For a time this web of upscale homes seems to have flourished; Baranco and the various owners of the Morehouses—who paid Baranco's Institute what might be called a franchise fee—apparently made a good deal of money from the seminars and houses, whose value was enhanced by the labor of their occupants. The presumed decline of the Morehouse movement has not been tracked in any of the standard communal surveys.[65]

SERVICE COMMUNES

Many other communities than those discussed above undertook specific social missions. A communal version of a nursing home, for example, was started about 1970 as the Share-a-Home Association in Winter Park, Florida; the eighteen residents (aged 70 to 95) paid in proportionate percentages of their incomes, hired a house manager and other workers, and lived comfortably for less than half of what a comparable commercial nursing home would have cost. Like other communes this one had a battle over zoning, which it won when the communards were adjudged a legal family.[66] A different kind of service was undertaken by the COPS (Committee on Public Safety) commune in Berkeley, which had three communal houses and provided several services to the leftist political movements of the late 1960s. COPS ran a movement print shop, doing paid work for commercial customers (such as concert promoters) and free printing for impoverished political groups, and also inherited from the defunct Olompali Ranch commercial-scale bakery equipment that it used to bake hundreds of loaves of bread a week for free distribution.[67] Still another commune, informally known as Kaliflower, published a newsletter that it distributed to all of the Bay-area communes in the late 1960s and early 1970s. Many other communes provided other countercultural communications services, as in the frequent case in which an urban commune published that locale's principal underground newspaper. In sum, the predominantly urban secular communes were enormous in number and incredibly diverse in their interests and activities.

7

Ends and Means
Communal Ideologies, Economics, and Organization

By definition, communes have purposes; otherwise they would simply be transient groups of roommates. Inevitably they have economic arrangements, if only loose ones, because even the communes avowedly opposed to American capitalism and materialism have to deal with financial issues. And communes have structures—if not formal bylaws, hierarchies, and governmental systems, then at least informal arrangements by which the complexities of interpersonal interaction can be ordered. In this chapter we explore some of the diverging and converging paths in which the communes of the 1960s era pursued their ideas, their social visions, their economic needs and desires, and their self-government.

Communal Ideologies

The American 1960s era saw a massive outpouring of sharp questioning of Received Truth—anything not apparent through the new generation's own experiences—as well as of long-accepted social institutions and practices. By the middle of the 1960s the civil rights movement, the beat generation, and a host of cultural phenomena ranging from science fiction to early rock and roll music had opened the postwar generation to new ways of looking at life and ideas. The arrival of psychedelics, the questioning of traditional sexual behavior and sex roles, and an unpopular war catalyzed a great refusal to accept the existing order. The cultural hippies and the political New Leftists, distinct but inseparable types, brought new agendas to the American table.

The ideologies of the countercultural 1960s-era communes were essentially the ideologies of the dissenting culture salted with traditional American rural idealism.[1] Writing specifically about the new communards, Bennett Berger, Bruce Hackett, and R. Mervyn Millar aptly summarize the countercultural point of view:

> They want to possess and consume as little as they need rather than as much as they can be induced to want. They affirm the present, the immediate, the NOW, over careful future planning and anticipated future gratification. They value the "natural" . . . over the civilized, the synthetic, the contrived. . . . Although they have and recognize leaders, their modes of relationship to each other affirm brotherhood and egalitarianism rather than hierarchy. They prefer the primitive to the sophisticated, transcendent ecstasy to order and security. . . . Their impulse is to share as much of their lives as they can with the community of their brothers and sisters, sometimes even beyond the point where it threatens those areas of privacy and reserve to which many communards are still at least partially attached. They want to share a mutually dependent communal fate without the obligatory constraints of social bonds; indeed, they depend upon the affirmation by their brothers and sisters of the value of personal expressiveness to enable each of them to exercise an unbounded freedom to do his thing; to engage, above all, in a spiritual search for personal meaning, for health and happiness, for self and selflessness, for transcendence and godhood.[2]

Or, as Jerry Garcia put it much more succinctly, "We would all like to be able to live an uncluttered life, a simple life, a good life and think about moving the whole human race ahead a step, or a few steps, or half a step."[3]

Some religious communes and others more or less removed from the hip world had certain specific ideological centers, and some groups espoused no real purpose but common living. Harvey Baker of the Dunmire Hollow community in Tennessee recalled an early meeting in which each of his fellow commune-founders told the reasons they had for participating in the venture; and when they finished, "we looked and there was not a single thing that everybody said that was the reason for their being there. There's kind of a pool of overlapping interests and reasons but no one thing you could point to."[4] But it was hardly possible to escape the spirit of the time—the spirit that was rejecting the materialistic old culture and seeking to rebuild society from the ground up, the spirit of ecstasy, expressiveness, naturalness, interconnectedness, and getting back to essentials. For the communal pioneers everything led inexorably toward community; as John Sinclair declared, "We have to see that it's all connected, that we are not going to be free *individually* until *all* people are free *collectively*. Dig it."⁵

Several themes in particular were crucial to the building, operation, and self-image of the communes as outposts of a new outlook on life: rejection of the dominant order, rural idealism, open land, egalitarianism, community, and environmentalism.

REJECTION OF THE DOMINANT ORDER

Basic to just about everything most of the 1960s-era communes stood for was a belief that the United States, and more generally the Western world, had become hopelessly, hideously corrupt—derailed from the lofty goals that the nation had embraced at its founding, and now not so much the world's hope as the world's oppressor. The nation was owned and operated by a political and economic elite that made war on small countries, oppressed American minorities, perpetuated widespread poverty, and had no vision, no ability to embrace nature or to seek real satisfaction, let alone to be open to new psychedelic expansions of the mind. Bruce Taub and other members of the Earthworks commune moved to their remote site in Franklin, Vermont, in 1970 seeking

to help create a society that would provide an alternative to the despair and destruction we were experiencing in our culture, our country and our environment. We were upset about the state of world affairs and had set about in a manner we acknowledged to be experimental to improve them. We were particularly opposed to our government's military violence, to the competitive behaviors we felt were inherent in capitalism, and to the selfish male dominated non-cooperative values we then believed were wrongly engendered by the nuclear family. The Vietnam holocaust was to us a source of daily pain. So too was the perceived destruction of our natural environment and the permanent annihilation of other living species. We hoped we could make things better. We intended to be social reformers and pioneers, not escapists.⁶

At the heart of it all was a rejection of greed, of material desire, and ultimately of individualism, at least the anticommunitarian American kind. Patch Adams, the communal physician, well expressed the typical communitarian attitude: "Greed is one of society's worst malignancies. . . . Unless greed and its symptoms are excised, society will perish."⁷ America, the counterculturists argued, enunciated ideals of generosity and spiritual values but in fact was thoroughly, hypocritically committed to materialism and possessiveness. More than any other people in the world, Americans clung to private gain and self-centeredness. Cutting through that powerful social current came a new generation who believed that individualism had to be curbed for the common good. What was finally required, and what the communards sought, was (in Raymond Mungo's phrase) "a death of the ego."[8]

The grand and impossible goal was nothing less than the rebuilding of society from the ground up, and in the exuberance of the American 1960s era that somehow did not seem impossible. Mungo again: "There is no adventure greater than ours. We are the last life on the planet, it is for us to launch the New Age, to grow up to be *men* and *women* of earth, and free of the walking dead who precede us."[9]

RURAL IDEALISM: THE FLIGHT FROM THE CITY

Western society is mainly urban, and therefore many more communes operated in the cities than in the countryside. Rural romanticism was nevertheless a key element in the great 1960s-era communal surge; only a relative handful would have built their communes in the middle of the metropolis had all else converged to make rural living easily possible. The literature of the alternative culture is awash in thundering critiques of the depravity of urban life as well as the kind of sentimental optimism that has made the agrarian ideal a cultural staple ever since the rise of cities.

Certainly it was not difficult for anyone to see grim prospects for the cities in the 1960s era. The automobile, riots, pollution, the high cost of living, alienated work, widespread poverty, crime, political corruption, and a thousand other ills afflicted not only countercultural dropouts but just about everyone else on the urban scene. Allen Cohen, editor of the *San Francisco Oracle* before he left the city to live at Table Mountain Ranch, predicted that "[i]n 10 years, all these cities are either going to be ghost towns, or we will be taking them apart for the pieces."[10] Raymond Mungo, after years of vigorous political activity, concluded that he and his friends were, in the city, "living in the heartland of death and failure, incapable of either reforming the decaying establishment or dealing it the final blow."[11] Hippies and radicals had never found an acceptable urban niche.

The beckoning green countryside offered quite a contrast to all of that. Nancy Nesbit spelled it out in the *Modern Utopian:*

Although it seems hard to imagine, we can survive without electricity, central air conditioning, and modern plumbing facilities. We can move into the woods with nothing but a few basic supplies such as we would take on an extended camping trip.

Plant a garden, get up and watch the sun rise, open your head to what Nature has to say. Create a new life and home where a truly peaceful existence is possible for yourself and a few friends. . . .

Let's stop and look at Nature and our earth NOW before we are so far away from her that we'll never get back. Invest in some land in the country, build a log cabin, grow your own vegetables, forget that future vice-presidency at the local computer programming office.[12]

The lure of the countryside also meshed well with countercultural fascination with Native Americans, who were frequently seen as embodying a profound nature wisdom long lost to nonnative peoples. Word that a new Indian tribe was forming met with enthusiasm in the early 1970s when Sun Bear, a Chippewa from Minnesota, reached out to non-Indians who wanted to live in old Native American ways and founded the Bear Tribe.[13] The Indian connection would continue through the 1960s communal era; good relationships with local Indian tribes were developed at several communes, such as Morning Star East in New Mexico, and even absent a direct local Indian connection, communards in many places lived in tepees, wore loincloths while hoeing their crops, and came together for peyote rituals.

OPEN LAND, GOD'S LAND

The majority of 1960s-era communes had some kinds of standards for residency, but the ideal of open land, enunciated at several of the earliest post-1960 communes, was powerful and was embraced (at least intermittently) at hundreds of communes. Even where the commune was not open to all or where bad experiences led members of a particular commune to close a previously open door, the idea of private property, of land ownership, did not sit well with many 1960s-era communards. As Pam Hanna, veteran of several communes, wrote, "Parceling up Mother Earth is a foreign and ludicrous concept to so many Indians, which is perhaps why hippies and Indians usually got along well."[14] An Oregon communitarian found land ownership not unlike slavery:

It seems very weird to think of land as property, stuff that can be owned, bought and sold; and I don't think anyone here thinks of it that way. Even though of course that idea is built in to the legal framework of this country, and we have to act within that framework. (Compare: nowadays everyone agrees that it's weird to treat human beings as property, to buy and sell them, but a little more than a century ago that idea was still part of our legal code.)[15]

Specific circumstances sometimes tested the grand ideal. Tolstoy Farm was firmly committed to open membership, but when one person shot up the communal house and threatened the lives of people who happened to be there one day, he was driven to the edge of the property and told not to return.[16] Nevertheless, some of the most passionate believers in open land never gave up that ideal, and a few bits of communal turf remain quietly open to all today. Lou Gottlieb, whose Morning Star Ranch was perhaps the most famous of all the bastions of openness, believed in the concept to the end of his days: "How does title filed at the county seat give anyone the ethical right to collect a tax from someone who wants to live at a given set of coordinates on the earth's surface?"[17] Vivian Gotters, an early Morning Star resident, has never purchased land and years later still has serious problems with the concept of private ownership.[18]

EGALITARIANISM

The generation that grew up with the civil rights movement was by and large committed to the concept of human equality—racial equality, certainly, and theoretically sexual equality, although as in the case of race, equality of gender took some time to settle in. The theory here was not generally in question; in the vast majority of communes, equality of all persons was accepted doctrine. (A few religious communes rejected gender equality in principle, and a few right-wing political and/or religious communes embodied some degree of racism, but such communities were in a decided minority.)

In fact the 1960s-era communes were quite racially homogeneous: they were overwhelmingly white. African Americans were not for the most part attracted to the communal scene, just as they were not much attracted to hip culture generally; it may be that a group long familiar with poverty due to racism would not likely embrace voluntary poverty, egalitarian or not. Thus blacks tended to be found only rarely in communes. Where they did join, however, they often made an impact in the larger local community. The Padanaram community, for example, was located in southern Indiana, an old hotbed of the Ku Klux Klan. The community named an early African American member as its purchasing agent, and merchants in nearby Bedford quickly decided that this black man making large purchases was welcome in their stores. "He broke the race barrier in Bedford," claims Daniel Wright, Padanaram's founder.[19]

Plenty of women lived in communes, and the rise of modern feminism came during the heyday of 1960s-era communalism. Implementing the revolution of women's rising expectations was never easy or quick, however. At a few communes deliberate steps were eventually taken to strive for real functional equality, as at Twin Oaks, which emphasized having women do mechanical work and men do child care and cooking. That was overwhelmingly the exception rather than the rule, however (as we will see in chapter 9).

In a few cases a more radical egalitarianism was sought, sometimes aggressively, by communal groups that sought to avoid any differentiation of effort among members of widely varying backgrounds and skills. Earthworks, in Vermont, pursued such a path for a time:

No matter how skilled or unskilled a commune member was, for example, we believed every person was required to learn to perform every task as an equal, whether that was pounding nails, shovelling manure, operating machinery, or mopping the floor and caring for the children. ("Give a person a fish and you feed him/her for one day. Teach a person to fish and you feed her for a lifetime.") I remember the shocked disapproval of two men visiting from an Israeli kibbutz as they watched ten or twelve healthy and potentially productive adults standing around doing nothing as one inexperienced communard tried to back the hay wagon up the ramp to the barn for unloading at the height of the haying season. Efficient we were not.[20]

Communal egalitarianism was the standard ideology and goal. It was not usually fully achieved, but it is fair to say that the communes were well ahead of American society as a whole on the matter.

TRIBALISM, WARM COMMUNITY, AND NEW/OLD FAMILY STRUCTURES

A basic impulse that drew a great many of the new communards to live collectively was a desire to recreate the close and warm communities that were once the essence of human social life. Here again the image of traditional American Indians was often invoked; their tribes were seen as cohesive and rewarding social units, well deserving of emulation. The language of "family" and "tribe" was common in the communes, as the members sought (in their view) to create new family and social structures—which actually more nearly meant to recreate some very old structures lately forgotten.[21]

"Family" is a term that surfaces again and again in interviews with and writings of the communards—paradoxically, to some degree, because almost always the new communitarians had rejected their families of birth in favor of new friends. As Marty Jezer wrote of the literary hippie clan at Packer Corner,

> The idea that we are a family is important to the people on the farm. This sense of family wouldn't be so much a part of our present awareness if we didn't each carry within us memories of what our family life was in the past; where it broke down and ceased being meaningful and how, now, it can be reconstructed to that end. We've all, symbolically or literally, left home and rejected our pasts. . . . In retrospect, we seemed to be running not as much *from* our families, but in search of family, looking for the sense of community and family life we once knew but, in the end, found lacking at home. As we reclaim this sense of community life, we rediscover the tribal soul and within ourselves become family men and women once again.[22]

In some cases the sense of being in a new family in a wholly new world led communards to take new names, which in some cases they kept even after leaving the community. The practice of new initiates' taking of new names has been followed in committed religious communities of many faiths for several millennia, and continued in the 1960s era in Hindu, Sikh, Sufi, Buddhist, and some Christian communes, among others. It also surfaced in several secular communes. At Drop City everyone had a whimsical Dropper name (Curly Benson, the Drop Lady, Clard Svensen, Larry Lard). The Source Family was led by Yahowha, and later Makushla; members were given names such as Mercury and Electra. Even today many joining Twin Oaks start using new names and change them from time to time if they like.

In some cases the pursuit of new family relationships led not to the breaking but rather to the nurturing of ties with one's birth family. In several cases parents of commune members became friendly with the young venturers and sometimes helped them to learn essential rural skills. In some cases older parents moved in, and the young communards often found that the historic task of taking care of one's ailing parents was not as difficult in a communal setting as it would be in a modern nuclear family. At Black Bear Ranch the mother of one member moved in to live out her final days, and the story of her dying as related in the commune's book *January Thaw* is a touching tribute to the larger spirit of community.[23] As one rather surprised reporter observed,

These hippies, these rebels, these dropouts, left to their own devices, what have they done? What new and dangerous thing have they done? Why, they have fashioned a life composed of community, hard work, the family, religion. They have re-created (in their own image, to be sure) an old knowledge fired by a new passion, born of original discovery. They have given new life to old, old needs.[24]

ENVIRONMENTALISM AND VOLUNTARY PRIMITIVISM

Most of the 1960s-era communards, in their critique of contemporary society, focused a great deal of their scorn on technology, which in the process of supposedly helping humans live better material lives had made them slaves to work and had precipitated the environmental crisis. In the environmentalism that was central to the outlook of the majority of the communes, technology itself was frequently seen as a villain, and in many cases the new communards—the rural ones most frequently, but sometimes urban ones as well—attempted to step backward from modernity into a primitive past. As a *Newsweek* writer wryly observed, "On the day two Americans harnessed technology to land on the moon 25 members of New Mexico's New Buffalo commune harvested wheat by hand—'the way the Babylonians did 3,000 years ago.'"[25]

This embracing of voluntary primitivism took widely varying forms at different communes. At Tolstoy Farm in Washington in its early days the members "were pretty poor, trying to grow our own food, build our own shelter, use old tools and equipment. It took a lot of time and energy to get by. It occupied us and challenged us," founder Huw "Piper" Williams recalled.[26] Rico Reed, a long-time Tolstoy resident, lived without electricity until he could install a photovoltaic system and had solar and wood-fired hot water.[27] Another Tolstoy resident found such a simple task as bathing to be quite challenging, especially in winter, when she would have to gather and melt snow, heat the water, and only then take a bath; not surprisingly, she took showers in town friends' homes whenever she could.[28] Hundreds of communes had no plumbing, electricity, or telephones; some of the remote ones could be inaccessible other than by foot or horseback for weeks or months at a time. The lack of modern amenities was sometimes life-threatening, as when most of the members of Cold Mountain Farm had to take a harrowing ride into town behind an old tractor—their only functioning vehicle—while several of them were gravely ill with hepatitis.[29]

Some communes, including most of the urban ones, did not reject technology, and some embraced it wholeheartedly. And quite a few followed some kind of idiosyncratic middle path, rather as some Amish do when they use tractors in their barns but not their fields. At the Farm, in Tennessee, early efforts to farm with horses gave way to the acceptance of more modern machinery, and the attempt to be self-sufficient led to the creation of the Farm's own telephone system and an extensive state-of-the-art ham and citizens' band radio network. Indeed, the CB radio project became so important at the Farm that members wrote a book on the subject, published it at the Farm's own Book Publishing Company, and sold a bundle of copies.[30] The Farm's environmental concern eventually spawned one of its many cottage industries, the production of sophisticated radiation detectors.

Communes often became centers of the preservation of nature and the development of environmentally sensitive technologies. Most rural communes engaged in organic gardening and preserved their unimproved lands and forests. Alpha Farm took an unusual step toward preserving wild nature: one part of its land is closed to all human entry, even that of members and wilderness lovers. Urban communes, their members well aware that by living communally they were reducing their impact on the planet, often became centers of recycling and environmental political activism. The Droppers of Drop City developed several imaginative alternative energy schemes and lived in energy-efficient domes. Black Bear Ranch and Dunmire Hollow developed hydroelectric power systems to meet at least part of their energy needs. The Farm in Tennessee used passive solar energy for its school and other buildings, and today one of its service businesses is the Ecovillage Training Center, a school for how-to work in low-impact living. The environmental theme was an early and consistent one in a great many communes, and even where large environmental projects were not pursued, the low per-capita impact on resources that communal living entails made communal settlements environmentally friendly.

The Economics of Community

A disdain for money was prominent in the 1960s cultural critique. Jerry Rubin advised people to "use your money as toilet paper,"[31] and in 1967 when he, Abbie Hoffman, and others threw dollar bills from the visitors' gallery at the New York Stock Exchange and declared that "Money is over,"[32] horrified Exchange officials immediately installed a pane of glass along the front of the gallery to keep such an "exorcism" from happening again. Despite their widespread belief that the American worship of money was sadly misplaced, however, the 1960s-era communards could hardly avoid dealing with filthy lucre. Communal property usually had to be bought or rented, and money proved hard to eliminate even in the Aquarian new society that the communards were building. The communal world had an economic dimension, like it or not.

BUYING THE LAND, PAYING THE RENT

Communal real estate was acquired in a remarkable variety of ways. In several cases angelic intervention made a community possible: one or more persons of means purchased land and donated it to a group for communal use, or a property owner who retained title let a given communal group settle on a piece of land without charge. In more cases, however, the usual market involved in residential life prevailed, and communards took out mortgages or paid rent for their facilities.

Angelic intervention came with surprising frequency. In the 1960s era communal consciousness was widespread, and inevitably it affected some persons with money as well as many without. In several cases a single person, or two or three of them, simply bought the land, handed it over to the group, and that was that. As noted in chapters 3 and 4, one benefactor, at least, funded two communes: Rick Klein, giving his inheritance away, purchased New Buffalo but still had money left over; a year or so later, when the Libre founders were trying to figure out how to raise the monumental sum of $12,600 to buy their 360 acres, he stepped in again and paid the tab. In many cases the identities of the donors are not well known; in the 60s Communes Project interviews several interviewees noted that their communes were bought with inheritances or other private money, but saw little point in lionizing the donor, because, after all, that would be contrary to the spirit of truly unselfish generosity that the 1960s era stood for. At Tolstoy Farm the founders hit up a friend with a nice inheritance for a loan to help with the land purchase but were unable to repay it, whereupon the lender let the loan become a gift—which nicely complemented a gift of land that the group had already received from the parents of cofounder Piper Williams.[33]

One of the most creative funding efforts went into the purchase of Black Bear Ranch in northern California. Several of the group trying to raise the money went to Hollywood and collected some $15,000 from various entertainment-industry supporters, although high "expenses" meant that they returned with far less than that. Others took up the cause and raised the bulk of the $22,500 price of the land in various ways, including one large unexpected angelic gift and the proceeds from a major LSD deal. Eventually they had enough to close the purchase, and managed to scratch out monthly cash payments for some time thereafter to pay off the balance.

Monthly payments, or rent, were a fact of life at a great many communes. The residents of Packer Corner, after coming up with a $5,000 down payment, spent twenty years paying off the balance at $225 per month, which was a lot for such an impecunious group but, as Marty Jezer commented, "provided some focus" for the Packer Corner family.[34] Sometimes raising even fairly modest amounts of money proved impossible; at Lila, in New Mexico, for example, angel Charles Lonsdale contributed a substantial down payment but asked members to prepare to pay, many months later, $500 each toward a $10,000 payment that would be due on the balance. As the deadline approached many members had not raised their shares and had drifted away, leaving Lonsdale holding the bag. End of Lila.[35]

Some communes happened into free land to use. The New Yorkers who ended up at Cold Mountain Farm had been looking for land to rent or buy when they heard about an unoccupied house and acreage that they could use free if they would clean up many years' worth of accumulated filth and neglect—a task they happily undertook.[36] At Earthworks, in Vermont, a sympathetic absentee landlord not only donated the use of the property but even kept paying the taxes on it.[37]

And in some cases very much money just wasn't necessary. As we have seen, the Drop City Droppers bought their six-acre plot for $450 and built their amazing domes for next to nothing. Communal life didn't have to be expensive.

PAYING THE BILLS

The communal cost of living was almost always low, but somehow even minimal costs for food and utilities had to be met, and this—like obtaining a place to live—was done in a variety of ways. In some cases (especially in the Christian communes, although not always even there)[38] all assets and income were pooled, and somehow, especially when one or more members held outside jobs, money to pay basic expenses usually materialized. In other cases members kept most of their income and paid fixed dues to a common kitty. Still other systems fell between those extremes, involving a loose pooling of money and crisis management as circumstances dictated.

Somehow, the spirit of sharing usually raised the necessary money. Virginia Stem Owens remarked of her communal experience in New Mexico that "whatever other supply of money trickled in—from families back home, part-time jobs in Santa Fe, hidden hoards—it was shared with astonishing nonchalance."[39] Another communitarian observed, "If we've all been sitting around talking about how the tiller or the chain saw is broken, and we need fifteen dollars to fix it, and you have fifteen dollars, then you want to throw it in."[40] As long as people didn't spend much, no system was needed. But the lack of a system also made some members hedge their bets in quite a few communes, putting some money into the kitty but holding onto the rest for personal use. Those private stashes sometimes became bones of contention and undoubtedly the lack of group commitment they reflected helped bring some communes to premature ends.[41]

Countercultural mysticism posited what was sometimes called "the flow," the remarkable ability of money or needed supplies to appear—"to manifest," to use the argot—when needed. Often the flow included little bits of money from members' parents—"love money," as it was called at New Buffalo.[42] John Nelson remembered the flow as working almost like magic at Wheeler's Ranch: "Some situation would develop, and then from out of the blue a solution would show up. Just when you thought you were going to succumb to junk food deficiencies, someone would show up with 40 gallons of ice cream to lay on the community. Or when you thought you just couldn't go another day without meat, someone would come and they'd bring 150 chickens to the place."[43]

Sometimes the flow could be miraculously precise in supplying someone's needs. Judson Jerome quotes a visitor to a commune in his *Families of Eden*:

I mentioned to one woman that I desperately needed birth control pills; I'd run out and had discovered the day before that my prescription couldn't be filled in Canada. She said, "Carol just threw away a six months' supply." . . . I fished the pills out of the trash pile and found they were the very type I'd used for years. I thought of offering to pay her for them, but decided that hippy ethics dictated against offering money for something the Flow had obviously brought to me.[44]

Except where a commune had angelic support or a larger constituency that contributed to the support of the communal core members (as in the case of the Himalayan Academy, most of whose members tithed ten percent of their incomes to support the smaller group of communal monks),[45] outside jobs helped meet day-to-day expenses in most places. In rural communes members sometimes worked for nearby farmers; other jobs ran the gamut, from waiting tables to sex-industry employment.[46] Members of the Finders in Washington, D.C., often worked at outside jobs, although the community advocated only short-term and temporary work in order to preserve the spontaneity that would be compromised by permanent employment.[47] Some communities worked hard to be self-supporting through cottage industries, with varying degrees of success. In a few cases they could make some money from their creativity, as in the case of the Droppers of Drop City who sometimes earned money from light shows they put on for rock bands.[48] At Packer Corner the two successful books of Raymond Mungo, *Famous Long Ago* and *Total Loss Farm*, produced an income of as much as $50,000 per year, money that was shared in loyal communal fashion. (One year Mungo decided to declare eighteen dependents for income tax purposes, and survived an audit over the issue—for indeed he was supporting that many other members.)[49] At Millbrook during one financial crisis the community essentially decided to market itself, organizing programs for paying guests that would feature lectures, light shows, and other heady entertainments.[50] Downhill Farm did fairly well manufacturing log flower planters that were sold through specialty stores.[51] The Alamo Foundation made fancy clothing favored by country-western music stars and ran several retail businesses. In a few cases specialty agriculture was remunerative, although for most communes the agricultural operation was at most large enough to meet the community's own basic needs. Jesus People USA operated several businesses that supported the community of several hundred, always with the stipulation that the businesses had to conform to the community's high ethical standards both in their intrinsic nature and in their methods of operation.[52] The Farm in Tennessee was also big enough to have several industries, including book publishing and soy-based food production. The Sunburst community of Santa Barbara had such a prolific agricultural operation that for a time it was said to be the largest purveyor of organic foods in the country. More than a few of the more remote communities quietly grew marijuana, in some cases on a scale large enough to provide a nice financial cushion as well as a source of personal pleasure.

Governmental support—welfare, commodity foods, and food stamps

—amounted to economic bedrock in some communities and was completely shunned in others. Several communities hated the very thought of
any entanglement with the government, especially a government as corrupt as America's was perceived to be at the time, and others wanted to
strive sincerely for self-sufficiency. When Stephen Gaskin learned that several persons on the Caravan to the new Farm in Tennessee were receiving
welfare payments he put an end to the practice, and the Farm, for all its
economic woes, never went on the dole. At other communities, however,
public support was accepted and sometimes eagerly embraced; at still others such assistance was bitterly debated.[53] In the early days of Table Mountain Ranch, most of the cash that entered the community came from
welfare, one resident reported.[54] When Sonoma County, California, declined to participate in the federal commodities food program in which
various surplus foods were given to persons in need, the denizens of
Wheeler's Ranch would load up the Ranch's school bus with residents,
drive north to Humboldt County, and come back with a busload of free
food.[55]

Although the purpose of welfare and food stamps was to provide basic
support and nutrition for low-income persons—and surely many communards were nothing if not low-income—officials in many jurisdictions
took offense at the voluntarily poor who seemed to be sponging off of the
government. In the case of food stamps Congress, in antihippie outrage,
amended the law in 1971 to keep stamps from going to any person in a
household in which residents were not all related to each other. The
amendment was contested and in 1973 was nullified by the Supreme
Court, which found it "clearly irrelevant to the stated purposes of the
[Food Stamp] Act and not rationally furthering any other legitimate governmental interest."[56] In northern New Mexico, where antihippie sentiment was strong and sometimes boiled over into violence, one bone of
contention was that huge numbers of hippies seemed to be on welfare—
even though one study identified welfare recipients as only 4% of the hippie population, whereas 5.2% of all New Mexicans were on welfare.[57]
Whatever the actual facts and statistics, however, hippies and communards generally attracted a good deal of scorn when they received government benefits.

One other source of income was rare but did come into play in a few
cases: crime. That strain of 1960s culture that saw private property and
selfishness as evil sometimes went a step further and reasoned that if excess

wealth were immoral, then redistributing that wealth could be acceptable, even necessary. Petty thievery thus became "instant socialism."[58] Probably the most frequent crimes that supported communes and their residents were fairly minor abuses of government benefits, as in the illegal conversion of food stamps to cash, or the reported case at Wheeler's Ranch in which a woman who had never even been pregnant was collecting welfare benefits for herself and four children.[59] In some few cases, though, the moral calculus went farther than that; as one commune-oriented author wrote,

Our thing to do is to liberate stuff you need, or even sometimes, stuff you don't. Alternatively called stealing, lifting, or ripping off, I like the somewhat more optimistic name for this practice—liberating. If you want to get into this, and you should, examine yourself closely. Raise your consciousness. Question your views of morality. I honestly believe that if I need something it should be mine, or my family's and that I shouldn't have to pay for it. I honestly believe that when I go into nearly any store and pay for something *I* am being ripped off. . . . I never rip off things around the corner and I won't at any country grocery store where people treat you like a human being.[60]

Presumably the author would not have been impressed with someone who visited her commune in the Ozarks and ripped off the hosts. But in any event crime as communal support was rare.

SIMPLE, SIMPLE LIVING

Basic to the communal economic equation was low outgo. Communes are inherently economical, especially when they are striving for self-sufficiency, and with some attention to spending the need for money could be quite small. One visitor calculated that New Buffalo was supporting some dozens of residents on $40 per week for food and utilities,[61] and a team of Berkeley researchers calculated that the communes that they studied needed about $40 per resident per month to get by.[62] Cold Mountain Farm never spent over $25 per week for food, even when the population hit thirty.[63] More than a few communards, in fact, had chosen the lifestyle mainly because of its low cost. Sara Davidson told of a family that was going broke in the suburbs and in desperation moved to Tolstoy Farm, where they built their own house, grew much of their own food, and did much better than they had in town.[64] Rico Reed, who also lived at Tolstoy for many years, found simple living politically attractive: "I intentionally wanted to live in poverty to avoid contributing to the war effort. And I wanted to shape my life so that it would become less and less dependent upon money. We actually got to the point where 95% of our diet was from what we raised ourselves."[65] Glenn Lyons could live on very little at Black Bear Ranch in part because he built his own home—starting with a tree that he cut by hand into lumber.[66] The members of Packer Corner dug their own well by hand, an extravagant undertaking that would have been wildly impractical for anyone operating in a cash economy and was a comedy of errors for impecunious communards.[67] Alternative energy projects and gardening helped keep life cheap, but so did lowered expectations and a Thoreau-like determination to keep everything as simple as possible.

Scavenging, incidentally, helped as well. Americans throw away tremendous quantities of useful goods, as many a dumpster diver knows, and one who stands patiently between the thrower-away and the landfill can soon acquire just about any necessity of life. The residents of Sunrise Hill cleaned out a lumber mill and carted home great loads of "firewood, lumber, garden-sawdust, ancient tools, and useless relics."[68] Residents of hundreds of communities dismantled abandoned buildings and used the free materials to build their own structures.[69] As a Heathcote scavenger concluded, "Trashmongering imparts a deep understanding of why Solomon, in all his glory and with all his money could never quite match the wardrobe of the lilies of the field. The Lord helps those, they say, who help themselves."[70]

It was also important to keep spending as low as possible, and that forced economy sometimes led to conflicts. The more remote rural communes without telephones and reliable vehicles offered their members little chance to spend much money, but most communes had frequent financial temptations—and disagreements. At the Clivendon House Club in the Germantown neighborhood of Philadelphia, the community experienced a major crisis when a member spent $60 (of her own money—but that did not matter when the issue was simple living) on a nice coat. People spent money on many other things, of course, but that was a large amount—and a *coat*, which could be obtained for next to nothing at a thrift store?[71] And even when the whole community had a clear need, sometimes the money just wasn't there to be spent. Stephen Diamond wrote of a Montague Farm member who ordered fifty sheets of wallboard, delivered, for $250—when the communal bank account contained exactly $34. The hapless deliveryman had to return most of the load to the lumber yard.[72] At Jesus People USA, even a legitimate need often had to wait for funds; as Jon Trott described the process of getting a pair of shoes, "You go in to the money ladies and say, 'I'd like to get my name on your shoe list, because I am in need of a new pair of shoes.' And they go, 'Oh, okay,' and they put you on there, and they'll work their way down to you. It might be a week and it might be a couple of months, but you'll get your need met, depending on how desperate you are or where you are on the list."[73] At Tolstoy Farm even the smallest expenditure had to be put to a vote; Cat Yronwode remembered a case in which a man, responding to a female member's request for money for tampons, asked, "Why should we spend money for tampons? Women have done without tampons for years." Even toothpaste was sometimes regarded as a nonessential at Tolstoy, where people *really* lived cheaply.[74]

Occasionally financial decisions had ethical dimensions, as at Cold Mountain Farm, where a "great chicken dispute" raged:

> The chicken crisis involved all sorts of things. Did we need eggs? Wasn't wheat germ good enough? Was it morally right to take eggs from chickens? Wasn't it cruel to keep chickens caged? If we didn't cage them, how would we keep them out of the garden? Were we really saving money on eggs, if we had to spend money on the chickens, chicken wire and all kinds of feed? Who was going to take care of them and feed them every day? Who was going to plant an acre of millet and an acre of corn for them? Who would build the chicken coop and how would we find time to build it with all the other things that needed to be done?[75]

Probably the most universal and intractable of spending problems involved long distance telephone bills. Poor communities couldn't afford the bills that seemed to appear out of nowhere, and where individuals were supposed to record their calls for later payment they often forgot. At least two communes—Millbrook and Morning Star Ranch—finally solved that one by installing pay telephones.

Whatever the system of getting and spending money, many communes had chronic financial problems that were the chief cause of their shutting down, although, as John Hall has observed, communal economic failure was "usually part of a broader complex of problems."[76]

Keeping It Running: Government and Leadership in the Communes

In governmental systems the communes ranged from highly structured to utterly anarchical. A great many of the communes proclaimed their commitment to unstructured equality, and when the commune members had good personal chemistry minimal structure could work quite well. When Carolyn Adams Garcia encountered more structured communes after living in the Grateful Dead house in the Haight-Ashbury, she was taken aback by what she saw: "That whole business about process was all news to me. For us, [leadership rested with the one] who shouted most and had the best joke."[77] Hugh Gardner, in fact, in his study of thirteen communes, concludes that at least in the early years of the 1960s era—years, incidentally, of national economic prosperity and optimism—the less structured communes actually lasted longer than more rigid ones, contrary to the widely quoted hypothesis of Rosabeth Moss Kanter that long life was directly related to commitment-inducing structures.[78] In the long run, however, systems and structures, formal or informal, seem to have grown up in most communes that lasted very long. As Kat Kinkade of Twin Oaks once argued, power within groups is inevitable, so "[o]ur job is not to escape it but to control it. . . . We have to learn to deal with political power without holding our noses."[79]

Some communes, especially religious ones, had charismatic leaders whose authority was the basis of all structure. At the Farm the charismatic authority of Stephen Gaskin was for a time nearly absolute; a basic condition of living permanently at the Farm was accepting Stephen as one's spiritual teacher, and inevitably his authority in all kinds of situations was strong. One former Farm resident recalled that his total commitment to the community began to slip over such a mundane matter as Stephen's musical abilities:

Stephen became the second drummer in our band. I saw that he wasn't a fully enlightened drummer. It was so obvious that he was wrong. I mean rock'n'roll's pretty basic, if you can count to four. He couldn't make it from one to four without screwing up in the middle. But he insisted on playing drums. I couldn't find ways in the most simple musical terms to explain to him how to correct it, I couldn't get the words out of my mouth—I would just get choked up. He had a tremendous power over vibrations in the room; he was a teacher of truth. And, the strange phenomenon that I started to realize was that you couldn't tell the truth to him if it was about him![80]

Despite Stephen's considerable charismatic authority he was never accused of any bad faith, but only of being, finally, an imperfect human being. He always lived in conditions at least as primitive as those endured by other Farm members, and when some admiring followers built him a nice house while he was on a road trip, he refused to live in it, going back to his long-standing tent.[81] When lesser Farm elders decided to depose him, he soon accepted their verdict and despite his demotion from both temporal and spiritual leadership remained at the Farm, now more nearly one among equals.

Other leaders with charismatic authority exercised their influence more subtly than did Stephen Gaskin. Lou Gottlieb remained the leader of Morning Star Ranch not only because he was the legal owner of the property (his efforts to give it to God notwithstanding) but also by the immense force of his personality. Bill Wheeler was characterized as the "benevolent king of the land" by one Wheeler's resident,[82] but his leadership brought him more grief than pleasure as he defended his piece of open land against ongoing complaints from neighbors and local public authorities. Communal leaders could be authoritarian and abusive: for example, Laurence Veysey has described at some length the humiliation of an innocent member accused (completely unjustly) by a despotic leader of trying to kill a fellow commune member,[83] and the leader at the Lower Farm in New Mexico was suspected of killing two residents.[84] Given the numbers of communes, leaders, and members, however—and the number of mental cases who landed in communes—such cases of abuse seem to have been remarkably rare. In any event leaders did not always have the clout that they sought to exercise; as Richard Longstreet observed of the Sunburst community, in which leader Norman Paulsen seemingly had enormous authority, "all of these announcements and guidelines and rules and decisions were pretty much ignored by anybody who didn't want to follow these rules."[85]

For communes without charismatic leaders—the great majority—just figuring out how to structure things could be difficult. Robert Houriet, who visited many communes at the peak of the 1960s era, saw case after case in which communes disdained leadership and then couldn't figure out how to function effectively; he concluded that "if you don't have leadership you flounder."[86] Many communes striving to function without leaders used consensus government and endless—often daily—meetings, often expending far too much energy on process. Allen Cohen, reflecting on consensus decision making at Table Mountain Ranch, came to consider it "a methodology that I grew to hate, because we had some people on various issues who would not give it up. It became a real obstacle to progress."[87] Rico Reed was even more vehement about the tediousness of group decision making at Tolstoy Farm:

We were so hung up on consensus that community meetings took forever. I often lost patience with meetings and went ahead and did something instead. Usually, the people who knew the least about the subject would be the pushiest about getting their way. We'd have to do it enough their way to get their consensus; therefore, the project was half doomed to start with if it required any expertise.[88]

On the other hand, at some places consensus did work, eventually. Alpha Farm, founded by Quakers long steeped in the consensus process, has prospered since the early 1970s and its cofounder has conducted workshops for groups around the country on making the seemingly difficult system work.

A great many communes that began without rules adopted, at a minimum, a work-rotation schedule, often with some kind of wheeled chart for assigning duties. And even the most anarchistic commune could adopt an occasional rule that made inescapable common sense: Black Bear Ranch, a member recalled, faced with sanitation problems, enacted a firm rule against sitting on the kitchen counter, and then another that "you couldn't turn the handle on the cream separator, because it used to drive people crazy when people would sit in the kitchen and play with the handle on the cream separator. Those were the two rules. We decided we had to compromise and allow some rules to happen."[89] In such basics, if nothing else, foes of regulations found their limits.

8

The People of the Communes

A decentralized movement with hundreds of thousands of members could be expected to have a great deal of variety among its participants. Communards came from both urban and rural backgrounds and from all socioeconomic levels, and they ranged widely in age. At the open-land communities where no one was asked to leave, at one time or another just about every kind of person was present; the more structured communities, on the other hand, tended to attract members who had something in common with each other, and the range of diversity encompassed in an individual commune was sometimes fairly limited.

Race, Class, and Family Ties in the Communes

Two categories in which diversity was *not* substantial were race and social class. The communes of the 1960s era were overwhelmingly white and predominantly middle class.

The civil rights movement was just winding down as the communes were heating up, and certainly in the overwhelming majority of cases the communards considered themselves entirely open to accepting nonwhite members. Few nonwhites, however, were interested. One communal observer of the early 1970s wrote that she had been in contact with over 150 communes in New England, and she had never encountered a single "third-world person" in any of them.[1] Her experience was a bit extreme; communards of color did exist in several places.[2] But extensive anecdotal evidence makes it clear that almost all communes were very largely white places, and what appears to be the most thorough social scientific study on the situation confirms that impression: Angela Aidala and Benjamin Zablocki, surveying sixty communes in the early to mid-1970s in several scattered geographical locations, found that nonwhite commune membership was less than 1%, compared to 12% nonwhite in the American population as a whole at that time.[3] Probably the largest African American participation in communal living came with the occasional organization of an all-black or nearly all-black commune—as in the cases of the Black Panthers, who operated communes in several cities for a time, and Oyotunji Village, located in South Carolina and dedicated to establishing an outpost of African Yoruba culture in the new world.[4] One anomaly was the Peoples Temple, a racially integrated, predominantly African American communal movement; it stood virtually alone in its racial composition among its fellow communes. Statistically the all-black communes and the Peoples Temple were not large or long-lived enough to make a great impact on the overall makeup of the white-dominated communal world. Some communes had Asian or Hispanic members, but again their numbers were low.

The hippies of the 1960s era were overwhelmingly white, and the standard explanation of this demographic fact is that the counterculturists were divesting themselves of materialism, of all the meaningless goods with which they had been brought up, whereas nonwhites typically had been social have-nots, without all of those meaningless goods, and were searching for a share of the material good life that they had never enjoyed. Material conditions in the communes were if anything even less bourgeois than they were in the urban hippie enclaves, so by the prevailing explanation of the whiteness of hip it is not surprising that few nonwhites joined communes.

On the whole communards were also substantially middle-class in background. Most reporters and social scientists who had much on-site contact with commune residents found their subjects to be overwhelmingly from middle-class families.[5] Although Aidala and Zablocki found that a significant minority of communards came from working class, less-than-college-educated backgrounds, they concluded that commune members were far more typically of middle-class upbringing (as measured by parents' education and occupations) than were Americans as a whole. Of the communards themselves, nearly four times as many (52% versus 14%) had college degrees as did all Americans in their age group.[6]

Moreover, the communitarians in the 1960s era overwhelmingly came from intact nuclear families.[7] A great many parents disapproved of their children's dropping out of middle-class life into the netherworld of sex and drugs that they supposed comprised the 1960s-era hip and communal scenes, but in the long run family ties usually were either not severely injured or at least later repaired. Many 60s Communes Project interviewees told of receiving bits of money from home (if not from parents, then from a sympathetic grandmother or aunt, perhaps) or other tokens of ongoing relatedness. Even parents who despaired of their grown or nearly-grown children often came to visit, to take in the whole mind-blowing scene for themselves, and often left appeased, having seen perhaps less appealing kitchen sanitation than they would have preferred but at least no visible orgies or heroin-shooting parties. Indeed (as we saw in the previous chapter), in a few cases parents actually moved into the commune—occasionally because they simply found it all liberating and appealing, but probably more often due to aging or infirmity, given that communal mutual care worked as well for older adults as it did for their children. Occasionally a parent would embrace the communal scene wholeheartedly, as did one mother who arrived at Wheeler's Ranch to visit her daughter. A few days later, Ramón Sender wrote, "Imagine my surprise when I spotted her at a Sunday Feast, lying naked on the ground, wriggling ecstatically to the beat of the black conga drummers beside her. She had taken the name 'Morning Star' and was apparently having a marvelous vacation. She stayed on for some weeks and became a good friend of the community."[8] On the communards' side the communes actually fostered some appreciation of family ties. Working through the difficult processes of making a new family operate and seeing the vagaries of dealing with the many different personalities who made up the family/commune put a new light on the birth family for many who had left their childhood homes repelled by the banality and emptiness of middle-class American life. As Marty Jezer concluded after getting settled at Packer Corner, "Living on the farm has enabled me to look back at my family with a fondness that I once found impossible and to begin to reconcile my present with the past."[9]

Going Communal: How Joining Worked

The spirit of the 1960s era was communal, and the romantic desire to create a new and loving intentional community from the ground up propelled myriads of persons communeward. At the same time, the larger culture was harsh toward the young dissenters, what with endless drug busts and other police actions as well as loudly voiced antipathy toward hippies, and the idea of setting up an isolated enclave of like-minded persons was appealing for the peace and quiet it promised. But every individual communitarian had his or her own reasons for joining as well. Many single mothers found communal living, where sharing of child care was readily available, a godsend. Many who took up specific spiritual paths found intentional community of the faithful a logical and rewarding manifestation of religious commitment. Some had larger social or personal goals, and saw communal life as a means for working for social change or personal transformation. Some simply wanted to "get real," as in the case of an academic, a committed socialist and good scholar, who found his campus-focused world too theoretical, too intense, too encouraging of a wrong lifestyle, and joined the politically revolutionary Black Bear Ranch: "I bought a house and a car and a laboratory full of equipment, in sum, a place in the mainline economy. I couldn't make that make sense. I saw the kids when I was alarm clock sleepy in the morning and worn-out uptight in the evening. . . . I didn't perceive a contradiction in socialist principle, but I did feel a fuck-up in life style."[10]

Once a commune had been established the question of figuring out a basis on which to admit new members usually came quickly to the fore. The hundreds of open land communes had no such problems, of course — "the land either accepted you or rejected you," said Coyote of Wheeler's Ranch.[11] The majority that were not freely open, though, needed procedures for sorting people out. Frequently the system was so loose as to be a nonsystem. Stephen Diamond asked, "How do you decide (*guess* is a better word) whether or not the new person will not only 'fit in' but also add to the group mind and experience?" and answered in a word, "Vibrations."[12] A former member of the Family of the Mystic Arts described the process of joining as "somewhat cosmic."[13] Elaine Sundancer described the informality of the process:

Will and Claudia—I'm not sure I have it right, but I think that they came here because Claudia was an old friend of Mary who was an old friend of Mark—who had been his girlfriend in high school. When they arrived Mark and Anne had already left, but of course we told them to stay for supper. Claudia and I sliced potatoes together while I told her how worn out I was by strange faces all the time, how my heart had dropped down when I saw another strange car (theirs) pulling up the driveway. Somehow, while I told her this, we got to be friends. . . . Before supper we all gathered, holding hands around in a circle, to chant. Will was on my right. When the chanting ended, I was still sitting with my eyes closed, and I felt him kiss my hand. How did it happen? I don't know how it happened. Will and Claudia were visiting us, and they felt good, and after a while they weren't visiting, they were just family.[14]

The Mulberry Family, in Richmond, Virginia, probably had a fairly typical process of joining. As one member described the process,

You had to come to several family meetings and they made it clear that they wanted to take a look at you and see if you were a tolerant person, see if you were willing to live under the kinds of restrictions that were in place in terms of public and private spaces and communal eating. Are you willing to take your turn at being on a committee? At going grocery shopping? At yard work? At maintenance?[15]

Libre, in Colorado, had a fairly strict set of requirements for membership, including convincing the existing members sitting as a "council" that the petitioner would be able to provide his or her own unobtrusive housing. As Jim Fowler recalled, "Some people came to a council and they'd be run off by the whole process. But if somebody really persevered they could live here, whether they wanted to be agreeable or not. If they wanted to be disagreeable and live here, they still could do so. It just took longer."[16] Similarly Table Mountain, as Allen Cohen recalled, nominally had waiting periods for membership and meetings for approving applicants, but the rules kept shifting: "The rules were agreed upon, but they kept varying anyway. Always there would be several people who were closed, and several who were open and wanted to embrace everyone. And usually what would occur would be somebody would be so persistent that they would just stay."[17] Some groups did manage to be stricter about membership. Downhill Farm in Pennsylvania had a six-month provisional membership after which a prospect had to be accepted by consensus.[18] Many religious communes required all residents to be committed to the specific spiritual path involved and, if an authoritative spiritual leader were involved, to get personal clearance from said leader. Somehow, people came, people went; some communes remained populated and overpopulated, and some dwindled. The chemistry of membership was complex.

Misfits and Eccentrics on the Scene

In daily communal life socioeconomic background mattered much less than personality. Community involves close, intense relationships, and it can bring out the best or the worst in a given individual.

Most of this volume deals with persons of high idealism who contributed, or at least tried to contribute, to communal life in a positive way. Communitarianism, however, has historically also attracted social misfits, and they have often been a serious burden on community—indeed, have in many cases brought the whole experiment crashing down. The Shakers regularly had "Winter Shakers," slackers with no other attractive life options who would show up in the fall professing sincere interest in Shaker life, find warmth and food for the winter, and then leave in the spring when the season of the hardest work began. Robert Owen's heralded experiment in open-door communitarianism at New Harmony in the 1820s drew so many slackers and misfits that the whole well-financed, well-conceived project collapsed in less than two years. Even communities with rigorous screening programs for new members were not immune to finding in their midst persons who would cause them considerable grief.

If difficult persons in the ranks plagued the orderly nineteenth-century communal societies, one might well expect that the problem could only have been larger in the 1960s era, when hundreds or thousands of communes had open-door policies, turning away no one. A good many of the problem cases were simply down-and-outers—those persons, sometimes mentally ill, who never could quite get it together, to use the expression of the day. Usually they were not directly harmful, but often they could not contribute to communal life, and typically they required a great deal of attention—which a commune trying to get the firewood in for winter could hardly afford. A few of the most optimistic communards could see a good side to the worst of people; Lou Gottlieb, who certainly had his share of freeloaders at Morning Star, pronounced the "basket cases" to be "the highest, because they test you. They test your capacity to love."[19] Most, however, found them millstones.

Sometimes the situation could be turned around. Judson Jerome described the case of a young woman who had run away from an abusive home at twelve and had since been a prostitute and drug addict, frequently in jail; a rural commune that gave her both personal support and breathing room seems, almost miraculously, to have turned her life around overnight.[20] Richard Marley noted that at some point during the first winter the more industrious members of Black Bear Ranch realized that they were in bad need of firewood and "we had a whole bunch of dependent people there, helpless, half of them reading comic books all day, waiting for someone to light the fire, who would rouse themselves when they smelled something cooking." So,

we founded the Black Bear Get-With-It Party, and we wrote a credo and went and nailed it up like Martin Luther on the door of the main house. It said, "We came up here to take over the world, to take over our own lives, and as a first step, we're announcing that we're going to take over Black Bear Ranch." It caused great consternation. Our tactic was to get up at the first light, have a bowl of porridge, and get to work and work all day—unheard of, right? Never mind smoking dope, you know—get to work.

Gradually more and more of the slackers started showing up for the work projects, and "it turned the whole experience around. It uplifted the whole tenor of life at the Ranch that winter."[21]

Some of those who showed up at communes were harmless but more than a little offbeat. A one-time member of Morning Star East recalled a fellow communard

that they called Crazy Bill who lived in a hole in the ground at Morning Star. He was supposedly an ex–particle physics major and he supposedly was working on teleportation. He lived in this hole in the ground at Morning Star. He ate nothing but pancake mix with syrup but he didn't cook pancakes, he ate handfuls of it. He would basically disappear in this hole for months and then he would come out. He never took a shower, he never bathed, he never did anything. When it snowed up there they would lose track of where Bill was because all he had was a trap door going into his hole, until one day the snow would move and Bill would come out of his hole.[22]

A Wheeler's resident recalled a former career military officer known to Wheelerites as Crazy David, among whose eccentric beliefs was one that

the thing that was wrong with humans is that they were always lying down, and everybody should stand up. So he built this place where he would invite us all for dinner, and it had walls that were at a slant, in a circle, with a table in the middle. So you would bring your dish and put it on the table, and then you'd lean against the wall to eat dinner. He built himself a platform that was at a slight angle to sleep on, and he really could sleep that way. Also, he believed in running everywhere, not walking.[23]

Some of the more unconventional communards and commune visitors had pronounced dietary quirks. At Hidden Springs in New Hampshire, one member considered cooking a waste of time and would only eat food directly from cans.[24] Albert Bates, writing of the Farm in Tennessee, recalled that the Farm once had a "'Tomatarian,' meaning that he ate only tomatoes. We sent him to work on a farming crew, but it was difficult to get much work out of him because he'd take a tomato break every few minutes. He even talked with tomatoes in his mouth. I guess if you are living on tomatoes, you have to eat a heck of a lot of them."

But the Farm, like many communes, could also be a good therapeutic center, and sometimes real healing took place. Another Bates vignette:

One visitor indicated that he was deaf and dumb, so we sent for someone who knew sign language. After they tried signing with him, he wrote that he didn't know how to sign and wasn't really deaf. After several hours of our being really friendly with him, he started talking! He had acted deaf and dumb for years because he was severely inhibited. We sent him to join the farming crew, and he was a better worker than the Tomatarian. He eventually became outgoing, having many stories to tell from the years he was deaf and dumb.[25]

Some who were attracted to the communes were outright criminals—occasional political revolutionaries (Black Panthers, Weather Underground members needing places to hide from the law), but probably more often more garden-variety criminals who also discerned good cover in the free-form communes. Wheeler's Ranch, for example, discovered that two residents who had been there for six months were escaped convicted murderers from San Quentin when a huge posse showed up one day to locate them. For better or worse, advance word of the raid had reached the Ranch and the objects of the search were gone, never having caused any problems during their long sojourn among the hippies.[26]

Others were not so locally innocuous. Communes were victimized by miscreants in their midst whose transgressions ranged from petty theft—someone stole a large larder of organic baby food from a mother who had spent all summer canning it by hand at Wheeler's Ranch—to murder. Morning Star Ranch, for example, had a troublesome character known as Mystery. As Lou Gottlieb and Ramón Sender recounted the tale,

He was a large, African American male who conformed in every detail to that vicious stereotype about African American males and the size of their male-generative organ. Every time the sheriff would show up, Mystery was nude and he had a blue ribbon that he would tie around his thing, so that the sheriff could see this is the winner. But he had a real klepto streak; things did disappear, and you'd confront Mystery and say, "My dope stash disappeared, Mystery." He'd say, "Well, that sure is a mystery." And we'd say, "Yeah, that sure is a mystery, isn't it, Mystery?"[27]

Sometimes communes saw more serious crimes on their premises; child molestation occurred in a few cases, and open violence cropped up from time to time. The professedly pacifist-anarchist Tolstoy Farm had an incident in which a member—an escaped mental patient, as it turned out—in a jealous rage got a shotgun and shot up the communal living room, terrorizing the gathered members until he was physically subdued.[28] Hugh Gardner, a peripatetic scholar who visited many communes, left Reality Construction Company in fear of his life "after a night spent in a sweat-filled sleeping bag while one of several psychopathic personalities in residence at the time walked around in the dark randomly shooting a rifle at targets unknown, some not very far from my head."[29] And in many more cases communes found themselves with members or visitors who were unstable and threatening, even when they did not in the end commit the criminal acts of which they were surely capable. As Marty Jerome said of two residents at Downhill Farm, "You don't know what they're going to do to themselves or somebody else. We had a couple of persons who were very bad, and everybody sighed in relief when it was over."[30]

In several cases bad behavior on the part of members—or, probably more frequently, of transient droppers-in at open communes—was the direct cause of a commune's demise. The Church of the Five Star Ranch, several miles south of Taos, functioned for a time as intended after its founding in a rented rural house in 1967, but as more and more persons arrived the scene became dominated by parties and drugs; the more transient residents took to stealing from the longer-term residents, even filching the woodstoves. When winter arrived, with no food, no rent money, and no stoves, the residents scattered—the less savory of them trashing the premises on their way out.[31] William Kephart has recounted a similar story about an open-door New Jersey commune that grew tomatoes on a commercial scale:

Half-a-dozen guys joined up—said they were from some commune in California. Two days after they joined, they all got drunk, started tearing the place up and smashing the windows. Then they went out to the tomato fields, and started running in their bare feet. Said they were making tomato wine. Up and down the rows they went squashing thousands of tomatoes. The rest of us watched while they spoiled practically the whole crop. Big Sam [the commune's leader] wouldn't let us do anything. He said the only way people learn is by self-realization. . . . The minority can sure spoil it for the majority.[32]

Even more troubling, sometimes, were the communally-based criminals who perpetrated their antisocial acts away from the communal premises and brought local wrath down on the innocent as well as the guilty back at the commune. One Wheeler's Ranch resident would borrow a truck and go into town at night, breaking into and burglarizing businesses and stashing the stolen goods in a remote corner of the Ranch. The local authorities finally solved the series of burglaries, about which other Ranch residents had not known but which certainly did not boost local public relations.[33] Shoplifters from local communes plagued merchants in several towns.

The more stable commune residents sometimes dealt with malefactors in their midst personally and decisively. Tolstoy Farm lost several houses to fires, usually accidental ones but in two cases probably arson fires set to keep unwanted current or prospective residents from having places to live at the Farm.[34] Libre saw one of its residents go to prison after being busted for an extensive marijuana-growing operation and decided that he should not return; because Libre had no central living facility and required each member to supply his or her own home, members dismantled his house and that was that.[35]

Getting Along

Criminal and antisocial behavior aside, the chemistry of interpersonal relations in communes has always been as complicated as the human spirit from which it arises. Few communes functioned smoothly in their early days, and a good many foundered over questions of personal interaction. Over time, however, many worked out relatively harmonious systems in which members managed to get along as they sought the communal good.

When personal relations worked out communal life seemed like the best thing on the planet. Many 60s Communes Project interviewees and many who have written of their communal days cite the closeness of the multifaceted group of friends as a wonderful memory (or an ongoing reality, in some cases). Often, it seems, the warm personal closeness glows more robustly in retrospect than it actually did when it was supposedly happening. As Joyce Gardner wrote after leaving Cold Mountain Farm, "Our heads are so full of our communities' shortcomings that we do not verbally express what our bodies show: the goodness of this way of life, sharing together, and being close to the land."[36] But idealized or not, communes did produce an intimacy that is rare in a society that is usually so atomized into singles, couples, and nuclear families. As Allen Cohen reflected, "The quality of intimacy that we had with each other, the quality of knowing each other through thick and thin and round and round was so much more intimate than daily routines, even with friends. It was the most intimate life I'd ever led."[37]

When it all did work well, what made it happen? What engendered closeness? Some communes had group LSD trips that helped to define a common outlook and to certify the whole group as countercultural—as exploring consciousness by thumbing its collective nose at majoritarian society and its laws. Others believed that the necessary closeness could be achieved through long, intensive meetings, encounter groups, and interpersonal marathons; and in some cases, as in that of Synanon, that kind of process in fact did weld strong communities.

The communal chronicler who called herself Elaine Sundancer, reflecting on the best of times at her commune, came to believe that

it had to do with the special situation we were in. We were living very close together, and yet everyone was free to leave. Free, because we hadn't made any commitment to each other, any long-term promise to stay, and also free in a practical sense: we were all mobile, had all left the city recently, had friends and jobs to which we could return. No one was trapped. . . .

At the farm, we're living so closely together that any bad vibes you put out get bounced right back at you. One person, if he dumps his self-pity or depression on other people, can send the whole house into a tailspin. We're so close to each other, we resonate to each other. And one person who's in a good mood can bring the whole house up. It's a closed system: what you put in, you get back. Under these circumstances, "love your neighbor" isn't a moralistic preachment, it's simple self-interest.[38]

On the other hand, all of the good will and high ideals that members brought to their communal experiences did not by any means always produce the kind of closeness so treasured by those for whom it did manage to work. Indeed, physical proximity often proved intolerable, and huge numbers of the communes did not long endure—indeed, often foundering on exasperating interpersonal relations. One veteran of two communal houses in the Boston area compiled a list of fifteen reasons why he thought they both proved short-lived, citing lack of clear communal goals and structures but also aggravations of shared space, irritating personal habits, members' overexposure to each other, and members' finding that in many cases they really didn't like each other once they got well acquainted.[39]

Over and over small quirks proved major elements in communal downfall. Patsy Richardson joined the Freefolk community in Minnesota with the great optimism characteristic of the time and was disillusioned when small matters became overwhelming:

What hung us up was whether we should eat all our honey in the fall or ration it through the winter; whether we should tie the cow or let her move around the barn; whether we should fence the garden around front or back; whether we should restrain the kids or let them clobber each other. And it wasn't the fence or the honey that really mattered. It was partly the fact that we had no other personal creative challenges to divert our energies.[40]

The small matters were indeed stalking horses for much larger, often unspoken, issues, and they were sometimes handled astoundingly ineptly. Gordon Yaswen saw the beginning of the end of the noble experiment of Sunrise Hill, one of the earlier 1960s-era communes, in its bungling of its first major interpersonal dispute. Two men could not stand each other; the community, rather than concluding that one or both should leave, decided that the whole community should leave and find a new site—a solution that was financially daunting and evasive of the issues inherent in the situation. (The community in this case did not actually move; one of the conflicted members resigned, and in any event the community would soon be dissolved.)[41]

Sometimes the personality conflicts would stem from major demographic shifts, as when communes merged. When members of Spring Hollow Farm in Tennessee decided to join their neighbors at the Farm, they sold their old land and donated the proceeds, $72,000, to the Farm—only to see it expended in ways that they considered frivolous and to find themselves outsiders in a commune that had already developed a rich, idiosyncratic culture.[42]

One bone of contention in a fair number of communities was dogs. Conflicts between dog-lovers and those not so enamored of four-legged companionship are older than the pyramids, and they afflict communes just as they do countless neighborhoods everywhere else. Black Bear Ranch, like many other communes, had a dog problem—and solved both it and the problem of getting winter food (when the commune was snowed in) with a single blow, as Art Downing recalled:

Lots of people decided to stay in the winter, and of course everybody had brought their fucking dog! They got part way into the winter and were going out to the world to get supplies and pack them back in, and they were bringing in hundreds of pounds of dog food, okay? It dawned on them that this was not productive, it didn't make a lot of sense. And so the dogs became food. They had a long, long meeting, and if you wanted your dog to live, you could leave. So they ate all the dogs.[43]

At Frogge Hollow in Ohio the dogs solved their own food shortage by attacking and eating the community goat.[44] As dedicated as Bill Wheeler was to not having rules at Wheeler's Ranch, he did at least attempt to ban dogs, and part of the time he succeeded in keeping the canine population at a minimum. However—perhaps as a result of the ban on dogs—the Ranch soon became flooded with cats, many of which became wild and invaded community food stores. The Wheeler's cats also became part of one Ranch neighborhood's diet—and fashion, some of the cat pelts being made into clothing.[45]

A final note on interpersonal conflicts in the communes: a great many marriages failed to survive communal life. Sociologists who have collected statistics typically figure the divorce rate of those who moved into communal settings to have been as high as 50% within the first year.[46] Several separate but converging social dynamics seem to have conspired to bring marriages down quickly. The communes that embraced the 1960s-era ethic of liberated sexuality often provided opportunities for spouses to experiment with other lovers, often with negative results for marriages. Many communes resonated with the emerging women's movement, and the women's groups that encouraged their participants to reexamine their social and marital roles—combined with the male recalcitrance that often greeted those early intellectual explorations—probably contributed to a good many dissolutions. For marriages already in trouble, a commune could provide the structure necessary to encourage a dependent partner to go it alone. As one team of scholars observed, "An empty shell couple has little reason to remain together within a commune."[47] Christian and other religious communes usually stressed stable marital relationships and presumably experienced lower rates both of sexual experimentation and of divorce than did their secular counterparts, although they were certainly not immune to the pressures felt by the rest of society in those unorthodox times.

Coming Apart

In a great many cases personality and other conflicts led individuals to leave their communes (communal attrition has been estimated at about 50% per year)[48]—and often to communal dissolution as well. Many communards, however, did not thus lose their faith in intentional community; more typically, to judge from the 60s Communes Project interviews, they remained intrigued with the communal ideal and open to further involvement in its working out. Indeed, many a person went from one commune to another, searching for just the right one, hoping next time to find or to develop a more finely tuned formula that would lead to real communal stability.

In a number of cases a commune would split, usually with a larger faction retaining the old site and the other striking out for new premises. An early case of that occurred at Drop City, when controversial Dropper Peter Rabbit joined two regular community visitors to withdraw and to found Libre on new principles. The Stelle Community represented a split in the communal Lemurian Fellowship, and then itself experienced schism when it deposed its founder and saw him and some of the faithful withdraw to Texas to found the Adelphi Community. The fact that new community could emerge from communal disillusionment is strong testimony to the commitment to their ideals of many who walked the communal path.

Children in Community

With few exceptions the communes of the 1960s era had children present—often lots of them. To be sure, a few of the middle-class urban communes swore off the distraction of small members, a few celibate communities did not admit dependents of adult members, and some communes that did allow children nevertheless limited their numbers on grounds of economics or want of facilities, turning away prospective members who were parents. (In a few cases communes went so far as to control fertility, requiring group consent for a member to have a baby, which meant that sometimes a pregnant member was given the option of having an abortion or leaving.)[49] Usually, however, children were fully present and constituted a major element in the communal equation. Children were typically considered part of the communal family, children of all the adults and siblings of all other children, although usually birth or adoptive parents actually retained primary *de facto* responsibility for their well-being. Parents were frequently convinced that a commune made an ideal setting for childrearing, with its extended family of adults with good values, many other children for playmates, built-in cadre of childcare providers, and—in the case of rural communes—wildlife to watch, creeks to play in, animals to care for, and all kinds of other positive diversions. The normal hazards of rural life seem not to have caused too many injuries; Kenoli Oleari recalled Black Bear Ranch as "for an anxious mother, a death-trap waiting to happen" with its unfenced pond and general lack of childproofing, but he noted that over many years only two children were injured—one who was burned when he stepped into a bucket of hot water waiting to be used in the sweat lodge, and another who broke his arm falling from a loft.[50] Many communal parents avowed that they couldn't imagine rearing children any other way.[51]

Several scholars studied communal children during the height of the 1960s-era commune boom, and their findings tended to support the optimistic assessments of the communal parents. Three psychiatric researchers concluded, for example, that "children in the communes tended to be more relaxed with adult strangers, and less dependent on their mothers, than are children in nuclear families" and that in most cases communes displayed "warmth, concern, and dedication to the children."[52] Medical student Charley Johnston, who visited communes to study children in the early 1970s, found that the majority of them "demonstrated a high degree of maturity, self-confidence, and self-reliance," that "early psychological maturation seemed the rule," that "the children deal effectively with unfamiliar or traumatic experiences," and that they were "interpersonally adept for their ages." Although some communes clearly did better jobs of raising children than others, his conclusion was that for communes that took childrearing seriously "the reward has been children who demonstrate self-confidence, openness, warmth, independence and maturity."[53]

A book-length investigation of communal childrearing reached similar conclusions. John Rothchild and Susan Wolf, interested in learning what effects "enlightened" 1960s-era parenting was having on children, spent several months visiting urban and rural, religious and secular communes, and they were surprised at what they found: "While we began the book with the suspicion that a hippie child is a wild child, we ended up believing that well-behaved children are the most radical alternative to American society. The farther away from regular families and cities and careers that we get, the less obnoxious and self-centered the kids get."[54] At the Farm in Tennessee Rothchild and Wolf had trouble reconciling their own overall distaste for the commune with the dramatic changes for the better in their own two children that they observed almost overnight: "It is a little like seeing the miracle and then turning down the religion."[55] For all the seeming chaos of the communal scene, they concluded, children fared enormously better there than did their noncommunal peers in the world at large.

Interviewees in the 60s Communes Project who grew up in the communes generally had rosy memories of their halcyon years in the cultural vanguard, with plenty of playmates, exposure to slices of the culture that most children never got to see, and endless adventures. Many have gone on to advanced education and successful careers; on the whole no downside to communal upbringing is readily apparent, and many are proud of their communal past, even if they are not planning to repeat it. Quite a few have taken exception to their past in one way, however: by changing unusual names. Parents caught up in the mystic and iconoclastic spirit of the time gave their children names such as Oran, Morning Star, Rama Krishna, Ongo Ishi, Star, Ora Infinita, Tala, Howdy Dogood, and Waska Curly Arrow Hawk Archuleta John Lamb,[56] and upon reaching legal age many of these children chose more conventional nomenclature. Even Lou Gottlieb's son Vishnu changed his name to Bill.

As positive as childrearing was in many cases, some problems did crop up, of course. A few communes rejected normal parenting and let their children grow up without direction or sometimes even much assistance. Sean Gaston described a year at Strange Farm during which, at age six, he was "completely wild" and had to fend for himself:

French toast was the only thing I knew how to cook and that was how I kept myself alive. It actually turned into a Lord of the Flies situation. We had lice in our hair and were basically living in the forest. My mother told me she went through the forest one day and found this pit that had been dug by some of the kids with a tree bent back with a rock on it designed to sort of kill one of the other kids.[57]

In a few cases child abuse did occur, probably no more often than in the larger society but just as unfortunately. Both Siva Kalpa and Tolstoy Farm had cases in which child molesters turned up in their midst, members have reported, and there were undoubtedly other places where abuse occurred as well. Even a microsociety that considers itself unusually enlightened is not immune to such human pathology, as history has proven repeatedly. And of course the normal hazards of life were present in communes as elsewhere; some children suffered disabling injuries, and some died. Lesser traumas existed as well, sometimes ones that seem petty but loomed large in the lives of those they were afflicting, as in the case of a sixteen-year-old girl who lived at a Sufi commune that had no other children near her age. Regarded as a child by the adults and not having any peers, she was glad to leave the communal part of her life.[58]

One situation that prevailed at a number of communes may have had a lasting negative impact on children, although long-term measures are hard to come by. Many communes rejected ageism and thus considered children, at least in theory, full equals in the commune, unrestricted in their behavior.[59] Children, sometimes young children, could smoke marijuana, drink alcohol, and take LSD at some communes. In a few cases children were allowed to engage in sexual acts with each other, sometimes because adults encouraged it but more typically because—as one former member recalled of her fellow communards—"[p]eople didn't give a shit about children's sexual activities with other children. They just didn't care."[60] What kind of long-term toll such tolerance may have taken on children can only be a matter for speculation. The now-adult communal children interviewed for the 60s Communes Project generally tend to minimize such activities and in any event seem in the main not permanently adversely affected by their indulgences.

CONFLICTS OVER CHILDREN

The presence of children at a commune was not always a unifying phenomenon. Even the stereotypically easygoing, permissive hippie parents of the 1960s era did not all agree on the care and treatment of children, and some adults were driven to distraction by others' children. In some communes some of the parents would regard their offspring as children of the commune as a whole (and thus try not to show them favoritism) while other parents were possessive and protective of their own children; children would thus get contradictory signals, and adults could have serious conflicts over it all.[61] In many cases a few children managed to drive a lot of other people to despair, as Joyce Gardner made clear in describing two sisters, aged four and six, at Cold Mountain Farm:

The only emotion which these kids inspired in most of us were anger and annoyance. Most of us felt that we should in fact try to let them work *through* their hangups and hopefully eventually come out the other side. Let them yell "penis" and "vagina" at the top of their lungs in order to hear the echo bounce off the mountains. Let them throw Raggedy Anne into the cellar and elaborate upon her tortures while chanting, "No, you *can't* come out of the cellar!" all day long. Maybe we could have managed that all right.

But what no one seemed to be able to endure were the howls and wails which rose from the lungs of one sister after the other, time after time, all day long, and particularly on rainy days of which there were many, locked up with them in the house all day long.[62]

Children could be a great communal strength or they could spell disaster. In more ways than one were communes classrooms.

BIRTHING

The 1960s-era drive for the natural and organic over the plastic and artificial, along with the general understanding that dehumanized American culture tended to deprive persons of authentic experiences in all kinds of life situations, led to a widespread interest in home birth. Communes, the places where the new culture was being worked out most vigorously, were natural centers of the new birthing movement, and a good many of them did see babies delivered on the premises.

Morning Star Ranch never planned to become a home-birth center any more than it planned any other part of its existence, but seven pregnant women did end up delivering their progeny there. Perhaps his upbringing as a physician's son had something to do with it, but Lou Gottlieb made himself a competent midwife: "Hey, open land, open cervix, the girls used to say. It is a natural process, the live birth, and it should be a joyous, wonderful party. The hippies did devise something terrific: when a mother had a contraction she'd go 'om,' and somebody'd go 'om om om' and we'd have a nice chord. Women in contraction—terrific."[63] Gottlieb's characteristic optimism notwithstanding, not every birth was easy. Some mothers had crises, as in the case of one who tore during delivery at Black Bear Ranch and developed a near-fatal fever before antibiotics (the communal medicine kit was well stocked, fortunately) saved her and the tears healed.[64] The lack of complete medical facilities at hand undoubtedly cost a few infant lives.[65] Few mothers who experienced home birth regretted it, however.

Home birth was typically an ecstatic group occasion. It was so powerful at Table Mountain Ranch that two members collaborated on a book
entitled *Childbirth Is Ecstasy,* an evocation and celebration of the wonder of
childbirth in poetry and photographs.[66] In many communities various little rituals came to surround the event. Sometimes a tree would be planted
for each baby born and the placenta put in the hole for fertilization. At
Black Bear members ritually ate the afterbirth of each child born there.
"We ate a lot of placenta," Elsa Marley recalled.[67] Her then-husband
Richard commented, "It was very far out to eat the first two or three pla-
centas, but at one point I remember saying 'I've eaten enough placenta to
last me for the rest of my life.' We ran out of ways to eat it until someone
said, 'Scramble eggs and put in placenta!' I'm serious, and it was good. A
lot of kids were born at the Ranch."[68] In complete dedication to the art and
science of delivering babies no commune surpassed the Farm in Tennessee,
where the birthing clinic became an institution central to the whole enterprise. Farm birthing began before there was a Farm—on the Caravan that
took the pioneers, several pregnant women among them, from San Francisco to Tennessee. Ina May Gaskin emerged as the head midwife; with no
background for the job, she delivered nearly a dozen babies on the Caravan and continued the work at the Farm. Her own baby—she, the midwife, had no midwife of her own—died shortly after birth on the Farm,
and with that she redoubled her efforts to perform her job as nearly perfectly as possible, learning science as well as art. Over time the Farm's midwives became famed for their expertise, and their statistics for successful
births became excellent; an extensive medical study comparing Farm and
hospital births concluded that the former were "accomplished as safely as,
and with less intervention than, physician-attended hospital deliveries."[69]
Home birth and midwifery publications still emanate regularly from the
Farm, now a pillar of the American home birth movement.

EDUCATION

Parents who moved into community were usually skeptical, to say the
least, about the viability of the institutions of the prevailing society, and
misgivings about conventional educational institutions in the United
States were legion. As Herb Goldstein described the outlook at Downhill
Farm in Pennsylvania, "Some wanted to homeschool because they wanted
their kids to do better than they could if they went to public school. And
for some it was a political concept: the establishment stinks, and we

shouldn't be raising kids to easily be assimilated by it."[70] Although some communes enrolled their children in the local public schools, sometimes simply for convenience and sometimes in an attempt to forge good relations with the neighborhood, a good many did their own private schooling—or, in some cases, no real schooling at all. In a few cases education was the principle around which the community was organized, and when outsiders were admitted to classes for a fee it could become an "industry" that provided communal income as well.

The largest of the communal schools must have been the Farm school (Tennessee), which was supplied by the fertile Farm population with hundreds of students. The Farm put a good deal of energy into providing the elementary school with one of the best buildings at the Farm, a solar-heated structure with classrooms, a library, and a media/computer center. Soon a high school was added in a separate, adjacent building. The quality of the Farm's school program has been demonstrated by Farm children who transferred to public schools or went on to college and almost always excelled.[71]

Serious schooling requires a major commitment of time, energy, and money, and a good many communes found that once the alternative school got under way, they were not up to the task. Commune after commune started a school with high expectations, only to see it founder fairly quickly due to insufficient adult energy addressed to the task.[72] Tolstoy Farm built a nice schoolhouse over several years, ending up with an eighteen-sided domed building, but after further years of valiant effort the last of the volunteer teachers wore out and the experiment came to a close.[73]

At Nethers, in Virginia, the story was happier, if not lengthier. A group of neighbors started a private school in 1970 and soon began to move to the site. The free-form school had a variety of classes and activities geared to the readiness and willingness of students to learn, and it functioned as the community's focus for five or six years.[74] At Hearthshire, in Covelo, California, the Hearth School functioned for several years after 1971, similarly at the heart of an intentional community. At least one alternative high school operated communally in the 1960s era—Pacific High School, located in the Santa Cruz Mountains in northern California and housed in several domes built by community members between 1969 and 1971. Pacific tried to eliminate the distinction between teachers and students and for several years was a center of technological innovation as well as of alternative education.[75]

The People, Yes

Communes could not have been more or less than the people who founded and joined them. At their best they were populated with wonderful, creative individuals who in their bedrock values and endless generosity pointed to a better future. But not everyone who ended up on the communal scene was that kind of model cooperator. Indeed, wildly disproportionate numbers of communards were exactly the kinds of persons who were not needed. Communes have always attracted some of the highest-minded idealists in our human ranks, but they also attract freeloaders, cranks, and low-lifes—and often enough of the latter, unfortunately, to bring it all crashing down. Even in the communes that screened their new members fairly carefully, incompatible people sometimes ended up wreaking havoc on communal life.

The problem was not new in the 1960s era, obviously, but is one that has always plagued communes. Horace Greeley, the reformer and newspaper publisher who was a leading supporter of intentional community in the latter part of the nineteenth century, saw the problem clearly:

A serious obstacle to the success of any socialistic experiment must always be confronted. I allude to the kind of persons who are naturally attracted to it. Along with many noble and lofty souls, whose impulses are purely philanthropic, and who are willing to labor and suffer reproach for any cause that promises to benefit mankind, there throng scores of whom the world is quite worthy—the conceited, the crotchety, the selfish, the headstrong, the pugnacious, the unappreciated, the played-out, the idle, and the good-for-nothing generally; who, finding themselves utterly out of place and at a discount in the world as it is, rashly conclude that they are exactly fitted for the world as it ought to be. These may have failed again and again, and been protested at every bank to which they have been presented; yet they are sure to jump into any new movement as if they had been born expressly to superintend and direct it, though they are morally certain to ruin whatever they lay their hands on. Destitute of means, of practical ability, of prudence, tact and common sense, they have such a wealth of assurance and self-confidence, that they clutch the responsible positions which the capable and worthy modestly shrink from; so responsibilities that would tax the ablest, are mistakenly devolved on the blindest and least fit. Many an experiment is thus wrecked, when, engineered by its best members it might have succeeded.[76]

Over a century after Greeley's utterance, Gordon Yaswen, reflecting on the downfall of Sunrise Hill, reiterated those sentiments:

It is said that happy people do not volunteer to go to War. Neither, I say, do they join Communities. The roots of this unhappiness may lie in either themselves, or their world. We at Sun Hill did not know how to determine one from the other, and so we hardly tried; we accepted virtually all who came. But I think that we at Sun Hill tended to assume that each others' various inadequacies to live in the Mass-Society were due to the faults of that Society, and not to those of the individuals in question. Therefore, we of course assumed that such inadequacies (or "hangups") would straighten themselves out within the "healthy" context of our Utopia. This—needless to say—was naive.[77]

As a footnote to Greeley and Yaswen, beyond the matter of the inevitability of communes' attracting misfits and ne'er-do-wells, communes are also often weakened by their strongest members in a manifestation of what I call the communal paradox. An optimal intentional community must be populated by persons who are generous, giving, compromising, self-denying, and always interested in the welfare of the group over their personal interests. In real life, however, many of those attracted to the high idealism of community have been strong-headed, willful, and reasonably sure that their perceptions and interpretations are the correct ones—in short, individualists who are natural leaders, not self-effacing followers, whose egos can hardly permit them to be the equals of all others. Kat Kinkade, discussing changes in the organizational structure of Twin Oaks, characterized her own role in the paradox more candidly than have most:

Not only had I believed that a community should be guided by the wisest heads available, but it was clear to me that I was one of them. I saw in myself the qualities I thought of as essential—"agility of mind, reasonableness of judgment, commitment to the goals of the Community, and sharp self-awareness," and as far as I could see, I had them in more generous measure than most members. I also had a strong desire to be in charge.[78]

Twin Oaks has survived, but on the shoals of human pride and will has many a community foundered.

9

Doing It
Daily Life in the Communes

At some communes the wake-up gong rang before dawn, and every day was ordered and task-oriented. At the most anarchistic places daily life was utterly unstructured, except as individuals chose to join with others in working on group projects. Over time, just as communes sorted their personnel and evolved into functional groups of compatible persons, they came up with ways of living that made it all work.

Central to it all, really, was the ongoing project of melding separate and often strong-willed personalities into a real *community*. As one participant-observer noted at the time, any subway rider knows that physical closeness doesn't automatically imply emotional solidarity—and people's solidarity was, after all, what it was all about.[1] Central to the community-building process was the sense of dropping out of a decadent society and building a new and better order on the ashes of the old. The more perceptive of the commune-dwellers clearly understood the process of coming together and knew that it happened by direction, not accidentally. Marty Jezer wrote of coming to realize at Packer Corner that

You can't force community in a night, a day, or even a year. Love is not all you need; to claim to love everyone fully and equally is an insult to their individuality and is not to be believed. . . . Love, honesty, patience, tolerance, and the ability to take an incredible amount of shit and let it all pass are among the qualities required to forge a community. It ain't easy.[2]

Despite the difficulties, in many cases togetherness did emerge from the confluence of many former strangers united by their vision of a new social order. Little bits of daily life, some now long forgotten, helped to push it along, as in the communes where everything—right down to clothing and sometimes even toothbrushes—was shared. At Oz in Pennsylvania dirty clothes were tossed into a corner of a room called the "free store" and anyone who wanted to use a garment could take it down to the creek, wash it, and wear it until it got too dirty again.[3] At Stelle, in Illinois, members maintained private finances, paying dues to support the community, but they had a great community-building device in their general store, a self-service twenty-four-hour facility run on the honor system.[4] In a thousand small ways did community thus shape up.

Sometimes group solidarity emerged quickly, fortified by the headiness of the experiment that the pioneers were undertaking. As Peter Rabbit of Drop City and Libre wrote, "While everyone is working together on actual construction the energy is centered, there is fantastic high spirit, everyone knows what he is doing all the time."[5] Gordon Yaswen wrote of an unforgettably wonderful first communal summer at Sunrise Hill, when

there was still the first flush of excitement and infatuation, and a strong sense of self-importance and self-confidence permeated the community. . . . [There was] a sense of something *more* than just a COLLECTION of beautiful people; our groupness was an entity in its own right; an entity composed of our separate beings combined, and therein was a joy I had never sampled before.[6]

The Physical Facilities

Communes had physical structures that ranged from the transient (tents, tepees, cars, vans, and buses) to the immense (large urban apartment buildings and hotels). One common theme, though, was tightness of space. Communes weren't *required* to be overcrowded, but many were. Crowding was often the direct cause of creative construction projects—persons who couldn't stand the jam-packed main house often built their own little shelters far enough away for a modicum of privacy but near enough to hear the dinner bell.

Drop City, with its cluster of car-top domes, certainly had architecture whose funky distinctiveness was never surpassed. That original inspired dozens of other communes, and even now domes are probably more common in communes than just about anywhere else.[7] But other equally imaginative and low-cost structures were domes' equals in hip creativity. A-frames were simple to build and became popular in many places as small houses. Where the climate permitted, adobe was virtually free and therefore an ideal building material, and the communards eagerly embraced it. Larry and Pam Read's "Meadowboat" at Morning Star was a hexagonal structure that seemed to hover in the air over a hillside. Nearby John Nelson built a minuscule house into a ten-foot redwood stump. Many of the shelters at Tolstoy Farm were built of salvaged materials; one resident reported erecting a workable house for a net cash outlay of sixty-five dollars. Often self-taught builders constructed solid, useful structures, although sometimes disaster struck. At Libre a new member family decided to use a ridgepole running between two boulders for roof support and then fill in the space between the boulders for the house. But when it rained, water came rushing down the arroyo between the boulders, washing away house and contents. Another Libre resident spent months building a precise model of the dome he planned to build, only to have it blow out of his pickup truck and be reduced to toothpicks on the windshield of a Greyhound bus.[8]

Where existing buildings, notably barns and chicken coops, were present they were often remodeled into housing. Sometimes a small commune could all be housed in one structure; extreme examples of that could be found at the Family of Taos, whose fifty or so members all lived in one small home, dormitory-fashion, and at the Red Rockers commune in southern Colorado, where around two dozen members all lived in a large one-room dome. Often rural communards had a farmhouse into which they all packed themselves—typically a barely habitable building, perhaps one without utilities and in some cases virtually intolerable in the winter. The residents of Montague Farm in Massachusetts realized how cold their house got when they discovered ice forming in the kitchen.[9]

Crowding could be intense, and privacy nearly nonexistent. The Brotherhood of the Spirit (later the Renaissance Community) in Massachusetts built a large dormitory but attracted so many members that soon several hundred were living in it, cheek to jowl. Some communities, in fact, specifically set out to minimize privacy. The Aloe Community, for example, deliberately put its bathtub in the heavily used main room; as a friend of the community later recalled, "They were supposed to take their baths out there where anybody could walk in and see them at any time. They decided that personal privacy of this kind was uncommunitarian."[10] Similarly the Brotherhood of the Spirit had a facility called "toilet city," which consisted of several "toilets in a semi-circle, and there were no stalls, so everybody got to sit across from each other. But it didn't last."[11] Moreover, where large numbers slept in a single room, it followed that sexual activity became more or less public as well (as will be discussed below).

Sometimes the packed and public accommodations seemed to work out well. An urban communard in Washington, D.C., was quoted as commenting in 1970, "I thought privacy was a basic human need, like hunger. Well, it's not."[12] Richard Fairfield, visiting what appears to have been Rockbottom Farm, marveled at "how seldom, with so many people living so close (about a dozen people in a 10-room house), anyone ever argues or bickers."[13] But others reacted in quite an opposite fashion. Ken Kesey, after breaking up the informal commune that had gathered on his Oregon farm, called congenial togetherness part of the "Communal Lie":

> You can't have any of your friends over, you know? There's no way to be a host. You can't go visiting, for fear somebody'll get your bed. It gets so bad it's terrible. And the worst thing about it is that it's with your best friends. . . .
> When people are pressed together for long times like that, it like homogenizes them, it breaks down that sense of space. Without that, we don't know who we are. We're into each other's drawers, we're stumblin' over each other.[14]

Communal living was, like having children, the best and the worst all at once. Crowding made people close and it drove them crazy.

Visitors

As if crowding were not bad enough with only members present, many communes were swamped with visitors—including friends of members, strangers who wanted to check out the scene, and tourists simply interested in ogling the weird hippies. The problem of visitors has long been an agonizing one for communes, especially for the larger and more stable ones that (given the high turnover that most communes experience) depend on a steady influx of new members for survival. A great many communities tried to control the visitor flow by keeping their profiles as low as possible, shunning news coverage, listings in communal directories, and other publicity. Indeed, for the many communities that were out of compliance with zoning and land-use laws a low profile was essential, and keeping visitors away became basic to communal survival.

Oz, in western Pennsylvania, was one of the communes that tried to accommodate all visitors, with less than satisfactory results. As Robert Houriet recounted,

> Sunday afternoons, [the townspeople] packed their kids into the family auto and went to gape. The slow procession of cars, with children's faces pasted to the windows, crept past the farm, churning up a continual dust cloud. Some days more than a thousand cars filed past, so many that state police had to be assigned there to direct traffic and post "no parking" signs along a strip of road. . . .
>
> Hippies came from as far away as Cleveland and Pittsburgh, and much occurred without the family's knowledge that they were nonetheless held responsible for. One night, for example, two teeny-boppers set up what amounted to a tent of ill repute on the grounds. Naturally, many of their clients spread the word throughout the county that the hippies supported themselves by selling their own women.[15]

Unwanted publicity often opened the floodgates. Cold Mountain Farm managed to exist fairly quietly in New York state until, to its members' great astonishment, an article on the community appeared in the *East Village Other*—"as if we hadn't enough trouble discouraging people we *knew* from coming up," as one member lamented. The community was ambivalent about dealing with the invasion, and the combined problem of visitors and strained relations among members undermined the whole community, as "the warmth and trust and sharing between us began to die. Whatever tribal or family feelings we had were gone."[16]

Gordon Adams found the worst moments of life in the Church of the Creative in Oregon to coincide with visitors who arrived with "a big dog, quantities of drugs, and really out of place lifestyles."[17] At Packer Corner, according to Marty Jezer, invited friends alone "often turned the farmhouse into a rural version of a crowded subway car, making decent conversation and worthwhile visits impossible." Beyond the visits of friends, in one four-month span alone, the farm suffered incursions by

> Sunday "hippy watchers," high school runaways, newspaper and magazine reporters from both the underground and establishment press, a local farmer who was frightened because his eldest son had expressed a desire to live like us, peace activists passing through, local freaks, a state policeman, hitchhikers wanting a place to spend the night, dropouts wanting a place to live, groups of people planning to start their own communes and schools, and a well-scrubbed young couple who wanted to interest us in manufacturing Ho Chi Minh sandals, which they would market for us, as a cottage industry.[18]

As difficult—and as frequent—as any other groups of visitors were reporters and sociologists looking to write about communes. At Downhill Farm Herb Goldstein got so fed up with sociologists interested in sex, drugs, and nudity that he took to bouncing the question back on the researcher: "People would come down and do interviews and ask us about our sex habits, but were rather shocked when I would turn the question around and ask them! 'Wait a minute! I don't have to say that! I don't live in a community!' And so to me the question was, 'Why does living in a community lessen my right to privacy?'"[19] Lucy Horton, a staff member on a major communal research project who also gathered recipes for her communal cookbook,[20] sometimes found more visitors and researchers than communards. Her project director, Judson Jerome, relates this anecdote from her travels:

The house was deserted. She wandered until she found the sweat hut (bent saplings covered with rugs, burlap, and mud.) Sure enough, steam was seeping out of the entrance flap, so she peeled off her clothes and popped in, finding the hut full of naked people. "Are you from the commune?" one asked. None of them were; they were all visitors. We fantasized that they might have answered in chorus: "We're all sociologists."[21]

The Body

A persistent theme within the larger 1960s-era cultural critique was the rejection of modern society's dalliance with the artificial, the plastic, the processed. The new consciousness called for a return to the natural, the unashamed, the organic, the raw and unprocessed—and for as much local self-reliance as possible, rather than dependence on massive industrial production of food, energy, medical services, and the like. The affirmation of the natural began with the human body.

NUDITY

Nowhere were nature and the body more radically affirmed and (to the rest of the culture) shockingly exhibited than in nudity, which was tolerated and sometimes encouraged at a great many secular communes, urban and rural, and at some religious ones. Gilbert Zicklin, a communal researcher in the late 1960s, concluded on the basis of studying about twenty communes that young people in the counterculture were more at home in their bodies and felt more positively about them than "straight" young people. From the communal bathrooms and toilets to the communal bath house or sauna, from the occasional open farters and belchers to the ever-present naked children, from work-a-day hot-weather gardening in the nude to the idyllic frolic of nude swimming, from long hugs and friendship kisses to mutual massages, one finds acceptance, sometimes halting, sometimes aggressive, of bodily exhibition, bodily functions and bodily pleasures, and all this in the name of greater naturalness.[22]

In some communities nudity was practically the order of the day, as at Morning Star Ranch and Wheeler's Ranch, where the mild climate and prevailing outlook combined to make unclothedness routine. At Wheeler's, in fact, one woman was so imbued with the philosophy of unclothed naturalness that, as one who was there recalled, "she decided that since you went around naked most of the time anyway, when she had her period she'd just let herself flow, and not even try to stop it and control it."[23] In Cambridge, Massachusetts, the Cambridge Commune—popularly called the Lewd Family—made a political statement of its members' constant nudity, some of which could be seen from outside the premises; following complaints by neighbors, commune members were tried and acquitted on charges of lewd and lascivious behavior.[24] At the Quicksilver newspaper commune in Washington, D.C., members dealt with an unwanted *Washington Post* reporter by showing up for breakfast in the nude just to be outrageous.[25]

In both city and country nudity could cause problems with neighbors. As Herb Goldstein recalled of his days at Downhill Farm,

We had a hard time having any facade of being straight or something, because neighbors might come down the road, and we'd be in our garden nude. We had an outdoor shower without any curtain around it. People did not express any problems with nudity. The only problem might be what it did socially. I remember trying to show an insurance agent around the place who was evaluating us for fire insurance, and we kept turning a corner and running into a naked person.[26]

Most communities that tolerated nudity found it a real contributor to communal solidarity. As Gordon Yaswen wrote of Sunrise Hill, "The practice of group nudity in the community proved itself a genuinely valuable instrument for the promotion of a sense of warm and frank familiarity among the members. It was—moreover—a symbolic act of communion with—and trust in—each other which helped to cement us."[27] When circumstances forced its curtailment or abandonment, community seemed to suffer. That is what happened at Cold Mountain Farm:

One day one of the guys went into town and was chatting with one of the neigh-boring farmers when the neighbor just casually mentioned, "You know, you can see everything from that hill up there. People are talkin'." . . . It was terrible to compro-mise, but most of us began to wear clothes again. That was a great loss. It had been such a pleasure to be among ten stark naked people unselfconsciously planting corn in the field. . . . We had all kinds of bodies, of all colors and sizes, and we had grown used to these basic differences without embarrassment. That was important for people who had been raised to regard their bodies with shame.[28]

FOOD

Mealtime was the great gathering occasion in most communes. At many of the agricultural communes the day's work was laid out at break-fast, and lunch and dinner brought everyone together from far-flung tasks. In the urban communes breakfast tended to be a rushed cup of coffee and lunch was usually *in absentia*, but dinner was prime communal time, glue that held the community together. At the Mulberry Family community in Richmond, Virginia, dinner was so important that the group adopted a rule mandating the use of chopsticks at all dinners, on the theory that it slowed things down and fostered conversation.[29] So central was the din-ner-table conversation that Verandah Porche of Packer Corner mused, "Maybe that's what they can put on my tombstone: 'Had great conversa-tions here.'"[30]

In her extensive communal visiting Lucy Horton saw endless debates over the permissibility of eating refined sugar or meat and great belief in using a lot of garlic, which was believed to have medicinal properties. The chief topic of conversation in communes was food, not sex or God, and of all the volumes on the shelf of cookbooks (which every commune had) the favorite was *The Joy of Cooking*.[31] Horton concluded that food was no less than "the key to understanding the communal experiment."[32] Some religious communes, particularly the Asian ones, had their own dietary regulations, as in the case of the International Society for Krishna Con-sciousness, which forbade the eating of meat or eggs (among other re-strictions). The Havurah communities tended to keep kosher, and some Judaizing Christian communities declined to use pork. Several com-munes dedicated themselves to macrobiotic diets, although typically they dropped that focus over time.

Food was not always of gourmet quality. Horton noted that after sev-eral culinary disasters the Theatre of All Possibilities in New Mexico adopted a rule that all cooking had to be done from cookbooks.[33] Con-sumption could be unstructured as well, as in the case of a pie contest held by a commune near Taos: it turned out that the commune did not have plates on which to serve the products of the contest, and the whole scene dissolved into a grubby mess.[34]

In a few cases, especially in communes that disdained both jobs and food stamps, the food was consistently slim and poor. Footbridge Farm in Oregon had "really meager fare," one member recalled, often unadorned rice and vegetables in small quantities; when someone managed to slaughter an animal, "we would just gorge."[35] When food ran low and people got hungry at Cold Mountain Farm, one member killed a groundhog and made a stew out of it:

That big pot of stew sat on the stove and people thought about it and talked about it and went to bed without dinner. In the middle of the night a couple of us woke up and had a little. Next day some of us had some for lunch. Only four people remained staunch in their vegetarianism, and mostly they didn't condemn the rest. Each of us worked it out our own way.

Still, the diet wasn't satisfying. Subsistence living was one thing, but we all felt damned hungry.[36]

HEALTH, HEALING, ILLNESS

Belief in organic, natural living did not perfectly protect communards from illness, and unsanitary conditions contributed to epidemics of hepatitis and other diseases that afflicted dozens, if not hundreds, of communities. To be sure, Rico Reed commented that during an early, grueling winter at Tolstoy Farm no one got sick—despite the fact that "they were poor and living on a lousy diet"—because the community was isolated and no diseases were carried in from outside.[37] That, however, was a decidedly uncharacteristic situation. In community after community epidemics, once introduced, laid a lot of persons low.

Hepatitis was the scourge of the rural communes, especially those with poor sanitation facilities or with dubious water supplies. The Hog Farm in New Mexico for a time drew its water from an open irrigation ditch and used it without any purification, soon ending up, predictably, with a hepatitis epidemic. The grimmest story in Joyce Gardner's account of life at Cold Mountain Farm describes the way in which hepatitis ran rampant through the commune, bringing some machinery-shunning residents close to death for lack of a good way to get to town for treatment.[38]

Other diseases took their toll as well. Bill Wheeler itemized staphylococcus, ringworm, threadworm, scabies, lice, and persistent colds as plagues that afflicted the residents of Wheeler's Ranch. But faith in the natural was undimmed through many a medical crisis:

With professional medical treatment unavailable, people turned to folk and Indian remedies: sulphur for scabies, radishes and ginseng for hepatitis, aloe vera for herpes, bay leaf tea and arrowroot starch for dysentery, golden seal for skin infections. And garlic for warding off colds, expelling worms and aiding the body in fighting any viruses passing through. Studying Miwok tribal customs brought the ranch another wonderful way to cure winter ailments. A sweat lodge was built out of bent branches covered with plastic behind the barn on the side of the West Canyon.[39]

Urban communes, despite presumably better water supplies than some rural enclaves had, suffered similarly. Staffers at the Haight-Ashbury Free Medical Clinic found that the crashpad communes contributed disproportionately to their patient load, with repeated cases of chronic relapsing hepatitis and venereal diseases—some of which, untreated, had rendered young women sterile.[40]

Although wide-open sexual activity was much less common than the popular image of the communes would have it, enough sexual freedom was present that in several communes sexually-transmitted diseases could run rampant. Wheeler's Ranch once had an impromptu orgy that liberally spread around an unspecified disease; as one participant recalled, "The Community Hospital was blown away when we pulled up in the school-bus with forty people all coming in to get shots."[41] At Black Bear Ranch one member developed a venereal disease and the communards decided that they had to trace his sexual contacts to treat those who had been exposed:

We made up a chart with who slept with who, just go down and put a little "X" on it, and it turned out that I think we had to treat everybody. But the funny thing was, people would look at the chart and say "Joe, you bastard, you cheated on me with that bitch?" And I remember coming up and going, "Look at that son of a bitch Michael, he screwed everybody! And look at me, I got no marks next to my name!"[42]

Sex and Drugs

The countercultural phase of the 1960s era was probably best known for an anything-goes attitude toward sex and drugs. Publicly spurning both the longstanding agreement in polite society to pronounce sexual activity legitimate only when undertaken by two married persons of the opposite sex and the more recent agreement to condemn the use of any drugs other than a certain few for pleasure, the hippies and a great many others at the time embraced an ethic of "whatever turns you on" and "if it feels good, then do it as long as it doesn't hurt anybody else." Sex was fun; drugs brought pleasure and exploration of the mind.

Several communes became magnets for those who would live without hedonic limits. For better or worse the image of the commune as a refuge for—or a cesspool of, depending on your point of view—such forbidden activities came to prevail among the general public, and the most straight and disciplined of communes were often presumed to be harboring such behaviors as much as were the outright hippies. The actual facts of the matter were mixed, as was always the case in communal America; some communes did have an anything-goes attitude, but a great many more decidedly did not.

COMMUNAL SEX

Sex was not as universally wide open in communal America as public perception had it. Most communities endorsed neither utter licentiousness nor celibacy, letting members work out their own sexual lives. As Richard Seymour remarked in his memoir of life at Compost College (a California commune), "What's there to say? How's sex in your neighborhood? Some of us are married. Some aren't. Some of us sleep together. Some don't. . . . We've had group showers and a lot of touching, but no orgies."[43] Virginia Stem Owens spoke for legions when, in a memoir of her days at Moriah in New Mexico, she asserted that "[w]hat we desired was innocence, not debauchery"—although she probably spoke for just as many more when, a page later, she admitted that there was also "a certain amount of prowling instinct inhabiting some of our hearts."[44] Many couples lived in communes in fairly stable fashion (although, as we have seen, the communal divorce rate was high); many more lived rather as much of the rest of contemporary culture was living, in a state of serial monogamy. Those who had more than one sexual partner often were acting furtively, even though secrecy was next to impossible in a commune. Open, frequent shifting of partners was rare; outright group sex, in the form of orgies and the like, was even rarer—although at one time or another just about anything imaginable happened in some commune somewhere.

Those who wrote about the 1960s-era communes often testified that they found communal sex much more mundane than the communes' public image suggested. In his study of eighty communes Benjamin Zablocki found that persons who joined communes experienced major *decreases*— often in the neighborhood of 50%—in the frequency in their lives of all of the following behaviors: having more than one sexual partner at a time, homosexual conduct, open marriage, and group marriage. Participation in public or group nudity also went down, although less drastically, and the percentage who were celibate went up moderately.[45] The decline in nontraditional sexual activity probably reflects the large presence of religious communities within the greater communal world; many who opted for spiritually disciplined communitarianism voluntarily restricted their previously more liberal sexual ways. Those who went from sexual activeness to celibacy or to marital monogamy certainly would influence the overall numbers. But even in the secular, countercultural communes that seemingly embodied the sexual revolution, sexual activity was sometimes diminished. Gordon Yaswen reports that at Sunrise Hill in Massachusetts members were interested in all kinds of intimacy and open relationships but that the commune's "sexual mores were in practice more conventional than they were in theory."[46] Indeed, sometimes a view of communal relationships as familial made sex seem incestuous and therefore taboo. According to one member of the 25 to 6 Baking and Trucking Society (a gay commune in New York City),

I think one reason why so many of us here have been able to live together relatively peacefully is that our relations have not been genitally sexual. I'm sure that it would have been harder, if not impossible, for me to feel as comfortable and close to those I live with as I do, if we'd all been sleeping together. The couples have been monogamous. . . . The single people have gone outside the house for sex. It's an incest taboo—too close to be genitally involved.[47]

Sometimes the crowded conditions of a communal household did not provide enough privacy for meaningful intimacy to be achieved. Even when this did not constitute an insurmountable obstacle, lack of privacy certainly made sex less secretive than usual in many rural communes and some urban ones. This scrap of dialogue was gathered at one of the warehouse communes in San Francisco:

WOMAN: It used to make me feel funny, hearing you and —— make love. "There they go again," I used to tell myself. Now I don't pay any attention.

MAN: We certainly can hear everything you do. Christ, you two make the whole building shake.[48]

In the early winters at Black Bear Ranch living space was so scarce that floors became covered with wall-to-wall sleeping bags at night. One resident remembered "looking over and seeing this woman sucking this guy's joint. No privacy at all, but it didn't make much difference. A couple here, over here another couple; it just happened. I didn't care if there were 80 people around me. What difference did it make? If I wanted to fuck, I'd fuck, and if they wanted to fuck, then fuck."[49]

Communal sexual activity that was not celibate or strictly monogamous most frequently imitated sexual conduct in the larger society in its surreptitious extramarital couplings, serial monogamy, and premarital relationships. But it clearly did push the boundaries. Charles Gruber said of the Abode of the Message, a Sufi commune in New York state, that

It was fertile ground for coupling and uncoupling because it was kind of an experiment in the works. But then there were some interesting other combinations besides coupling up. One evening at the Abode one person said, "I think it's time we talk about triangles," and someone said, "That sounds like a good idea; I've always been interested in Pythagoras."[50]

Some communes were dedicated to unconventional sexual and marital relationships and worked out whole new structures of relationships. The Farm, for all its encouragement of conventional marriage, once experimented with "four-marriages"—two men, two women, each man and each woman a couple, with Stephen and Ina May Gaskin joining one such relationship. That pattern was fairly short-lived, however. Threesomes existed in many places with greater or lesser success. Group marriages, as we have seen, were tried only rarely.

In a few cases sexual gratification for the males—as opposed to interpersonal relationships—was structured into communal life. For example, a highly structured secular commune at one point decided that a fully planned community dedicated to meeting the needs of all members should deal with men's sexual needs. Thus, a kind of prostitution in which women could earn labor credits for liaisons with men was tried briefly. As things turned out, everyone was too embarrassed to use the system much, so it quietly collapsed. A less formal situation prevailed for a time at Wheeler's Ranch, when a sympathetic woman from Morning Star who styled herself a Love Goddess would visit every week or two to couple with the needy males.

The looser countercultural communes, most frequently the rural ones, simply had no rules and saw a kaleidoscope of sexual activities occur.

Olompali Ranch in California was one of the most open of the communes, sexually, its members admitting to few inhibitions. One visitor
from Morning Star recalled walking into the kitchen and seeing a couple

lying on one of the tables in the "69" position, giving each other head. And I said,
"Oh, sorry!" And they said, "No, it's all right! Come on in, we'll be through in a
minute. Don't worry about it, sit down and talk a while!" And so, between slurps
we talked and bullshitted, having a good visit while they sucked each other off.[51]

Certainly there were some extravagant sexual scenes. Public sex, indiscriminate coupling, and orgies did occasionally occur. But for all the sensationalism that that image of communal life raised, the reality was that in
most communes things were decidedly mundane, and most communes
probably spent more time trying to dispel misperceptions about their sexual activities than doing anything very exotic.

What is here called the 1960s era (the late 1960s and early 1970s) was
the period in which homosexuality was just emerging from the closet.
Even though the alternative culture certainly embraced tolerance of same-
sex activity much more readily than did the culture as a whole, it still took
hippies and other cultural dissenters some time to cope with the change.
Most of the communes of the time seem to have had a predominantly heterosexual orientation. In time many gay men and lesbians founded their
own communes; the first wave of these was predominantly lesbian, and
several founded before 1975 still exist in various locations, especially southern Oregon. Gay male communes are much more a post- than a pre-1975
phenomenon, which is why they are so inconspicuous in this volume.

COMMUNAL DRUGS

Toleration, if not outright advocacy, of at least some of the drugs that
became fashionable in the 1960s was practically universal at the countercultural communes and fairly common in the middle-class urban collectives. In religious communities the picture was mixed, but by no means
universally abstinent: some religious communities banned drug use, with
greater or lesser success; others typically discouraged it but did not attempt to enforce actual rules as long as use did not present communal
problems; a few saw drugs as useful for spiritual progress and eagerly embraced the psychedelic (or, perhaps more precisely, entheogenic) experience. The 60s Communes Project interviews revealed a background of
widespread use of marijuana and the principal psychedelics (LSD, peyote,
and psychoactive mushrooms) among those who eventually joined com-

munes, and in many cases experimentation in alteration of mind was a predisposing factor that drove persons toward intentional community. A sense of the oneness of all things was a typical part of the psychedelic experience, and the marijuana-induced high tended to make one feel warm and expansive at least toward one's fellow users. Most drug use also had a deconditioning effect that was enhanced by the illegality of the substances: it tended to make users question the received wisdom that they had been taught from childhood, because the fact that such obviously pleasurable and useful substances were outlawed clearly demonstrated the moral bankruptcy of the dominant society.[52] The fact that these magical substances were illegal also propelled the flight into community; a sense of being an outlaw fraternity often developed among those who were at risk of prosecution for their pursuit of chemical ecstasy. A few communes— but only a few—became major dealing centers; the Brotherhood of Eternal Love of Laguna Beach, California, was perhaps the most notable of them, its members importing hashish from Afghanistan and distributing major psychedelics as well as taking them regularly.[53] Rural communes provided, in many cases, good locations for growing marijuana and sometimes producing other substances. Community and psychedelia were natural allies; indeed, in the communes in which marijuana and psychedelic use was widely tolerated, LSD and its analogues sometimes neared sacramental status, framing major community events.

Drug use was not usually without its limits, however. Most counterculturists distinguished between "dope" and "drugs"—the former (i.e., marijuana and the psychedelics) being positive, mind-expanding, uplifting, but the latter (most of the refined opiates, amphetamines, usually cocaine, and often alcohol, among other substances) habituating, narcotizing, and socially counterproductive.[54] Most communes thus disdained "drugs."[55] Indeed, users of "drugs" in this sense were the bane of many communes, more than a few of which collapsed because they could not rid themselves of the alcoholics and junkies in their midst. "Dope," however, was something else; at the peak of the 1960s era its acceptance was perhaps the single most important delineator between straight, traditional society and the new alternative outlook.

That is not to say that all or most communes were centers of substance consumption or magnets for the druggiest members of society. The Stelle Community in Illinois, for example, was not interested in attracting hippies and had a middle-class dress and behavior code (men had to be clean shaven, women had to wear dresses, marijuana was forbidden).[56] Zablocki, who as we have seen found lessened, not increased, sexual activities among those who joined communes, came to similar conclusions about drug use.[57] Drugs may have been widely tolerated, but the commune had work to do, and in many cases communes were under such intense scrutiny from neighbors and law enforcement that abstention became a simple matter of self-preservation.

Sometimes impecunious communes would lack the wherewithal to obtain the substances in which they otherwise would have indulged freely, but (as in other areas of life) the "flow" often managed to supply people's needs. Visitors frequently were prime sources, a fact that made the endless stream of curiosity-seekers slightly more bearable. At Earth People's Park in Vermont, one resident said,

> We even actually at one time had our own dope commissioner, a large generous dope pusher who lived on the east coast and for some reason was benevolent enough to supply large amounts of drugs to Earth People's Park. I remember one time he came with a briefcase with probably 80 different kinds of hash oil, all labeled. We spent probably a good two weeks doing nothing but smoking different kinds every night.[58]

Where conditions made covert agriculture feasible, marijuana-friendly communards often tried growing their own—usually just for the commune's own use, but sometimes for sale. At a community in Tennessee a sheriff's deputy, patronizing a woodworking shop run by one of the members, walked by a garden that had several plants in it but didn't happen to see them. Later, "when he became sheriff, the drug surveillance helicopters came over our place pretty heavily, because he suspected us even though he missed his chance. But those of us who were not excited about growing pot on our land had the ammunition by then to persuade people to stop doing it."[59] Inevitably, some communes were raided on drug charges. Olompali Ranch, where dope use was certainly common, was raided twice in quick succession, with many arrests each time. Both raids had their comic moments, as when the residents, hearing that the police were coming in, scooped up hundreds of marijuana cigarettes and threw them out a second-story window—right onto the waiting officers.[60] Sometimes the guiltiest managed to evade capture, as during a raid at Tolstoy Farm in 1966 in which the culpable marijuana growers managed to evade the police but sixteen less guilty householders who just happened to be there at the time were arrested.[61]

Sometimes the police were so anxious to crack down on the hippie communes that they pounced—only to fail to find any forbidden substance at all. At Black Bear Ranch, one resident recalled, when six carloads of police showed up on a drug raid, "it was just like outer space. They came in and pulled up a bunch of baby tomato plants, thinking they were marijuana."[62] But the outcome could still be bad for the community; George Hurd noted that when a raiding party failed to find any drugs at Oz in Pennsylvania the officers busted the persons there "for encouraging idleness, a statute that probably had never been enforced before."[63]

Down on the Farm

As we have seen, communes had a variety of ways of keeping afloat financially. Many of the rural communities intended to earn most or all of their keep by farming, meeting their own food requirements and perhaps providing marketable excess. In most cases, however, farming was far less than lucrative, and only a few communes actually managed to grow most of what they needed; fortunately, they could usually supplement their own produce with purchased groceries or government commodities. In a few situations grim poverty and dogged determination led to a kind of monotonous self-sufficiency in which communards made it through the winter on the sparsest of diets; at the Farm the early winters were famous for diets that were mainly soybeans, in various forms, and Tolstoy Farm had a "wheatberry winter" early on that was later recalled with grimaces. For that matter, even in more prosperous situations food was sometimes fairly dull and predictable. Sometimes a member's allergies or aversion to certain spices prohibited the use of whole categories of foods or flavors. Robert Houriet found the food at Frog Run Farm so bland—"I mean, there is a place for salt and pepper, you know?"—that he often ducked out for a Snickers bar on the sly and developed a lifelong aversion to tofu.[64]

The new ruralists frequently set to farming with great gusto, but in almost every case very few of them knew much about how to make it work; most had grown up in cities, after all. Even the basics were elusive: What crops grew well in this climate and soil? How much water would be needed? How did one keep livestock under control? How should weeds and insects be controlled, and should chemicals be used or not?

Many tragicomic stories came from the learning curve of the incipient agronomists. Ayala Talpai got a milk cow for her community of Bodega

Pastures, California, and found that it took her over half an hour to milk it—and that she got odd little spots in the milk to boot. Finally she asked for help from a professional dairyman neighbor; after finding the cow in good shape, the neighbor asked Talpai, "'Well, how long do you take to milk?' And I go, 'Oh, about 35 minutes.' And he goes, 'Well, that's what the problem is. Those flecks you're seeing in the milk, that's butterfat. You're churning the milk, honey.' I must have been a great story all around town for months later."[65] At Packer Corner, Verandah Porche learned not to milk barefooted when the cow stepped on her toes, fracturing two of them: "Now I can tell when the weather is changing by a stiffness in the pinky and next toe."[66] Earthworks, in Vermont, had an excellent stand of sugar maple and decided to exploit it; eventually they produced over 150 quarts of maple syrup, which they marketed in New York City—earning, by the estimate of member Bruce Taub, maybe fifteen cents per hour. The profit of the undertaking was severely undermined by the misadventures of the neophyte crew:

We were gathering heavily flowing maple sap on a glorious sunny day, temperatures in the high forties, using a three hundred gallon tank being drawn by our team of horses on a dray through deep snow. Dozens of people were tromping through the woods pouring sap from the tap buckets into gathering buckets and unloading those buckets joyfully and speedily into the horse drawn tank. As we drove the first fully loaded tank back toward the sugar house the dray hit a hidden rock and tipped over pitching the gathering tank off the dray and onto its side. Though we only lost about twenty or thirty gallons of sap, the tank was far too heavy for us to right and reset on the dray, even with all the people power we had. So we set about unloading the sap we had gathered in the tank back into the gathering pails and then retraced our steps through the snow to the trees we had just harvested where we poured the sap back into the very buckets we had just unloaded. It was as if someone had taken a movie of our operation and was now playing the reel in reverse.[67]

And so it went. Cold Mountain Farm members bought a tractor and based their planned summer's activities on its anticipated use, only to find it inoperable just when it was most needed and when the only person capable of fixing it was on an extended absence from the farm.[68] Hidden Springs members' attempt to raise purebred goats foundered when the offspring "came up mongrel, oops!"[69] Self-sufficiency did not come easily.

On many a rural commune perhaps the greatest spectacle, often laced with trauma, was the slaughtering of animals. At Packer Corner one member, dispatched to dispatch a rooster, was found an hour later talking to the chickens he could not bear to harm.[70] At Black Bear Ranch the killing of Siegfried the hog was an all-community event, a sort of communal ritual following the text of the USDA pamphlet "Let's Butcher a Hog."[71] Neighborly assistance sometimes proved crucial: at the killing of Sophie the cow at Earthworks, a visitor helped get the victim in position to be shot and a surgeon who just happened to drop in at the proper moment oversaw the dissection of the beast.[72] Like most 4-H kids who suffer tragic separation when the animals that they have raised almost as pets are sold for slaughter, the communal animal stewards did not usually take great joy in the final portion of their task.

Householder Yogis

"If you figure out who is going to carry out the garbage, everything else will seem simple." Thus did Judson Jerome quote an anonymous long-time communitarian, and the observation is apt.[73] The little chores of daily life became some of the principal centers of contention in a great many communes—and in fact the proximate cause of the breakup of more than a few. Peter Coyote spoke for legions when he declared: "Who will empty the garbage, clean the toilets, and do the dishes are mundane but vital questions. . . . If I prefer washing my face in a clean sink and someone else doesn't, it is a difficult issue to resolve from an ideological position."[74]

The pattern of operations varied, as always, from one commune to another. A fair number, especially among the communes committed to gender equality, worked out a systematic rotation of chores for all adult members, often after a chaotic early period in which little got done reliably. In some communes a few devoted workhorses would simply do far more than their share, day after day. In a few places a near-miracle occurred: things just got done, without schedules or acrimony. In some communes not much got done at all.

In the most satisfying of circumstances the work, or at least important parts of it, would simply get done without formal job assignments or rancor. At Packer Corner no very formal system was ever instituted—"What decisions? What organization? There were none"—but through the good chemistry of the gathered Farmers the essentials got done: "Every night (almost) the dishes were done by some new face at the sink. No kitchen manager. No list tacked onto the fridge or over the sink specifying dishwasher, bottle cleaner, sweeper, etc."[75] At Wheeler's Ranch, one resident (an escaped convict on the lam, the residents would learn from the police after he had moved on) made it his job to inspect the rather primitive water lines daily, checking them for leaks. Another resident, forever after known as Garbage Mike, took it upon himself to be the picker-up of litter.[76] Often slackers were present, but if the others could get the necessary chores done without too much aggravation, then all could still be well. At Black Bear Ranch, according to Kenoli Oleari, "The issue of carrying their load was not a big one. It was kind of okay for people to do whatever they did, and some people didn't do as much as other people. There was some grumbling about it, but it seemed like everybody more or less did something. When something needed to be done, we'd organize a crew."[77]

Sometimes lack of organization became frustrating. Gordon Yaswen wrote of the "Phenomenon of the Unlabelled Jar":

The various jars, cans, cups, and plates in which things were stored (both in the refrigerator and upon the kitchen shelves) were at first rarely labelled. The confusion they caused was way out of proportion to their value. Since no one knew what was in them and for what end they were destined, no one wished to disturb them, and so with each use or cleaning of countertops and refrigerator shelves, they were shuttled back and forth, and cleaned around. When . . . some courageous soul wished to solve their mystery, it might just take asking everyone in the entire Community about them before such could be done—carrying them all about the house in the process. Often (only after such lengthy process) its contents were summarily thrown out—having first received the OK of every adult member of the Community. Just as often, such containers waited until their very stench made such discarding crucial.[78]

That kind of neglect, unfortunately, sometimes had more serious consequences. Yaswen's tale of omission concludes with the note that two car engines were ruined for lack of attention. At Tolstoy Farm members bought a cow and proclaimed the establishment of a cow co-op—only to find that many wouldn't help milk. Inattention was such that the cow was not even confined properly; a neighbor finally captured it while it was on the loose and sold it at auction.[79] Often the larger tasks fell completely by the wayside: the sugarhouse, a grand scheme at Packer Corner, never got built; the badly needed additional accommodations at Sunrise Hill never got much beyond land-clearing and foundation-laying.

In a few cases, however, tasks were performed to excess. Sunrise Hill, finding itself in need of firewood, organized a massive effort to get it rounded up. The result, Yaswen noted sardonically, was "so prodigious a woodpile that it virtually equalled the house it was to heat. When I visited Sun Hill for the last time, it was still very much there."[80]

At the other end of the spectrum, some communities organized their work quite thoroughly. Most frequently some kind of list or wheel of chores was used to spread the work around fairly. A few communities developed more elaborate work credit systems in which members could have some choice about the work they did but had to contribute a fixed number of hours (or credits) per week. Twin Oaks, Virginia, and East Wind, Missouri, were and are sister communities that use a work-credit system, and their high level of organization may have something to do with the fact that they are both quite alive and well after more than a quarter-century of existence. Their flexibility and willingness to innovate may also be a key to long-term survival; in the early days of Twin Oaks, for example, as the community reported in its newsletter,

We had breakfast scheduled for 8:00, but it was rarely ready before 9:00, because the breakfast cook couldn't get out of bed, either. . . . Then someone suggested we set the clock back, just like Daylight Savings Time, and for the same purpose. . . . The odd thing is that it worked. We are still a little late getting up, but we are late an hour earlier than we used to be, and therefore use an extra hour of scarce and valuable sunlight for the outdoor work.[81]

Women's Work

As noted in an earlier chapter, the 1960s era saw a historic revival of American feminism, and the questioning of the roles to which women had traditionally been assigned by society went on in the communes as elsewhere. Any revolution takes time to succeed, and the new women's movement was often met in communal America with the same kind of bewilderment and hesitation that it experienced elsewhere. The fact that communal founders and dominant leaders were overwhelmingly male undoubtedly contributed to the general inertia on that score. Many of the new feminists—not wanting to be forever assigned to cooking rice and tofu in communal kitchens any more than they wanted forever to cook meat and potatoes in middle America—had trouble understanding why it should take very long for supposedly enlightened, progressive males (and some females, for that matter) to come to their gender-role senses. Kit Leder reflected on her experiences in a rural commune in 1969 in that vein:

Even though there was no society-dictated division of labor, even though we had complete freedom to determine the division of labor for ourselves, a well-known pattern emerged immediately. Women did most of the cooking, all of the cleaning up, and, of course, the washing. They also worked in the fields all day—so that after the farm work was finished, the men could be found sitting around talking and taking naps while the women prepared supper. In addition to that, one of the women remained in camp every day in order to cook lunch—it was always a woman who did this, never a man. Of course, the women were excused from some of the tasks; for example, none of us ever drove a tractor. That was considered too complicated for a woman.[82]

Some dissatisfied women left communes over such issues, and the early 1970s saw the founding of a number of women's communes, many of them predominantly lesbian and several of which still survive. In a few cases, as at Black Bear Ranch, some women moved into a separate building where they could have separate space within the larger commune.[83] In some places, some of the time, women who so chose could get out of the kitchen and elect to perform traditionally male tasks, although that did not always provide anyone with complete, immediate satisfaction. A woman at Black Bear joined a firewood crew but found that that didn't solve all gender-related problems:

It's physically very difficult for me to handle a forty-pound saw. I can do it, but not for long. The massiveness of it decreases my skill and accuracy a lot. The men use the big saws, the women use the small saw. It is hard to avoid the macho snobbery that goes along with greater strength. . . . The fact that the men controlled the mechanical power in the situation made the whole thing out of balance.[84]

Gender realities in the larger society also could define roles for communal women. The Digger communes, for example, became expert at scavenging for food, getting much of it from surpluses at public produce markets, and women were essential to making the system work. As Peter Coyote wrote, "The Italians who controlled the market simply would not give free food to able-bodied men, and consequently the women became our conduit to this basic necessity, which afforded them power and high status in our community."[85]

However, the fact that communes did not perfectly liberate women did not mean that communes were invariably no better than the larger society on gender issues. The simple fact that many women lived in close proximity made communes an easy place for women's groups to develop, and consciousness raising among women (and sometimes men) was thus widespread. One team of researchers found that "women in many of the urban communes studied tended to be noticeably stronger and more independent than traditional societal expectations of them" and that "many were deeply involved either actively or philosophically in the women's liberation movement."[86] A female communard in Maryland spoke for many of her peers when she wrote, "The men and women at Toad Hall have enabled each other to move outside of male-female roles and expectations. . . . Our community arrangement offers the support and acceptance necessary in a society which alienates us from who we are and where we want to go. We don't have all the answers—but we are picking up some good leads."[87]

As one might guess, gender roles tended to be both more traditional and more clearly delineated in religious than in secular communes. Jon Wagner's edited volume of case studies, limited though its sample is, finds that women's roles in religious communities were usually circumscribed, with situations ranging from some gender-role distinction to "an explicit ideology of female subordination."[88] Most Christian communes seem to have maintained traditional gender roles,[89] although exceptions did exist: the Sojourners Community, for counterexample, has long been committed to full equality, has usually had women among its pastors, and has regularly had men do domestic work.[90] At the Farm in Tennessee a certain traditionalism joined with biology and ideology to mitigate in favor of traditional work assignments during the commune's early years, at least: with a disdain for most kinds of birth control and a great enthusiasm for children, Farm women tended to be pregnant or nursing a good deal of the time. As Ina May Gaskin observed, "That meant they weren't out on the construction crews."[91]

Life of the Spirit

Most communes of the 1960s era had at least a modicum of religious and ritual life, diffuse though it often was. The many specifically religious communities of course had beliefs and practices distinctive to their own traditions: Christians worshipped together, prayed privately and together, and studied the Bible; Zennists meditated and took lengthy retreats; Hindu-oriented groups meditated and attended spiritual teaching sessions; members of the Farm heard Stephen Gaskin preach on Sunday mornings and tried to live their inclusive faith in the warp and woof of their lives. Sometimes the religious focus would change periodically; at the Sunburst community in California, as a member recalled, "People were doing a sort of 'religion of the month' for a long time. Everyone was into Judaism for a while; everyone was into Hinduism for a while. There was a period when everyone was wearing ceremonial robes for special occasions."[92]

Some counterculturists, stereotypes to the contrary, just attended nearby churches. Adam Read, who spent his infancy at Morning Star and Wheeler's Ranch and grew up in the commune country around Taos, recalled that his mother always went to church, children in tow.[93] Beyond such structured patterns, however, many communards simply communed with nature, talked endlessly of spiritual matters, and dabbled in religious and ritual activities ranging from astrology to Ouija boards to sun yoga. Belief in psychic phenomena was widespread.[94] Some communards disdained organized and traditional religiosity yet felt that spiritual concerns guided many of their actions. Art Downing spoke of his life in several communes in the San Francisco Bay area, including the Diggers:

"Religious" wouldn't have worked for my vocabulary. I would've considered our approach to what we were doing as being spiritual. I mean, we were really invested in the notion of karma yoga, and service, good works for the sake of doing good works. And that tied, for us, in with the notion of "free." That was as religious as we got. We didn't spend a lot of time meditating. Our approach was to do good work, to create stuff, for the sake of creating, as karma yoga.[95]

Gordon Yaswen wrote of Sunrise Hill's having a religiosity that was "a fact felt by us all" but "undefined and mostly uncodified"; it coexisted with specific members' commitments to Zen, Quakerism, and Russian Orthodoxy.[96] And some communards pursued a private spirituality that related little to the rest of the life of the commune. At Wheeler's Ranch, which had several deeply spiritually-oriented residents within a community that had no common religious focus, one man disappeared into a canyon for three months; he returned half-starved, announcing that he had seen God.[97]

Group rituals, whatever the overall spirituality of the community, were often important to communal cohesion. Sometimes they were as simple as a blessing before meals. Lucy Horton in her communal travels found pre-meal rituals in many communes, including Atlantis, in Oregon:

The food was placed on the floor, and the group sat around it in a circle, holding hands. First we chanted "om" for a few minutes and recited the Lord's Prayer. Then several members recited another prayer. It went: "From the point of light within the mind of God, let light stream from the center, where the will of God is known. Let purpose guide the little wills of men, the purpose which the masters know and serve. From the center, which we call the family, the race of man, let the plan of love and light work on. And may it seal the door where evil dwells. Let light and love and power restore the plan on earth. Om shanti."[98]

Group meditation was also popular at a great many communes; its lack of particularistic religious content made it suitable for all but the most hardened skeptics.

Rituals could be tied to recurring occasions, or they could just arise spontaneously. Major ceremonial events (weddings, new-baby observances) were typically full of ritual festivities that might include chanting, circle dancing, incense-burning, singing, and the use of visual decorations including homemade God's eyes, wildflowers, and fantastic clothing.[99] Robert Houriet describes the unscheduled rituals of the Oz commune in Pennsylvania as "happenings"—"Once, in the midst of a thunderstorm, they did a rain dance to the accompaniment of recorders, a clarinet and a saxophone."[100] In Vermont, an outside historian recorded a rain dance at Earthworks that worked:

Our area suffered a dry spell during July or August, as a usual occurrence, so they did something about that. We heard sounds of musical instruments and human hoots and hollers (hellos) ringing out over the summer evening air. They were performing a rain dance. Too bad not one of us saw it. Anyway it did rain, a whacking old Vermont thundershower. Lightning struck very near their house so we chuckled and all said, "They overdid the thing," but the rain was a benefit.[101]

Because the use of marijuana and psychedelics was often considered fraught with religious importance, rituals and ceremonies sometimes accompanied the ingestion of the divine substances. One member of Siva Kalpa recalled the smoking ritual as the most important of the ceremonies that the group observed:

Smoking the chillum was a big ritual. It's a clay pipe, and you would mix ganga, which is high-grade marijuana, with tobacco, and everybody would sit in a circle. One person would have the chillum and light it, and there was a whole lot of ritual with that. You'd make a little ring with rope and light that first, and then put it on top of the chillum and tap it down, and smoke would go all over the place, and everybody would chant a phrase meaning "Arise Shiva, Lord of Oblivion," or, as [the group's guru] Ciranjiva expressed it, "Wake up you self oblivious gods and goddesses." That was the main ritual we practiced, and in the early days there was a circle every morning.[102]

Communal Art and Culture

The young communards were typically a well-educated and creative lot, and their communes were easily disposed to become cultural centers for the alternative society. Many communes had good musicians, painters, sculptors, writers, and other artists among their numbers, and the creation of art was a frequent undertaking and sometimes an important component of the communal economy—indeed, the economic backbone (such as there was) at Libre, Packer Corner, AAA, the Grateful Dead house, Trans-Love Energies, East Hill Farm of the Rochester Folk Art Guild, and dozens of other communities. Their creative contributions were often substantial; much influential rock music (and some folk music) was created in communal settings, and what may have been the very earliest underground comic books were created by the communitarians of Drop City and Libre. The COPS commune in Berkeley printed imaginative posters for everything from rock concerts to political rallies. In short, the artists' colonies of nearly a century earlier were recapitulated in a new generation. As Art Downing reflected, "We were trying to incorporate artistic expression into almost everything. I had visions of building just a simple rustic cabin, but then realized, 'Absolutely not, that's way too ordinary. You have to come up with something beautiful.' In very large measure art was what it was about. We wanted to live and have art all around us."[103]

Any and all artistic media were embraced. The communes of southern Colorado, many of them devoted primarily to art, often came together in the early 1970s for grand theatrical events at the huge Red Rockers dome; after the demise of the commune, the dome lived on for years as the common theater of the other communes in the area, with all sorts of elaborate productions—overtly sexual skits, comedy sketches, silly stuff. Sometimes the events would go on for days, with dances and feasting. Music was always available from the several commune-based bands in the area.[104] In other places creativity was simpler, as at Hidden Springs in New Hampshire, where members poured cooking oil into the record player to hear the music play at varying speeds.[105]

The one cultural element, if it can be called that, that was missing at a great many communes was television. In place after place television was either banned outright or relegated to individual rooms and its presence minimized.[106] One survey found that "there is an almost total lack of television in the psychedelic communes. Members who spoke about television stigmatized it."[107] Tolstoy Farm was tv-free in its early years, but finally the tube began to creep in—and with that, Rico Reed lamented, Tolstoy's common social life veered sharply downhill.[108]

In the absence of television, reading fared well in most cases. The typical commune had a library or at least a shelf of books on such topics as self-sufficient living and occult/New Age philosophy. Fiction often ran to utopianism and fantasy, with such works as Robert Heinlein's *Stranger in a Strange Land* and J. R. R. Tolkien's trilogy *Lord of the Rings* front and center.

Getting Along with the Neighbors

Most middle Americans were not pleased, to say the least, about having a commune pop up in the neighborhood. To the staid majority of the population the new culture of the 1960s was ominous, if not downright terrifying, and communes represented the worst fears of many a householder. Most persons had never visited a commune, but that didn't keep them from thinking that they had a pretty good idea just what was happening in those dens of iniquity. Hippies, after all, were known for sex, drugs, refusal to work, lack of grooming and hygiene, loud animalistic music, and hedonism, were they not? Even hostile neighbors tended to take an intense interest in the new situation; at Wheeler's Ranch, and undoubtedly in many other places, one neighbor regularly took in the scene through binoculars. Press coverage hardly helped; although reporters were far from universally hostile, the news business instinctively looks for headlines, and innuendoes about sex, drugs, and nudity often made it into the obligatory story about the new local commune. Thus has it ever been; rumors of terrible atrocities and acts of fanaticism have circulated at least since the first Shakers began to be noticed in the 1770s and 1780s. "Commune" is not always a benign term.

Given such prevailing sentiments, newly founded communes were often faced with delicate problems of public relations. Over time, however, the conflicts tended to drop away. As communitarians and neighbors got to know each other it became clear that the population on each side was composed of people, and gradually relations usually became cordial, if not warm. In some cases communes that survived went on to become pillars of their larger local communities.

Simple rumors and stereotypes greeted the communal pioneers in a great many places. At Black Bear Ranch the original settlers had little contact with the scattered local residents, but years later, when tensions had eased, an early communard asked a neighbor, "What did people think about us when we first came up there?" The two-word answer: "Charles Manson."[109] Sometimes an innocent event would spark rumors, as when visitors noticed that the poor inhabitants of the Lyman Family's Benton Farm had a house full of Thomas Hart Benton paintings worth, probably, millions—so were the Lymans a gang of art thieves? (Actually, Benton's daughter was a member of the community, and Benton had donated the works now hanging on the walls.) Art Kleps recounted a scene at Millbrook in which Bill Haines threw a rifle belonging to a community resident into the lake to get rid of it: "Just as he was pitching it in a carload of Bungalow visitors passed over the bridge where he was standing, in his robes, which must have given them all something to think about as they sped on their way."[110]

Other prejudices aside, countercultural communards did sometimes threaten cherished values of some persons who saw them move into the neighborhood. The residents of western Sonoma County, California—who were so incensed at the seeming invasion that they saw—were largely prosperous, and a permanent enclave of open land might have threatened their lofty property values. Right within the city of Chicago the members of Jesus People USA were amazed to find a cross burning beside their building one night; it seems that a Ku Klux Klan chapter was headquartered nearby, and it took exception to JPUSA's interracial marriages.[111]

There were, naturally, a few exceptions to the pattern of hostility from neighbors. Freefolk in Minnesota boasted fine relations from the beginning:

A community surrounding our community has developed, partly because we are living in an area where money is scarce. The divergence in ways of life isn't that great. Bartering, trading, exchanging labor is a frequent occasion. We are able to help some of our neighbors and they often help us, giving us the skim milk they would otherwise throw out, teaching us stuff you won't find in books. Another major reason we have a good thing going with our neighbors, besides the fact that we really dig people and try to make friends, is that the community has grown slowly, giving people a chance to get used to us, to know that we are friendly, "hard-working, honest folk, even if they do look a bit weird."[112]

Similarly, Springtree Community started out happily:

Our new neighbors here in rural Virginia are gentle, friendly and helpful people. Our ignorance in such matters as tractors, goats, thistle eradication and dairying is abysmal, and we have gotten good advice from the experienced farmers around us. We have explained about our community and found them receptive to the idea.

They agree with us about the horrors of city living and realize that one of the farmer's greatest difficulties is finding reliable labor. The sharing of tools and labor is a common practice in our part of the world, and we have received many kind offers of assistance from our new friends and neighbors.[113]

Sometimes, especially in rural areas, some of the neighbors were themselves idiosyncratic—to say the least—and by comparison the communards did not seem so strange. Residents of Frogge Hollow in Ohio recalled a neighbor who deliberately trashed his property to keep his taxes down and bathed once a year, coating himself afterwards with turpentine and vaseline.[114]

Occasionally relations would go well for a time and then be soured by some real or perceived miscreancy on the part of a communard. Lou Gottlieb, for example, said that Morning Star's problems with its neighbors were aggravated by several ill-conceived acts by commune residents, as in the case in which a neighbor's show horse got an unwanted haircut. A well-intended young resident saw a heavy mane over the horse's eyes that she presumed kept the horse from seeing clearly, so one day she went over to the pasture next door and clipped the offending hair. That trimming ruined the animal for several years as a competitor at horse shows, and its owner was irate.[115] Members of the Farm (Tennessee) decided to dispose of a huge mountain of tires by burning them—only to see smoke and soot settle over the entire area. The perpetrators were briefly locked up, one of them recalled, "for our own protection, lest the town come to lynch us."[116] A member of the Church of the Creative in Oregon decided to try to get rid of rattlesnakes by starting a grass fire, which got out of hand and brought out the local fire department; "It was not good for our reputation," a member lamented.[117] Tolstoy Farm had long been viewed with suspicion by some nearby residents—many of whom had never heard of Leo Tolstoy and called the farm "Tolstory"—and after the commune's first dope bust, Piper Williams recalled, "Tolstoyers weren't allowed in some of the restaurants" in nearby Davenport.[118] In Chicago, Jesus People USA committed the "error" of bloc voting against a well-established incumbent in an aldermanic election and paid a hefty price: as John Trott recounted the story, "We saw more city inspectors than we had ever seen in our entire time in uptown before that. We were nickel and dimed to death, practically, over every last little building violation they could find."[119]

Sometimes even when most neighbors were skeptical, one or two would break through the veil of suspicion and befriend the new communitarians. The settlers of Cold Mountain Farm, seeking free fertilizer, offered to clean out a neighboring farmer's barn for the manure, and he was so gratified that he showed up a few days later with his huge tractor to prepare their land for planting.[120]

Occasionally a community would be goaded into a confrontational response; at the Himalayan Academy in Nevada, for example, after repeated harassment by motorcyclists a burly member fired several shotgun blasts into the air over one contingent's heads, and the hassles ceased immediately.[121] More typically, however, communes undertook public relations offensives to reduce local tension. The Packer Corner settlers, Marty Jezer noted, made it a point to open "communications with as many local people as possible. We talked to the town selectmen, shopped in local stores, and said 'Hello,' and 'Good morning,' as if we were at a Be-In greeting fellow freaks." As a result, the "hippy farm" soon did not seem so strange after all.[122] Siva Kalpa members in California made a point of improving their urban neighborhood—picking up trash, building playground equipment, repairing their buildings, and throwing block parties for everyone's enjoyment. Soon, one member found, "We were pretty popular with people in the neighborhood. They thought we were a little strange, but they liked us."[123]

Often that was not the case, however, and several localities took active legal steps to keep communes from operating. At Oz thirty-four adults were charged with contributing to the delinquency of minors and operating a disorderly house; they left the area to avoid a hostile trial.[124] On Nantucket the local government adopted several anticommunal ordinances that banned, among other things, occupancy of one building by more than five persons.[125] In many places the vehicle for legal action against communes was the building inspector or local public health officer; at Cold Mountain, to name only one example, in a visit of just a few minutes the health inspector told the community that it would have to get a toilet, a spring house, and a refrigerator.[126] The various legal pretexts for suppressing communes were often of dubious constitutionality, and sometimes were overturned. Zoning restrictions against communes (but not against conventional families and other more familiar situations) often had no rational basis and could not withstand a legal challenge. Anticohabitation and antifornication statutes violated the constitutional mandate of equal protection of the laws. Regulations that denied food stamps and welfare benefits to communards had no legally legitimate purpose; they were discriminatory and violative of freedom of association.[127] Fighting city hall, however, was often difficult for the communal victims of such legal crusades.

In the more extreme cases hostile neighbors committed violence against communes with acts ranging from minor vandalism to murder. The Brotherhood of the Spirit in Massachusetts had some of its vehicles shot at.[128] Hip communards at Magic Valley in Oregon were variously shot at and greeted with antihippie signs in local stores, and their free store mysteriously burned down.[129] Someone sprinkled nails in the driveway at Downhill Farm.[130] Barry Laffan recounted an incident in which a desperately ill Johnson Pasture resident who was driven to the local hospital was refused treatment because of his place of residence; the nurse who finally examined him at the next closest hospital, sixty miles away, asserted that he had almost died from dehydration and lack of timely medical attention.[131]

THE WORST-CASE SCENARIO: VIOLENCE AT TAOS

Nowhere did violence against communes flare more vigorously than at Taos, where the perceived inundation of a traditional community by waves of down-and-out hippies caused deep cultural conflict—at its worst leading to the murder of a member of one of the many communes in the area. In fact, the inundation was far more perceived than real, hippies most of the time probably numbering fewer than a thousand; in such delicate contexts, however, perceptions can be extremely important. The worst vibes came from Chicanos, most of them poor, who felt threatened by the immigrants who came from prosperous backgrounds but were living in poverty. Among other things, the Chicano economy depended heavily on the white tourist trade, and some feared that the hippies would scare the affluent tourists away. But beneath such generalized fears lay a deep-seated contradiction in American culture. An observer offered this assessment in 1970:

Roughly 25 per cent of the Chicanos in Taos are unemployed. Consequently, many are dependent on welfare and food stamps for survival. Their poverty is generations old—stretching back even to the Mexican rule—and for many of them dependency on the government for survival is simply a bitter fact of life.

Combined with the Chicanos' low economic status is an education—or, rather, an indoctrination—which teaches them to value and respect, to honor and emulate, the American Middle-Class Way of Life, where success and happiness are measured in terms of greenbacks, two-car garages, college educations, and barbeque pits in manicured backyards. At the same time, they are reportedly taught that hippies are disease-ridden, sex-crazed dope fiends, communist conspirators who are out to rip off the Great White American Way. The result—frustrating to say the least—is that the Chicanos in Taos (whose children comprise 87 per cent of the county's students) are taught to value a life-style which they haven't a beggar's chance of attaining.[132]

Those kinds of tensions led to a long string of legal and illegal antihip and anticommunal actions. The following are just a few of the many instances of violence that occurred over a short span of time in 1969 and 1970: The Volkswagen van of a commune was dynamited by night; later a building on the property was burned to the ground. Hippies were brutally beaten up on the street on many occasions. A hitchhiking longhair was sentenced to jail for possession of a "concealed weapon"—a tiny pocketknife. Vehicles were shot up in various situations. Anonymous phone calls threatened arson and murder. A hippie woman was gang-raped. A macrobiotic restaurant was destroyed. A sign appeared on a Taos building: "The only good hippie is a dead hippie. Kill."[133] To the extent they could, some communes took defensive actions; the Family, for example, posted a guard all night in its free school building after some of its windows were broken out. Richard Fairfield reports that to visit the Family's rural house he had to call ahead and then blink the lights on his car when he neared the premises.[134]

The hostility toward the hip newcomers was much less pronounced among the Indians (the second-largest ethnic group in the area), who apparently were less threatened by the new settlers and often appreciated the hip fascination with Indian culture. Indeed, Indians often accepted overtures of friendship from communes and visited frequently. At Morning Star East, for example, Taos Pueblo Indians helped to establish and lead a peyote church. Eventually there was some intermarriage between hippies and Indians.

At the Church of the Five Star Ranch, the hip presence even became the stuff of Indian legend. The commune was located at the Ponce de Leon hot springs, and the local Indians, far from being put off by the hippies who bathed there in the nude, often joined them. The hip presence was good luck, the Indians said; the springs had been cool when earlier owners had tried to establish a resort there, but warmed up again when the communal Five Star band appeared.[135] The hippies' good luck, however, did not endure. Five Star's open-door policy attracted low-life transients who did both physical and psychological damage, and finally (according to one member) a group of Chicanos came and told the remaining residents to leave. They apparently were acting without legal authority, but the last desperate Five Star members did not argue the point.[136]

The nadir of the conflict came with the murder of Michael Press, a hip resident of the Kingdom of Heaven commune at Guadalupita, New Mexico, on August 5, 1970, and, on that day and the next, the beating of three other members and triple rape of yet another. Two years later several of the perpetrators received mild sentences on reduced charges.[137] But by then the peak of the conflict had passed. Many communards had left the area, and the ones who remained were moving steadily down the road toward normalized relations.

CONTEMPT FOR STRAIGHT SOCIETY

Critics of the hippies would say that they brought much of the hostility that they experienced on themselves, and to some extent that may have been true. Although many kinds of nonviolent antisocial behavior might often be deemed within the range of conduct that should be tolerated in a free society, a fair number of communitarians—especially the countercultural ones—did sometimes go out of their way to offend persons whose values and way of life differed from their own. Most 1960s-era communes, after all, stemmed from opposition to the existing culture, and the new generation's critique of the Establishment way of life could sometimes be visceral.

Countercultural attitudes toward sex and drugs were certainly taken by society's more conservative majority as a slap in the face. The idea that one could have a happy, fulfilling life without working at a job was jarring to many who had punched a clock for decades. The American controversy over the war in Vietnam reached its peak during the era of commune-building, and many regarded the communes as unpatriotic—even criminal, given that they occasionally harbored draft resisters. In some communes sex with children and the use of drugs by children was countenanced to some degree, and no self-respecting Middle American could tolerate those kinds of things.

Sometimes communards simply did not show common sense in their dealings with others. A member of a southern Colorado commune recalled a communal party at which one member, high on the DMT that he was distributing freely, began to have sex in the middle of the floor with another man's wife—with several visiting Chicano neighbors watching.[138] Communes may not have deserved all the antipathy that they received, and a great many were certainly innocent of grave social abuses; sometimes, though, their lack of social graces did contribute to their public relations problems.

10

Moving On

The story of the 1960s-era communes has been diverse in every detail, and that diversity applies as much to the end of the phenomenon as to anything else. Some communes went out with a bang, some with a whimper, and some are still going—robustly or feebly, publicly or privately, with the same leadership and ideals that they had two or three decades ago or heading in some new direction.

The stories of the closing of many individual communities have been recounted in the chapters above. Sometimes—particularly in the case of communes that operated with open-door policies—noncontributing or destructive members overwhelmed the hard-working idealists who had typically founded the community. Drop City in its latter days was little more than a motorcycle gang's hangout, and the founders (who still had legal control of the property) eventually managed to evict them, shut the place down, and then sell the property to a neighbor. Five Star was afflicted by new members who plagued the more stable veterans and brought the house down around them with theft and vandalism. That general pattern was played out dozens, probably hundreds, of times.

Sometimes communities succumbed to internal tensions. Living with others is not usually easy, at least for those who have not been socialized in that lifeway from birth; if it were, communal living, given its manifest advantages, would be the norm of the human race, not an odd exception.

The little quirks and small (or large) character flaws that kept domestic life from being as harmonious as members hoped often in the end tore things apart. Sometimes the commune was formally, ceremoniously dissolved; more often members peeled away one by one, and finally nothing that could be called a community existed any more. The highest idealism, it seems, often cannot overcome human pettiness. Freefolk, in Minnesota, closed through attrition, and Patsy Richardson composed the commune's elegy:

Maybe we could have made it together, adapted to meet our various separate and collective needs, if we could have tuned into what was happening sooner. But we were blinded by dreams, I think. Trapped, living so closely. And saddest of all, unable in a year and a half to learn to talk to one another, to tell each other straight what it was we felt or thought, to be open about our needs and our hurts. Bitterness grew and silence grew till it filled up the clearing and now we're all gone except for the winter birds and the rabbits.[1]

The process of shutting down was often somewhat random in direction. As Robert Houriet characterized the dissolution of Frog Run Farm, "It sort of fizzled. It just lost energy. It reached the point where people said, 'What are we doing here?' 'Well, maybe we should sell the place.' 'Well, we can't do that.' 'Well, why not?' 'Well, maybe you're right. Why not?'"[2]

Sometimes the proximate cause of a commune's breakup was a simple loss of facilities. Those that occupied rented buildings were subject to eviction, and in the crunch some either could not find suitable replacement facilities or deemed the search not worth the effort. The Clinton Farm in Kansas, occupying donated space, was closed when the Army Corps of Engineers condemned the land for a reservoir. Sometimes a private owner tired of communal problems and simply booted the company out, as Michael Duncan did with Morning Star East and Reality Construction Company near Taos. Several communes disbanded after they lost major buildings, as in the case of the Garden of Joy Blues in Missouri, which (like Brook Farm over a century earlier) could not survive the destruction by fire of its principal residence.

Some communes were dependent on specific leaders and failed to survive their departure. When Ulysses S. Grant left the Lower Farm on the lam after two residents were murdered, no one could keep any residual communal scene together. Sometimes a leader chose to take what had been a communal group in a different direction, as in the case of the Guru Maharaj Ji, who dissolved the Divine Light Mission, closed its ashrams, renounced his guru status, and became simply a public lecturer. Kerista effectively dissolved (long after the 1960s era) when most of the members disavowed the longtime leadership role of Brother Jud.

External pressure took its toll in quite a few cases. Oz, in Pennsylvania, only survived for a few months before strong pressures from the local authorities finally drove everyone away. Morning Star Ranch made a valiant effort to survive, but the county's bulldozers were relentless. MOVE, in Philadelphia, got the ultimate termination notice when city law enforcement agents bombed its house, killing most of the members present.

More broadly, the tenor of the times changed; the spirit of the 1960s— which engendered community more massively and dramatically than ever before in American history—moved on. The war in Vietnam wound down and the military draft ceased, taking a good deal of wind out of the sails of radical politics. For better or worse, idealism took a beating. The books that guided a generation had once been about rejecting materialism and seeking higher consciousness, but those titles were replaced with new ones about manipulating other people and winning at all costs. Somehow the great promise of the 1960s era and of communal living just didn't make it—not completely, at least. As early as 1971 the eminent counterculturist Stewart Brand, the creator of the *Whole Earth Catalog,* joined Ken Kesey in branding some cherished communal beliefs and propositions the "Commune Lie," shoals on which communes were doomed to founder:

> We'll let other people take care of us.
> We'll let God take care of us.
> Free lunch. (Robert Heinlein)
> The Tragedy of the Commons. (Garret Hardin)
> We'll all be honest.
> We'll all be selfless.
> No rules.
> Possessions are bad. Privacy is bad. Money is bad.
> We've got the answer.[3]

All of the communes did not close, and those who wanted to continue the life (and were worthy of it) could easily do so. For many, though, it was time to leave. As Charles Gruber reflected after leaving the Abode of the Message, "We had come and done what we needed to do. It was time to take all this studying we had been doing and apply it to the outside world. It was time for something different."[4] And anyway, who said that all communities would last forever? Maybe the opposite was true. Rosabeth Moss Kanter noted that the ideologies of most communal groups "say that nothing should be forever, that change is part of life."[5]

The Communal Survivors

Hundreds of communes founded in the 1960s era—not to mention the communal dream itself—are alive and well at the beginning of a new millennium. Several dozen of them are listed in the 1995 *Communities Directory*,[6] along with quite a few more founded before 1965; although not as many communes exist today as did in the early 1970s, several thousand of them still do operate in the United States—more, almost certainly, than at any time in American history other than the 1960s era. Thus, the 1960s-era surge of community has had a lasting impact.

Like the reasons for communal closure, the "why" of communal survival could be debated endlessly. Each case has its own explanation. Many revised their operations to reflect changing circumstances and maturing perspectives on community and through change managed to prosper. Some of the spiritual communes had specific, focusing beliefs and practices that remain in place today, the community operating much as it did a quarter-century ago. Many of the secular communities have become somewhat decentralized (if they were not so earlier), giving members a good, sustainable mixture of freedom and togetherness. Quite a few of them have moved from fully collective ownership of land and buildings to a land trust situation in which individuals have their own homes but the underlying land is held in common and new members still must be approved by the community as a whole. Hugh Gardner, in his 1978 investigation of what made communes survive or die, concludes that close sharing, "supposedly the essence of what communes are all about," actually tended to shorten communal life spans, and that "the level of sharing typically diminished over time if the group survived. In essence, modern communards were always individualists more than communalists."[7] Jim Fowler of Libre opined in 1996 that his community's robust survival has to do first and foremost with the fact that from the beginning it gave members a lot of space: "We have respect for individual family privacy. We're not in each other's face twenty-four hours a day."[8]

The Farm, in Tennessee, once the largest of the 1960s-era communes, survived its radical restructuring and depopulation in the 1980s and has since settled into a comfortable ongoing existence that looks likely to endure for a long time to come. It has survived, Albert Bates believed, because of a "willingness to work it out. We've been through pretty hard times together. There's a certain amount of sentimentality toward seeing it succeed. That, coupled with skills gained over twenty-five years, working out different forms of consensus building and interaction and conflict resolution, makes the formula for keeping it going."⁹ Most of the two hundred or so current residents of the Farm profess to retain their old 1960s ideals, and indeed the good works continue, with the Farm's social service foundation Plenty, various projects promoting environmentalism and sustainable ecovillage living, and a public-interest law firm still going strong. Farm members continue to spread their ideals by publishing books, delivering babies, distributing vegetarian foods—and operating a dyeworks that still produces the most flamboyant tie-dyed t-shirts on the planet. The 1960s era meshes well with the 1990s at the Farm.

Similarly strong in continuing their ideals are the half-dozen or so communities that make up the Federation of Egalitarian Communities, the flagship of which is Twin Oaks, still thriving with about one hundred members in Virginia. The Federation communities still pool all income, strive for true equality for all adults, and live simply and cheaply. They all avoid or downplay competitiveness, acquisitiveness, and television. Turnover tends to be high, but new seekers of community always seem to be ready to fill the vacancies. Twin Oaks has had a good deal of construction activity in the 1990s, as has its offshoot community Acorn. Ganas, an associate member of the Federation, recently bought a large old hotel in the Catskills for a retreat and conference center. Egalitarian community is doing well.

The Sojourners Community in Washington, D.C., still publishes its magazine, provides services to the poor and homeless, and generally continues to challenge liberals and conservatives alike with its evangelical Protestant faith and progressive political activism. Membership has been small in recent years, but the ongoing core members are devout in their commitment to their faith-driven agenda.

The Hog Farm has changed but is as alive as it was when it achieved overnight fame as the Please Force at Woodstock. No longer do its members live on buses and travel endlessly; now they mainly live in a large house in Berkeley and at Black Oak Ranch, their extensive spread three hours north of the city. Members pursue all kinds of private occupations. Wavy Gravy, ever the clown, still presides over Camp Winnarainbow every summer at Black Oak, and the charitable works continue, especially through Seva, the Hog Farm organization that fights blindness in poor countries. The Hog Farmers may be aging and becoming more sedentary, but the old vision is largely intact.

And so the stories go. Most members of the communes that have survived the 1960s era are content and glad that they chose the way of life they did. The communal presence in America today is larger than many would suspect because communities tend to be quiet, shunning the publicity that was often so disastrous in the early days.[10] In other cases they are not very obvious simply because they have blended so well into their local surroundings that they seem part of the natural landscape, no longer an oddity. Sometimes privacy is assiduously pursued because the old bugaboo, zoning laws, still haunts many a community. Although after all these years the local officials tend to know pretty much what the real situation on a given piece of property is, communes whose very existence is illegal have not forgotten the bulldozers at Morning Star and seek to call as little attention to themselves as possible. Several 60s Communes Project interviewees asked to remain anonymous because they did not want to jeopardize their current communal situations.

On the other hand, a determined minority of ongoing communitarians advertise their way of life quite publicly and even travel the country preaching the gospel of communal living. In the mid-1980s a group of devoted advocates, most of whom had settled into community during the 1960s era, refounded the old Fellowship of Intentional Communities— renaming it slightly as the Fellowship for Intentional Community—and began holding semiannual meetings around the country at which communards could compare notes and seekers of community could meet veteran practitioners of the art. At this writing the FIC is working zealously to promote some old ideals among a new communal generation.

THE FATE OF THE EARTH

Most communal property not still functioning in something like its original fashion is now in private, noncommunal hands. Many of the communities rented (or were given the use of) land or buildings, and the owners went on to use the real estate for other purposes. The dozens of communal houses of the Haight-Ashbury are mostly still there, functioning as private homes and apartments. Many of the rural communes were working (or abandoned) farms before the communards arrived and have reverted to their former status.

Occasionally the sadness of communal decline has given way to a happier ending. Earth People's Park as a concept arose in the wake of the Woodstock festival in 1969, promulgated as a permanent enclave of open land that would forever keep the wonderful Woodstock vibes alive.[11] The land finally secured in 1971 was a 592-acre tract in Vermont, its purchase price having been raised by Hog Farmers and friends through a series of public appeals and benefit events, including a grand party on the land itself in the fall of 1971.[12] Soon forty or fifty settlers were on the land living in the houses, domes, tepees, and log cabins that they had built. The word of open land spread and Earth People's Park experienced what several other open-land communities had seen earlier: among those who chose to stay there were some decidedly unenlightened beings. The land sat very near the Canadian border, making it a natural place for draft resisters to cross, and it attracted less idealistic lawbreakers as well. Over time things went downhill, and eventually "a wedge of biker-junkies" (as cofounder Wavy Gravy called them) muscled out the other residents and began to sell timber off the heavily wooded property for drug money and profit.[13] In September 1990, federal agents raided the premises, finding a good deal of marijuana, a bit of LSD, and a number of weapons.[14] Following the raid the government seized the land pursuant to the drug laws. However, Governor Howard Dean claimed the land for the state of Vermont.[15] With that it became a state park. It has a campground, so once again anyone can stay there—just not indefinitely. Wavy Gravy has pronounced it the best of possible outcomes.[16]

Several communal sites sit in abeyance and may yet revert to collective use. Several members of Packer Corner, for example, live in the farmhouse and in other structures on the land as well as in the surrounding neighborhood, and the property is still owned by the old communards for the common good. Those no longer resident are hardly forgotten; as the current residents say, a lot of persons have refrigerator rights: they can come to visit and open the refrigerator, "and if you can find something, it's yours. That's always been something we wanted to preserve."[17] Community remains subject to revival.

Some communal sites sit empty, as if waiting for a new generation to arrive. In southern Colorado, the domes of Drop City, unmaintained, gradually collapsed—the last enduring to the late 1990s in precarious condition before it was demolished. At Morning Star one can see foundations and remnants of buildings, although on the whole the bulldozers did their job effectively. Few local historical societies seem to have undertaken the preservation of these distinctive memorials of an unusual moment in history.

Michael Duncan, who still lives on the property where Morning Star and Reality operated for a time, was surprised to see several government officials head up his excruciatingly rugged driveway in the early 1990s. It seems they had identified a previously undetected piece of Indian art—a large thunderbird etched into the ground—on his property from a satellite photograph. The story elicited guffaws in Taos for years thereafter. The "art" was actually the outline of the old Reality Construction Company communal building, which was indeed built in the shape of a Native American peyote bird. After the Reality members had left the building quickly deteriorated, and a few years later a new group of communards at Magic Tortoise, a few miles to the north, salvaged Reality's adobe bricks for their own buildings. Their good scrounging job left only the building's outline on the ground. Well, hippies always did admire Indians.

MORTALITY

The 1960s era was the epoch of youth. Never trust anyone over thirty. Mind the generation gap. May you stay forever young.

As things turned out, the clock and the calendar kept turning, and the young generation has reached middle age. Inevitably, death has overtaken some of the 1960s generation and in time will claim a few more.

Several of the surviving communes have cemeteries. The one at the Farm in Tennessee has dozens of graves—quite a few of them the final resting places of babies, because even the best birthing system can't prevent all infant mortality. As Ina May Gaskin reflected, "We bury the person usually the following day. There's no embalming. There's no funeral home. Nobody's really making a profit off it, which means that the energy stays with the community." When a man died, having been preceded in death by his wife, he left funeral instructions that included having the whole community shout, "Hey, Helen, Joe's here!"[18]

The Hog Farm's Black Oak Ranch came with a three-grave cemetery, and several of their own number have been added to it. As Wavy Gravy has intoned at Hog funerals, "Fate is like a kick from a blind camel. If it's a hit, you're dead; if it's a miss you live until you're senile."[19]

Several of the notable figures, including founders, of the 1960s-era communes have thus passed from the scene. In the short time since the 60s Communes Project began, several interviewees have died. Marshall Bloom, a key energizer of Packer Corner Farm, committed suicide not long after he and his comrades settled on the land. Max Finstein, the co-founder and early leading light of New Buffalo, died several years ago, as did Judson Jerome, the communal scholar and cofounder of Downhill Farm. Mitch Snyder, the energetic activist of the Community for Creative Nonviolence, committed suicide in 1990. John Affolter, a lifelong communitarian who founded the May Valley Cooperative Community and the Teramanto Community, died in 1997.

Lou Gottlieb, the prophet of open land at Morning Star Ranch, died very quickly of cancer in July 1996. His old friends are all convinced that in his enlightened way he knew just when to die because by doing it when he did he saved a life. It seems that his son Tony was scheduled to fly to Paris just about then and held a ticket for travel on a TWA 747. When word of his father's impending death reached him he canceled his plans. The plane on which he was to fly exploded just out of Kennedy Airport, killing all aboard. Lou Gottlieb has died; Tony Gottlieb lives.

AGING

Elsewhere many of the ongoing communitarians are planning for retirement. Alpha Farm has revised its work schedule to reduce the load for those over 60 and let them quit required work entirely at 70.[20] At Sandhill Farm some planning for old age was done early on—the young communards planted hundreds of walnut trees that by the time many members reach retirement age should be ready for harvesting.[21] The Mulberry Family upon selling its urban buildings in 1986 put the proceeds into a socially responsible mutual fund; members contemplate the possibility that they may be reunited in retirement some years hence—in a house without stairs.

The most ambitious of the communal retirement plans is Rocinante (alluded to in chapter 5 above). On an acreage adjacent to the Farm, Stephen Gaskin and friends are building a hippie retirement community of small cabins with wheelchair-accessible facilities, including a community building and clinic. They look forward to a happy retirement in the company of their fellow superannuated counterculturists.

Looking Back

Those who lived the communal life have largely fond memories of it all, whether they still live communally or not. Fewer than half a dozen of the hundreds of former commune members contacted by the 60s Communes Project declined to participate in interviews, and overwhelmingly the reaction of those contacted was great enthusiasm for the preservation of what they almost all thought was a high point in American history as well as in their own lives. If nothing else, as Sunny Ridge (Oregon) alumna Shannon Perry remarked, having lived in a 1960s-era commune "makes for some great stories."[22] Although some found it all exhaustingly intense (Robert Houriet called communes "pressure cookers—everything is intensified in a commune"),[23] most also remembered the experience as exhilarating. Don McCoy called his time at Olompali Ranch "a life changing experience and a change for the better and the most colorful time in my life." Dennis Duermeier, who lived in several communal situations, said in 1995, "Everything I am has come out of that experience. Everything I really hold dear and what I consider important, the way I think I should live, really grew out of that experience. There was a feeling that the door was wide open to anyone who came in. There is a certain ineffable beauty when a group situation works. I don't know what else to call it but magic."[24] And the persevering communards have certainly found it all worthwhile; few regret the lives they have chosen. Jim Fowler, who has lived at Libre for just about all of his adult life, notes that while he has never had any kind of financial security, "I feel real wealthy in other ways. Without this I don't feel like I would have had such a gentle life; I don't think my children would be so happy."[25] Jenny Upton of Shannon Farm relishes "the pleasure of knowing my life turned out totally different than my parents or I thought it would be. I was born and bred to marry well, and live comfortably, raising my children and being a supportive wife. And instead I've started a business in somewhat of a man's world and built my own house. I lived in the woods and hauled my water and did all that stuff for a while."[26]

Most 60s Communes Project interviewees were asked whether, in the simplest of terms, the communes in which they had lived had been successes or failures. Surprisingly few said failure, even when their communes had been chaotic, loaded with freeloaders, and short-lived. Just about everyone regarded the time on the commune as a great learning experience, and for that if nothing else it succeeded. Marlene Heck spoke for legions in describing her experience with the Mulberry Family in Virginia:

It sounds trivial and trite, but living with a lot of people I learned about tolerance and saw people in their complexity. I learned to be able to confront people who were doing things I didn't like in a nice way and not to feel that I had to yell at them or that I had to burst into tears to catch their attention. When you live in a group, you find out things don't always run to your satisfaction, and you work on resolving problems and conflicts.[27]

Robert Houriet, who saw as much of the scene as anyone, was less sanguine than some, seeing both success and failure in the communes:

One learns, sometimes, more from one's failures than one does by coasting on one's supposed successes. It's incomplete analysis which looks only at success and does not recognize failure and discontinuity. When communes were great, they were really great, but when they were bad they were really bad. There was a downside to the whole movement that was as low as it was high.[28]

But John Curl of Drop City rejoined, "Since all life has to end in death, I don't think you should consider that a failure. That Drop City lasted as long as it did and did what it did made it very successful, amazingly successful."[29]

The fact that many communes were quite short-lived of itself does not necessarily mean they failed. As two California scholars of communes noted in the early 1970s, the seemingly high "failure" rate for communes was "probably no higher than [that of] other forms of small enterprise."[30] Lucy Horton called Frog Run Farm "a tremendous success" that just "evolved out of existence."[31] After living nearly thirty years at Libre, Dean Fleming concluded: "This has all been a magnificent experiment. Just because some communities didn't last doesn't mean they failed. To me it's the most tremendous success I could imagine. It's about taking responsibility for every detail of your life. What it could mean to anyone else, I don't know. This way of life does attract madness."[32] Human nature tends to let one remember the positive experiences, while the negative ones fade or even become funny. Joyce Gardner found that after moving back to the city from Cold Mountain Farm she came to appreciate the high moments of community that at the time had been obscured by the mundane realities of daily life. In retrospect the shortcomings dwindled, and she finally was able to appreciate things that,

because they were such basic and simple things, were so often overlooked and taken for granted. The way we all worked and lived together without any power or authority structure, simply following our own consciousness of what should be done each day. . . . The way that children are cared for communally, with the men also caring for them, without any stigma about child-rearing being effeminate. . . . And nudity, bodies of all shapes, so readily accepted just as a part of nature. And no power! Only a natural hierarchy of skill, experience, and knowledge.[33]

RIGHT LIVELIHOOD

For the most part the interviewees have a positive attitude toward the communal experience and the whole 1960s era as a grand time to be alive—but they are not mired in nostalgia. They are mostly still trying to work out the better parts of the 1960s vision by being good parents, responsible progressive citizens, and doing work that has social value. One of the most striking overall characteristics of the 60s Communes Project interviewees is that a generation later they are overwhelmingly involved in occupations and activities that Buddhists would call "right livelihood." They are teachers, health care workers, computer workers, artists, monks and nuns, social workers, midwives, organic farmers, health food store employees, small entrepreneurs, and the like. Neither of two physicians that we interviewed were in remunerative practices. The relatively few lawyers were almost all doing public interest and environmental legal work. Avocationally the interviewees were environmental activists, social change activists, writers for progressive publications, and pursuers of personal transformation. Nowhere did we encounter stockbrokers, corporate lawyers, corporate executives, or anyone in full-tilt pursuit of great wealth. Of the relatively few communards who have gone on to careers in business management, some, at least, have been influenced by their 1960s communal heritage; John Schaeffer, for example, founded and built the alternative-energy firm Real Goods as an outgrowth of his communal experiences at Compost College and Rainbow.[34]

Some literature following up on the 1960s era has portrayed many former counterculturists as upwardly mobile professionals who have exchanged their tie-dyes for power suits. Our experience, however, was exactly the opposite. Of course our sample may not be random; we made our contacts mainly by word of mouth (and modem) from the informal networks of current and former communards, and in any event it stands to reason that of all the persons to some degree involved in countercultural activity in the 1960s era, the most deeply dedicated were those who joined communes. They were the ones who tried to live their ideals as fully as possible, and those ideals seem largely not to have vanished. Nor have countervailing lifestyle choices disappeared entirely; a fair number of former communards still indulge themselves in a toke of marijuana now and then, and a few here and there still experiment with various forms of sexual openness.

Others conducting similar followup projects on the 1960s-era communards have confirmed our findings. Howard Lieberman recently tracked the later lives of many former members of communes in southern Vermont: "With some exceptions, the people I have been able to locate, regardless of occupation or economic situation, share a view of the world that is community oriented; looking beyond the merely expedient to something more global. . . . This broader view seems to be a common thread that runs through the lives of all the people I was able to find."[35] Many have carried their 1960s-era values into their later lives in small but important ways. John Neumeister, formerly of Footbridge Farm, was incorporating passive solar features and limited electrical consumption into the modest new house he was building in the woods at the time of his 60s Communes Project interview. Rico Reed, the longtime Tolstoy Farm resident, is involved in efforts to promote environmentalism in politics. His communal experience taught him to live on little money, and "because we didn't waste our money, we were able to afford those trips to state committee meetings, and be involved in the political process of the country."[36] Gene and Jo Ann Bernofsky have never lost the idealistic and artistic zeal that led them to found Drop City, and Gene has become an environmental activist in Montana who makes films about corporate depredations of the state's mountains and forests and rivers. He recently said that "we struggle for survival about half the time, and the rest of the time we try to do important things."[37] Malon Wilkus, formerly of East Wind and the mastermind of that commune's successful nut butter business, now co-manages an employee-owned investment banking firm that helps workers buy out their companies.

Beyond the matter of employment, many report that they grew as persons in their communal experiences. In his autobiography Lou Gottlieb tells the story of a young man who read about Morning Star while in a mental hospital in New York state: "He told me that he packed his bags shortly thereafter and came to Morning Star Ranch. He stayed about six months, got his head together, enrolled at Stanford University in their pre-med curriculum, graduated and went to medical school at Emory University in Atlanta. I scarcely knew he was there."[38]

THE COMMUNES' IMPACT ON THE LARGER SOCIETY

Tens of thousands of communes with hundreds of thousands of members constituted a large social phenomenon—or a small one, when one considers that those who even dabbled in communitarianism constituted a minor fraction of one percent of the American population. They attracted a lot of press attention for a year or two but soon drifted back out of public consciousness. Did they have any real and lasting impact on the larger society?

Many of those interviewed for the 60s Communes Project believe that they did. The communes' impact is hard to separate from the overall impact of the countercultural 1960s era, but they do seem to have made some difference in American life. Perhaps the largest impact has been in American eating habits. Whole and natural foods were scarcely known in the United States in, say, 1960; now natural-food specialty stores can be found everywhere, and the typical commercial supermarket carries quite a few natural foods as well. Foods once thought of as weird hippie fare—yogurt, rice and beans, tofu, whole-grain bread, high-fiber vegetables—are now well recognized as components of a healthy diet. Many of the principal natural food stores had communal origins and are still run cooperatively today. Puget Consumers Co-Op, for example, the large natural food cooperative in the Seattle area, was founded by John Affolter at his intentional community, the May Valley Cooperative.

Health care has also changed as a result of what happened in the 1960s era. Public receptivity to holistic health and to alternative therapies ranging from chiropractic to naturopathy to aromatherapy has expanded enormously since a generation rose up and challenged the world to question received wisdom. Ina May Gaskin has noted that the countercultural—and especially communal—interest in home birth has led to much more humane hospital birthing centers.[39] Some specific healing centers, including several ongoing free clinics, had important roots in 1960s-era culture and in some cases specifically in communes, as in Vermont, where the People's Free Clinic grew out of a health collective that traveled from commune to commune.[40]

The communes of the 1960s era reflected the alternative culture's scorn for centralized authority, and Stewart Brand has argued that that scorn spawned the internet and the personal computer revolution.[41] The era's notions of openness, of inclusiveness, have had a lasting impact in the spiritual world, with the increasing spread of alternative religions (i.e., spiritual paths outside the traditional American mainstream), multiculturalism, and gender liberation. The sexual revolution of the 1960s era seems to have left a permanent legacy of liberalized sexual mores; AIDS has cer-

tainly inhibited the wide-open sexual freedom idealized by counterculturists, but acceptance of sexual activity other than strictly marital heterosex
is widespread in modern life. Even though the political pendulum has
swung in a conservative direction in the later twentieth century, in some
places where the communal presence was strongest a progressive political
presence remains vigorous. Vermont, a major 1960s-era communal magnet, has elected and reelected a professed socialist, Bernie Sanders, to
Congress.

HOW DID THE KIDS FARE?

Were the children at risk in the heyday of the communes? Sometimes
youngsters were not supervised very closely, and in the rural communes,
especially, hazards were everywhere. Many parents were decidedly lax
about discipline. In the end things tended to work out well, however.
Communal children learned some important skills—how to get along
with many others in close proximity, for example—and often became self-
sufficient at an early age. Most parents who raised their children on communes are happy with the ways that their offspring have turned out, and
the children themselves—now solidly into adulthood, of course—tend to
see their time at the commune as having been free and blissful (although
most are not seeking communal living for themselves). As one mother
who raised children at Drop City and Libre later commented, "The kids
turned out to be bright, creative, interesting and full of life. It's almost as
if being exposed to all the wildness back then de-mystified that way of life
for them. They don't seem particularly interested in it now." Her daughter
has gone on to be a doctor and her son a carpenter.[42] Dan Questenberry,
who still lives at Shannon Farm, theorizes that the children who grew up
in the most back-to-the-land primitive families are "the ones that have
grown up and turned into Young Republicans. They weren't about to do
what their parents did."[43]

No one has followed the children of the communes more closely than
Sylvia Anderson, who lived at the Farm in Tennessee for several years as
well as in other communal settings. Eventually settling in northern California in a loose countercultural colony that included several former Farm
members in its number, Anderson stayed connected with the many second-generation Farmers in her neighborhood and across the country,
eventually starting a newsletter, *Whirling Rainbow News,* to help that Farm
generation keep in touch.[44] As she has concluded, "These kids are here to

be world servers, you know, and are a generation of Avatars. I think a lot of them are here to do a lot of good work for the planet and for the species."[45]

Virtually no one interviewed for the 60s Communes Project, including the minority who would not consider living communally again, regretted having gone through the experience. It should not be surprising, then, that quite a few former commune-mates still keep in touch. Sometimes they live near each other, either near the old commune or somewhere else. Venerable loyalties can still be strong; when one of the members of the extensive network of former communitarians in southern Vermont was dying, Verandah Porche and Marty Jezer wrote a single fund-raising letter to the extended old communal family and, as Porche put it, "we raised $8,000 with no effort at all. It was just people considering it a privilege to do something. If there's one legacy from all of this communal stuff, it's the loyalty, that people know each other."[46]

Communal reunions occur from time to time, where possible usually at the old site. An informal memorial gathering for Lou Gottlieb shortly after his death in July 1996 took place in the exquisite redwoods of Morning Star Ranch—property that as far as Gottlieb was concerned forever belonged to God. The Mulberry Family of Richmond, Virginia, sold its communal houses years ago, but members continue to gather for annual reunions elsewhere in the vicinity. Several communes had twenty-fifth-anniversary celebrations in the 1990s. The Family of the Living Arts (formerly Family of the Mystic Arts) in southern Oregon, still going as a community, considers all former residents (now numbering over two hundred) to be members and can attract over one hundred of them to a summer reunion, where old and new members confer about maintaining the land and buildings. That kind of connectedness, by no means unusual, is a lasting commentary on the depth of community that often developed even in communes that seemed unfocused and anarchical.

Some communes, although residentially defunct, still hold onto their archives (or have deposited them in research libraries). Former (sometimes current) members of the Farm, the Mulberry Family, the Renaissance Community, the Family of the Living Arts, and undoubtedly many others have ongoing newsletters. Ramón Sender, the first resident of Morning Star Ranch, now edits a newsletter (in print and electronic versions) for Morning Star and Wheeler's Ranch alumni as well as one for former members of the Bruderhof commune in which he lived briefly in the late 1950s.

GETTING BACK TOGETHER

Most of the communal veterans interviewed for the 60s Communes Project said that they would consider living communally again—under the right conditions. Several mentioned community as an attractive option for retirement. A survey of former 1960s-era communitarians conducted by Angela A. Aidala in the mid-1980s similarly found 12% of them definitely seeking to return to community and 59% open to the possibility—in addition to 8% still (or again) living communally at the time of the survey.[47] In all, 79% were at least interested in giving community another try, a percentage that suggests that the communal experience, at least in retrospect, must have been a rich one for most who lived the life. Of course some would do things a bit differently next time around; many of those who have actively contemplated starting anew in some kind community say that they would prefer some level of private facilities and generally a combination of communal and individual features in their domestic lives. Many of the communities that have been started since the 1960s era have reflected that preference; the land trust communities, in particular, balance commonness and privacy in various ways. One of the most important new developments of the 1980s and 1990s has been cohousing, a modified land-trust arrangement (often urban or suburban) in which members have private homes but high levels of shared other facilities, usually including many meals in common.[48]

Piper Williams, who as the founder of Tolstoy Farm vigorously supported keeping the land open to all, eventually came to believe that unrestricted access was not adequately workable, and his later community, Earth Cycle Farm, was less open. "We should have had our beliefs agreed on, and accepted people who shared those beliefs," he has since said. But such is the fruit of experience. "At the time we didn't really know what would work. It was a revolutionary act to say, This space is open to anybody who thinks they have a better idea and wants to try to work it out.'"[49]

The Ark and the Lighthouse

Most communes in American history have seen themselves as either arks or lighthouses. For those expecting some monumental upheaval—nuclear war, environmental catastrophe, premillennial tribulations—to overwhelm the world, the commune can serve as an ark, a place where the few remnant faithful can gather to try to endure the storm together. For those who see the contemporary world as a moral cesspool, a commune can be a place where one may separate oneself from all the decadence in the larger culture and perhaps raise one's children in a wholesome atmosphere impossible to find in "the world." Arks are by their nature communal, and in any event those who seek to endure the severest of disasters should have more resources at their disposal than a single individual or nuclear family is likely to be able to muster. Many of the communes of the American past have been arks.

The communes of the 1960s era, however, were predominantly of another type. They were lighthouses, edifices built by persons convinced that they had found a better way to live than most people knew. They were demonstration projects that would show the world just how wonderful life could be if only humans would abandon selfishness, greed, and materialism. In many cases the communards did not just happen into some congenial situation; they were out to save the world by forging a whole new way of living. One communard wrote that she and her companions were "people who want to build a new way of life, set up an example of how things will maybe be after the revolution."[50]

The language seems fanciful, but the vision inspired millions, some of whom still work toward the goals articulated in thousands upon thousands of communes. The great communal heyday is over; the dream lingers. Jerry Garcia, musician and communard, years later recalled the great soaring of the communal spirit:

There was a moment when there was a vision; there was a very wonderful vision, see it had to do with everybody acting in good faith, it had to do with everybody behaving right. It was really a moment, it was like a breath there for a moment, it was like an open door, Oooh look, you know . . .[51]

Afterword
Communal Life after 1975

This volume and its predecessor have outlined the story of communal living in the first three-quarters of the twentieth century; what remains is the telling of the story of the remainder of the century. My hope is that soon after century's end I will be able to complete the story begun in these first two volumes. Much gathering of information awaits me, however, and a bit of time to provide some historical perspective also will be needed before that work can be completed, or even properly begun.

Given that the completion of this work is thus several years away, I here include the briefest of notes on the course that American communitarianism has take since 1975.

Continuity. As has been made clear repeatedly in the preceding pages, much of what happened communally between 1960 and 1975 has not run its course. Hundreds of communes founded during that period, and some founded earlier, are very much alive today, as are hundreds founded more recently but on principles (and sometimes in locations) that epitomize the 1960s era. That is the largest component of the ongoing communal story: the same communities and their ideological descendants are still carrying the communal torch. This survey has organized intentional communities loosely by founding date, but it has tracked the stories of individual communes to their ends or present status and thus has included a good deal of information on what happened after 1975.

A right turn. The most distinctive new emphasis in post-1975 community has been what Michael Barkun has called the dark side of community, the growth of communitarianism within the political ultraright in the United States. The 1980s and 1990s have seen a rise in the visibility of antigovernment, antitax, and racist sentiments, and one strand of this rightist ascendancy has been the Christian Identity movement. Simply put, Identity here refers to the belief that Anglo-Saxon and/or other northern European peoples (and not the contemporary Jews) are the true descendants of ancient Israel and as such God's chosen people. Other peoples, the theory has it, are inferior. In practice Identity tends to be a white-supremacy movement, and it has spawned several communes, notably in Idaho and in the Ozarks of Missouri, Arkansas, and Oklahoma. Although the communal adherents of Identity doctrine are not terribly numerous, they have received a good deal of press attention, especially because of their putative connections to certain violent acts (such as the bombing of the federal courthouse in Oklahoma City in 1995) committed by individuals of ultrarightist conviction.

Maturity. The 1960s era saw the flourishing of communes overwhelmingly populated by the young—teenagers, in many cases. More recent communitarianism has ceased to be the domain of the young. Indeed, as we have seen, one of the chief growth areas of communitarianism in recent years has been among persons who have retired or at least are contemplating retirement.

New communities. New religious leaders continue to found communal enclaves; in the post-1975 period Christian groups have almost certainly been the most numerous intentional communities in the United States, and Asian and other religions have continued to establish new communal centers as well. Idealistic secular communities continue to be founded with regularity. The phenomenal explosion of the 1960s era may be over, but communal activity since then has continued at a much higher level than most persons realize.

Resources

The reader who seeks to know more about intentional communities since the 1960s era can readily find a good deal of information, because several individuals and organizations still track the ongoing communal saga. The foremost resource is the *Communities Directory,* the most recent edition of which was published in 1995. This volume lists over five hundred active communities of various statuses (some are new and/or small communities not yet on secure footings; many are older, well established centers of communitarianism); its coverage tends to be stronger on secular communities and weaker on religious groups. Earlier editions have information on yet other communities, some of which endure and some of which do not. The publisher of the *Communities Directory*, the Fellowship for Intentional Community, also publishes *Communities: Journal of Cooperative Living*, a quarterly periodical that contains updates and corrections to *Directory* listings as well as articles on a wide range of topics of interest to communitarians, community-seekers, and scholars of communitarianism. For communes not found in these sources, try consulting the *Encyclopedia of American Religions.*

The principal organization promoting scholarship about intentional communities is the Communal Studies Association (CSA), which maintains its headquarters at the Amana Colonies in Iowa. The CSA publishes a journal, *Communal Societies*, that contains articles on past as well as contemporary communities, and it also publishes a semiannual newsletter. The association's annual meetings, held at historic communal sites, are attended by contemporary communitarians as well as by scholars and historic preservationists. A loosely affiliated organization, the Center for Communal Studies, is headquartered at the University of Southern Indiana and maintains an archive of communal literature.

Many communities, federations of communities, scholarly organizations, and other interested groups and individuals maintain pages on the World Wide Web. Such postings are constantly changing but may usually be reached through standard internet search routines.

The extensive world of Christian communities virtually defies systematic cataloging, but some informal connections exist among many of those communities of believers. A list of 148 Christian communities is included in David Janzen's 1996 book *Fire, Salt, and Peace*. Janzen lists one Hutterite colony; that largest of Christian communal movements now has around four hundred colonies in the United States and Canada with over 40,000 members in all.

None of the lists of communities active after 1975 or of the other resources mentioned above is remotely comprehensive. Thousands of communities are known to be active at this writing, but no single roster contains greatly more than five hundred entries. Many communities do

not publicize themselves because they want to avoid the inundation by curiosity-seekers that afflicted so many 1960s-era communes, because they
want to maintain their spiritual isolation from the corrupt outside world,
because they are in conflict with local land-use and zoning laws—and
probably, in a very few cases, because they have something to hide. The
world of community is marvelously complex; no one can expect to explore it fully.

   In short, a good deal of information on intentional communities since
1975 is already available. My goal is to bring much of it together in my final volume in this series in a few years. In the meantime, these resources
should help those with more immediate curiosity to pursue their interests
in contemporary American communal life.

Appendix
Notes
Selected Bibliography
Index

Appendix
American Communes Active 1960–1975

A complete and accurate list of communities active in the United States in the 1960s era would be impossible to construct. This roster, drawn from various directories of communities, the 60s Communes Project interviews, and other sources, is fragmentary and undoubtedly fraught with errors. It represents, however, the most complete list of 1960s-era communities thus far published. It includes all known groups meeting the definition of intentional community provided at the beginning of this volume, except for the established canonical religious orders of the Catholic, Episcopal, and other similar churches (all of whose histories have generally been well recorded elsewhere) and a very few groups that live in violation of local zoning ordinances and whose identity needs to be protected. It is divided into two parts, one a list of communes founded earlier and still in operation in 1965, and the other a list of communes founded between 1965 and 1975.

Many communes were known by more than one name, either simultaneously or sequentially. This list provides the most frequently used name in the main entry and other names in cross-reference.

Many anonymous, pseudonymous, and nameless communes are not listed here. However, when a street address is known but a name is not, the address is used as a communal name, reflecting the common practice among 1960s communards of naming communities after locations; see, for example, the entry for 345 Michigan (alphabetically at "three") below.

The presence of multiple locations in a citation indicates either a communal movement with more than one location or successive locations for a single commune (including, in some cases, post-1975 locations for communes in operation past that date). Single entries are provided for each of several communal movements with multiple locations, such as the Hutterites and the Bruderhof.

The dates given here are reported opening and closing dates of communities where they are known or conjectured, or dates during which a given community was reported active. Pairs of dates (or a date and a question mark) represent dates of founding and dissolution. A single date (without a hyphen) represents a date or general time period at which a community was reported to be active. Dates reflect the period during which each group practiced communal living, not necessarily its entire period of existence. Where no dates are given, they are unknown.

A few federations of communities and other organizations promoting community living are included on this list; they may not themselves have been communities.

Additions and corrections to this list are welcome. Please send them to Timothy Miller, Department of Religious Studies, University of Kansas, Lawrence, Kansas 66045.

COMMUNES FOUNDED BEFORE 1965,
STILL OPERATING IN 1965

Amana Society
Amana, Iowa
1854–ongoing

Ananda Ashram
Monroe, New York
1964–ongoing

Arden
Arden, Delaware
1900–ongoing

Aum Temple Desert Sanctuary
Newberry Springs, California
1956–?

Bethany Fellowship
Bloomington, Minnesota
1945–ongoing

Bethany Mennonite Brethren Church
Freeman, South Dakota
1953–ongoing

Bhoodan Center of Inquiry.
See Ma-Na-Har
Community

Brotherhood of the White Temple (Shamballa Ashrama)
Sedalia, Colorado
1946–ongoing

Bruderhof
Rifton, New York, and
other locations
1954–ongoing

Bryn Athyn
Bryn Athyn, Pennsylvania
Ca. 1890–ongoing

Bryn Gweled Homesteads
Southampton,
Pennsylvania
1940–ongoing

Camphill Movement
Several locations
1961–ongoing

Cassadaga
Cassadaga, Florida
1894–ongoing

Castalia Foundation
Millbrook, New York
1963–67

Catholic Worker
Various locations
1933–ongoing

Cedar Grove
New Mexico
Ca. 1960–?

Celo Community
Burnsville, North Carolina
1937–ongoing

Children of Light
Dateland, Arizona
1949–ongoing

Christian Homesteading Movement and School
Oxford, New York
1961–?

Christian Patriots Defense League
Illinois, Missouri, West
Virginia
Early 1960s–?

Christ's Church of the Golden Rule
Willits, California
1943–ongoing

Church of God and Saints of Christ
Belleville, Virginia
1901–ongoing

Church of the Golden Rule
San Jose, California
1962–?

Church of the Saviour
Washington, D.C.
1946–ongoing

Circle Pines Center
Delton, Michigan
1938–?

The Colony
Burnt Ranch, California
1940–ongoing

Community Service, Inc.
Yellow Springs, Ohio
1940–ongoing

Co-op Homesteads
Suburban Detroit
Late 1940s–ca. 1978

Davidian Seventh-Day Adventists
Waco, Texas, and other
locations
1930s–ongoing

East-West House
San Francisco, California
Late 1950s–ongoing

Ecumenical Institute. See
Institute of Cultural
Affairs

Emissary Communities
Loveland, Colorado, and
other locations
1939–ongoing

Esoteric Fraternity
Applegate, California
1880s–ongoing

Fairhope
Fairhope, Alabama
1895–ongoing

Father Divine's Peace Mission Movement
New York City; Philadel-
phia, Pennsylvania; and
elsewhere
1920–ongoing

Free Acres
Berkeley Heights, New
Jersey
1909–ongoing

Glen Gardner. See St.
Francis Acres

Gorda Mountain
Gorda, California
1962–68

Gould Farm
Monterey, Massachusetts
1913–ongoing

Green Valley School
Orange City, Florida
1962–?

Heaven City
Harvard, Illinois, and
Mukwonago, Wisconsin
1923–60s

Hilltop Community
Bellevue, Washington
1951–ongoing

Himalayan Academy
Virginia City, Nevada;
Kapaa, Hawaii
1962–ongoing

House of David and Mary's
City of David
Benton Harbor, Michigan
1903–ongoing

Humanitas
Orange City, Florida
Early 1960s–?

Hutterites
South Dakota and
elsewhere
1874–ongoing

ICC
Ann Arbor, Michigan
1937

Institute of Cultural Affairs
(Ecumenical Institute)
Chicago, Illinois, and
other locations
1954–ongoing

International Babaji Yoga
Sangam. See Kriya Babaji
Yoga Sangam

Israelite House of David. See
House of David

The Joseph House
Philadelphia, Pennsylvania
1963–?

Koinonia
Baltimore, Maryland
1951–85

Koinonia Farm
Americus, Georgia
1942–ongoing

Koreshan Unity
Estero, Florida
1894–ca. 1965

Kriya Babaji Yoga Sangam
New York City; Norwalk,
California
1952–?

Krotona
Hollywood and Ojai, Cali-
fornia
1912–ongoing

Latter Day Saints:
Glendenning (Order of
Aaron; Levites)
West Jordan and Murray,
Utah
1956–ongoing

Latter Day Saints: Kilgore
(Zion's Order)
Mansfield, Missouri
1953–ongoing

Latter Day Saints: LeBaron
Various locations
1920s–ongoing

Latter Day Saints: Woolley
(Short Creek)
Colorado City, Arizona
1928–ongoing

Lemurian Fellowship
Ramona, California
1941–ongoing

Levites. See Latter Day
Saints: Glendenning

Lily Dale
Lily Dale, New York
1879–ongoing

Love Valley
Love Valley, North
Carolina
1954–ongoing

MacDowell Colony
New Hampshire
1907–ongoing

Ma-Na-Har Community
(Bhoodan Center of Inquiry)
Oakhurst, California
1953–?

Mary's City of David. See
House of David and
Mary's City of David

Maverick
Woodstock, New York
1904–ongoing

May Valley
Renton, Washington
1957–77

Medway Forest Commune
California
Ca. 1963–?

Melbourne Village
Melbourne, Florida
1947–60s

Mennonite Voluntary
Service
Many communal locations

Merry Pranksters
La Honda, California;
Pleasant Hill, Oregon
1963–69

Millbrook. See Castalia
Foundation

Mohegan Colony
Peekskill, New York
1923–69

Montrose
Montrose, Colorado; Pal-
isades, Colorado
1950–67

New England CNVA Farm
Voluntown, Connecticut
Early 1960s–80s?

Oakknoll Homestead

Olive Branch
Chicago, Illinois
1876–ongoing

Oneida Community
Sherrill, New York
1848–ongoing

Order of Aaron. See Latter
Day Saints: Glendenning

Order of St. Michael
Gary, Indiana; Crown
Point, Indiana
1954–72

Parishfield
Brighton and Detroit,
Michigan
1948–67

Pendle Hill
Wallingford, Pennsylvania

People of the Living God
New Orleans, Louisiana;
McMinnville, Tennessee
Ca. 1950–ongoing

*Polaris Action Farm.
See* New England
CNVA Farm

*Powelton Neighbors
(Powelton Village)*
Philadelphia, Pennsylvania
Early 1970s

Pumpkin Hollow Farm
Craryville, New York
1937–ongoing

Quarry Hill
Rochester, Vermont
1946–ongoing

Ramakrishna Monastery
Orange County, California
1949–ongoing

Reba Place
Evanston, Illinois
1957–ongoing

St. Benedict's Farm
Waelder, Texas
1956–ongoing

St. Francis Acres
Hampton, New Jersey
1947–68

*Salem Mennonite Brethren
Church*
Bridgewater, South
Dakota
1956–?

Savitria
Baltimore, Maryland

*Seventh Elect Church in the
Spiritual Israel*
Ballard, Washington
1917–90s

*Shakers (United Society
of Believers)*
Mount Lebanon, New
York, and other locations
1774–ongoing

Shamballa Ashrama. See
Brotherhood of the White
Temple

Shiloh Community
Chautauqua County, New
York; Sulphur Springs,
Arkansas
1941–ongoing

Short Creek. See Latter Day
Saints: Woolley

Skyview Acres
Pomona, New York
1948–ongoing

*Society for the Preservation of
Early American Standards*
Oxford, New York
1961–?

*Sullivan Institute/Fourth
Wall Community*
New York City
1957–92

Sunrise Ranch. See
Emissary Communities

Sycamore Community
State College,
Pennsylvania
Ca. 1956–?

Synanon
Santa Monica, California;
other locations
1958–91

Tanguy Homesteads
Glen Mills, Pennsylvania
1945–ongoing

Temple of the People
Halcyon, California
1903–ongoing

Tolstoy Farm
Davenport, Washington
1963–ongoing

*United Cooperative
Industries*
Los Angeles and
Wildomar, California
1923–?

*United Society of Believers in
Christ's Second Appearing.
See* Shakers

The Vale
Yellow Springs, Ohio
1959–ongoing

Van Houten Fields
West Nyack, New York
1937–?

Vedanta communities
Various locations
1900–ongoing

Vivekananda Society
Chicago, Illinois
1930–?

*WKFL Fountain of
the World*
San Fernando Valley,
California, and Homer,
Alaska
Late 1940s–80s

Whitehall Co-op
Austin, Texas
1949–?

Woman's Commonwealth
Belton, Texas, and
Washington, D.C.
1879–1983

Yaddo
Upstate New York
1926–ongoing

*Zion Mennonite
Brethren Church*
Dinuba, California
1957–?

Zion's Order. See Latter
Day Saints: Kilgore

COMMUNES FOUNDED 1965–1975

*AAA (Triple A—
Anonymous Artists of
America)*
Huerfano Valley, Colorado
?–ongoing

*AAO (Actions Analysis
Organization)*
Boston and Somerville,
Massachusetts
Mid-1970s

Abba's Way
Oregon
1970s

Abeika
Montgomery, Alabama

Abode of the Message
New Lebanon, New York
1975–ongoing

Acorn (People's Farm)
Browns, Alabama
Mid-1970s

Acorn Hill House
Krumville, New York
1970s

Active Acres Coop
Dodgeville, Wisconsin
Ca. 1971–?

*Adventure Trail Survival
School*
Black Hawk, Colorado
1970

Afterbirth Farm
Champaign/Urbana,
Illinois
1970s

Agape Community
Liberty, Tennessee
1972–?

Agape Fellowship
Chicago, Illinois
1970s

Agape House
Washington, D.C.
Early 1970s

Agape Inn
Eugene, Oregon

Agora Community
St. Paul, Minnesota
Mid-1970s

Ahimsa Community
Parsons, Kansas
Ca. 1965–?

*Alamo Christian
Foundation*
Hollywood and Saugus,
California; Alma, Arkansas
1969–ca. 1994

*Alexander Berkman
Collective Household*
Seattle, Washington
1970s

Aliya Community
Bellingham, Washington
1975–?

Alleluia
Augusta, Georgia
1970s–90s?

Aloe Community
Cedar Grove, North
Carolina
1974–ca. 1979

Aloha
Honolulu, Hawaii

Alpha Farm
Deadwood, Oregon
1972–ongoing

Alta
Northern Oregon
Ca. late 1960s

Alternative Community
New Haven, Connecticut
Mid-1970s

*Alternative Futures
commune*
San Francisco, California
Ca. 1970–?

Alternative Lifestyles
Minneapolis, Minnesota
1972–?

Alternatives, NW
Oroville, California
1972–?

Alton Farm
Iowa

Amazing Grace Family
Evanston, Illinois
Mid-1970s

American Landuist Society
Southern California
Ca. 1970

American Playground
Washington, D.C.
Late 1960s

Amitabha Ashram
Kansas
1967–69

Ananda Marga
Denver, Colorado, and
other cities
1969–ongoing

*Ananda World
Brotherhood Village*
Nevada City, California
1968–ongoing

Anaphia Farm
West Virginia

Ancient Builders. See
Builders

Andorra II
Daly City, California
1971–?

Anima. See Bass Creek
Commune

Animal Farm
Northern California

*Anonymous Artists of
America. See* AAA

Another Place
Greenville, New
Hampshire

Ansaaru Allah Community
(later *Nuwambian Nation
of Moors*)
Brooklyn, New York;
Eatonton, Georgia
1973–ongoing

Ant Farm
Berkeley/Sausalito
Early 1970s–?

Ant Farm
Space City, Texas
Ca. 1970

Antioch Farm
Mendocino, California

Any Day Now
Philadelphia, Pennsylvania
Ca. 1970–?

Apocalypse Farms
Walden, Vermont
1971–?

Appalshop
Whitesburg, Kentucky
Mid-1970s

Appletree/Appletree Co-op
Boulder, Colorado; Cot-
tage Grove, Oregon
1974–?

Apple Tree Acres
Blowing Rock, North
Carolina
1973–?

Apple Tree Canyon
Sonoma County,
California
Ca. 1970–?

Aquarian Foundation
Seattle, Washington

*Aquarian Research
Foundation*
Philadelphia, Pennsylvania
1969–?

Aquarius Project
Berkeley, California

Arcata House
Arcata, California
Late 1960s

L'Arche Erie
Erie, Pennsylvania
1972–?

L'Arche Syracuse
Syracuse, New York
1974–?

Archuletaville
Redwing, Colorado
1970s?

Arcology Circle
San Francisco, California
Mid-1970s

Arcosanti
Mayer, Arizona
1970–ongoing

Areopagus
Santa Barbara, California
Early 1970s

Arica Institute
Several locations
Late 1960s?

The Ark. See Free State of
the Ark

Ark (Hearthstone Village)
Springfield, Massachusetts
Mid-1970s

Arrakis
Jeffersonville, New York
Early 1970s

Arunachala Ashram
New York City
1966–ongoing

Aryan Nations
Hayden Lake, Idaho
1973–ongoing

Ashburnham
Brookline, Massachusetts

The Assembly
Goshen, Indiana
1974–?

Association for Social Design
Boston, Massachusetts
Ca. 1970–?

Association of Communes
Philadelphia, Pennsylvania
Early 1970s?

Atkins Bay Farm
Phippsburg, Maine
1970–?

*Atlanta Community
(Atlanta Avenue)*
Atlanta, Georgia
1970s

Atlantis
Oregon

Atlantis I
Saugerties, New York
Ca. 1970–?

Atmaniketan Ashram
Pomona, California; Lodi,
California
1972–?

Aum. See Holiday Commune

Aurora Glory Alice commune
San Francisco, California
Late 1960s?

Austin Community Fellowship
Chicago, Illinois
1973–early 1980s

Avenanda Ashram
New York State

Babaji Yoga Sangam
Norwalk, California
Mid-1970s

The Backbench
Philadelphia, Pennsylvania
Ca. 1970–?

Bad Manners
Lawrence, Kansas
Early 1970s

Badhi Manda
Jemez Mountains, New
Mexico
1974–?

Bahai House
Colorado

Bailey Farm Community
Winona, Minnesota
Mid-1970s

Balanced Life Center
Davisburg, Michigan
1970–?

The Banana Patch
Maui, Hawaii
Late 1960s

Bandidos
Taos/Penasco, New
Mexico, area

Barkmill Hollow Commune
Airville, Pennsylvania
Mid-1970s

Bartimaeus Community
Berkeley, California
Late 1960s–?

Bass Creek Commune
Stevensville, Montana
1968–?

Basta Ya House
St. Louis, Missouri

Batavia Community
Batavia, Ohio
Mid-1970s

Bayland Family
Campbell, California
1972–?

Beacon Hill Free School
Boston, Massachusetts
Mid-1970s

The Bead Game
New York City; Lost
Nation, Vermont
1960s

Beansprout
Cambridge, Massachusetts
Mid-1970s

Bear Tribe
Sacramento, California
Mid-1970s

Bear Tribe
Reno, Nevada
Early 1970s

Bear Tribe
Harriman, New York

Bear Tribe Medicine Society
Spokane, Washington
1970–ongoing

Beaumont Foundation
La Puente, California
Ca. 1970

Beaver Run Farm
Bedford, Pennsylvania
Mid-1970s

Bee Farm
Ashland, Oregon
Mid-1970s

Bees Land
Northern California

Beit Ephraim Chavurah
New York City
Ca. 1973–?

Belly of the Whale
Princeton, Illinois
Early 1970s–?

Benton Farm. See Lyman
Family

Berachah Farm
Petaluma, California
Early 1970s–?

Berachah House
San Anselmo, California
Early 1970s

Beraiah House
Costa Mesa, California
Early 1970s

Berkeley Poets Commune
Berkeley, California
Mid-1970s

Berkeley Tenants Union
Berkeley, California
Late 1960s

Berkeley Tribe commune
Berkeley, California
Early 1970s

Beth El
Oregon
1970s

Beth-El Village
Alpena, Michigan
Mid-1970s

Bibs Family
Vermont

Bierer House
New York City
Early 1970s

Big Foot
Mendocino County, California

Big Gray Community
Brooklyn, New York
1975–95

Big House East
Lawrence, Kansas
Early 1970s

Big Island Creek Folks
Pipestem, West Virginia
Early 1970s

Big Springs Farm
Cheney, Washington
1970s

Big Wheels Ranch
Montgomery, California
1971–?

Biotechnia. See Synergia Ranch

Birdsfoot Farm
Canton, New York
1972–ongoing

Black Bear Ranch
Forks of Salmon,
California
1968–ongoing

Black Flag
New Hampshire
Early 1970s

Black Oak Ranch. See also
Hog Farm
Laytonville, California
1982–ongoing

Blocks Farm
Cottage Grove, Oregon
Ca. 1970

Blood Kin of Christ.
See Sons and Daughters of Jesus

Blue Fairyland
Berkeley, California?
Ca. 1970–72

Blue Gargoyle
Chicago, Illinois
1970s–90s?

Blue Mountain Ranch
[pseud.]. See Black Bear Ranch

Blue River
Virginia
1974–?

Blue Sky Vegetarian
Commune
Allison Park, Pennsylvania
Mid-1970s

Blue Star
Deadwood, Oregon
1970s

Blue Stream Community
Boston, Massachusetts,
area
Ca. 1970–?

Bodega Pastures
Bodega, California
Ca. 1971–ongoing

Body of Christ
Various locations
Ca. 1970–ongoing

Bonsilene
New Haven, Connecticut
Mid-1970s

Borsodi Homestead
Smithville, Oklahoma
1967

H. Bosch Farm
Pedro, West Virginia
Early 1970s

Boston Commune
Boston, Massachusetts
1974

Brandywine Community
Land Trust
Olympia, Washington
Late 1970s

Bread and Roses
Philadelphia, Pennsylvania

Bread Tree
Philadelphia, Pennsylvania

Breadloaf
New Mexico

Briceland Cafe and
Truck Stop
Briceland, California

The Bridge
Newton, Kansas
Mid-1970s

Bridge Mountain
Ben Lomond, California
Mid-1960s–?

Brills' commune
Boston, Massachusetts,
area
Early 1970s

Brook
Charlottesville, Virginia
Mid-1970s

Brook House
West Charleston, Vermont
Early 1970s

Brooklyn Commune
Brooklyn, New York

Brotherhood Family
Oregon

Brotherhood of Eternal Love
Laguna Beach, California
1966

Brotherhood of the Spirit. See
Renaissance Community

Brotherhood of the Sun.
See Builders

Brotherhood of the Way
Fairfax, California
Mid-1970s

Brownville Artist Colony
Republic, Washington
1968–?

Brush Brook Family
Oregon
Early 1970s

Bryn Athyn
South Strafford, Vermont
1967–69

Buddhist Association of the USA
Bronx, New York

Builders
Santa Barbara, California;
Oasis, Nevada
1969–ongoing

Busey St. Commune
Urbana, Illinois
1970–73

Butler Hill
Monroe, Oregon

Butternut Farm
Western Oregon
Early 1970s

Butterworth Farm (Octagon House; The Octagon)
Orange, Massachusetts
1973–?

Cabbage Lane
Wolf Creek, Oregon
1972–?

Calabash Farm
Southern Vermont

Cambridge Commune (Lewd Family)
Cambridge, Massachusetts
Ca. 1970–?

Cambridge Cooperative Club
Cambridge, Massachusetts
Mid-1970s

Camp Joy
Boulder Creek, California
Ca. 1971–?

Camphill Village USA
Kimberton, Pennsylvania
1972–ongoing

Campus Improvement Association. See CIA House

Canaan Farm
Canaan, New York

Canaan on the Desert
Phoenix, Arizona
Early 1970s–ongoing

Candy Ass House
Seattle, Washington

Canyon
Canyon, California

Carl Street House
San Francisco, California

La Casa Grande Colectiva
Urbana, Illinois
1970–?

The Castle
Minneapolis, Minnesota
Early 1970s

Cat City
Cleveland, Ohio
Early 1970s

The Catacombs
Chicago, Illinois
Early 1970s

Cathedral of the Spirit. See Renaissance Community

Catholic Resistance
Washington, D.C.
Late 1960s–?

Cat's Cradle
Oregon

Cave Hill
California

CaveCampKids Commune
Williams, Oregon

Cedar Bend
Aripeka, Florida
Late 1960s–?

Cedarwood/Cedarwood Technical Center
Louisa, Virginia
Mid-1970s

Celebration of Life Community
Jackson, Mississippi

Celebration of Life Community, See Laos

The Center
Criglersville, Virginia
1971

Center for Christian Renewal
Washington, D.C.
Late 1960s

Center for Ecological Living
Pacheco, California
Ca. 1971–?

Center for Family Experimentation
San Jose, California
Mid-1970s

Center for Feeling Therapy
Los Angeles, California
1971–80

Center for Living
Phoenicia, New York
Late 1960s

Center for Peace and Life Studies
Muncie, Indiana
1972?

Center for the Examined Life (Center for Psychological Revolution)
San Diego, California
1966–?

Center for the Living Force. See Pathwork Phoenicia

Center for the Next Step
San Diego, California
Mid-1970s

Centers for Change
New York City
Mid-1970s

Cerro Gordo
Cottage Grove, Oregon
1973–ongoing

Changes
Chicago, Illinois
Mid-1970s

Chapel Hill Fellowship
Chapel Hill, North
Carolina

Chardavogne Barn
Warwick, New York

Chavurat Aviv
Cleveland, Ohio
Ca. 1973–?

*Chelsea Commune (New
Learning Community)*
New York City
1968–?

Chestnut Hill
Washington, D.C.
1970s

Chicago Religious House
Chicago, Illinois
1968–?

Chilaway House.
See Job Chiloway House

Children Kansas
Florence, Kansas
1972

*Children of God
(The Family)*
Many locations
1968–ongoing

Children of God Soul Clinic
Jesus movement

*Children of the Valley
of Life*
Eugene, Oregon
1973

China Grade
Big Basin, California
Ca. 1968–?

Chinook Learning Center
Clinton, Washington
1972–ongoing

The Chosen Family
New Mexico
Late 1960s/early 1970s

Christ Brotherhood
Eugene, Oregon
1969–?

Christ Community
Grand Rapids, Michigan
1973–1990

Christ Family
Hemet, California; mobile
1960s–ongoing

*Christ of the Hills
Monastery*
San Antonio, Texas
1972–ongoing

*Christananda Adl Shakti
Ashram*
San Jose, California
Mid-1970s

Christian Brotherhood
Omaha, Nebraska
Early 1970s

*Christian Conservative
Community*
Early 1970s

Christian House
Vacaville, California
Early 1970s

Christian House
Athens, Ohio
Early 1970s

*Christian World
Liberation Front*
Berkeley, California

Christ's Household of Faith
St. Paul, Minnesota
1970s–ongoing

Chrysalis Community
Helmsburg, Indiana

Chuckanut Drive
Blanchard, Washington

Church of Isla Vista
Santa Barbara, California
1969–?

Church of the Creative
Creswell, Oregon

Church of the Divine Birth
Harrisburg, Pennsylvania
Mid-1970s

Church of the Earth
Sonoma County,
California
1972–?

*Church of the Five Star
Ranch. See* Five Star

*Church of the Living
Word—Shiloh*
Kalona, Iowa
Late 1960s

Church of the Messiah
Detroit, Michigan
Late 1960s–?

*Church of the Northern
Lights*
Homer, Alaska

Church of the Redeemer
Houston, Texas
Late 1960s–late 1970s

Church of the Servant King
Gardena, California
Ca. 1969–?

*Church of Unlimited
Devotion (Spinners)*
Sonoma County,
California

Church Street
New York City

*CIA House (Campus
Improvement Association)*
Lawrence, Kansas
Late 1960s

Circle of Friends
North Carolina
1973–?

City Island Commune
Bronx, New York

City of Light
San Francisco; Santa Fe,
New Mexico
Late 1960s–?

City of Love
Fairfax County, Virginia
Late 1960s–?

Clan Pax (Peace Tribe)
Chicago, Illinois
1970

Clayton House
San Francisco, California
Early 1970s

Cleveland Jesus Center
Cleveland, Ohio
Early 1970s

Clinton Farm
Lawrence, Kansas
1970s

Clinton Street Commune
Brooklyn, New York
1970

Clivenden House Club
Philadelphia, Pennsylvania
1971–

Close Farm
Meadville, Pennsylvania
1970

Cloverdale
Cloverdale, California

Coagulators
Eugene, Oregon
Mid-1970s

Cold Comfort Farm
Olympia, Washington
Ca. 1973–?

Cold Mountain Farm
Hobart, New York
1967–68

Colorado Avenue House
Boston, Massachusetts,
area
Early 1970s

Common Choice community
Peoria, Illinois
Mid-1970s

Common Circle
Lake Forest, Illinois
1971–?

Common Roads 721
1971

The Commune
East Palo Alto, California
1966–?

The Commune
Brooklyn, New York
1972–76

Commune Association
Philadelphia, Pennsylvania
Early 1970s

Commune-occasion.
See U-Lab II

Communitarian Village
Oroville, California
Mid-1970s

Communitas
Yellow Springs, Ohio
Early 1970

The Community
Arlington, Virginia
1966–?

The Community
Pacific Northwest

Community Association
Lake Dorena, Oregon
Mid-1970s

Community Covenant
Church. See Covenant
Community Church

Community Design
Institute
Denver, Colorado
1971–?

Community for Creative
Nonviolence
Washington, D.C.
1970–ongoing

Community for Urban
Encounter
Chicago, Illinois
1969–?

Community of Communities
Late 1960s–early 1970s

Community of Jesus
Orleans, Massachusetts
1970–ongoing

Community of the Simple
Life. See Starcross
Monastery

Community of Zen
Sharon Springs, New York
Mid-1970s

Community X
Saginaw, Michigan
Ca. 1970

Compost College
Boonville, California
Early 1970s

Concord
Snowflake, Arizona
Mid-1970s

Consciousness Village
(Campbell Hot Springs)
Sierraville, California
1974–?

Contemporary Mission
St. Louis, Missouri
1968–?

Coomb's Farm
Troy, Maine

Cooperative College
Community
Cambridge, Massachusetts
1975–?

Cooperative Humanist
Society
Madison, Wisconsin
1970

COPS Commune (Commit-
tee on Public Safety)
Berkeley, California
Late 1960s

Cornucopia. See Vision
Foundation

Cosmic Circle
California
Late 1960s

Country Women
Albion, California
Mid-1970s

Covenant Community
Church
Missoula, Montana
Late 1960s

Crabapple
Florence, Oregon
1975–?

Crabapple Corners
New Hampshire
Early 1970s

Crook's Creek
Sunny Valley, Oregon
1969–?

The Crossing
Philadelphia, Pennsylvania
Mid-1970s

Cro Research Organization
(CRO Farm)
Veneta, Oregon
Ca. 1966–early 1970s

Cumbres
New Hampshire
1969–71

Cummington Community
of the Arts
Cummington,
Massachusetts
Mid-1970s

Cushing Street
Boston, Massachusetts,
area
Early 1970s

Cynergia
Cerrillos, New Mexico
Early 1970s

Daddy Dave's Love
Commune
Colorado or New Mexico

Dandelion Collective
Syracuse, New York

Dandelion Hill
Newfield, New York
Mid-1970s

Dawes Hill Commune
West Danby, New York
Mid-1970s

Dawn Horse Communion
Middletown, California
Mid-1970s

Dayspring
(Four Chimneys Farm)
Himrod, New York
1975–?

Daystar
Various locations
Mid-1970s

Daytop Lodge
New York State

DeCloud Family
Kansas City, Missouri

Deep River Community
Deep River, Washington
Ca. 1971–?

Deep Run Farm
York, Pennsylvania
1975

Democratic Revolution in
(or Republic of) Vermont.
See Packer Corner

Denver Space Center
Colorado
Mid-1970s

Derby House
Berkeley, California

Desiderata
Texas
1975–ongoing

Dharma Masa
Stone County, Arkansas
1970s–?

Diakonia Farm/Diakonia
Partners
Barnstead, Maine
1972–?

Dietrich Bonhoeffer House
Chicago, Illinois
Early 1970s–?

Diggers
San Francisco, California
1966–?

Dinky Universal Church
Stanford, California
Mid-1970s

Dionysian Society
Durham, New Hampshire
Ca. 1971–?

Disciples of Thunder
Elko, California

Divine Information Center
Tampa, Florida
Mid-1970s

Divine Light Mission
Denver, Colorado, and
other locations
Early 1970s–80s

Divine Right
Early 1970s

DOE Farm (Daughters of
the Earth)
Norwalk, Wisconsin
Mid-1970s

Dog Town
West Oakland, California
Late 1960s–?

Dome House
LaConner, Washington

The Domes
Placitas, New Mexico
Late 1960s

Dorje Khyung Dzong
Farisita, Colorado
1973–ongoing

Downhill Farm
Hancock, Maryland
1971–79

Dragon Eye
Berkeley, California

Dragonwagon
Ava, Missouri
Ca. 1974–?

The Dreamers
Vermont

Drop City
Trinidad, Colorado
1965–73

Drop South
Placitas, New Mexico
Late 1960s–?

Dulusum Farm
Salwaka Valley area,
Oregon

Dunes Beach
Oxnard, California

Dunmire Hollow
Waynesboro, Tennessee
1974–ongoing

Dunrovin

Earth, Air, Fire and Water
Franklin, Vermont

*Earth Cycle Farm (Earth
Cyclers; Waukon Institute)*
Edwall, Washington
1975–ongoing

Earth Family Farm
Gardner, Colorado

Earth Home
Oregon

Earth House
Providence, Rhode Island
Early 1970s

*Earth/Life Defense
Commune*
California

Earth People's Park
Norton, Vermont
Early 1970s–ca. 1993

Earthmind
Saugus, California
Mid-1970s

Earth's Rising Coop
Monroe, Oregon
1970–?

Earthward Bound
New Haven, Kentucky
Ca. 1975–?

Earthwonder Farm
Blue Eye, Missouri
Mid-1970s

Earthworks
Franklin, Vermont
1970–74

Earthworm
Champaign, Illinois
Mid-1970s

East Hill Farm. See
Rochester Folk Art Guild

East Ridge Community
Callicoon, New York
Late 1960s–?

*East River Community
(East River Farm)*
Guilford, Connecticut
Mid-1970s–?

East Street Gallery
Grinnell, Iowa

East Wind
Jamaica Plain,
Massachusetts
Mid-1970s

East Wind
Tecumseh, Missouri
1973–ongoing

The Eater Family
Coquille, Oregon
Early 1970s

EC2
Kalamazoo, Michigan
Ca. 1970

Eckankar
Las Vegas, Nevada
Mid-1970s

*Ecumenical Monks.
See* Christ of the Hills
Monastery

Eden West. See Genesis

Edge City
Missouri Ozarks
Ca. 1974–?

El Centro
Santa Fe, New Mexico
Early 1970

El Shaddai House
Bellaire, Texas
Early 1970s

Elfhome
New Hampshire
Early 1970s

Elixer Farm
1970s

Ellis Island
Los Angeles, California
Mid-1970s–ongoing

Emerald City
Chicago, Illinois
Mid-1970s

Emmanuel Farm
Sumas, Washington

Emmaus House
New York City

Empire Lakes Trip
Oregon

Enchanted House
San Francisco, California

Encones
New Mexico, near the
Hog Farm
Late 1960s–?

Encounter Ranch
Grass Valley, California
Early 1970s–?

Entitas
Reno, Nevada
Mid-1970s

Entropy Acres
Barton, Vermont

Entwood
Jamesville, Ohio
1972–?

Equitable Farm
Little River, California
Early 1970s–?

Esalen Institute
Big Sur, California

Essene Community
Grand Rapids, Michigan
Early 1970s–?

*Ethiopian Zion Coptic
Church*
Star Island, Florida

Ethos
Little Rock, Arkansas
Early 1970s–?

Evenstar
Oregon coast

Everything for Everybody
New York City
Mid-1970s

Exchange
715 Ashbury, San Francisco, California
1970

Expanded Family
New York City
Late 1960s–?

Experimental Cities
Mid-1970s–?

Fairview Mennonite House
Wichita, Kansas
1971–?

The Family
Chicago, Illinois, and Los Angeles, California
Late 1960s/early 1970s–?

The Family
Taos, New Mexico
Ca. 1967–?

The Family
Ithaca, New York

The Family
Bronx, New York
1968

The Family
New York City
Ca. 1970

Family Circus
San Francisco, California
Ca. 1971–?

Family Dog commune
San Francisco, California
Late 1960s–?

Family Farm
Barboursville, Virginia
Early 1970s–?

Family of Christ. See Sons
and Daughters of Jesus

Family of Friends
North Bergen, New Jersey
1974

*Family of Full Measure.
See* The Family (Taos)

A Family of Peace
Philadelphia, Pennsylvania
1969

*Family of the Living Arts.
See* Family of the Mystic
Arts

Family of the Mystic Arts
Sunny Valley, Oregon
1970

Family of the Three Lights
Skagit County,
Washington
1969–71

*The Family Possession of
Great Measures. See* The
Family (Taos)

Family Synergy
Los Angeles, California
1971–?

Family Tree
Dallas, Texas
Ca. 1971–?

The Fanatic Family
Cave Junction, Oregon

Far Valley Farm. See
Helpless Farm

Farallones Institute
Occidental, California
1976

Fare-the-Well Center
Huntington,
Massachusetts
1974–?

Farkle Farm
Warrington, Pennsylvania
Ca. 1970–?

The Farm
Lawrence, Kansas

The Farm
Wawa, Minnesota

The Farm
Summertown, Tennessee;
branches in Fulton, Missouri; Canaan, New York;
Bitely, Michigan; Wisconsin; Texas; Florida
1971–ongoing (all branches
defunct)

The Farm
Takilma, Oregon

Farm Coop
Natchitoches, Louisiana
1976

Farming Commune
San Bernardino, California
1970

Fayerweather
Freeport, Maine
1976

FBS
Charlottesville, Virginia
1975

Feathersfield Farm
Albany, Georgia
1976

*Federation of Communities
in Service*
Knoxville, Tennessee, and
other locations
1970

Fellowship Community
Spring Valley, New York
1967

Fellowship House
Chicago, Illinois
Early 1970s

Fellowship House
Philadelphia, Pennsylvania

Fellowship House and Farm
Philadelphia and
Pottstown, Pennsylvania
Early 1970s

Fellowship of Believers
Silver Spring, Maryland
1960s–?

Fellowship of Friends
Dobbins, California
1972

Fellowship of Hope
Elkhart, Indiana
1971–?

Felton Guild
Felton, California
1970–?

Ferry Sisters
(Ferry Street House)
Eugene, Oregon
1969–?

Fertile Hills Community
Chapel Hill, North
Carolina
1974

Fiddler's Choice
Franklin, New Hampshire
1972

The Finders
Washington, D.C.
Ca. 1970–ongoing

Firehouse Theatre People
and Friends Home
St. Paul, Minnesota
1970

First Baptist Church
Chula Vista, California
1974

First Street Fellowship
Louisville, Kentucky
1976

Five Star (Church of the
Five Star Ranch)
Ranchos de Taos, New
Mexico
1967–ca. 1970

507 Atlanta Avenue
Atlanta, Georgia
1971–?

Flatrock Community
Tennessee?

Floating Lotus Opera
Company
Berkeley, California

Floyd's Big House
Lawrence, Kansas
Early 1970s

Fly Away Home
Oregon
Mid-1970s

Flying Frog Farm
Bowling Green, Kentucky
1972–?

Folly Farm
Grande Ronde, Oregon
Mid-1970s

Footbridge Farm
West of Eugene, Oregon

Forgotten Works
Wolf Creek, Oregon

Fort Greene Commune
Brooklyn, New York
1970

Fort Hill Community.
See Lyman Family

Fort Hill Faggots
for Freedom
Roxbury, Massachusetts
1969–ongoing

Fort Mudge
Dexter, Oregon
Ca. 1967–?

4711 Warrington
Philadelphia, Pennsylvania
Ca. 1970–?

Foundation of Revelation.
See Siva Kalpa

The Foundlings
Eastern Iowa

Four Chimneys Farm.
See Dayspring

Four Winds Farm
Hood River, Oregon
1974–ongoing

Four Winds Village
Tiger, Georgia
1969–ongoing?

Franciscan Fraternity
Chicago, Illinois
Mid-1970s

Franklin Commune. See
Earthworks

Fraternité Blanche
Los Angeles, California
Mid-1970s

Free Farm
Putney, Vermont
Early 1970s

Free Growth Farm
Rock Camp, West Virginia
Mid-1970s

Free State of the Ark
Stowe, Vermont
1974

Free Vermont
Putney, Vermont
1972

Freefolk
Pennington, Minnesota
Ca. 1968–70

Freshwater
Lovingston, Virginia
1975–?

Friends of Perfection. See
Kaliflower

Friends Southwest Center
McNeal, Arizona
1974–?

Friendship House
Boise, Idaho
Mid-1970s

Frog Run Farm
East Charleston, Vermont
Mid-1970s

Frogge Hollow
Andover, Ohio
1968–72?

Full Circle Farm
Bronson, Michigan
Mid-1970s

Full Circle Farm
Beavertown, Pennsylvania
Early 1970s–?

Furies Collective

Furry Freak Brothers
Taos, New Mexico, area

G. Gregory Foundation
Hicksville, Long Island,
New York
Ca. 1972–?

Gabriel's House. See
Raphael's House

Galahad's (crash pad)
New York State

Galaxy K Commune
St. Petersburg, Florida
Early 1970s

Garberville House
Garberville, California

Garden of Joy Blues
Birch Tree, Missouri
1972–?

Tim Gardiner (or Gardner)
Des Moines, Iowa
1969–?

Gate 5
Sausalito, California
1970

Gates of Heaven.
See Godsland

The Gathering
Schuyler, Virginia
1969–?

The Gemeinschaft Group
Harrisonburg, Virginia
1973–?

Genesis (Eden West)
Southern California
Early 1970s

Genesis 1:29
Cleveland, Ohio

Georgeville Trading Post
Georgeville, Minnesota
Ca. 1969–?

Gesundheit/Gesundheit
Institute
Hillsboro, West Virginia
1971–ongoing

Girls' House
Early 1970s

Gita Nagari Village
(ISKCON Farm)
Port Royal, Pennsylvania
1975–ongoing

The Glorified Hamburger

Goat Farm
Eugene, Oregon
Early 1970s

God's Army
Kerman, California
Ca. 1968–76

God's Valley. See Padanaram

Godsland (Gates of Heaven)
Kettle, Kentucky
1972–?

Good Earth Commune
Southern Oregon
1971

Good Earth Communes
San Francisco, California
Early 1970s–?

Good Earth Homestead
Dobbins, California
1972–?

Good Times Commune
(GTC)
Berkeley, California
1969–?

Goodlife Community.
See Harrad West

Gopherville
Humboldt County,
California

Gorg Family
Keaau, Hawaii
Mid-1970s

Gospel Outreach
Eureka, California
1971–?

Grady Street House
Athens, Georgia
1970s

Grailville Community
Loveland, Ohio
Mid-1970s

Grand Street Aristocrats
New York City
Late 1960s

Graniteville Commune
Graniteville,
Massachusetts
Mid-1970s

Grant Street House
1514 Grant, Berkeley,
California
Ca. 1968–?

Grasmere
Rhinebeck, New York
Ca. 1973–?

Grassroots Collective
Syracuse, New York
1973–?

Grateful Dead commune
710 Ashbury, San Francis-
co, California
1960s

Grateful Union-Earth
Guild
Cambridge, Massachusetts
Mid-1970s

Green Gulch Farm
Marin County, California
1972–ongoing

Green Mountain Red
Franklin, Vermont

Green Tower Community
Altura, Minnesota
1972–?

*Green Valley School
(Humanitas)*
Orange City, Florida
Early 1970s

Greenbriar
Elgin, Texas
1969–ongoing

Greenbrook Road
Boston, Massachusetts,
area
1972

Greenfeel
Barre, Vermont
Ca. 1969–71

Greenfield Ranch
Mendocino County,
California
Ca. 1972–ongoing

Greenhouse
Goleta, California
Mid-1970s

Greenhouse
Lawrence, Kansas

Greening Life Community
Shermans Dale,
Pennsylvania
1972–?

The Grotto
Rolla, Missouri
1970s?

The Group, Inc.
St. Louis, Missouri
Early 1970s?

The Grove

Grove Groovers
Plaistow, New Hampshire
Mid-1970s

The Guild. See Felton
Guild

The Guild of Colorado

Hacienda Canyon
Forestville, California
Late 1960s–?

*Hamilton Street Resistance
House*
Philadelphia, Pennsylvania
Ca. 1970–?

Hamse Community
Stewart, Ohio
Mid-1970s

Happening House
San Francisco, California
Late 1960s

Happy Hollow
Bay area, California

*Happy Sun Rhubarb
Trucking Farm*
Evansville, Minnesota
Early 1970s

*Harbin Hot Springs
(Harbin; Harbinger; Heart
Consciousness Church)*
Middletown, California
1971–ongoing

Harbinger. See Harbin
Hot Springs

Harbingers Commune
San Francisco (Haight-
Ashbury)
Late 1960s

Hardscrabble Hill
Orland, Maine
Mid-1970s

*Hargobind Sadan Ashram.
See* Spiritual Community,
Inc.

Harmony
San Bernardino, California
Early 1970s

Harmony Heart community
Williams, Oregon
Mid-1970s

Harmony House
Seattle, Washington
Ca. 1971–?

Harmony Ranch
Oxford, Connecticut
Early 1970s

Harrad
Arlington, Massachusetts

Harrad
Venice, California
1970

Harrad Community
San Francisco, California
1969–?

Harrad L.A.
Los Angeles, California
1970

*Harrad West (later Goodlife
Community)*
Berkeley, California
1969–?

Harvest House
San Francisco, California
Ca. early 1970s

Harwood House
Oakland, California
Mid-1970s

Haskell House
Lawrence, Kansas
Ca. 1975–78

Havurat Shalom
Somerville, Massachusetts
1968

Head
Minneapolis, Minnesota

Healing Arts Family
Madrid, New Mexico
Mid-1970s

Healing Waters
Eden, Arizona
1970s

*Healthy-Happy-Holy
Organization. See* 3HO
New Mexico

Heart
Kenmore, Washington
(Seattle area)
1960s

Heart Consciousness Church.
See Harbin Hot Springs

Hearthshire
Covelo, California
1967–ongoing

Hearthstone Village. See Ark

Heathcote Center
Freeland, Maryland
1965–ongoing

Heaven's Gate
Various locations
Ca. 1972–97

Heerbrook Farm
Community
Lancaster, Pennsylvania
Mid-1970s

Heifer Hill
West Brattleboro,
Vermont
1974–?

Helpless Farm (later known
as Far Valley Farm)
Southeastern Ohio
Ca. 1970

Here and Now. See One
World Family

Hickory Farms
Whitmore Lake, Michigan
1975–?

Hickory Hill
Tallahassee, Florida
1970s

Hickory Hill
Tappan, New York
1970

Hidden Springs
Rockmart, Georgia
Mid-1970s

Hidden Springs
South Acworth, New
Hampshire
Late 1960s–ca. 1972

High House
Philadelphia, Pennsylvania
1970

High Ridge Farm
Southern Oregon
1968–?

High Top Commune
Virginia
1969–?

High Valley Farm
High Valley, Washington
1971–mid-1990s

Highland Center.
See Rabbity Hill
Farm/Highland Center

Highland Community
(Highlander School)
Paradox, New York
Early 1970s–?

Hill House Foundation
for Centering
Charlemont,
Massachusetts
Early 1970s

Himalayan Institute
Honesdale, Pennsylvania
1971–ongoing

Hippocrates Health Institute
Boston, Massachusetts
Early 1970s

His House
Indianapolis, Indiana
Early 1970s

Hoedads
Mobile, Pacific Northwest
Tree planting

Hog Farm
Sunland, California;
Llano, New Mexico;
Berkeley, California
1965–ongoing

Hogg Farm Community
New York City
1970

Hogwild
Rutherfordton, North
Carolina
1974–early 1980s

Hohm Community
Tabor, New Jersey;
Prescott Valley, Arizona
1975–ongoing

Hoka-Hey
Redway, California

Holiday Commune (Aum,
Om)
Ben Lomond, California
Ca. 1967

Holy Earth
California
Ca. early 1970s

Holy Order of MANS
San Francisco, California,
and other places
Early 1960s–ongoing

HOME
Maine

The Homestead
New Hampshire

Hong Kong West 1/2
Way House
Northern California
Early 1970s

Hop Brook Commune
Amherst, Massachusetts
Mid-1970s

Hosanna House
Eugene, Oregon
Early 1970s

Hoskins
Mt. Sterling, Kentucky
1970

The House
Oakland, California
1972–?

House of Acts
Novato, California
1967–?

House of David
Seattle, Washington
Late 1960s–?

House of Dawn
Early 1970s

House of Elijah
Yakima, Washington
1970s

House of Esther
Seattle, Washington
Early 1970s

House of Immanuel
Sumas, Washington
Early 1970s

House of Joshua
Early 1970s

House of Joy
Portland, Oregon
Early 1970s

House of Judah
Atlanta, Georgia

House of Judah
Grand Junction, Michigan
1971–ongoing

House of Lavendar
(Lavendar House)
Milwaukee, Wisconsin
1968–ongoing

House of Life
Buffalo, New York
Early 1970s

House of Love and Prayer
San Francisco, California
Early 1970s–?

House of Miracles
Costa Mesa, California
Ca. 1968

House of Peace
Albuquerque, New
Mexico
Early 1970s

House of Prayer
Pontiac, Michigan
Early 1970s

House of Rebekah
Early 1970s

House of Ruth
Early 1970s

House of the Risen Son
Chicago, Illinois
Early 1970s

House of the Risen Son
Eugene, Oregon
Late 1960s

House of the Seventh Angel
Nevada City, California
Ca. 1968–69

Huckle Duckleberry
Sandpoint, Idaho

The Huggs Family
Pownal Center, Vermont
Early 1970s

The Human Dancing
Company
Ashland, Oregon
1967–?

Humanitas. See Green
Valley School

Humble Bottom
Santa Rosa, California
1970

Hunger Farm
Monterey, Massachusetts
Early 1970s

Hungry Hill
Creswell, Oregon
Ca. 1970–?

Hunter's Lodge
Troy, Virginia
1973–?

Hurrle
Manhattan, Kansas
1970

Hyde Park Friendship
House
Boise, Idaho
Mid-1970s

IAMU Community Farm
Elizabethtown, New York
Ca. 1970–?

IC
Seattle, Washington
1970

Ilarne
Crockett, California
Mid-1970s

IM. See Iris Mountain

In Search of Truth (ISOT)
Santa Cruz and Canby,
California
1969–ongoing

Indian Camp
Leslie, Arkansas
Early 1970s

Ingleside
Cincinnati, Ohio
Mid-1970s

Inner Life Fellowship
Community
Cambridge, Wisconsin
Mid-1970s

Innisfree Village
Crozet, Virginia
1971–ongoing

Insane Liberation Front
Long Beach, California
Ca. 1975–?

Insight Meditation Center
Barre, Vermont
1975–ongoing

Institute for Environmental
Activities
Lake Samish, Washington
Ca. 1972–?

Institute Mountain West
Denver, Colorado
Mid-1970s

Institute of Eco-Technics
San Francisco and Oak-
land, California

Institute of Human Abilities. See Morehouse communes

Intentional Family
Stillwater, New Jersey
1974–?

The Interaction Center
Washington, D.C.
1971–?

International Center for Self-Analysis
North Syracuse, New York; Rochester, New York
Early 1970s

International Community of Christ
Reno, Nevada

International Ideal City
Boonville, California
Early 1970s

International Society for Krishna Consciousness
Various locations
1966–ongoing

Invitation Center
Anna Maria, Florida
Mid-1970s

Iris Mountain (IM)
Unger, West Virginia
Early 1970s–?

Isla Vista Demystification Collective
Goleta, California
Ca. 1971–?

Island
Providence, Rhode Island
Early 1970s–?

Island Earth
Clinton, Washington
1972

Island of the Red Hood Commune
West Virginia
Ca. 1968–?

Island Pond Community. See Messianic Communities

ISOT. See In Search of Truth

Israel Family. See Love Israel

Ithaca Project
Ithaca, New York
1972–?

Ithilien
Sheridan, Oregon
Mid-1970s–ongoing

J'Ananda
Elk, California
Mid-1970s

J. C. Light and Power Company
Los Angeles, California
Early 1970s

Jawbone Flats (The Mines)
Mehama, Oregon

Jeremiah Family of Christ

Jesus Christ Light and Power Company
Los Angeles, California

Jesus Name Lighthouse
Loleta, California
1970–?

Jesus People Army
Seattle, Washington

Jesus People USA
Chicago, Illinois
1974–ongoing

Jewish Socialist Community
New York City
Mid-1970s

Job Chiloway House
Philadelphia, Pennsylvania
Early 1970s

Johnson Pasture
Guilford, Vermont
Ca. 1970–?

Johnston Center for Individualized Learning

Jonah House
Baltimore, Maryland
Mid-1970s

Jordan River Farm
Huntly, Virginia

Joshua Tree
Philadelphia, Pennsylvania

Journey Family
New York City
Mid-1970s

Jubilee Brotherhood
Colorado Springs, Colorado
Mid-1970s

Jubilee House
Oregon
1970s–?

Julian Woods
Julian, Pennsylvania
Ca. 1973

Jump Off Joe
Sunny Valley, Oregon

Jupiter Hollow
Weston, West Virginia
1970s–ongoing

Kahumana Farm and Community
Waianae, Hawaii
1974–?

Kailas Shugendo
San Francisco, California
Mid-1970s

Kaliflower
San Francisco, California

K'an Ts'ui Ferro-cement Boat Building commune
Bellingham, Washington
1975–?

Karma Dzong
Boulder, Colorado
1972–ongoing

Karma Farm
Madison, Wisconsin?

Karme-Choling. See Tail of
the Tiger

Karmu
Cambridge, Massachusetts
1972

Karum Group, Inc.
Bellingham, Washington
Mid-1970s

Katharsis
Nevada City, California
1974–?

Kauchema Community
Colorado mountains
1971–?

KDNA commune
St. Louis, Missouri
1970s

Kearney Street
Manhattan, Kansas
Ca. 1970–?

Kelly Road House
Whatcom County,
Washington
Late 1960s

Ken Keyes Center. See
Vision Foundation

Kerensa Co-Op Community
Menlo Park, California
Mid-1970s

Kerguelen Isles
College Park, Maryland
1970

Kerista
San Francisco, California
1971–ongoing

Keystone
Carrolton, Georgia
Early 1970s

Kibbutz Micah
Pennsylvania
1972–?

Kingdom of Heaven
Guadalupita, New Mexico
Ca. 1970

KIRK
Garvin, Minnesota
1972

Kittamaqundi Community
Columbia, Maryland
Mid-1970s

Koinonia Community
Santa Cruz, California
Early 1970s

Kripalu Yoga Ashram
Sumneytown,
Pennsylvania
1972–ongoing

Krishna
Siskiyou County,
California

Kuntree Bumpkin
Whitmore Lake, Michigan
1975–?

La Jolla
Truchas, New Mexico

Laetare Partners
Rockford, Illinois
1970–?

Lake Village
Kalamazoo, Michigan
1971–ongoing

Lama Foundation
San Cristobal, New
Mexico
1967–ongoing

The Land
New Hampshire

The Land at Sabina's
Mendocino, California

Land of Oz. See Oz

Landlovers
Portland, Oregon
Mid-1970s

Laos
Washington, D.C.
Ca. 1970–?

Laramie Street
Manhattan, Kansas
Ca. 1970

L'Arche communities. See
L'Arche under A

Last Chance
Davenport, California

Last Ditch Homestead
Pass Creek, Huerfano Val-
ley, Colorado

The Last Resort
Taos, New Mexico, area
Late 1960s

Laughing Coyote Mountain
Black Hawk, Colorado
1970

Lavender Hill
Ithaca, New York

Law Commune
Palo Alto, California
Early 1970s

Law Commune
New York City
1970

Law Commune of Flym
Geller Miller and Taylor
Cambridge,
Massachusetts
Mid-1970s

Law Commune of Haroz
Katz Rockwell and Faber
Cambridge,
Massachusetts
Mid-1970s

League for Community
Berkeley, California
1967

Leicester Commune
Kenmore, New York
Ca. 1971–?

Leslie Community/
Leslie Folks
Leslie, Arkansas
Mid-1970s

Lewd Family. See Cambridge Commune

Leyden Society
Western Massachusetts

Liberty Hall

Liberty House
Jackson, Mississippi
1970

Liberty House
New York City
1969

Libre
Gardner, Colorado
1968–ongoing

Lichen
Wolf Creek, Oregon
1971–ongoing

Life Center Association. See
Philadelphia Life Center

Lifestyle Associates
Ellicott City, Maryland
Mid-1970s

Light Morning
Virginia
1974–ongoing

Light of the Mountains
Leicester, North Carolina
Mid-1970s

Lighter Side of Darkness
House
Springfield, Illinois
Early 1970s

Lighthouse Christian
Ranch. See Jesus Name
Lighthouse

Lila
El Rito, New Mexico
Ca. 1969

Limekiln Creek
Big Sur, California, area
Ca. 1967

Limesaddle
Oroville, California
Early 1970s–?

Linda Vista
Oracle, Arizona
1968–?

Lindisfarne Assn.
Southampton, New York
Mid-1970s

L.I.O.N. Community
Tampa, Florida
Early 1970s

Little River House
Little River, California
Early 1970s

Living Communion
Association
Cloverdale, California
Mid-1970s

Living Love Center.
See Vision Foundation

Living Springs
Southern Oregon
Ca. 1970

Lonaku
San Francisco (rural), California
Early 1970s–?

Long Branch Environmental Education Center
North Carolina
1974–?

Long Cliff People's Collective
Sunnybrook, Kentucky
1975–?

Long John's Valley
New Mexico

Long Leaf
Melrose, Florida
Mid-1970s

Longreach
Cloverdale, California
Late 1960s–?

Lookout Farm
Napanoch, New York

Lorian Foundation
Belmont, California
Mid-1970s

Lorien
El Rito, New Mexico
1969

Lorillard Children's School

Love
Highland, New York
Early 1970s

Love Inn
Freeville, New York
Early 1970s

Love Israel
Seattle and Arlington,
Washington
1968–ongoing

Love Story Commune
Terre Haute, Indiana
Mid-1970s

Lower Farm
Placitas, New Mexico
1970s

Lunasi
Columbia Cross Roads,
Pennsylvania
1974–ongoing

Lyman Family (Fort Hill Community, Benton Farm)
Boston, Massachusetts;
Frankfort, Kansas; other
locations
1966–ongoing

The Lynch Family
California
1960s/70s

Lyons Valley Cooperative
Talmage, California

McAllister Street commune
San Francisco, California

Maccabee Farm
Louisa, Virginia
Mid-1970s

MacCauley Farm
Lopez Island, Washington
Ca. 1974–92

McGee Street House
2611 McGee, Berkeley,
California
Ca. 1968

Mad Brook Farm
East Charleston, Vermont

Madhave Family
Longmont, Colorado
Mid-1970s

Madison Community Coop
Madison, Wisconsin
1968–?

Madre Grande
Dulzura, California
1975–ongoing

Maggie's Farm
Portland, Oregon
Ca. 1968–?

Magic Animal Farm
Naturita, Colorado
1971–?

Magic Bus
Oregon

Magic Forest Farm
Takilma, Oregon
Early 1970s

Magic Land
St. Petersburg, Florida
Early 1970s

Magic Mountain
Seattle, Washington
Late 1960s–?

Magic Mountain Farm
Cave Junction, Oregon
1970

Magic Tortoise
Taos, New Mexico, area
Late 1960s–?

Maharaj Ashram
Santa Fe, New Mexico
1969–71

Main Street Gathering
Portland, Oregon
Mid-1970s

Maitri
Connecticut
1974–?

Makepeace Colony
Stephens Point, Wisconsin
Early 1970s

Malachite Farm
Gardner, Colorado

Mama Keefer's Boarding House
Eugene, Oregon

Manera Nueva
Taos, New Mexico, area

Manifest Sons
Portland, Oregon
Early 1970s

Mann Ranch
Ukiah, California
Early 1970s

The Manor
Upstate New York
1973

Mansion Messiah
Costa Mesa, California
Early 1970s

Manson Family
Topanga, California, and
other locations
Late 1960s

Many Commune
Cambridge, Massachusetts
1970

Many Hands
Ann Arbor, Michigan
Mid-1970s

Maple Hill commune
Vermont

Maple Street Household
Evanston, Illinois
1973–74

Maple Tree Farm
Lanesville, New York
Early 1970s

Maranatha House
San Jose, California
Early 1970s

Maranatha House
Washington, D.C.
Early 1970s

Marblemount Outlaws
Washington State
Early 1970s

Marengo House
Pasadena, California

Marion Mennonite Brethren Church
Hillsboro, Kansas
Mid-1970s

Mariposa School/ Community
Ukiah, California
Ca. 1970–?

Martha's Housing Cooperative
Madison, Wisconsin
1970s

Martindale
Brookville, Maryland
1970–ca. 1975

The Master's House
Lansing, Michigan
Early 1970s

Matagiri Sri Aurobindo Center
Mt. Tremper, New York
Mid-1970s

Maui Zendo
Maui, Hawaii
1969–80s

Maya
Mendocino County, California

Maya Commune
(Maya House)
Coconut Grove, Florida
Early 1970s

Mayday Farm
Guilford, Vermont
1970–?

Meadowlark Farm (Mead-
owlark Healing Center)
Hemet, California
Late 1960s–?

The Meadows
Mendocino, California

The Meadows
Takilma, Oregon
1970s–ongoing

Medical Opera
Bay area, California;
Huerfano Valley, Colorado

The Meeting
Minneapolis, Minnesota
Early 1970s

Meeting School
Rindge, New Hampshire
Early 1970s

Memphis Fellowship
Mid-1970s

Mendocino Farm and
Folk School
Sebastopol, California
Mid-1970s

Messiah's World Crusade.
See One World Family

Messianic Communities
Island Pond, Vermont,
and other locations
Ca. 1972–ongoing

Meta Tantay
Carlin, Nevada

Metelica Aquarian Concept.
See Renaissance Community

Mettanokit
Greenville, New Hampshire
Early 1970s–?

Miccosukee Land Co-Op
Tallahassee, Florida
1973–ongoing

Michael's Family
Taos, New Mexico, area
1969

Midwest Collective
Chicago, Illinois
Mid-1970s

The Milk Farm

Milkweed Hill
Vermont

Mimbres Hot Springs Ranch
San Lorenzo, New Mexico
1970s–ongoing

Mime Troupe
San Francisco, California

The Mines. See Jawbone
Flats

Mineral Hot Springs
San Luis Valley, Colorado

The Mining Claim
Southern Oregon

Minnesota Commune
Minneapolis, Minnesota
1971–?

Mirkwood
West of Eugene, Oregon
Ca. 1970–?

Mississippi House
St. Louis, Missouri

Mist Mountain Farm
Mist, Oregon
Mid-1970s

Mizpah Brethren
Frances, Washington
1970s–?

Moieté
Seattle, Washington, area
1971–?

Mon Nid

Mon Repose

Monan's Rill
Santa Rosa, California
1973–?

Monarchy of Christiania
Santa Barbara, California
1970–?

Moneysunk Farm

Montague Farm
Montague, Massachusetts
1968–?

Moon Garden
Oregon
Early 1970s

More Institute
Los Angeles, California
1974

Morehouse (or More House)
communes
California and other
locations
Ca. 1967–?

Moriah
Northern New Mexico
Early 1970s

Morning Glory Community
Arnold, Missouri

Morning Star Community
New York City
Mid-1970s

Morning Star East
Taos, New Mexico
1969–72

Morning Star North
Sand Point, Idaho
Ca. 1974

Morning Star Ranch
Occidental, California
1966–73

Morning Town Pizza Parlor
Seattle, Washington
1969–early 1980s

Morningside
Birmingham, Alabama
Mid-1970s

Morningside House
Arlington, Massachusetts
1967–68

Morningstar Family
Smartville, California
Mid-1970s

Morningstar Ranch
Kihei, Maui, Hawaii
Mid-1970s

Mother of God
Gaithersburg, Maryland
1970s

The Motherlode
Oregon

Mt. Philo
Ferrisburg, Vermont
Early 1970s

Mountain Family
Oroville, California
1970s–ongoing

Mountain Grove
Glendale, Oregon
1969–?

Mountain Wolf
Northern California

Move
Philadelphia, Pennsylvania
1971–ongoing

Movement for a New Society.
See Philadelphia Life
Center

Moxie
Pittsburgh, Pennsylvania,
area

Mu Farm
Yoncalla, Oregon
Early 1970s–?

Mud Farm
Eugene, Oregon
1974–80

The Mud People
New Orleans, Louisiana
Early 1970s

Mulberry Family (Mulberry
Group, Inc.)
Richmond, Virginia
1972–80s

Mulberry Farm/School
Pettigrew, Arkansas
Early 1970s–?

Mullein Hill
West Glover, Vermont
Mid-1970s

Mushroom Farm
California
Early 1970s

Mustard Seed
Lawrence, Kansas
Early 1970s

Mystical Christian
Community
1971

Namaste Farm
Sandpoint, Idaho
Mid-1970s

Narrow Ridge and the
Community Market
Voluntown, Connecticut;
Newaygo, Michigan
Ca. 1967–?

Nasalam
Duvall, Washington
1969–?

Naturalism
Chicago, Illinois
Ca. 1970–?

Naturalism
Los Angeles, California
Mid-1970s

Nature Farm
Putney, Vermont

Nearing farm
Vermont

Nethers Community
and School
Woodville, Virginia
Ca. 1972–77

Neverland Commune
Menlo Park, California
1970

New Adult Community
San Diego, California
1970

New Age Farm

New Alchemy West
Pescadero, California
Mid-1970s

New Beginnings
Community
Dutton, Arkansas
Mid-1970s

New Buffalo
Arroyo Hondo, New
Mexico
1967–ca. 1996

New City
Maine

New Community Project
Cambridge/Boston, Mass-
achusetts
Early 1970s–?

New Community School
Coburn, Pennsylvania
1972

New Covenant Fellowship
Athens, Ohio
1972–ongoing

New Creation Fellowship
Newton, Kansas
1971–?

New Dawn
Willits, California

New Education Foundation.
See Mountain Grove

*New England Committee
for Nonviolent Action
(CNVA) Farm*
Voluntown, Connecticut
1962–72

New Hamburger
Plainfield, Vermont
Ca. 1970–ongoing

New Harmony Homestead.
See Freefolk

New Jerusalem Community
Cincinnati
1971–?

New Learning Community.
See Chelsea Commune

New Life
Philadelphia, Pennsylvania
1970s

New Life Community
California
Ca. 1972–?

New Life Cooperative
Kalamazoo, Michigan
1972

New Life Farm
Ozarks

New Slant
Chappaqua, New York
Early 1970s

New Swarthmoor
Clinton, New York

New Utopia Commune
Northern San Diego
County
1971

Newsreel commune
San Francisco, California;
Washington, D.C.; New
York State
Late 1960s–?

1957 Biltmore St., NW
Washington, D.C.
Late 1960s

Noah's Ark
Harrison, Maine
Late 1960s–?

Nomads
Santa Monica, California
Mid-1970s

Nordeca
Bellingham, Massachusetts
1970

Norn House

*North Mountain
Community*
Lexington, Virginia
1972–?

Northeon Forest
Easton, Pennsylvania;
Tucson, Arizona
1975–?

Northern Lights
Oregon

*Northridge Christian
Fellowship*
Springfield, Ohio
Mid-1970s

Now House
Northern California

Nyingma Institute
Berkeley, California
1973–ongoing

Oak Valley Herb Farm
Camptonville, California
Mid-1970s

Oakwood Farm
Bethel, Missouri

Obiji Farm
Lawrence, Kansas
Early 1970s–ongoing

Ocean Spring House
North of Seattle,
Washington

Octagon House.
See Butterworth Farm

Odiyan
Sonoma County,
California
1975–ongoing

*The O'Haile Mountain
Family*
Woodstock, New York
1972

Ohana Aloha Village
Waimanalo, Hawaii
Early 1970s–?

Ohmega Salvage
Berkeley, California
1975–?

Old Day Creek Commune
Skagit County,
Washington

Old McCauley Farm. See
MacCauley Farm

Old Phoenix Gold Mine
Cave Creek, Arizona
1970

Old Solar Farm
Oxford, Connecticut
1970s

Olema
Olema, California

Olompali Ranch
Novato, California
1967–69

Om. See Holiday

Om Foundation
Carmel, California
Mid-1970s

Om Shanti
Mendocino County,
California

Omega House
Sioux Falls, South Dakota
Early 1970s–?

Omen
Tucson, Arizona
1970

One Life Family
Santa Monica, California
1974–?

One World Family
San Francisco, Berkeley,
and Santa Rosa, California
1968–ongoing

Oneida II
West Mifflin, Pennsylvania
Early 1970s

Onion Farm
Oregon
Ca. 1970

Open
Seattle, Washington
Mid-1970s

Open Door Community
Atlanta, Georgia
Late 1960s

Open End
Marin County, California
1971–?

Open House Community
Lake Charles, Louisiana
1971–?

Open Space
New Hope, Pennsylvania
Mid-1970s

Open Way
Seattle, Washington, area
1971–?

Oquitadas Farm
Northern New Mexico
1972–?

Oracle House
San Francisco, California
Early 1970s

Orange House
Oroville, California

Order of St. Michael
Crown Point, Indiana
Early 1970s

Oregon Extension
Lincoln, Oregon
1975–?

Oregon Family
Oregon
1972

Oregon Women's Land
Trust
Roseburg, Oregon
1975–?

Orphalese Foundation
Denver, Colorado
Early 1970s

Ortiviz Ranch
Huerfano Valley, Colorado

The Outpost
Minnesota?
Early 1970s

OWL Farm/Oregon
Woman's Land
Roseburg, Oregon
1975–?

Oyotunji Village
Sheldon, South Carolina
1970–ongoing

Oz
Harmonsburg, Pennsylva-
nia
1968

Pacific High School
Santa Cruz Mountains,
California
1969–?

Packer Corner Farm (Total
Loss Farm)
Guilford, Vermont
1968–ongoing

The Pad
Ithaca, New York

Padanaram Settlement
Williams, Indiana
1966–ongoing

Padma Jong
Dos Rios, California
1974–ongoing

Padma Ling
Berkeley, California
1971–ongoing

Pah⁺na
Topanga, California
Ca. 1971–?

Pahana Town Forum
Cottage Grove, Oregon
1972–?

Pahania
Santa Barbara, California
Early 1970s

Panther Mountain
Commune
Shandaken, New York
1970

Paradise Ranch
Southwestern U.S.

Park Place Commune
Brooklyn, New York
1969

Parker Farm
West Townshend,
Vermont
Early 1970s

Passage Farm
Seven Foundations,
Virginia
Mid-1970s

PASS, Inc.
San Francisco, California
Mid-1970s

Pastures. See Bodega
Pastures

Pathwork Phoenicia (Center
for the Living Force)
Phoenicia, New York
1972–?

Pea Pod. See Dome House

Peace Action Farm
Stanfordville, New York
Early 1970s

Peace, Bread, and
Land Band
Seattle, Washington
1972

Peace Farm
Carson County, Texas

Peace House
Pasadena, California
1969

Peacemakers Community
Costa Mesa, California
1967–?

Peach House
Pasadena, California
1970

Peking Man House
Oakland, California
Early 1970s

People
Allston, Massachusetts
Mid-1970s

People's Architecture
Berkeley, California
Early 1970s

People's Christian Coalition
Deerfield, Illinois
Mid-1970s

People's Farm
Browns, Alabama
Mid-1970s

People's Information Center
Brooklyn, New York
1971

Peoples Temple
Redwood Valley, Califor-
nia; Jonestown, Guyana
Early 1970s–78

Pepperland
Hillsborough, New
Hampshire
1972

Perserverance Furthers
Berkeley, California
Early 1970s

Pest House
New Hampshire

Peter Gray's Valley
Taos, New Mexico, area

Philadelphia Fellowship
Philadelphia, Pennsylvania
Mid-1970s

Philadelphia Life Center
Philadelphia, Pennsylvania
1971–ongoing

Phoenix Family
Taos, New Mexico, area
Ca. 1970–?

Pie in the Sky
Marshville, Vermont
1970s

Pig Farm
Colorado

Pigs and Fishes
California; Colorado

Pine Terrace Nine
New York City
1972–?

Pinebrook Community
Wayne, Pennsylvania

The Pit
Seattle, Washington
1972–73

Pitt River Tribal Council
Bieber, California
Mid-1970s

Placitas
Placitas, New Mexico
Late 1960s

Plate Rock Ranch
Northern California

Pleasant House
Boulder, Colorado
Late 1960s

Plow Creek Fellowship
Tiskilwa, Illinois
1971–ongoing

Plowshare Collective
South Minneapolis,
Minnesota
Mid-1970s

Polaris Action Farm. See
New England Committee
for Nonviolent Action
Farm

Pomo Tierra
Yorkville, California
Late 1960s–ongoing

Port Chicago Vigil
San Francisco, California
1970

Portland Group
Portland, Oregon
Early 1970s

Portola Institute
Menlo Park, California
Late 1960s–early 1970s

Poseidon
San Francisco, California

Post-American Community
Deerfield, Illinois
1971

The Pottery
Penrose, Colorado

Prag House
Seattle, Washington
1972–ongoing

Pragtree
Arlington, Washington
1972–ongoing

Prairie Dog Village. See
Gopherville

Prajna Family
Ojai, California
1972–?

*Prema Dharmasala and
Fellowship Association*
Bedford, Virginia
Mid-1970s

Pretty Boy Floyd Associates.
See Montague Farm

Pride Family
California/mobile

*Primal Scream Radical
Ministry*
Brookline, Massachusetts
1972

Princeton commune
Princeton, New Jersey
Ca. 1972

*Process Church of the Final
Judgment*
Various locations
1966–74

Project Artaud
San Francisco, California
1969–?

Project One
San Francisco, California
Ca. 1971–late 1980s?

Project Place
Boston, Massachusetts

Project Two
San Francisco, California
1972–?

Providence Hammock
Florida Everglades

Providence Zen Center
Providence and Cumber-
land, Rhode Island
1972–ongoing

Prudence Crandall House
California
1972–?

Psychedelic Sheep Ranch
Hesston, Kansas
Late 1960s

Pulsa
Early 1970s

Purple Rose. See U-Lab II

Putney commune
Putney, Vermont
Ca. 1970

Pygmy Farm
Buena Vista, Colorado

Quaker Commune
Brooklyn, New York
1970

*Quaker Resistance House.
See* Any Day Now

Queenschapel House
Hyattsville, Maryland
1975

Questers
Cathedral City, California
Ca. 1970

Quicksilver
Washington, D.C.

Quiet Village
Sebastopol, California
Early 1970s

*Rabbity Hill Farm/
Highland Center*
Dalton, Pennsylvania
1974–?

Radical Action Coop
New York City
Late 1960s–?

Ragged Mountain Ranch
Sperryville, Virginia
Early 1970s

Rainbow
Philo, California
Early 1970s

Rainbow Commune
Woodstock, New York
Late 1960s–?

*Rainbow Family of Living
Light (Rainbow Family)*
Itinerant
1972–ongoing

Rainbow Farm
Drain, Oregon
1969 or 1970–present

Rainbow Farm
Selma, Indiana
1973

Rainbow Mist
Five Rivers, Oregon
?–ongoing

Rainbow People's Party
Ann Arbor, Michigan
1966–?

*Rajarajeshwari Peetham
(Sivananda Ashram of Yoga
One Science)*
Stroudsburg, Pennsylva-
nia; Woodbourne,
New York
1968–ongoing

*Raja-Yoga Math
and Retreat*
Deming, Washington
1974–ongoing

Ralph's House
Santa Cruz, California
1968–70

Ramona Land Church
Ramona, California
1967–?

Rancho Diablo
California

Ranchos Colorados
Orinda, California

Range Line commune
Columbia, Missouri
Early 1970s

Raphael's House
660 Cole Street,
San Francisco, California
Ca. 1969–?

Rat Creek
Cottage Grove, Oregon
1970 or 1971–ongoing

Rattlesnake Gulch
Early 1970s–?

Raven Rocks
Beallsville, Ohio
1970–?

Ravendale
Mendocino, California

Ray Kelley commune
Sedro-Woolley,
Washington

*Reality Construction
Company*
Taos, New Mexico
1969–72

Red Barn
West Virginia

Red Clover Farm
Putney, Vermont
1971–?

Red Family/Red Fist House
Berkeley, California
Late 1960s–?

Red Fox Cooperative
Oakland, California
Early 1970s

Red House
Forest Knolls, California

Red Rockers
Farisita, Colorado
1969–early 1970s

Redbird
Vermont
1974–79

Re-education Foundation
San Francisco, California
Mid-1970s

*Reina del Cielo/Shambala
Community*
Lexington, Virginia
1972–?

Rejoice Always
San Francisco, California
Early 1970s

Religious Society of Families
Frewsburg, New York
1963–?

*Renaissance Community
(Cathedral of the Spirit,
Brotherhood of the Spirit,
Metelica Aquarian Concept)*
Leyden, Massachusetts;
Guilford, Vermont; Gill,
Massachusetts
1968–ongoing

Renewal House
Los Angeles
Early 1970s

Repose
Oregon
Ca. early 1970s

Resistance commune
Brooklyn, New York
Late 1960s–?

Resistance commune
Chicago, Illinois
Late 1960s–?

Resistance commune
Topanga, California
Late 1960s–?

Resistance Commune
Seattle, Washington
1970

Resistance House
Philadelphia, Pennsylvania

Resource One
San Francisco, California
Mid-1970s

Resurrection City, USA
Browns, Alabama
20 acres
Ca. 1970–?

Revolver
New York City
Ca. 1972–?

Ridge Street commune
New York City
Ca. 1970–?

Rio Del Norte
Taos, New Mexico, area
Early 1970s

Rippey's Orchard
Glenwood, Missouri
Ca. 1973

Rising Sun Tribe
New York City
Late 1960s

Rising Sun Tribe
Miamisville, Ohio
Late 1960s–?

Rivendell
Maysville, Arkansas
1970s

Rivendell Cooperative
Lansing, Michigan
1974–?

*River Farm (Brandywine
Forest)*
Deming, Washington
1971–82

Road #721 Commune
Mendocino, California

*Roandoak of God Christian
Commune*
Morro Bay, California
1971–?

Rochdale Coop
New Haven, Connecticut
Mid-1970s

Rochester Ashram
Rochester, New York
Mid-1970s

*Rochester Folk Art Guild
(East Hill Farm)*
Naples, New York
1967–ongoing

Rock Creek
Deadwood, Oregon
Early 1970s

Rock Ridge Community
Dodgeville, Wisconsin
1971–ongoing

Rockbottom Farm
South Strafford, Vermont
1969–?

Rockridge
New Mexico
1970

*Rocky Mountain
Dharma Center
(Shambhala Center)*
Red Feather Lakes,
Colorado
1971–ongoing

Rogers
Mt. Sterling, Kentucky
Early 1970s

Rootworks
Wolf Creek, Oregon
1970s

Rose Foundation
New Mexico
Ca. 1968–?

*Round Mountain Co-
operative Community*
Ukiah, California
Early 1970s–ongoing

*Rowe Camp and
Conference Center*
Rowe, Massachusetts
1974–ongoing

Ruhani Satsang
Oakton, Virginia
Early 1970s

Runaway House
Washington, D.C.
Late 1960s

Russell Commune
West Lafayette, Indiana
Early 1970s–?

Rutland Square House
Boston, Massachusetts
1968–69

Sabot. See Wooden Shoe
Farm

*Saddle Ridge Farm [pseud.].
See* High Ridge Farm

Sadhana Foundation
Los Altos Hills, California
1972

Safespace Island
San Francisco, California
Ca. 1974

Saint Gregory's Abbey
Three Rivers, Michigan
Mid-1970s

St. James Community
Portage, Wisconsin
Early 1970s

St. John's Order
San Francisco, California
1971–ongoing

*St. Mark's Avenue
Commune*
Brooklyn, New York
1970

*Salem Communal
Brotherhood*
Rock City, Illinois
1960s–?

*Salmon Creek Family
(Valley of Life)*
Big Sur area, California
Late 1960s–?

Salmon River House
California

San Francisco Zen Center
San Francisco, California
1969–ongoing

Sandhill Farm
Rutledge, Missouri
1974–ongoing

Sans Souci Temple
Los Angeles, California

Sant Bani Ashram
Franklin, New Hampshire
Mid-1970s

Santa Cruz House
Santa Cruz, California

Santa Fe Community School
Santa Fe, New Mexico,
and Paonia, Colorado
1968–?

*Santana Dharma
Foundation*
St. Helena, California
Mid-1970s

Sassafras
Boxley, Arkansas
1972–?

Sassafras Ridge Farm
Hinton, West Virginia
1972–ongoing

*Satchidananda Ashram.
See* Yogaville

Savitria
Baltimore, Maryland
Mid-1970s

Scatter Creek
McLouth, Kansas
1970s

Die Schöne Aussicht

School House
Shelbourne, Vermont
1971–?

*School of Light and
Realization (SOLAR)*
Sutton's Bay, Michigan
Ca. 1969–81

Scott Street Commune
San Francisco, California

Scupparnong Landings
Kill Devil Hills, North
Carolina
1972

SDS commune
Washington, D.C.
Late 1960s

*Sea and the East Utopian
Mission*
Berea, Virginia
1971

Seattle Liberation Front
Seattle, Washington

Seattle Workers' Brigade
Seattle, Washington
1970s

Sedgewick Commune
Bronx, New York
1969

S.E.L.F. Foundation
Los Angeles, California
1970

Seven Springs Community
Dillard, Oregon
Ca. 1971–?

Seven Springs Farm
Mountain Grove,
Missouri
1972–?

Sevenoaks Pathwork Center
Madison, Virginia
1972–?

1704 Q St. N.W.
Washington, D.C.
1969

1724 S St. N.W.
Washington, D.C.
1969

Shalom Community
Browns Summit, North
Carolina
1974–?

Shambala Community.
See Reina del Ceilo

Shangri-la

Shannon Farm
Afton, Virginia
1974–ongoing

Shantivanam
Easton, Kansas
Ca. 1972–ongoing

Share-a-Home Association
Winter Park, Florida
Early 1970s

Shasta Abbey, Zen Mission
Society
Mt. Shasta, California
Mid-1970s

Shekinah
Logsden, Oregon
1970s–?

Sheepfold House
Milwaukee, Wisconsin
Early 1970s

Shepherdsfield
Fulton, Missouri
1969–ongoing

Sherwood Forest Collective
Orange County, California
1970

Shiloh. See Church of the
Living Word—Shiloh

Shiloh Community
Sherman, New
Hampshire
1970

Shiloh Farms
Martindale, Pennsylvania

Shiloh Youth Revival
Centers
Eugene, Oregon, and
many other locations
1969–89

Shivalila
Lake Isabella, California
Ca. 1974–79

Short Mountain Sanctuary
Tennessee

Shotwell Street Commune
San Francisco, California

Shree Hridayam Satsang
Hollywood, California;
successor communities in
Fiji and elsewhere
1972–ongoing (successor
communities)

Siddha Yoga
Oakland, California;
South Fallsburg, New
York
1974–ongoing

Siva Kalpa (Foundation of
Revelation)
San Francisco, California
Late 1960s–ongoing

Sivananda Ashram. See
Rajarajeshwari Peetham

1616 22d Street
Washington, D.C.
1969

Sky Woods Cosynegle
Muskegon Heights,
Michigan
1972–?

Skyfields
Bluemont, Virginia
Late 1960s–early 1970s

Slaughterhouse Creek
Commune
Bonanza, Colorado
1970–ca. 1980

Slide Ranch
California

Small Earth Farm
Union, West Virginia
Mid-1970s

Society of Families. See
Religious Society of
Families

Sojai Farms
Pleasant Valley, New York
Mid-1960s

Sojourners Community
Washington, D.C.
1975–ongoing

Sollux
New Mexico
Ca. 1966

Solomon's Porch
San Francisco Bay area,
California

Sonoma Grove
1971–?

Sons and Daughters of Jesus
Arizona

Soul Inn
San Francisco (Haight-
Ashbury), California
1968–?

Source Collective
Washington, D.C.
Early 1970s–?

Source Family
Los Angeles, California;
Hawaii
Ca. 1970–ca. 1978

South Fork
On the Sacramento River,
California

Southern Rainbow
Cincinnati, Ohio
Mid-1970s

Southwest Georgia Project
Albany, Georgia
Early 1970s–?

Spanish House
Brighton, Massachusetts
1972–?

Spentalot

Spiral Wimmin
Kentucky
Mid-1970s

Spiritual Community, Inc.
San Rafael, California
1972–?

Spiritual Dawn Community
Tallahassee, Florida
Early 1970s–late 1970s

Spring Hollow Farm
Red Boiling Springs,
Tennessee
Ca. 1973–78

Spring Valley
California

Spring Valley
Spring Valley, New York

Springtree Community
Scottsville, Virginia
1971–ongoing

Springwater Village
Decorah, Iowa
Early 1970s

Square Pigeon

Squash Bug Farm
Big Springs, Kansas
1973–late 1970s

Sri Ram Ashrama
Benson, Arizona (earlier at
Millbrook, New York)
Late 1960s–ongoing

Star Mountain
California

Starcrest
North Carolina

Starcross Monastery
Annapolis, California
Mid-1970s

Stardance. See U-Lab II

Stardust
Costa Mesa, California
Mid-1970s

Stelle Community
(Stelle Group)
Stelle, Illinois
1973–ongoing

Stillpoint
Wetmore, Colorado
1971–?

Stillstone
Eugene, Oregon
1975–?

Stillwind Community
(Still Wind)
Sugar Grove, North
Carolina

Stires Associates
North Miami, Florida
Ca. 1972–?

Stone Mill Farm
Appomatox, Virginia
Ca. 1972–?

Stonehead Manor
Detroit, Michigan
Ca. 1970–?

Stoney Mountain Farms
Fremont, Missouri
Mid-1970s

STP Family
Various locations

Strange Farm
Virginia
Ca. 1973–?

Strawberry Fields
Malibu, California
Late 1960s

Street Journal
San Diego, California
1970–?

Suburban Partners
Durham, North Carolina
1970–?

Summerland collective
California
Early 1970s

Sun at Midday
Olalla, Washington
Mid-1970s

Sun Farm
Placitas, New Mexico

Sun Tribe
Reseda, California
Early 1970s

Sunburst. See Builders

Suneidesis Consocation
Buras, Louisiana
1975–?

Sunflower Farm
Amesville, Ohio
1975–?

Sunflower House
Lawrence, Kansas
1969–ongoing

Sunflower Life Center
Newton, Kansas
Mid-1970s

Sunny Ridge Occult Society
and Candy Store
Cave Junction, Oregon

Sunny Valley
Grant's Pass/Medford,
Oregon

Sunray Meditation Society
Huntington, Vermont
Mid-1970s

Sunrise
Mansfield, Missouri
1970s

Sunrise Communal Farm,
Full to the Brim
Evart, Michigan
1971–?

Sunrise Commune
Standardsville, Virginia
1971

Sunrise Community Land
Trust/Clear Light Farms
East Machias, Maine
Mid-1970s

Sunrise Farm
Bath, New York
Mid-1970s

Sunrise Hill
Conway, Massachusetts
1966–67

Sunset House
Seattle, Washington
1974–ongoing

Sunshower Farm
Lawrence, Michigan
1971–?

Sunstar
Cave Junction, Oregon
Ca. 1971–?

Sutter Street Commune
San Francisco, California
1970

Sweet Earth
St. Peter, Minnesota
Mid-1970s

Sweetwater Community
Guerneville, California
Ca. 1972–?

Switchboard
Washington, D.C.
Late 1960s

Symbionese Liberation Army
California
Early 1970s

Symphony of Souls in Christ
New York City/mobile
Early 1970s

Synergia Ranch
New Mexico

The Syndicate
Philadelphia, Pennsylvania
Early 1970s

Table Mountain Ranch
Albion, California
1968–ongoing

Tai Farm
California

Tail of the Tiger
(Karme-Choling Buddhist
Meditation Center)
Barnet, Vermont
1970–ongoing

Taize
Chicago, Illinois
Early 1970s

Takilma
Southern Oregon
Early 1970s–ongoing

Talsalsan Farm
Takilma, Oregon
1968

Taos Learning Center
Taos, New Mexico
Late 1960s

Tara
Ukiah, California
Mid-1970s

Tassajara Zen Mountain
Center
Big Sur, California
1966–ongoing

Taylor Camp
Kauai, Hawaii

Tecumseh Garden
Rutledge, Missouri
1974

Temenos
Shutesbury, Massachusetts

Temple Tribe
Portland, Oregon
Late 1960s–?

1090 Page Street
San Francisco, California
Late 1960s

Teramanto
Renton, Washington
1974–ongoing

Terra Firma Commune
New York City
1968

Terra Firma
Oregon

Terrarium
1970s

Terrasoumirma
Portland, Oregon

Theatre of All Possibilities.
See Synergia Ranch

Theleme
Akron, New York
1970

1309 and 1340 Tennessee
Lawrence, Kansas
Ca. 1967

30 Canal Street
Staten Island, New York

345 Michigan
Lawrence, Kansas
Mid-1970s

3HO New Mexico
Espanola, New Mexico
1971–ongoing

Threshold
Portland, Oregon
Ca. 1971–?

Thunder Mountain
Commune
Nevada

Thunder River
Trail, Oregon
Mid-1970s

Thunderhawk
Portland, Oregon
Mid-1970s

Tierra Verde Fellowship
Oakland, California
1971–?

Toad Hall
East Haven, Vermont

Together
Venice, California

Together
Brooklyn, New York
Early 1970s

Total Loss Farm.
See Packer Corner

Towapa
Placitas, New Mexico
1970s–ca. 1994

Training for Urban
Alternatives
New Haven, Connecticut
1975

Trans-Love Energies
Detroit and Ann Arbor,
Michigan
Late 1960s

Traprock Peace Center
(Woolman Hill)
Deerfield, Massachusetts

Travelling Promised Land
Itinerant
Ca. 1973–?

Treat Street House
San Francisco, California

Tree Frog
Southern Vermont
Early 1970s

Tree Frog
Penasco, New Mexico

Tree House commune
Oregon

Tribal Messenger Commune
Albuquerque, New
Mexico

The Tribe
Southern Colorado

Trillium Trout Farm
Ashland, Oregon
1970s

Trinidad House
Trinidad, California

Trout Lake Farm
Washington State
Ca. 1974–?

True House
South Bend, Indiana
1968–?

True Light Beavers
Woodstock, New York
1968–?

Truth Consciousness
Boulder, Colorado;
Rockford, Michigan;
Tucson, Arizona
1974–?

Tucson Mennonite
Fellowship
Tucson, Arizona

Turkey Ridge Farm
Delaware Water Gap,
Pennsylvania

Turning Commune
Stony Brook, New York
Ca. 1969–?

Twelve Tribes. See Messianic
Communities

21st Family
Oregon

25 to 6 Baking and
Trucking Society
New York City area
Ca. early 1970s

2620
Washington, D.C.

23rd Psalm House
Nashville, Tennessee
Early 1970s

Twin Oaks
Louisa, Virginia
1967–ongoing

Twin Pines
Santa Clara, California

The Two. See Heaven's Gate

Two Rainbows Community
Lowman, Idaho
Mid-1970s

Two Rivers Farm
Aurora, Oregon
1974–ongoing

U&I Community (United
and Individual)
Eldridge, Missouri
1974–?

Ujama
Lawrence, Kansas
Ca. 1971

U-Lab. See Kerista

U-Lab II (Stardance;
Purple Rose)
San Francisco, California
Mid-1970s

Uncle Sam

Underground Fellowship
Akron, Ohio
1970

Unification Church
Various locations
1960s–ongoing

United Order Family
of Christ
Denver, Colorado
1966–early 1970s

United Research Life Center
Black Mountain, North
Carolina
1970–?

Unity House
Chicago, Illinois
Early 1970s

Universing Center
Cottage Grove, Oregon
1973–?

University of the Trees
Boulder Creek, California

Upper Range
Huerfano Valley, Colorado

US
Washington, D.C.
1969

USA
Clawson, Michigan
Late 1960s–?

USCO
Occidental, California;
Garnerville, New York
1969

U.V. Family
Itinerant
1969–?

Valley Cooperative School
Dundee, Illinois
Mid-1970s

Valley of Life. See Salmon
Creek Family

Valley of Peace
Squires, Missouri
Mid-1970s

Vega Institute
Oroville, California
Mid-1970s

Villa Sarah
Altadena, California
1973–?

Villa Serena
Sarasota, Florida

The Village
Point Arena, California
1971–86

Village Design
Berkeley, California
Early 1970s

Village of Arts and Ideas
Berkeley, California

Village of Free Souls
Chicago, Illinois
1970

The Vineyard
Dallas, Texas
Ca. 1971–?

Virgil House
Hollywood, California
Early 1970s

Vision Foundation
1972–ongoing
Coos Bay, Oregon

*Vivekananda Monastery
and Retreat*
Fennville, Michigan
1966–?

Vocations for Social Change
Oakland, Hayward, and
Canyon, California
Late 1960s

Vonu Life
Cave Junction, Oregon

Vortex House
Lawrence, Kansas
Ca. 1970

Vrindavan Yoga Farm
Grass Valley, California
Mid-1970s

*Wailua University of
Contemplative Arts*
Kapaa, Kauai, Hawaii
Early 1970s

Wake Robin Farm
Vermont

Walden House
Washington, D.C.
1965

Walden III
Providence, Rhode Island
Early 1970s

Walkabout
Seattle, Washington

Walker Creek Farm
Mt. Vernon, Washington

Warehouse Family
San Francisco, California
Ca. 1970

Warm Fellowship
Mountain View, California
1975–?

*Washington Free
Community*
Washington, D.C.
Late 1960s

*Washington Free
Press commune*
Washington, D.C.
Late 1960s

The Way
New Knoxville, Ohio, and
other locations
Ca. 1971–ongoing

Weather Underground
Various locations
Late 1960s–early 1970s

The Weavers
Maine coast
Ca. 1968–?

Weed Mine Farm
Copake, New York
Mid-1970s

Welcome Home
Corrales, New Mexico

*Wellington Street, Seattle.
See* Candy Ass House

Wellman Road Big House
Oskaloosa, Kansas
Ca. 1970

Wendell Farm
Wendell, Massachusetts
Early 1970s

West Burke commune
West Burke, Vermont
1970

Wheel of Life Foundation
Kirkland, Arkansas
Ca. 1972

Wheeler's Ranch
Sonoma County,
California
1967–ongoing

White Buffalo
Paonia, Colorado
1973–ongoing

White House. See Five Star

White House
Yakima, Washington

White Lotus Study Center
El Cajon, California
Mid-1970s

*Whitten Hill Farm
Community*
Thorndike, Maine

Whole Health Foundation
Cardiff, California
1973–?

Willard Street House
San Francisco, California

Willits House
Willits, California

Willow
Napa Valley, California
Ca. 1973

*Windspirit Farm and
Music Community*
Kettle, Kentucky
1974–?

Wisconsin Family
Milwaukee, Wisconsin
Mid-1970s

*Wiscoy Organic Farm
Community/Wiscoy Valley*
Winona, Minnesota
Mid-1970s

Wolf Lake Refuge–Communities for Service
McGregor, Minnesota
1972–?

A Woman's Place
Lake George, New York
1974–82

Womanhill. See Willow

*WomanShare Feminist
Women's Land*
Grants Pass, Oregon
1974–ongoing

Women's Collective
Berkeley, California
1972

*Wonderland Civic
Association*
Boulder, Colorado
1970

Wood Street commune
San Francisco, California
Late 1960s

Woodburn Hill Farm
Mechanicsville, Maryland
1975–?

Wooden Shoe Farm
Canaan, New Hampshire
Early 1970s–?

Woodstock Commune
Saugerties, New York
1970

Woody Hill
Idaho

Woolman Hill
Deerfield, Massachusetts
Mid-1970s

Word of God Commune
Ann Arbor, Michigan
1968–ongoing

Word of God Community
San Fidel, New Mexico
Early 1970s–?

Work of Christ Community
Lansing, Michigan
1973–?

Xanadu
Los Angeles, California
Mid-1970s

Yahara Linden Co-op
Madison, Wisconsin
1974–?

Yarrow
Newark, New York
Mid-1970s

Yea God!
Ithaca, New York

Yellow Fire Puppet Theater
Washington, D.C.
1969

Yellow House
Forest Knolls, California

Yellow House
Mansfield, Pennsylvania

Yellow Submarine
Eugene, Oregon
1968–?

Yellow House Commune
New Hampshire
Early 1970s

Yin Palace
Palo Alto, California

Yoga Society of Rochester
Rochester, New York
1972–ongoing

Yogaville
Pomfret Center, Connecticut; Buckingham, Virginia
Ca. 1972–ongoing

Yogic Community
Early 1970s

Yoruba Village. See
Oyotunji Village

Young Ideas
Lagunitas, California
Ca. 1970–?

Z Fellowship
Atlanta, Georgia
1970s–early 1980s

Zen Center of Los Angeles
Los Angeles
1968–ongoing

*Zen Meditation Center
of Rochester*
Rochester, New York
1966–?

Zen Mountain Center. See
Tassajara Zen Mountain
Center

Zendik Farm
San Diego; Balstrop,
Texas; Florida
1969–ongoing

Zion's Inn
San Rafael, California
1969–?

Zocald
Tucson, Arizona
Mid-1970s

The Zoo
Newport, Oregon
Ca. 1965

Notes

ACKNOWLEDGMENTS

1. Yaswen's work was published by the author, now at 740 First Street, Sebastopol, California 95472.

INTRODUCTION

1. For a sketch of Plockhoy's Commonwealth, America's first known communal experiment following European settlement, see Timothy Miller, "Peter Cornelius Plockhoy and the Beginnings of the American Communal Tradition," in *Gone to Croatan: Origins of North American Dropout Culture*, ed. Ron Sakolsky and James Koehnline (New York: Autonomedia, 1993), 117–26. For an overview of the Labadist colony at Bohemia Manor see Bartlett B. James, "The Labadist Colony in Maryland," *Johns Hopkins University Studies in Historical and Political Science*, 17, no. 6 (June 1899): 7–45.

2. Paul Goodman and Percival Goodman, *Communitas: Means of Livelihood and Ways of Life* (New York: Vintage, 1960), 109.

3. Benjamin Zablocki, *Alienation and Charisma: A Study of Contemporary American Communes* (New York: Free Press/Macmillan, 1980), 4. The phrase "old standby" Zablocki attributed to Rosabeth Moss Kanter. For Kanter's ideas about commitment mechanisms, see Kanter, *Commitment and Community: Communes and Utopias in Sociological Perspective* (Cambridge, Mass.: Harvard Univ. Press, 1972).

4. See, among many examples, Stephen Gaskin, *Volume One: Sunday Morning Services on the Farm* (Summertown, Tenn.: Book Publishing Co., n.d.); Stephen [Gaskin] and the Farm, *Hey Beatnik! This Is the Farm Book* (Summertown, Tenn.: Book Publishing Co., 1974).

5. See, for example, Bennett Berger, Bruce Hackett, and R. Mervyn Millar, "The Communal Family," *Family Coordinator* 21, no. 4 (Oct. 1972): 419–27; David E. Smith and Alan J. Rose, "Health Problems in Urban and Rural 'Crash Pad' Communes," *Clinical Pediatrics* 9, no. 9 (Sept. 1970): 534–37.

6. Bill Kovach, "Communes Spread as the Young Reject Old Values," *New York Times*, Dec. 17, 1970; Benjamin Zablocki, *The Joyful Community* (Chicago: Univ. of Chicago Press, 1971), 300; Herbert A. Otto, "Communes: The Alternative Life-Style," *Saturday Review*, Apr. 24, 1971, 17; "Year of the Commune," *Newsweek* 74 (Aug. 18, 1969): 89.

7. William J. Speers, "Philadelphia's Communes," in *Utopia USA*, ed. Richard Fairfield (San Francisco: Alternatives Foundation, 1972), 134 (originally published in the *Philadelphia Inquirer*); James Nolan, "Jesus Freaks . . . out," in *Utopia USA*, ed. Richard

---

Some who were interviewed for the 60s Communes Project asked not to have their identities revealed. Several citations of interviews thus do not include names or dates that might cause the interviewee to be identified.

Fairfield (San Francisco: Alternatives Foundation, 1972), 44; Mark Perlgut, "Communal Living: Adventure in Relating to Others," *New York Times,* Nov. 28, 1971, A7; Mae T. Sperber, *Search for Utopia: A Study of Twentieth Century Communes in America* (Middleboro, Mass.: Country Press, 1976), 17.

8. Hugh Gardner, "Dropping into Utopia," *Human Behavior* 7 (Mar. 1978): 43; Patrick W. Conover, "An Analysis of Communes and Intentional Communities with Particular Attention to Sexual and Genderal Relations," *Family Coordinator* 24 (Oct. 1975): 454.

9. Judson Jerome, *Families of Eden: Communes and the New Anarchism* (New York: Seabury, 1974), 16–18. Jerome's method of counting is somewhat more complex than this summary reflects.

10. Several scholars and visitors have estimated communal membership within this general range. See, for example, Gilbert Zicklin, *Countercultural Communes: A Sociological Perspective* (Westport, Conn.: Greenwood, 1983), 40. Zicklin's estimate of membership was based on his own sample of twenty communes.

11. David Felton, "The Lyman Family's Holy Siege of America," *Rolling Stone,* Dec. 23, 1971, and Jan. 6, 1972.

12. John Rippey, 60s Communes Project interview, Mar. 22, 1996.

13. Elaine Sundancer [Elaine Zablocki], *Celery Wine: The Story of a Country Commune* (Yellow Springs, Ohio: Community Publications Cooperative, 1973), 29.

1. SET AND SETTING: THE ROOTS OF THE , 1960S-ERA COMMUNES

1. Robert Houriet, *Getting Back Together* (New York: Avon, 1971), 9.

2. Maren Lockwood Carden, "Communes and Protest Movements in the U.S., 1960–1974: An Analysis of Intellectual Roots," *International Review of Modern Sociology* 6 (spring 1976): 16; Helen Constas and Kenneth Westhues, "Communes: The Routinization of Hippiedom," in *Society's Shadow: Studies in the Sociology of Countercultures,* ed. Kenneth Westhues (Toronto: McGraw-Hill Ryerson, 1972), 191–94.

3. Art Downing, 60s Communes Project interview, Mar. 22, 1996.

4. Some, for that matter, would find the earliest prefigurings of hip much earlier—for example, among the second-century Adamites, who lived in isolation, worshiped in the nude, rejected marriage, and saw themselves as living in paradise. See Carl Bangs, "The Hippies: Some Historical Perspectives," *Religion in Life* 37, no. 4 (winter 1968): 498–508; J. H. Plumb, "The Secular Heretics," *Horizon* 10, no. 2 (spring 1968): 9–12.

5. Laurence Veysey, *The Communal Experience: Anarchist and Mystical Communities in Twentieth-Century America* (Chicago: Univ. of Chicago Press, 1978 [1973]), 33.

6. See John Robert Howard, "The Flowering of the Hippie Movement," *Annals of the American Academy of Political and Social Science* 382 (Mar. 1969): 43–55.

7. Paul Krassner, "The Parts That Were Left Out of the Kennedy Book," *The Realist* 74 (May 1967): 18; manifesto, *Fuck You: A Magazine of the Arts* 1 [1962]; Ed Sanders, *The Family: The Story of Charles Manson's Dune Buggy Attack Battalion* (New York: Dutton, 1971). On Sanders's early years in New York see "Peace Eye: An Interview with Edward Sanders," *Mesechabe: The Journal of Surre(gion)alism* (New Orleans) 14/15 (spring 1996): 30–32.

8. Murray Bookchin, "When Everything Was Possible," *Mesechabe: The Journal of Surre(gion)alism* (New Orleans) 9/10 (winter 1991): 1–7.

9. Quoted in *Billings (Montana) Gazette* Online, Sept. 15, 1996. Feldstein was living in retirement in nearby Paradise Valley, Mont.

10. See, for example, Walt Crowley, *Rites of Passage: A Memoir of the Sixties in Seattle* (Seattle: Univ. of Washington Press, 1995), 6.

11. On these themes see D. Lawrence Wieder and Don H. Zimmerman, "Generational Experience and the Development of Freak Culture," *Journal of Social Issues* 30, no. 2 (1974): 137–61.

12. See, among many other works, Alan W. Watts, *The Way of Zen* (New York: Pantheon, 1957).

13. Norman Mailer, "The White Negro," in *Voices of Dissent* (New York: Grove, 1958), 199.

14. Stephen Diamond, *What the Trees Said: Life on a New Age Farm* (New York: Dell, 1971), 73. For an elaboration of this line of thought see Hugh Gardner, *The Children of Prosperity: Thirteen Modern American Communes* (New York: St. Martin's, 1978), 5–7.

15. Bennett M. Berger, *The Survival of a Counterculture: Ideological Work and Everyday Life Among Rural Communards* (Berkeley: Univ. of California Press, 1981), 196.

16. On this point see James L. Murphy, *The Reluctant Radicals: Jacob L. Beilhart and the Spirit Fruit Society* (Lanham, Md.: University Press of America, 1989), 226.

17. Donald Wayne Bender, *From Wilderness to Wilderness: Celestia* (Dushore, Pa.: Sullivan Review, 1980).

18. On the interaction of Koinonia with 1960s-era communitarians see, for example, William Hedgepeth and Dennis Stock, *The Alternative: Communal Life in New America* (New York: Macmillan, 1970), 175–81.

19. Brother Arnold Hadd, 60s Communes Project interview, Feb. 9, 1996.

20. Asaiah Bates, 60s Communes Project interview, Sept. 12, 1996.

21. For Loomis's account of the development of Heathcote see Richard Fairfield, *Communes USA: A Personal Tour* (Baltimore: Penguin, 1972), 32–38. Other historical tidbits were published in various issues of the School of Living's publication *Green Revolution*; see, for example, 9, no. 12 (Dec. 1971): 3–7.

22. Herb Goldstein, 60s Communes project interview, July 17, 1996.

23. Elia Katz, *Armed Love* (New York: Bantam, 1971), 37–46. The aggressively negative tone of Katz's whole book leads one to discount his impressions somewhat.

24. On Sender's early experiences with the Bruderhof see Ramón Sender Barayón, "A Bruderhof Memoir," *KIT Newsletter* 9, no. 6 (June 1997): 6–10.

25. See John Curl, *History of Work Cooperation in America: Cooperatives, Cooperative Movements, Collectivity and Communalism from Early America to the Present* (Berkeley: Homeward, 1980); John Curl, ed., *History of Collectivity in the San Francisco Bay Area* (Berkeley: Homeward, 1982).

26. Al Andersen, 60s Communes Project interview, July 12, 1996.

27. Marty Jezer, "How I Came Here," in *Home Comfort: Stories and Scenes of Life on Total Loss Farm*, ed. Richard Wizansky (New York: Saturday Review Press, 1973), 44–45.

28. Ibid., 49.

29. H. Gardner, *Children of Prosperity*, 18.

30. Raymond Mungo, "Living on the Earth," *New York Times Book Review*, Mar. 21, 1971, 6–7; Christopher Lehmann-Haupt, "A Red Fox and a Bay Laurel," *New York Times*, Mar. 25, 1971, 37; "Her Hymn to Nature Is a Guidebook for the Simplest of Lives," *New York Times*, Mar. 26, 1971, 34.

2. THE NEW COMMUNES EMERGE: 1960–1965

1. Tom Wolfe, *The Electric Kool-Aid Acid Test* (New York: Farrar Straus and Giroux, 1968), 53; ellipses in original.

2. Extensive accounts of the bus trip (and of the larger Kesey/Merry Pranksters scene) are contained in Wolfe, *Electric Kool-Aid Acid Test*, 68–124, and Paul Perry, *On the Bus: The Complete Guide to the Legendary Trip of Ken Kesey and the Merry Pranksters and the Birth of the Counterculture* (New York: Thunder's Mouth, 1990).

3. Timothy Leary, *Flashbacks: A Personal and Cultural History of an Era* (Los Angeles: Tarcher, 1990), 204–6.

4. Quoted in Perry, *On the Bus*, 97. For a description of the differences in their approaches to LSD between the Merry Pranksters and the Millbrook psychedelic explorers, see Martin A. Lee and Bruce Shlain, *Acid Dreams: The CIA, LSD and the Sixties Rebellion* (New York: Grove, 1985), 124–25; Jay Stevens, *Storming Heaven: LSD and the American Dream* (New York: Harper and Row, 1987), 235.

5. Carolyn Adams Garcia, 60s Communes Project interview, July 15, 1996; Allen Ginsberg, "First Party at Ken Kesey's with Hell's Angels," *Collected Poems 1947–1980* (New York: Harper and Row, 1984), 374.

6. Carolyn Adams Garcia, 60s Communes Project interview; Gordon Adams, 60s Communes Project interview, Sept. 5, 1996.

7. Michael Goodwin, "The Ken Kesey Movie," *Rolling Stone*, Mar. 7, 1970, 24ff. For a chronological overview of Kesey's life with the Merry Pranksters see "Ken Kesey," in Ann Charters, *The Beats: Literary Bohemians in Postwar America*, vol. 1 (Detroit: Gale, 1983), 306–16.

8. That population count is provided by Ramón Sender, "Three Commune Fathers and One Mother," *Modern Utopian* 2, no. 6 (July–Aug. 1968): 8–9.

9. Rasa Gustaitis, *Turning On* (London: Weidenfeld and Nicolson, 1969), 99–109.

10. Lewis Yablonsky, *The Hippie Trip* (New York: Pegasus, 1968), 74–96.

11. Sender, "Three Commune Fathers and One Mother," 8.

12. Erling Skorpen, "The Himalayan Academy," *Modern Utopian* 3, no. 3 (summer 1969): 4.

13. Acharya Palaniswami, 60s Communes Project interview, July 7, 1997.

14. Fairfield, *Communes USA*, 160–62. See also Skorpen, "Himalayan Academy," 5.

15. On the establishment of the headquarters in Hawaii and a sketch of the movement's early days there see Richard Fairfield, ed., *Utopia USA* (San Francisco: Alternatives Foundation, 1972), 74–76.

16. Steve Trimm, "Pacifist Farm," *Modern Utopian* 2, no. 2 (Oct.–Nov. 1967): 27, 32. See also "Even Pacifism Requires Training," *New York Times*, Nov. 29, 1965, 37, 40.

17. Huw "Piper" Williams, 60s Commune Project interview, Sept. 9, 1996.

18. Huw "Piper" Williams, interviewed by Timothy Miller, Sept. 11, 1990. Subsequent unattributed quotations from Williams are also taken from this interview.

19. Houriet, *Getting Back Together*, 219.

20. Rico Read, lecture on Tolstoy Farm at the Celebration of Community, Olympia, Wash., Aug. 27, 1993.

21. Sara Davidson, "Open Land: Getting Back to the Communal Garden," *Harper's*, June 1970, 91–100 (the portion on Tolstoy Farm is on pp. 97–100; the balance is on Wheeler's Ranch).

22. Don Hannula, "Tolstoy Farm: 10 Years Later," *Seattle Times*, Apr. 1, 1973, E1; Rico Reed, 60s Communes Project interview, Sept. 10, 1996; quoted in Sara Davidson, *Real Property* (Garden City, N.Y.: Doubleday, 1980), 245.

23. *The 1990–91 Directory of Intentional Communities: A Guide to Cooperative Living* (Evansville, Ind., and Stelle, Ill.: Fellowship for Intentional Community and Communities Publications Cooperative), 158. A description of Tolstoy Farm can be found on p. 225 of the *Directory*.

24. Stevens, *Storming Heaven*, 193.

25. Ibid., 208.

26. For an account of early relations between the newcomers and the established citizens of the town of Millbrook see "Psychic Drug Testers Living in Retreat," *New York Times*, Dec. 15, 1963, 64.

27. Kleps wrote, from his own point of view, what is probably the most comprehen-

sive published history of Millbrook: Art Kleps, *Millbrook: The True Story of the Early Years of the Psychedelic Revolution* (Oakland, Calif.: Bench Press, 1977). He also published as the scripture of the Neo-American Church a remarkable piece of psychedelic literature entitled *The Boo Hoo Bible: The Neo-American Church Catechism* (San Cristobal, N.M.: Toad, 1971).

28. Ruby Tuesday, 60s Communes Project interview, Mar. 21, 1996. Tuesday was a college student who lived at Millbrook part-time.

29. On the financial problems and attempts to solve them see Stevens, *Storming Heaven,* 260ff.

30. For an eyewitness account of the April raid by a reporter who happened to be at the mansion at the time, see Marya Mannes, "The Raid on Castalia," *Reporter* 34, no. 10 (May 19, 1966): 27ff. On the raid and subsequent police pressure see Lee and Shlain, *Acid Dreams,* 117–18, and Stevens, *Storming Heaven,* 255, 270–71.

31. Most sources date the end of Millbrook as a community in 1967. On the final (1968) eviction see Kleps, *Millbrook,* 5. For a personal memoir of life at Millbrook, see Michael Hollingshead, *The Man Who Turned on the World* (New York: Abelard-Schuman, 1974 [1973]), chap. 5.

32. John Sinclair, 60s Communes Project interview, Nov. 26, 1996. The quotations from Sinclair in the following paragraph are also from this interview.

33. Rosabeth Moss Kanter, *Commitment and Community: Communes and Utopias in Sociological Perspective* (Cambridge, Mass.: Harvard Univ. Press, 1972), 40, 41, 194, 199, 200, 217.

34. "Directory of Intentional Communities," *Modern Utopian* 4, nos. 3 and 4 (summer–fall 1970): 61.

35. *Amity Circular* 1, no. 1 (Oct. 11, 1963?). A dictionary entry on the community is included in Foster Stockwell, *Encyclopedia of American Communes, 1663–1963* (Jefferson, N.C.: McFarland, 1998), 19–20, but the author does not disclose the source of his information.

36. "Listing of Communities," *Communities: Journal of Cooperative Living* 24 (Jan.–Feb. 1977): 46; "Ananda Ashram," *Communities Directory: A Guide to Cooperative Living* (Langley, Wash.: Fellowship for Intentional Community, 1995), 214.

37. Unattributed quotations in this section are taken from interviews conducted between 1984 and 1989, plus subsequent correspondence and telephone conversations. For a longer historical sketch of Drop City see Timothy Miller, "Drop City: Historical Notes on the Pioneer Hippie Commune," *Syzygy: Journal of Alternative Religion and Culture* 1, no. 1 (winter 1992): 23–38.

38. Baer never lived at Drop City but has worked at developing environmental architecture at his zome home outside Albuquerque since the 1960s. For an illustrated overview of his work see Norma Skurka and Jon Naar, *Design for a Limited Planet* (New York: Ballantine, 1976), 44–49.

39. Peter Rabbit (whose real name was Peter Douthit), shortly after moving to Libre, wrote a book about Drop City that has been widely taken as the commune's definitive history: Peter Rabbit, *Drop City* (New York: Olympia, 1971). Other Droppers dismiss the book as fanciful, but Rabbit maintains that most of what he wrote was taken from his own observations and from stories that he heard from the original Droppers.

40. On this point, as on many other factual ones, the Droppers disagree. Richert, for example, seriously doubts that Bob Dylan or Peter Fonda ever visited.

41. "Directory of Intentional Communities," *Modern Utopian* 3, no. 4 (fall 1969): 19.

42. Hedgepeth and Stock, *The Alternative,* 153–58.

43. H. Gardner, *Children of Prosperity,* 39–40.

3. COMMUNES BEGIN TO SPREAD: 1965–1967

1. For a chronology of Romney's early life see Wavy Gravy, *Something Good for a Change: Random Notes on Peace through Living* (New York: St. Martin's, 1992), 226–29.

2. Lou Gottlieb, manuscript autobiography, 298–99.

3. Quoted in Neal White and Peter Schjeldahl, "Living High on the Hog Farm," *Avant-Garde* 5 (Nov. 1968): 45.

4. For Romney's own account of the Hog Farmers' Woodstock see Wavy Gravy, *The Hog Farm and Friends* (New York: Links, 1974), 72–80.

5. Wavy Gravy, 60s Communes Project interview, Sept. 17, 1996.

6. Fairfield, *Communes USA,* 198–99.

7. Jim Shields, "Sheriff Says No to Pignic," *Anderson Valley Advertiser* (Boonville), Jan. 8, 1997, 1, 11; Jim Shields, "Supes OK Bigger Pignic," *Anderson Valley Advertiser,* Jan. 22, 1997, 8, 12.

8. Hugh Romney, "The Hog Farm," *The Realist* 86 (Nov.–Dec. 1969): 18.

9. Elsa Marley, quoted in Peter Coyote, "Playing for Keeps: The Free-Fall Chronicles," from the internet, Nov. 1996. See http://www.webcom.com/~enoble/diggers.html.

10. Judy Berg, "The Diggers," in Curl, *History of Collectivity,* 34.

11. On the development of the clinic see David E. Smith, *Love Needs Care: A History of San Francisco's Haight-Ashbury Free Medical Clinic and Its Pioneer Role in Treating Drug-Abuse Problems* (Boston: Little, Brown, 1971).

12. Allen Cohen, 60s Communes Project interview, Mar. 25, 1996.

13. Stevens, *Storming Heaven,* 305.

14. See Smith and Rose, "Health Problems."

15. Stephen A. O. Golden, "At a Commune for Diggers Rules Are Few and Simple," in *The Hippie Scene,* ed. Carolyn Barnes (New York: Scholastic Book Services, 1968), 92–99 (originally published in the *New York Times*). For a rather negative eyewitness report on Galahad's pad see Yablonsky, *Hippie Trip,* chap. 5. Yablonsky, who found little to like in most of the communes he visited, found Galahad's "violent and depressing," the "community insane asylum of New York" (116).

16. Sylvia Anderson, 60s Communes Project interview, Aug. 3, 1996.

17. "The Family," *WIN,* Jan. 1, 1969, 4–5.

18. Gottlieb received a Ph.D. in musicology from the University of California at Berkeley in 1958; his dissertation was entitled "The Cyclic Masses of Trent Codex 89."

19. Gustaitis, *Turning On,* 157.

20. Much of this early history has been recorded in "Home Free Home: The Story of Two Open-Door Sixties Communes, Morning Star and Wheeler's Ranch, as Told by Various Residents," ed. Ramón Sender Barayón, manuscript; a copy is at the library of the University of California, Riverside. Other details are from an early draft of Lou Gottlieb's manuscript autobiography, provided to me by Gottlieb before his death.

21. *The Morning Star Scrapbook* (Occidental, Calif.: Friends of Morning Star, n.d. [ca. 1973]), 2.

22. Lou Gottlieb, 60s Communes Project interview, Mar. 23, 1996.

23. Gottlieb, quoted in "Home Free Home," 13.

24. Sandi Stein, 60s Communes Project interview, Mar. 22, 1996; Pam Hanna, "Morningstar," manuscript (the author's name was changed by marriage from Read to Hanna).

25. Anonymous former Morning Star Ranch resident, 60s Communes Project interview, 1996.

26. Gottlieb, manuscript autobiography, 244.

27. Ibid., 317.

28. Don McCoy, 60s Communes Project interview, Sept. 18, 1996.

29. For a disciple's account of Ciranjiva and his teachings see Harvey Meyers, *Hariyana* (San Francisco: Omkara, 1979).

30. C. P. Herrick, "Population Explosion 1," *Modern Utopian* 2, no. 4 (Mar.–Apr. 1968): 8–9; Yablonsky, *Hippie Trip*, 191; "Lou Gottlieb on Motherhood, LSD, and Revolution," in *Modern Man in Search of Utopia*, ed. Dick Fairfield (San Francisco: Alternatives Foundation, 1971), 92.

31. Houriet, *Getting Back Together*, 140.

32. As quoted by Ralph J. Gleason, "A Limeliter's New Thing," *San Francisco Chronicle*; reprinted in the *Morning Star Scrapbook*, 19.

33. Gottlieb, 60s Communes Project interview, Mar. 23, 1996.

34. *Morning Star Scrapbook*, 137, 139.

35. Several communal groups in the United States had opened their land to all comers before Gottlieb did so; just three years earlier, for example, Tolstoy Farm had been founded in Washington state on such principles. Indeed, as was mentioned in chapter 1, land was deeded to God as early as 1864, when Peter Armstrong, founder of the Celestia community in Pennsylvania, gave his movement's six hundred acres "to Almighty God, who inhabiteth Eternity, and to His heirs in Jesus Messiah, to the intent that it shall be subject to bargain and sale by man's cupidity no more forever"; Bender, *From Wilderness to Wilderness*, 22, 24.

36. Lou Gottlieb to Timothy Miller, Apr. 6, 1994.

37. Gottlieb, manuscript autobiography, 214; Gottlieb, 60s Communes Project interview, Mar. 23, 1996.

38. Lou Gottlieb, quoted in "Home Free Home," 18.

39. Lou Gottlieb to Timothy Miller, Oct. 13, 1994.

40. Personal communication, 1996.

41. Gottlieb, 60s Communes Project interview, Mar. 23, 1996.

42. Bill Wheeler, quoted in "Home Free Home," 42.

43. Gay Wheeler, quoted in "Home Free Home," 49.

44. Bill Wheeler, 60s Communes Project interview, Mar. 24, 1996.

45. See, for example, H. Gardner, *Children of Prosperity*, 139.

46. Sara Davidson, *Loose Change* (Garden City, N.Y.: Doubleday, 1977), 241.

47. Sylvia Anderson, 60s Communes Project interview, Aug. 3, 1996.

48. See Bill Wheeler, "Wheeler Ranch: Open Land," *Green Revolution* 9, nos. 10–11 (Oct.–Nov. 1971): 10–11.

49. Bill Wheeler, quoted in "Home Free Home," 133.

50. See B. F. Skinner, *Walden Two* (New York: Macmillan, 1948). Earlier intentional communities based on specific utopian novels include, for example, Altruria, in northern California (based on William Dean Howells's *A Traveller from Altruria* [New York: Harper and Brothers, 1894]), and Freeland, in Washington state (based on Theodor Hertzka's *Freeland: A Social Anticipation* [London: Chatto and Windus, 1891; New York: Appleton, 1891] and its sequel, *A Visit to Freeland, or, The New Paradise Regained* [London: W. Reeves, 1894]).

51. See "Walden House," in *Journal of a Walden Two Commune: The Collected Leaves of Twin Oaks*, vol. 1 (Louisa, Va.: Twin Oaks Community, 1972), 3.

52. See H. Wayne Gourley, "A Utopian Answer: Walden House Plus Group Marriage," *Modern Utopian* 1, no. 1 (1966): 33–38.

53. Kat Kinkade, *A Walden Two Experiment: The First Five Years of the Twin Oaks Community* (New York: William Morrow, 1973), 26. Much of my discussion of Twin Oaks draws upon this book, along with Ingrid Komar, *Living the Dream: A Documentary Study of Twin Oaks Community* (Norwood, Pa.: Norwood Editions, 1983), and Kat Kinkade, *Is It Utopia Yet? An Insider's View of Twin Oaks Community in Its 26th Year* (Louisa, Va.: Twin Oaks Publishing, 1994).

54. For a discussion of the philosophy and practice of the Twin Oaks system of labor credits see "Labor Credits," *Modern Utopian* 4, no. 1 (winter 1969–70): unpaginated; for a discussion of the agonies involved in setting up variable labor credits see "What Is a Labor Credit," *Journal of a Walden Two Commune*, vol. 1, 3–4.

55. For a characterization of Twin Oaks "dating," meaning fairly casual sexual relationships, see Gareth Branwyn, "Gareth's Story," in Patch Adams with Maureen Mylander, *Gesundheit! Bringing Good Health to You, the Medical System, and Society through Physician Service, Complementary Therapies, Humor, and Joy* (Rochester, Vt.: Healing Arts, 1993), 147.

56. Vince Zager, "Twin Oaks," in *A Guide to Cooperative Alternatives*, ed. Paul Freundlich, Chris Collins, and Mikki Wenig (New Haven, Conn., and Louisa, Va.: Community Publications Cooperative, 1979), 160.

57. Jon Wagner, "Sex Roles in American Communal Utopias: An Overview," in *Sex Roles in Contemporary American Communes*, ed. Jon Wagner (Bloomington: Indiana Univ. Press, 1982), 38.

58. The Walden Two model inspired quite a few other communal groups in the 1960s era. For a list of several such communities in planning stages around 1970 see Houriet, *Getting Back Together*, 307.

59. Gordon Yaswen, "Sunrise Hill Community: Post-Mortem," mimeographed essay, 2nd ed., 1970, 1–2. Abridged versions of Yaswen's evocative account appear in several other publications; see, for example, Jerry Richard, ed., *The Good Life* (New York: New American Library, 1973), 140–72; Rosabeth Moss Kanter, ed., *Communes: Creating and Managing the Collective Life* (New York: Harper and Row, 1973), 456–72.

60. Robert Heinlein, *Stranger in a Strange Land* (New York: Putnam's, 1961). For a brief statement of the use of the book by the communards at Sunrise Hill see Houriet, *Getting Back Together*, 38.

61. Yaswen, "Sunrise Hill Community," 6–7.

62. Joyce Gardner, *Cold Mountain Farm: An Attempt at Community* (N.p., 1970), 1.

63. On Bryn Athyn see Houriet, *Getting Back Together*, 39–53. Rockbottom Farm appeared for several years in various directories and lists of communes; see, for example, "Commune Directory," *Communities* 7 (Mar.–Apr. 1974): 36.

64. Fairfield, *Communes USA*, 164–76, 180–85.

65. Hedgepeth and Stock, *The Alternative*, 73.

66. Fairfield, *Communes USA*, 193.

67. "Ahimsa Community," listing in *Modern Utopian* 3, no. 4 (fall 1969): 22.

68. Jim Fowler, 60s Communes Project interview, Aug. 22, 1996.

69. Personal communication from Joe Peterson, Aug. 1993.

70. See, for example, "Declaration of Creation," *Avatar* n.d. [1968], 3. On page 2 are printed the words "BUT MEL LYMAN IS THE AVATAR and all that has been communicated has come from Mel." For more of Lyman's pronouncements and information on the group's early history see Paul Mills, "Mel Lyman: An American Avatar," in Fairfield, *Utopia, USA*, 77–83, 100.

71. The most unfavorable piece of publicity was David Felton, "The Lyman Family's Holy Siege of America," in *Mindfuckers*, ed. David Felton (San Francisco: Straight Arrow Books, 1972), which compared the group unfavorably with the Manson Family. See also Bruce Chatwin, *What Am I Doing Here* (New York: Viking, 1989), 36–41. One of the few later articles about the group is "Once-Notorious '60s Commune Evolves into Respectability," *Los Angeles Times*, Aug. 4, 1985, 10–14.

4. OUT OF THE HAIGHT AND BACK TO THE LAND:
COUNTERCULTURAL COMMUNES AFTER THE SUMMER OF LOVE

1. Philip E. Slater, *The Pursuit of Loneliness: American Culture at the Breaking Point* (Boston: Beacon, 1970), 5.

2. Jan Hodenfield, "It Was Like Balling for the First Time," *Rolling Stone,* Sept. 20, 1969.

3. Information taken from a sign at Olompali State Park in 1996.

4. Sheila U.S.A., 60s Communes Project interview, Sept. 18, 1996.

5. Ibid.

6. Vivian Gotters, 60s Communes Project interview, Mar. 23, 1996.

7. Noelle Barton, 60s Communes Project interview, Sept. 15, 1996. The quotation in the following paragraph comes from this interview as well.

8. Richard Marley, 60s Communes Project interview, Sept. 13, 1996.

9. Coyote, *Sleeping Where I Fall,* 152.

10. *January Thaw: People at Blue Mt. Ranch Write About Living Together in the Mountains* (New York: Times Change, 1974), 21.

11. Berger, *Survival of a Counterculture,* 29–30.

12. Ibid., 30.

13. Allen Cohen, 60s Communes Project interview, Mar. 25, 1996.

14. "Alpha Farm," informational brochure, ca. 1995.

15. Caroline Estes, 60s Communes Project interview, July 18, 1995.

16. "The Commune Comes to America," *Life,* July 18, 1969, 16B–23.

17. Houriet, *Getting Back Together,* 197–98.

18. Jon Stewart, "Communes in Taos," in *Conversations with the New Reality: Readings in the Cultural Revolution,* ed. by the Editors of *Ramparts* (San Francisco: Canfield Press/Harper and Row, 1971), 216.

19. "Home Free Home," 143.

20. H. Gardner, *Children of Prosperity,* 116.

21. Ibid., 94–95.

22. David Ostroff, personal communication, 1996.

23. H. Gardner, *Children of Prosperity,* 100–101.

24. For further information, sometimes fragmentary, on these communes see the following sources: Church of the Five Star Ranch (commonly called Five Star or White House), "New Mexico Road," *Last Whole Earth Catalog* (Menlo Park, Calif.: Portola Institute, 1971), 244, and Sterling F. Wheeler, "New Mexico: No Mecca for Hippies," *Christian Century* 87 (July 1, 1970): 828–30; on the Furry Freak Brothers, Lucy Horton, *Country Commune Cooking* (New York: Coward, McCann and Geoghegan, 1972), 83–84; on the Kingdom of Heaven, "Home Free Home," 138.

25. Dean Fleming, personal communication, 1993.

26. David Perkins, "Commune," *Spirit Magazine: Rocky Mountain Southwest* 9, no. 1 (spring/summer 1996): 15.

27. Most of this information about the communes of Huerfano County was communicated orally by Dean Fleming and Sibylla Wallenborn on several occasions since 1994.

28. "Brotherhood of the Spirit: The Most Successful Commune in the U.S.A.," *Free Spirit Press* 1, no. 4 (n.d., ca. 1972): 33, 35.

29. For a popular-press account of daily life in the community see Patricia Curtis, "We Live in a Commune," *Family Circle,* Feb. 1973, 50, 52, 61, 118.

30. Houriet, *Getting Back Together,* 347.

31. Levi H. Dowling, *The Aquarian Gospel of Jesus the Christ* (London: Fowler, 1920 [1907]). The book has been published in dozens of editions.

32. Jerome, *Families of Eden,* 33.

33. Karol Borowski, who had access to the community's records, calculated peak membership at 260 in 1972, but in an oral presentation in 1995 provided a peak figure of 350 in 1980. See Karol Borowski, *Attempting an Alternative Society* (Norwood, Pa.: Norwood Editions, 1984), 93–94; Borowski's oral presentation was made at the International Communal Studies Association conference, Ramat Efal, Israel, June 1, 1995. Cris and Oliver Popenoe provide a figure of 365 but provide no source or date for it; Cris Popenoe and Oliver Popenoe, "The Renaissance Community: A Commune of the 1960s That Survived," in *Seeds of Tomorrow: New Age Communities That Work* (San Francisco: Harper and Row, 1984), 53.

34. "Renaissance Community Is Looking for New People," flyer, ca. 1993.

35. Laura Berg and Norman Toy, 60s Communes Project interview, Aug. 4, 1996.

36. Aura Bland, "'Hippies' in These Later Days," *Greenfield (Massachusetts) Reporter,* Sept. 17, 1988, 4.

37. Raymond Mungo, *Total Loss Farm: A Year in the Life* (New York: Bantam, 1971 [1970]).

38. The story of the heist and its aftermath is told in Raymond Mungo, *Famous Long Ago: My Life and Hard Times with Liberation News Service* (Boston: Beacon, 1970), chap. 9.

39. Verandah Porche and Richard Wizansky, "Skating Home from the Apocalypse," in *Home Comfort,* 29.

40. Marty Jezer, "Total Loss Economics," in *Home Comfort,* 150.

41. Among the many books, in addition to *Home Comfort* and Mungo's previously cited works, were Pete Gould, *Burnt Toast* (New York: Knopf, 1971); Verandah Porche, *The Body's Symmetry* (New York: Harper and Row, 1974); and Marty Jezer, *Fifty Years of Nonviolent Resistance* (New York: War Resisters League, 1973).

42. Marty Jezer, "The DRV," *WIN* 4, no. 1 (Jan. 1, 1969): 13.

43. Kathleen Burge, "88 Acres and a Lasting Dream," *Boston Globe,* July 14, 1996, 29, 34.

44. Stephen Diamond, *What the Trees Said: Life on a New Age Farm* (New York: Dell, 1971).

45. Ibid., 176.

46. Andrew Kopkind, "Up the Country: Five Communes in Vermont," *Working Papers for a New Society* 1, no. 1 (1973): 44–49.

47. "Shannon Farm Community," in *The New Age Community Guidebook: Alternative Choices in Lifestyles,* 4th ed. (Middletown, Calif.: Harbin Springs Publishing, 1989), 49; see also 60s Communes Project interviews with Dan Questenberry and Jenny Upton.

48. Harvey Baker, 60s Communes Project interview, Oct. 19, 1995.

49. "Introduction to the Federation of Egalitarian Communities," FEC booklet, 1994.

50. "Sharing the Dream," Federation of Egalitarian Communities introductory booklet, 1995.

51. Keith and Joel, "Intercommunities Inc.," *Communities* 7 (Mar.–Apr. 1974): 24–25. Other information on cooperation among communities was provided by Allen Butcher in personal communications on several occasions.

5. SEARCHING FOR A COMMON CENTER: RELIGIOUS AND SPIRITUAL COMMUNES

1. Robert S. Ellwood, Jr., *One Way: The Jesus Movement and Its Meaning* (Englewood Cliffs, N.J.: Prentice-Hall, 1973), 11–23.

2. Hiley H. Ward, *The Far-Out Saints of the Jesus Communes* (New York: Association Press, 1972), 48, 36.

3. For anecdotal accounts of sexual activity among the supposedly refraining believers see Ward, *Far-Out Saints of the Jesus Communes,* chap. 7. See also Roger C. Palms, *The Jesus Kids* (Valley Forge, Pa.: Judson, 1971), 42–43.

4. Joe V. Peterson, "The Rise and Fall of Shiloh," *Communities: Journal of Cooperative Living* 92 (fall 1996): 61. For a more detailed enumeration of the businesses, especially those located at the rural headquarters, see James T. Richardson, Mary White Stewart, and Robert B. Simmonds, *Organized Miracles: A Study of a Contemporary, Youth, Communal, Fundamentalist Organization* (New Brunswick, N.J.: Transaction, 1979), 21–37.

5. See Jeanie Murphy, "A Shiloh Sister's Story," *Communities: Journal of Cooperative Living* 92 (fall 1996): 29–32.

6. Peterson, "The Rise and Fall of Shiloh," 60–65.

7. For details of the Huntington Beach coffeehouse activities see Roy Wallis, *Salvation and Protest: Studies of Social and Religious Movements* (London: Frances Pinter, 1979), 54–55.

8. David E. Van Zandt, *Living in the Children of God* (Princeton, N.J.: Princeton Univ. Press, 1991), 37.

9. Anson D. Shupe, Jr., and David G. Bromley, *The New Vigilantes: Deprogrammers, Anti-Cultists, and the New Religions* (Beverly Hills, Calif.: Sage, 1980), 90. Shupe and Bromley place the founding of FREECOG in 1972; Van Zandt, in *Living in the Children of God* (37), dates the organization at August 1971.

10. Van Zandt, *Living in the Children of God*, 41.

11. Basic historical information on the Children of God/the Family has been published in a number of places. See, for example, David Millikan, "The Children of God, Family of Love, The Family," in *Sex, Slander, and Salvation: Investigating The Family/Children of God*, ed. James R. Lewis and J. Gordon Melton (Stanford, Calif.: Center for Academic Publication, 1994), 181–252.

12. For a characterization of the early Alamo movement in Los Angeles see Ellwood, *One Way*, 60–61, 83–85.

13. "The Pope's Secrets," pamphlet, Holy Alamo Christian Church, Consecrated, Alma, Arkansas, n.d.

14. The most comprehensive historical study of the Alamo community and the source of most of the information in this brief sketch is Rosalie A. Vaught, "The Tony and Susan Alamo Christian Foundation," M.A. thesis, Univ. of Kansas, 1996.

15. In 1984 state troopers raided the Island Pond community, removing over 100 children from the premises; for a press account of the raid see "Children of Sect Seized in Vermont," *New York Times*, June 23, 1984, 1, 6. For community members' own accounts of their repeated conflicts with the authorities and former spouses over childrearing issues see Jean Swantko and Ed Wiseman, "Messianic Communities, Sociologists, and the Law," and Isaac Dawson, "My Son Michael," both in *Communities: Journal of Cooperative Living* 88 (fall 1995): 34–35, 36–38.

16. John M. Bozeman, "The Northeast Kingdom Community Church in Island Pond, Vermont: Raising Up a People for Yahshua's Return," paper presented at the annual meeting of the Communal Studies Association, Oneida, N.Y., Oct. 9, 1994.

17. John M. Bozeman, "Jesus People U.S.A. after Twenty Years: Balancing Sectarianism and Assimilation," paper presented at the annual meeting of the Communal Studies Association, New Harmony, Ind., Oct. 16, 1993.

18. Jon Trott, 60s Communes Project interview.

19. Joe Roos, 60s Communes Project interview. On the outreach programs see Rose Berger, "Community Self-Portrait," in *Fire, Salt, and Peace: Intentional Christian Communities Alive in North America*, ed. David Janzen (Evanston, Ill.: Shalom Mission Communities, 1996), 145.

20. Among Wallis's several books are *The Call to Conversion: Recovering the Gospel for These Times* (San Francisco: HarperSanFrancisco, 1981), *Waging Peace: A Handbook for the Struggle to Abolish Nuclear Weapons* (San Francisco: Harper and Row, 1982), and *Who Speaks for God? An Alternative to the Religious Right—A New Politics of Compassion, Community, and Civility* (New York: Delacorte, 1996).

21. Kent Philpott, "Zion's Inn, Home for the Mangled," in *New Christian Communities: Origins, Style, and Survival*, ed. Michael Zeik (Williston Park, N.Y.: Roth, 1973), chap. 1.

22. Ward, *Far-Out Saints of the Jesus Communes*, 80.

23. Ron Bellamy and Joe Mosley, "Gentle Christians or Dangerous Cult?" *Eugene (Oregon) Register-Guard*, Nov. 6, 1981, 1E–2E.

24. Janzen, *Fire, Salt, and Peace*, 174.

25. Dave Jackson and Neta Jackson, *Glimpses of Glory: Thirty Years of Community: The Story of Reba Place Fellowship* (Elgin, Ill.: Brethren, 1987), 150–54.

26. *Communities Directory* (1995), 257, 267; Mark Shepard, *The Community of the Ark* (Arcata, Calif.: Simple Productions, 1990).

27. *Communities Directory* (1995), 229.

28. Jackson and Jackson, *Glimpses of Glory*, 161–62. See also Michael Harper, *A New Way of Living: How the Church of the Redeemer, Houston, Found a New Lifestyle* (London: Hodder and Stoughton, 1973); Graham Pulkingham, *Gathered for Power* (New York: Morehouse-Barlow, 1972).

29. Perhaps the best of the many works on the Peoples Temple is John R. Hall, *Gone from the Promised Land: Jonestown in American Cultural History* (New Brunswick, N.J.: Transaction, 1987).

30. See, for example, *Buddhist America: Centers, Retreats, Practices*, ed. Don Morreale (Santa Fe, N.M.: John Muir, 1988).

31. The founder's original name was Abhay Charan De. He took the spiritual name A. C. Bhaktivedanta Swami; his followers generally call him by the honorific "Prabhupada."

32. For a summary of the history and theology of the Caitanya movement see "Interview with Shrivatsa Goswami," in *Hare Krishna, Hare Krishna*, ed. Steven J. Gelberg (New York: Grove, 1983), 196–258.

33. Satsvarupa dasa Goswami, *Planting the Seed: New York City, 1965–1966* (Los Angeles: Bhaktivedanta Book Trust, 1980), 135ff. This is volume 2 of a six-volume biography of Bhaktivedanta entitled *Srila Prabhupada-lilamrta*.

34. Lou Gottlieb, Morning Star's founder and patron, always emphasized the fact that Morning Star was established by spiritual seekers, despite its reputation as an anything-goes haven of sex and drugs. Some left upon being exposed to ISKCON, he argued, simply "because it was the only trip around," the other 1960s-era Asian spiritual movements not yet having become established in the United States. Personal communication, Nov. 22, 1992.

35. For a synopsis of ISKCON's most serious crises see E. Burke Rochford, Jr., "Hare Krishna in America: Growth, Decline, Accommodation," in *America's Alternative Religions*, ed. Timothy Miller (Albany: State Univ. of New York Press, 1995), 218.

36. On ISKCON generally see, in addition to the works cited above, E. Burke Rochford, Jr., *Hare Krishna in America* (New Brunswick, N.J.: Rutgers Univ. Press, 1985); Larry D. Shinn, *The Dark Lord: Cult Images and the Hare Krishnas in America* (Philadelphia: Westminster, 1987).

37. Paramahansa Yogananda, *Autobiography of a Yogi* (Los Angeles: Self-Realization Fellowship, 1946).

38. Kriyananda, *Cooperative Communities—How to Start Them, and Why*, 5th ed. (Nevada City, Calif.: Ananda Publications, 1970), 1.

39. On the purchase and early development of the land at Ananda see John Ball, *Ananda: Where Yoga Lives* (Bowling Green, Ohio: Bowling Green Univ. Popular Press, 1982), 35–49.

40. Ball, *Ananda*, 89–96.

41. Ted A. Nordquist, *Ananda Cooperative Village: A Study in the Beliefs, Values, and Attitudes of a New Age Religious Community* (Uppsala, Sweden: Borgströms Tryckeri, 1978), 44.

42. *Communities Directory* (1995), 190.

43. Ananda's legal battles have been reported repeatedly in various alternative and specialized publications; see, for example, "Ananda Village Loses Lawsuit, Faces Financial Crisis," *Communities: Journal of Cooperative Living* 99 (summer 1998): 8; Mark Fearer, "A Fight over Yogananda's Teachings," *Nexus* (Boulder, Colo.), July/Aug. 1998, 16, 18.

44. Nordquist, *Ananda Cooperative Village,* 136.

45. Popenoe and Popenoe, *Seeds of Tomorrow,* 15.

46. For historical vignettes about Ananda conveyed through individual members' own stories of joining and living at the community, see Sara Cryer, *Reflections on Living: 30 Years in a Spiritual Community* (Nevada City, Calif.: Crystal Clarity, 1998).

47. Mark Juergensmeyer, *Radhasoami Reality: The Logic of a Modern Faith* (Princeton, N.J.: Princeton Univ. Press, 1991), 207.

48. H. Gardner, *Children of Prosperity,* 120–33.

49. For an introduction to Yogi Bhajan's thought see Siri Singh Sahib Bhai Sahib Harbhajan Singh Khalsa Yogiji [Yogi Bhajan], *The Teachings of Yogi Bhajan* (New York: Hawthorn, 1977).

50. James V. Downton, Jr., *Sacred Journeys: The Conversion of Young Americans to Divine Light Mission* (New York: Columbia Univ. Press, 1979), 5.

51. "Premie" means "lover"—i.e., one who loves the Guru.

52. For an introduction to the early Divine Light Mission and its leader see *Who Is Guru Maharaj Ji?* ed. Charles Cameron (New York: Bantam, 1973); Downton, *Sacred Journeys.*

53. J. Gordon Melton, *Encyclopedia of American Religions,* 4th ed. (Detroit: Gale Research, 1993), 906.

54. Eileen Barker, *New Religious Movements: A Practical Introduction* (London: Her Majesty's Stationery Office, 1989), 167–68.

55. Gene R. Thursby, "Hindu Movements Since Mid-Century: Yogis in the States," in *America's Alternative Religions,* ed. Miller, 201–4.

56. Swami Rama's story is told in Doug Boyd, *Swami* (New York: Random House, 1976). For an account of life at the Himalayan Institute's communal headquarters see Harriet S. Mosatche, *Searching: Practices and Beliefs of the Religious Cults and Human Potential Groups* (New York: Stravon, 1983), 222–51.

57. Gene R. Thursby, "Siddha Yoga: Swami Muktananda and the Seat of Power," in *When Prophets Die: The Postcharismatic Fate of New Religious Movements,* ed. Timothy Miller (Albany: State Univ. of New York Press, 1991), 165–81. On Muktananda's behavior see William Rodarmor, "The Secret Life of Swami Muktananda," *CoEvolution Quarterly* 40 (winter 1983): 104–11. On the controversies surrounding Chidvilasananda, see Lis Harris, "O Guru, Guru, Guru," *New Yorker,* Nov. 14, 1994, 92–109.

58. See, for example, among several other works, Alan Watts, *The Way of Zen* (New York: Pantheon, 1957); D. T. Suzuki, *An Introduction to Zen Buddhism* (New York: Philosophical Library, 1949); Suzuki, *Essays in Zen Buddhism* (New York: Grove, 1949).

59. Charles S. Prebish, *American Buddhism* (North Scituate, Mass.: Duxbury Press, 1979), 81–86. For reflections on the Zen Center's philosophy and activities see Richard Baker-roshi, "Sangha-Community," in *Earth's Answer,* ed. Michael Katz, William P. Marsh, and Gail Gordon Thompson (New York: Lindisfarne/Harper and Row, 1977), 44–57; reprinted in *Resettling America: Energy, Ecology and Community,* ed. Gary J. Coates (Andover, Mass.: Brick House, 1981), 123–35.

60. For a brief overview of the charges against Baker and his departure from the Zen Center see Helen Tworkov, *Zen in America* (New York: Kodansha International, 1994), 202–3, 234–47. For a member's account of how the Baker crisis affected the community see Katy Butler, "Events Are the Teacher," *CoEvolution Quarterly* 40 (winter 1983): 112–23. See also Sandy Boucher, *Turning the Wheel: American Women Creating the New Buddhism,* 2nd

ed. (Boston: Beacon, 1993), 245–56; Andrew Rawlinson, *The Book of Enlightened Masters: Western Teachers in Eastern Traditions* (Chicago: Open Court, 1997), 166–75.

61. For an illustrated history of Tassajara, see Paul Kagan, *New World Utopias: A Photographic History of the Search for Community* (New York: Penguin, 1975), 158–75. For a visitor's account of community life see Gustaitis, *Turning On*, chap. 9.

62. Edward Espe Brown, *The Tassajara Bread Book* (Boulder, Colo.: Shambhala, 1970); Edward Espe Brown, *Tassajara Cooking* (Boulder, Colo.: Shambhala, 1973).

63. Kenneth Turan, "Why Go to a California Zen Center? The Answer Is Simple," *Washington Post*, Mar. 16, 1997, E1, E5–E6.

64. Stephanie Kaza, "A Community of Attention," *In Context* 29 (summer 1991): 32. See also Rick Fields, *How the Swans Came to the Lake: A Narrative History of Buddhism in America* (Boulder, Colo.: Shambhala, 1981), 268, 366.

65. Popenoe and Popenoe, *Seeds of Tomorrow*, 20.

66. On the leadership crisis see Boucher, *Turning the Wheel*, 214–20.

67. Melton, *Encyclopedia of American Religions*, 4th ed., 989. For a synopsis of Seung Sahn's teaching see *Dropping Ashes on the Buddha: The Teaching of Zen Master Seung Sahn*, ed. Stephen Mitchell (New York: Grove, 1976).

68. Boucher, *Turning the Wheel*, 225–35.

69. Philip Kapleau, *The Three Pillars of Zen: Teaching, Practice, and Enlightenment* (New York: Harper and Row, 1966).

70. Fields, *How the Swans Came to the Lake*, 239–42.

71. Ibid., 252.

72. For a historical sketch of the Maui Zendo see Tworkov, *Zen in America*, 43–61.

73. Trungpa's account of his early life in and escape from Tibet is contained in his *Born in Tibet* (Boston: Shambhala, 1985).

74. For a note on the early evolution of the Rocky Mountain Dharma Center see Rick Fields, "A High History of Buddhism," *Tricycle* 6, no. 1 (fall 1996): 54–55.

75. Tom Clark, *The Great Naropa Poetry Wars* (Santa Barbara, Calif.: Cadmus, 1980).

76. Some basic information on the development of the communal institutions of Trungpa's Shambhala movement can be found in Fields, *How the Swans Came to the Lake*, 308–12.

77. "Only in America," *Tricycle* 6, no. 1 (fall 1996): 112–13. See also Prebish, *American Buddhism*, 123–25.

78. David G. Bromley and Anson D. Shupe, Jr., *"Moonies" in America: Cult, Church, and Crusade* (Beverly Hills, Calif.: Sage, 1979), 36.

79. Gisela Webb, "Sufism in America," in *America's Alternative Religions*, ed. Miller, 250–51.

80. Elizabeth Rechtschaffen, "Resettling the Shakers: The Abode of the Message, New Lebanon, N.Y.," in *Resettling America*, ed. Coates, 138.

81. Khabira Gruber, 60s Communes Project interview, Nov. 15, 1995.

82. For a sketch of the Abode during its first decade see Cris Popenoe and Oliver Popenoe, "The Abode of the Message: Sufis in the Footsteps of the Shakers," in *Seeds of Tomorrow*, chap. 5.

83. "Two Rivers Farm: A Search for Values," Two Rivers Farm introductory flyer, 1988.

84. Gerald B. Bubis, Harry Wasserman, and Alan Lert, *Synagogue Havurot: A Comparative Study* (Washington, D.C.: Center for Jewish Community Studies and University Press of America, 1983), 8; Bernard Reisman, *The Chavurah: A Contemporary Jewish Experience* (New York: Union of American Hebrew Congregations, 1977), 7.

85. One observer maintained that "rumors of drug-taking at the *havurah* seem greatly exaggerated." See Stephen C. Lerner, "The *Havurot*," in *Contemporary Judaic Fellowship in Theory and Practice*, ed. Jacob Neusner (New York: Ktav, 1972), 132.

86. Lerner, in "The *Havurot*," describes some worship practices at Havurat Shalom.

For a fuller description, see Arthur Green, "Some Liturgical Notes for Havurat Shalom," in *Contemporary Judaic Fellowship*, ed. Neusner, 155–60.

87. *The Jewish Catalog*, ed. Richard Siegel, Michael Strassfeld, and Sharon Strassfeld (Philadelphia: Jewish Publication Society of America, 1973). The section called "Communities" is on 278–88.

88. Bill Novak, "Havurat Shalom: A Personal Account," in *Contemporary Judaic Fellowship*, ed. Neusner, 239–70.

89. Several of these campus havurot and batim are identified in Jon Groner, "The 1973 Phenomenon—Jewish Residences," *Sh'ma* 3, no. 54 (May 11, 1973): 105–6.

90. The estimate of several dozen havurot is supplied by Bubis, Wasserman, and Lert, *Synagogue Havurot*, 13, although they note that there are no solid data either on the number of havurot or on their life spans.

91. Reisman, *The Chavurah*, 13.

92. Quoted from an early Lama descriptive brochure in Stewart, "Communes in Taos," 218.

93. *Be Here Now* (San Cristobal, N.M.: Lama, 1971).

94. See "Lama Sizes Up Devastation," *Albuquerque Journal*, May 7, 1996, 1ff.

95. For some years all Farm members subscribed to a vow of poverty that declared in part, "We have a common treasury. All money from whatever source is given to our bank which distributes the money according to need—to further our religious and educational purposes, and to provide everyone in our community with food, clothing, housing, and ordinary medical and dental supplies and services. No individual member of our Church owns property." See Rupert Fike, ed., *Voices from The Farm: Adventures in Community Living* (Summertown, Tenn.: Book Publishing Co., 1998), 9.

96. Stephen and the Farm, *Hey Beatnik!* (unpaginated).

97. Stephen Gaskin, "Om," in *Hey Beatnik!* (unpaginated).

98. For an overview of Stephen's teachings at the Monday Night Class see Michael Traugot, *A Short History of the Farm* (Summertown, Tenn.: The author, 1994), 6–10. (Available from the author at 84 The Farm, Summertown, Tenn., 38483.)

99. Stephen's talks on the Caravan and many photographs of the adventure were published as *The Caravan* (New York and Berkeley, Calif.: Random House/Bookworks, 1972).

100. "The Dope Statement," in *Hey Beatnik!* (unpaginated).

101. The Farm's argument that its use of marijuana should have been protected as the free exercise of religion, along with other documents relating to the case, is reproduced in *The Grass Case* (Summertown, Tenn.: Book Publishing Co., 1974).

102. Ina May Gaskin, 60s Communes Project interview, Oct. 19, 1995.

103. Stephen Gaskin, 60s Communes Project interview, Oct. 18, 1995.

104. One of the Farm's best-selling books came from its interest in avoiding artificial birth control; see Margaret Nofziger, *A Cooperative Method of Natural Birth Control* (Summertown, Tenn.: Book Publishing Co., 1976).

105. "Hey Ladies!" in *Hey Beatnik!* (unpaginated).

106. Another steady-selling Farm book emerged from the birthing program: Ina May Gaskin, *Spiritual Midwifery* (Summertown, Tenn.: Book Publishing Co., 1990 [1977]).

107. See Lillie Wilson, "The Plenty Project: Inside the Hippie Peace Corps," *New Age*, July 1981, 18–27.

108. Traugot, *Short History of the Farm*, 46–48.

109. Wilson, "The Plenty Project," 24–25.

110. Albert K. Bates, *Climate in Crisis: The Greenhouse Effect and What We Can Do* (Summertown, Tenn.: Book Publishing Co., 1990). This book contains a foreword by then-Senator Albert Gore, Jr., who at one point was an active ally of Farm environmentalists.

111. *Shutdown: Nuclear Power on Trial* (Summertown, Tenn.: Book Publishing Co., 1979).

112. Albert Bates, "Technological Innovation in a Rural Intentional Community," *Bulletin of Science, Technology, and Society* 8 (1988): 183–99.

113. Many of Stephen's talks were collected and published in book form. See, for example, Gaskin, *Volume One: Sunday Morning Services on The Farm.*

114. On family structures, including the early experiments in "four-marriage" (i.e., two couples together), see Traugot, *Short History of The Farm,* 24–25.

115. For anecdotes that illuminate some of the dissatisfaction that long-time members felt, see "Why We Left the Farm," *Whole Earth Review* 49 (winter 1985): 56–66.

116. Traugot, *Short History of the Farm,* 59.

117. "Operating Manual for the Second Foundation," brochure, 1993.

118. Stephen Gaskin, 60s Communes Project interview.

119. [Stephen Gaskin], "Rocinante: A Commune by and for Elders," *Whole Earth Review* 72 (fall 1991): 114–15.

120. Albert Bates, personal communication, Sept. 1998.

121. Information on the Ecovillage Training Center and other Farm projects can be found at http://www.thefarm.org.

122. Love Israel, 60s Communes Project interview, Sept. 6, 1996.

123. Serious Israel, 60s Communes Project interview, Sept. 6, 1996.

124. Linda Shaw, "Coming of Age," *Seattle Times/Post-Intelligencer,* Mar. 10, 1991, A6.

125. Stephen Clutter, "Twist in State Law May Aid Group's Dreams for Future," *Seattle Times,* Mar. 11, 1997, A1–A2; "Ex-Commune Leader Wants to Build Homes," *Oregonian (Portland),* Mar. 13, 1997, E11.

126. Information about the Love Israel Family not otherwise attributed comes mainly from Charles P. LeWarne, "The Love Israel Family: An Urban Commune Becomes a Rural Commune," paper presented at the annual conference of the Communal Studies Association, New Harmony, Ind., Oct. 17, 1993.

127. In 1993 the community reportedly had over 90 children under age 18; they were given summer jobs beginning at age 10. Troy Guthrie, "Commune's Future Lies with Children," *Times-Mail (Bedford, Ind.),* Oct. 18, 1993.

128. One scholar has argued that Padanaram embraces misogyny. The community vigorously disputes the charge, arguing that it is based on inadequate exposure to the community's daily life and on the scholar's disagreement with Padanaram's point of view. See Wagner, *Sex Roles in Contemporary American Communes,* chap. 7; letter from Daniel Wright to the National Historic Communal Societies Association, Apr. 18, 1988 (a copy is in the archives of the Center for Communal Studies at the University of Southern Indiana, Evansville, Ind.). See also Daniel Wright, 60s Communes Project interview.

129. Fairfield, *Communes USA,* 130–38; Hedgepeth and Stock, *The Alternative,* 117–26. Noonan has proclaimed his message in several books; see, for example, Allen-Michael [Noonan], *The Everlasting Gospel: To the Youth of the World* (Berkeley, Calif.: Starmast, 1973). The community's restaurants led to the publication of a cookbook: Kathryn Hannaford, *Cosmic Cookery* (Berkeley, Calif.: Starmast, 1974).

130. Robert de Grimston, *As It Is* (Chicago: Process Church of the Final Judgement, 1967), flyleaf.

131. The most complete study of the Process Church prior to its reorganization into the Foundation Faith is William Sims Bainbridge, *Satan's Power: A Deviant Psychotherapy Cult* (Berkeley: Univ. of California Press, 1978).

132. For a brief synopsis of the Process Church see David G. Bromley and Susan G. Ainsley, "Satanism and Satanic Churches: The Contemporary Incarnations," in *America's Alternative Religions,* ed. Miller, 405.

6. SECULAR VISIONARIES: COMMUNES FOR SOCIAL REFORM AND THE GOOD LIFE

1. Cynthia Arvio, "Take HEART—All Those in the Struggle," *Communities: Journal of Cooperative Living* 19 (Mar./Apr. 1976): 11.

2. Arvio, "Take HEART," 10; "Movement for a New Society," *Communities: A Journal of Cooperative Living* 8 (May/June 1974): 52.

3. James S. Best, *Another Way to Live: Experiencing Intentional Community* (Wallingford, Pa.: Pendle Hill, 1978), 27.

4. For an account touching on the later life of an ongoing MNS community see Jonathan Betz-Zall, "'Meta-Politics' at Bright Morning Star," *Communities: Journal of Cooperative Living* 100 (fall 1998): 43–44.

5. Rachelle Linner, 60s Communes Project interview, Dec. 4, 1995.

6. John Mintz and Barbara Carton, "Snyder Agrees to Deal on D.C. Homeless Shelter," *Washington Post,* Mar. 17, 1986, A1.

7. Chris Spolar and Marcia Slacum Greene, "Mitch Snyder Found Hanged in CCNV Shelter," *Washington Post,* July 9, 1990, A1.

8. Chris Spolar, "CCNV Looks to Its Strength," *Washington Post,* July 9, 1990, A1, A6.

9. Michael Ferber and Staughton Lynd, *The Resistance* (Boston: Beacon, 1971), chap. 6.

10. 60s Communes Project interview, 1996.

11. 60s Communes Project interview, 1996.

12. Kenoli Oleari, 60s Communes Project interview, Sept. 16, 1996.

13. *20 Years on the Move* [Philadelphia: MOVE, ca. 1991], 2.

14. John Anderson and Hilary Hevenor, *Burning Down the House: MOVE and the Tragedy of Philadelphia* (New York: Norton, 1987).

15. Tony Miksak, "Vocations for Social Change," *WIN* 4, no. 1 (Jan. 1, 1969): 7.

16. On the rarity of group marriage communes see Larry L. and Joan M. Constantine, "The Group Marriage," in *The Nuclear Family in Crisis: The Search for Alternatives,* ed. Michael Gordon (New York: Harper and Row, 1972), 206. Studies of such communes apart from the few that sought publicity are rare; for one example see David E. Smith and Alan J. Rose, "The Group Marriage Commune: A Case Study," *Journal of Psychedelic Drugs* 3, no. 1 (Sept. 1970): 115–19.

17. For early views at Kerista, see Robert Anton Wilson, "The Religion of Kerista and Its 69 Positions," *Fact* 2, no. 4 (July–Aug. 1965): 23–29, and John Gruen, *The New Bohemia: The Combine Generation* (New York: Shorecrest, 1966), 49–60.

18. On Kerista's life and ideas see *Polyfidelity: Sex in the Kerista Commune and Other Related Theories on How to Solve the World's Problems* (San Francisco: Performing Arts Social Society, 1984).

19. Mitch Slomiak, 60s Communes Project interview, Mar. 21, 1996.

20. Robert H. Rimmer, *The Harrad Experiment* (New York: Bantam, 1967 [1966]); Robert H. Rimmer, *Proposition 31* (New York: New American Library, 1968). Rimmer also wrote other books on the subject.

21. "Harrad West," *Modern Utopian* 4, no. 1 (winter 1969–70) (unpaginated).

22. Fairfield, *Communes USA,* 292–304.

23. Ibid., 317.

24. For a description of life and of sleeping and sexual arrangements in the house see Katz, *Armed Love,* 117–20.

25. Katz, *Armed Love,* 127.

26. The most complete account of Family life—by one who lived there in 1970—is Margaret Gloria Hollenbach, "'The Family': A Commune in Taos, New Mexico," M.A. thesis, Univ. of Washington, 1971. For a shorter overview of the life and history of the Family see John A. Hostetler, *Communitarian Societies* (New York: Holt, Rinehart and Winston, 1974), chap. 2.

27. Fairfield, *Communes USA*, 329; Katz, *Armed Love*, 123.

28. Kanter, *Commitment and Community*, 189.

29. "Greenfeel," *Modern Utopian* 4, no. 1 (winter 1969–70) (unpaginated).

30. Fairfield, *Communes USA*, 304–14.

31. H. Gardner, *Children of Prosperity*, chap. 11.

32. Sue, Nelly, Dian, Carol, and Billie, *Country Lesbians: The Story of WomanShare Collective* (Grants Pass, Ore.: WomanShare, 1976), 172.

33. For a concise description of arcology see Paolo Soleri, "The City of the Future," in *Earth's Answer*, ed. Katz et al., 72–77.

34. Several articles have been written on Soleri and Arcosanti. See, for example, Paul Preuss, "The Soleri Dream," *Human Behavior* 7, no. 7 (July 1978): 53–58. Soleri has described his ideas and Arcosanti, specifically, in his own books; see, for example, Paolo Soleri, *Arcology: The City in the Image of Man* (Cambridge, Mass.: MIT Press, 1969); Paolo Soleri, *Arcosanti: An Urban Laboratory?* 3rd ed. (Scottsdale, Ariz.: Cosanti, 1993).

35. For an article that provides an overview of Arcosanti but expresses frustration with the project's slow progress, see Sheri F. Crawford, "Arcosanti: An American Community Looking Toward the Millennium," *Communal Societies* 14 (1994): 49–66.

36. Bill Bishop, "State Files Lawsuit against Eco-Village," *Eugene Register-Guard*, June 27, 1997, 1B, 5B.

37. Cerro Gordo has published a good deal of information about itself; see, for example, the many issues of *Cerro Gordo Town Forum* and the *Cerro Gordo News*. See also *Cerro Gordo: Plans, Progress and Process* (Cottage Grove, Ore.: Town Forum, 1985), a booklet issued by the organization. One descriptive article by the community's founder is Christopher Canfield, "Cerro Gordo: Future Residents Organize to Plan and Build an Ecological Village Community," in *Resettling America*, ed. Coates, 186–213.

38. For an overview of notable ecovillage projects active worldwide in the early 1990s see *Eco-Villages and Sustainable Communities: A Report for Gaia Trust by Context Institute* (Bainbridge Island, Wash.: Context Institute, 1991).

39. For a detailed survey of the arts and crafts colonies, see chapter two of Timothy Miller, *The Quest for Utopia in Twentieth-Century America: 1900–1960* (Syracuse: Syracuse Univ. Press, 1998).

40. On Almanac House see R. Serge Denisoff, *Great Day Coming: Folk Music and the American Left* (Baltimore: Penguin, 1973 [1971]), 78–79.

41. For many vignettes of life at 710 Ashbury and at Olompali, see Rock Scully with David Dalton, *Living with the Dead: Twenty Years on the Bus with Garcia and the Grateful Dead* (Boston: Little, Brown, 1996) — although the reader should be warned that some associated with the Dead scene have decried the volume as having many inaccuracies. For photographs of band members at 710 Ashbury and Olompali see Jerilyn Lee Brandelius, *Grateful Dead Family Album* (New York: Warner, 1989), 31–44.

42. Carolyn Adams Garcia, 60s Communes Project interview, July 15, 1996.

43. John Sinclair, quotation on cover, *Berkeley Tribe*, July 17–24, 1970.

44. Popenoe and Popenoe, *Seeds of Tomorrow*, 80.

45. Beth Roy, "Human Ecology," *Ms.* 3, no. 2 (Aug. 1974): 94.

46. Peter Bartzchak, 60s Communes Project interview, May 25, 1996.

47. On Project Artaud see Stephen Kelly and Beck Dominic, "Project Artaud," *Communities: Journal of Cooperative Living* 18 (Jan./Feb. 1976): 4; on Project One see Roy, "Human Ecology"; on Project Two see "The City Community," *Alternatives Journal* 20 (Jan. 1–15, 1973): 1–2.

48. For a discussion of some of the specific circumstances under which persons joined urban communes see Albert Solnit, "Wear and Tear in the Communes," *Nation* 222 (Apr. 16, 1971): 524–27.

49. Carl Bernstein wrote of one family that had had trouble making ends meet on

$200 per week, but by moving to a communal house was doing much better on a mere $45. See Carl Bernstein, "Communes, a New Way of Life in the District," *Washington Post*, July 6, 1969, C1–C2. Bernstein found at least forty communes in Washington, principally in the inner city, with six to fifteen members each.

50. Rosabeth Moss Kanter, "Communes in Cities," *Working Papers for a New Society* (summer 1974): 36.

51. Mark Perlgut, "Communal Living: Adventure in Relating to Others," *New York Times*, Nov. 28, 1971, A7.

52. Eric Raimy, *Shared Houses, Shared Lives: The New Extended Families and How They Work* (Los Angeles: Tarcher, 1979).

53. Ann Hershberger, "The Transiency of Urban Communes," in Kanter, *Communes*, 485–91.

54. For sketches of individual communes not discussed here see *Exploring Intimate Life Styles*, ed. Bernard I. Murstein (New York: Springer, 1978); "Communal Living Comes in from the Woods," *Money*, Nov. 1976, 87–88; Pamela G. Hollie, "More Families Share Houses with Others to Enhance 'Life Style,'" *Wall Street Journal*, July 7, 1971, 1, 19.

55. "Commune in Disguise Flourishes in Suburbs," *New York Times*, Dec. 7, 1975, R1, R8.

56. Maitland Zane, "Living Together in California," *Nation* 211, no. 12 (Oct. 19, 1970): 361.

57. J. R. Kennedy, "Communes," *Fifth Estate* (Detroit), Aug. 6–19, 1970.

58. See Grace Lichtenstein, "Communal Living Here Lures the Untied but Lonely," *New York Times*, Dec. 7, 1970, 47, 89.

59. Kanter, *Commitment and Community*, 201–12; Lewis Yablonsky, *Synanon: The Tunnel Back* (Baltimore: Penguin, 1967 [1965]); Laurie Miller, "Inside Synanon," *Alternatives Journal* 24 (Mar. 1–15, 1973): 1; personal communications with former Synanon members. As of early 1999 a full study of Synanon by Rod Janzen was reported to be nearing publication.

60. Adams with Mylander, *Gesundheit!*

61. Zane, "Living Together in California," 360–63.

62. Jerry LeBlanc, "Communes for the Middle Class," *Chicago Tribune Magazine*, Apr. 21, 1974, 43–45, 48.

63. Laurence Veysey, "Communal Sex and Communal Survival: Individualism Busts the Commune Boom," *Psychology Today* 8, no. 7 (Dec. 1974): 73–78.

64. Reproduced in "Institute of Human Abilities," *Alternatives Newsmagazine*, undated "Commune Directory" issue (1971): 4–5.

65. One lengthy and rather skeptical article on the Morehouse movement is "Sgt. Bilko Meets the New Culture," *Rolling Stone*, Dec. 9, 1971, 40–46.

66. Marlise James, "A Commune for Old Folks," *Life*, May 1972, 53ff.

67. Kenoli Oleari, 60s Communes Project interview, Sept. 16, 1996.

7. ENDS AND MEANS: COMMUNAL IDEOLOGIES,
ECONOMICS, AND ORGANIZATION

1. See, for example, Charles Reich, *The Greening of America* (New York: Random House, 1970); Theodore Roszak, *The Making of a Counter Culture: Reflections on the Technocratic Society and Its Youthful Opposition* (Garden City, N.Y.: Doubleday, 1969).

2. Bennett Berger, Bruce Hackett, and R. Mervyn Millar, "The Communal Family," *Family Coordinator* 21, no. 4 (Oct. 1972): 421.

3. Jerry Garcia, quoted in Ron Piper, "Some Lives and Times of the Truly Psychedelically-Inspired Musical Icon of the 1960's," *Psychedelic Illuminations* 1, no. 8 (winter 1995–96): 36.

4. J. Harvey Baker, 60s Communes Project interview, Oct. 19, 1995.

5. John Sinclair and Robert Levin, *Music and Politics* (New York: World, 1971), 60.

6. Bruce Taub, personal communication, Jan. 1997.

7. Adams with Mylander, *Gesundheit!* 53.

8. Mungo, *Total Loss Farm,* 152.

9. Ibid., 173.

10. "Where Have All the Flower Children Gone? To Communes," *Washington Post,* Nov. 14, 1971, K11.

11. Mungo, *Famous Long Ago,* 94.

12. Nancy Nesbit, "Get Back to Where You Belong," *Modern Utopian* 4, nos. 3 and 4 (summer–fall 1970): 15.

13. On the appearance of the Bear Tribe see "Bear Tribe," *Alternatives Newsmagazine* [no. 1] (1971): 9–10. Sun Bear and others in the Bear Tribe have written several books on their work; see, for example, Sun Bear, Wabun, and Nimimosha, *The Bear Tribe's Self-Reliance Book* (New York: Prentice Hall, 1988).

14. Pam Hanna, computer bulletin board posting, 1996. Hanna's communal memoirs are posted at www.diggers.org/mstar_chron1.htm.

15. Sundancer, *Celery Wine,* 82.

16. Cat Yronwode, 60s Communes Project interview, May 29, 1996.

17. Lou Gottlieb, personal communication, Oct. 13, 1994.

18. Vivian Gotters, 60s Communes Project interview, Mar. 23, 1996.

19. Daniel Wright, 60s Communes Project interview, July 24, 1997.

20. Bruce Taub, personal communication, Jan. 9, 1997.

21. On the recovery of human tribalism in contemporary alternative cultures see Gary Snyder, "Why Tribe," in Richard, *The Good Life,* 135–39.

22. Marty Jezer, "How I Came Here," in *Home Comfort,* 37.

23. *January Thaw,* 86–90.

24. Gorkin, "Notes from New Mexico," *Rag* (Austin, Texas), July 10, 1969. Originally published in the *Village Voice.*

25. "Year of the Commune," *Newsweek,* Aug. 18, 1969, 89.

26. Huw "Piper" Williams, interviewed by Timothy Miller, Sept. 11, 1990.

27. Rico Reed, 60s Communes Project interview, Sept. 10, 1996.

28. 60s Communes Project interview, 1996.

29. J. Gardner, *Cold Mountain Farm,* 35–42.

30. *The Big Dummy's Guide to C.B. Radio* (Summertown, Tenn.: Book Publishing Co., 1976).

31. Jerry Rubin, "Rubin Raps: Money's to Burn," *Berkeley Barb,* Jan. 19–26, 1968.

32. Walter Bowart, "Casting the Money Throwers from the Temple," *East Village Other,* Sept. 1–15, 1967.

33. Huw Williams, 60s Communes Project interview, Sept. 9, 1996.

34. Marty Jezer, statement written for the 60s Communes Project, Nov. 7, 1995.

35. H. Gardner, *Children of Prosperity,* 93–101.

36. J. Gardner, *Cold Mountain Farm,* 3.

37. Bruce Taub, personal communication, 1996.

38. For a discussion of various economic arrangements in several typical Christian communities see Dave and Neta Jackson, *Living Together in a World Falling Apart* (Carol Stream, Ill.: Creation House, 1974), chap. 30.

39. Virginia Stem Owens, *Assault on Eden: A Memoir of Communal Life in the Early '70s,* 2nd ed. (Grand Rapids, Mich.: Baker, 1995), 94.

40. Sundancer, *Celery Wine,* 115.

41. See, for example, Yaswen, "Sunrise Hill Community," 17–18.

42. William Hedgepeth, "Maybe It'll Be Different Here," *Look,* Mar. 23, 1971, 70.

43. John Nelson, 60s Communes Project interview, Mar. 26, 1996.

44. Jerome, *Families of Eden*, 94.

45. Acharya Palaniswami, 60s Communes Project interview, July 7, 1997.

46. The sex industry provided relatively profitable employment for members of a number of communes. Robert Houriet, for example, told of a young woman at the Oz commune in Pennsylvania who modeled for a pornographic photographer. See Houriet, "Life and Death of a Commune Called Oz," in Kanter, *Communes*, 475; originally published in the *New York Times Magazine*, Feb. 16, 1969. The story of three communards' trip to San Francisco for a lucrative stint acting in a pornographic movie is recounted in "The Burgeoning of Real Goods: John Schaeffer," *The New Settler Interview* 107 (Oct./mid-Nov. 1997): 6.

47. John Rippey, 60s Communes Project interview, Mar. 22, 1996.

48. John Curl, personal communication, 1991.

49. Raymond Mungo, 60s Communes Project interview, Dec. 28, 1998.

50. Kleps, *Millbrook*, 70.

51. Marty Jerome, 60s Communes Project interview, Sept. 8, 1996.

52. Jon and Carol Trott, 60s Communes Project interview, Apr. 15, 1996.

53. See, for example, a discussion of High Ridge Farm's divided opinions about accepting and using food stamps in Sundancer, *Celery Wine*, 138–40.

54. Allen Cohen, 60s Communes Project interview, Mar. 25, 1996.

55. Bill Wheeler, 60s Communes Project interview, Mar. 24, 1996.

56. See United States Department of Agriculture et al. v. Moreno et al., no. 72-534, 413 U.S. 528; 93 S. Ct. 2821; 1973 U.S. Lexis 33; 37 L. Ed. 2d 782.

57. Sterling F. Wheeler, "New Mexico: No Mecca for Hippies," *Christian Century* 87, no. 26 (July 1, 1970): 829.

58. Steven V. Roberts, "Halfway Between Dropping Out and Dropping In," *New York Times Magazine*, September 12, 1971, pp. 44–70.

59. 60s Communes Project interview, 1996.

60. Crescent Dragonwagon, *The Commune Cookbook* (New York: Simon and Schuster, 1972), 154, 156.

61. Hedgepeth, "Maybe It'll Be Different Here," 70.

62. Bennett M. Berger, Bruce M. Hackett, and R. Mervyn Millar, "Supporting the Communal Family," in Kanter, *Communes*, 246.

63. J. Gardner, *Cold Mountain Farm*, 23.

64. Davidson, *Real Property*, 282.

65. Rico Reed, 60s Communes Project interview, Sept. 10, 1996.

66. Glenn Lyons, 60s Communes Project interview, Mar. 20, 1996.

67. Bob Payne, "Hemorrhoids in Paradise," in *Home Comfort*, 188–205.

68. Yaswen, "Sunrise Hill Community," 17.

69. For the saga of a community that built several buildings, including massive log structures, of salvaged materials, see Jock Lauterer, *Hogwild: A Back-to-the-Land Saga* (N.p.: Appalachian Consortium Press, 1993).

70. H. Lawrence Lack, "The Fine Art of Trashmongering," *Mother Earth News*, Nov. 1970, 13.

71. Michael Weiss, *Living Together: A Year in the Life of a City Commune* (New York: McGraw-Hill, 1974), 93.

72. Diamond, *What the Trees Said*, 37–38.

73. Jon Trott, 60s Communes Project interview, Apr. 15, 1996.

74. Cat Yronwode, 60s Communes Project interview, May 29, 1996.

75. J. Gardner, *Cold Mountain Farm*, 23–24.

76. John R. Hall, *The Ways Out: Utopian Communal Groups in an Age of Babylon* (London: Routledge and Kegan Paul, 1978), 35.

77. Carolyn Adams Garcia, 60s Communes Project interview, July 15, 1996.

78. H. Gardner, *Children of Prosperity*, 218–19, 244.

79. Kat Kinkade, "Power and the Utopian Assumption," *Journal of Applied Behavioral Science* 10, no. 3 (July–Sept. 1974): 402–14.

80. Walter Rabideau, in "Why We Left the Farm," *Whole Earth Review* 49 (winter 1985): 64.

81. Lynette Long and Michael Traugot, "Kissing Tree Lodge," in Fike, *Voices from The Farm*, 40–42.

82. 60s Communes Project interview, 1996.

83. Veysey, *Communal Experience*, 300–302.

84. Fairfield, *Communes USA*, 180–85.

85. Richard Longstreet, 60s Communes Project interview, Sept. 7, 1996.

86. Robert Houriet, 60s Communes Project interview, Dec. 7, 1995.

87. Allen Cohen, 60s Communes Project interview, Mar. 25, 1996.

88. Rico Reed, 60s Communes Project interview, Sept. 10, 1996.

89. Kenoli Oleari, 60s Communes Project interview, Sept. 16, 1996.

8. THE PEOPLE OF THE COMMUNES

1. Paula Rayman, "The Commune Movement: The Need to Revolutionize," *WIN* 9, no. 37 (Dec. 6, 1973): 8–9.

2. See, for example, Louie Robinson, "Life Inside a Hippie Commune," *Ebony* 26 (Nov. 1970): 88–98. Robinson provides a profile of Toni Frazer, a black woman from the South Side of Chicago who graduated from the University of Chicago, married a white man, and moved with him to the AAA commune in southern Colorado.

3. Angela A. Aidala and Benjamin D. Zablocki, "The Communes of the 1970s: Who Joined and Why?" *Marriage and Family Review* 17 (1991): 92.

4. A section on Oyotunji Village is included in the CD-ROM *On Common Ground*, developed by Diana Eck and the Pluralism Project and available from Columbia Univ. Press. See also Melton, *Encyclopedia of American Religions*, 4th ed., 852–53.

5. See, for example, H. Gardner, *Children of Prosperity*, 240; Patrick W. Conover, "Communes and Intentional Communities," *Journal of Voluntary Action Research* 7, nos. 3–4 (summer–fall 1978): 6.

6. Aidala and Zablocki, "The Communes of the 1970s," 92.

7. Zablocki, *Alienation and Charisma*, 97.

8. "Home Free Home," 86.

9. Jezer, "How I Came Here," in *Home Comfort*, 37–38.

10. *January Thaw*, 148.

11. Paul "Coyote" Otto, 60s Communes Project interview, May 27, 1996.

12. Diamond, *What the Trees Said*, 60.

13. 60s Communes Project interview, 1995.

14. Sundancer, *Celery Wine*, 62.

15. Marlene Heck, 60s Communes Project interview, Apr. 18, 1995.

16. Jim Fowler, 60s Communes Project interview, Aug. 22, 1996.

17. Allen Cohen, 60s Communes Project interview, Mar. 25, 1996.

18. Herb Goldstein, 60s Communes Project interview, July 17, 1996.

19. "Lou Gottlieb on Motherhood, LSD, and Revolution," in Fairfield, *Modern Man in Search of Utopia*, 92.

20. Jerome, *Families of Eden*, 223–24.

21. Richard Marley, 60s Communes Project interview, Sept. 13, 1996.

22. Morgan Morgan, 60s Communes Project interview, Sept. 13, 1996.

23. 60s Communes Project interview, 1996.

24. Maida Tilchen, 60s Communes Project memoir, 1997.

25. Albert Bates, "The Farm: Tie Dyes in Cyberspace," in *Shared Visions, Shared Lives,* ed. Bill Metcalf (Forres, Scotland: Findhorn, 1996), 78–79.

26. Bill Wheeler, 60s Communes Project interview, Mar. 24, 1996; "Home Free Home," 22.

27. Lou Gottlieb and Ramón Sender, 60s Communes Project interview, Mar. 24, 1996.

28. Cat Yronwode, 60s Communes Project interview, May 29, 1996.

29. H. Gardner, *Children of Prosperity,* 119.

30. Marty Jerome, 60s Communes Project interview, Sept. 8, 1996.

31. Sterling F. Wheeler, "New Mexico: No Mecca for Hippies," *Christian Century* 87, no. 26 (July 1, 1970): 829.

32. William M. Kephart, "Why They Fail: A Socio-Historical Analysis of Religious and Secular Communes," *Journal of Comparative Family Studies* 5, no. 2 (autumn 1974): 132–33.

33. 60s Communes Project interview, 1996.

34. Rico Reed, 60s Communes Project interview, Sept. 10, 1996.

35. Jim Fowler, 60s Communes Project interview, Aug. 22, 1996.

36. Joyce Gardner, "From Cold Mountain to Warm Vermont," *Modern Utopian* 3, no. 2 (Nov. 1968–Jan. 1969): 2.

37. Allen Cohen, 60s Communes Project interview, Mar. 25, 1996.

38. Sundancer, *Celery Wine,* 82–83.

39. Matthew Israel, "Two Communal Houses and Why (I Think) They Failed," *Journal of Behavioral Technology* 1 (summer 1971): 7–17.

40. Patsy Sun (Richardson), "Meanwhile in Minnesota . . ." *WIN* 6, no. 7 (Apr. 15, 1970): 12.

41. Yaswen, "Sunrise Hill Community," 9–10.

42. Craig Blaker, 60s Communes Project interview, July 21, 1995.

43. Art Downing, 60s Communes Project interview, Mar. 22, 1996.

44. 60s Communes Project interview, 1996.

45. Bill Wheeler, in "Home Free Home," 113.

46. Zablocki, *Alienation and Charisma,* 82.

47. Rosabeth Moss Kanter, Dennis Jaffe, and D. Kelly Weisberg, "Coupling, Parenting, and the Presence of Others: Intimate Relationships in Communal Households," *Family Coordinator* 24, no. 4 (Oct. 1974): 437.

48. Zablocki, *Alienation and Charisma,* 82.

49. Allen Butcher and his mate left East Wind community under exactly those conditions; see Butcher, 60s Communes Project interview, Aug. 23, 1996.

50. Kenoli Oleari, 60s Communes Project interview, Sept. 16, 1996.

51. See, for example, "Kids in a Commune," *WIN* 10, no. 6 (Feb. 21, 1974): 14–15.

52. Saul V. Levine, Robert P. Carr, and Wendy Horenblas, "The Urban Commune: Fact or Fad, Promise or Pipedream?" *American Journal of Orthopsychiatry* 43, no. 1 (Jan. 1973): 156.

53. Charley M. Johnston and Robert W. Deisher, "Contemporary Communal Child Rearing: A First Analysis," *Pediatrics* 52, no. 3 (Sept. 1973): 323–24, 326.

54. John Rothchild and Susan Berns Wolf, *The Children of the Counterculture* (Garden City, N.Y.: Doubleday, 1976), 9.

55. Ibid., 191.

56. These are all actual names given to communal children. See David E. Smith and James Sternfield, "The Hippie Communal Movement: Effects of Child Birth and Development," *American Journal of Orthopsychiatry* 40, no. 3 (Apr. 1970): 528; Gravy, *Hog Farm and Friends,* 158; and Jim Fowler, 60s Communes Project interview, Aug. 22, 1996.

57. Sean Gaston, "Chaos and Community: Memories of a 'Wild Child,'" *Communities: Journal of Cooperative Living* 84 (fall 1994): 29.

58. 60s Communes Project interview, 1995.

59. On this matter see Bennett M. Berger and Bruce M. Hackett, "On the Decline of Age Grading in Rural Hippie Communes," *Journal of Social Issues* 30, no. 2 (1974): 163-83.

60. 60s Communes Project interview, 1996.

61. On this matter see Levine et al., "Urban Commune," 155-56.

62. J. Gardner, *Cold Mountain Farm*, 19.

63. Lou Gottlieb, 60s Communes Project interview, Mar. 23, 1996.

64. Kenoli Oleari, 60s Communes Project interview, Sept. 16, 1996.

65. For one poignant story of a baby's death following a home birth see "A New Mexico Road," in *Last Whole Earth Catalog* (Menlo Park, Calif.: Portola Institute, 1971), 244.

66. Stephen Walzer and Allen Cohen, *Childbirth Is Ecstasy* (Albion, Calif.: Aquarius, 1971).

67. Quoted in Coyote, *Sleeping Where I Fall*, 153.

68. Richard Marley, 60s Communes Project interview, Sept. 13, 1996.

69. A. Mark Durand, "The Safety of Home Birth: The Farm Study," *American Journal of Public Health* 82 (1992): 450-52. Reproduced on a Farm web page at www.thefarm.org/charities/mid.html.

70. Herb Goldstein, 60s Communes Project interview, July 17, 1996.

71. Albert Bates, 60s Communes Project interview, Oct. 11, 1996.

72. See, for example, Sundancer, *Celery Wine*, 84-85.

73. Rico Reed, lecture at Celebration of Community conference, Evergreen State College, Wash., Aug. 27, 1993.

74. "Nethers Community School," *Alternatives Newsmagazine* (1971): 19, 23.

75. See Michael S. Kaye, *The Teacher Was the Sea: The Story of Pacific High School* (New York: Links, 1972).

76. Quoted in John Humphrey Noyes, *History of American Socialisms* (New York: Hillary House, 1961 [1870]), 653-54.

77. Yaswen, "Sunrise Hill Community," 4-5.

78. Kinkade, *Is It Utopia Yet?* 25-26.

9. DOING IT: DAILY LIFE IN THE COMMUNES

1. Ed Schwartz, "Why Communes Fail," *Fusion*, Nov. 12, 1971, 20-25.

2. Marty Jezer, "Psychic Farming: The Organic Method," in *Home Comfort*, 132.

3. Houriet, "Life and Death," in Kanter, *Communes*, 475.

4. Susan Fisher, 60s Communes Project interview, Apr. 17, 1996.

5. Peter Rabbit, *Drop City* (New York: Olympia, 1971), 148.

6. Yaswen, "Sunrise Hill Community," 6.

7. The communal domes also inspired a wave of literature on dome-building. See, for example, *Domebook 2* (Bolinas, Calif.: Pacific Domes, 1971); "Libre: Building Your Own Dome," in *Last Whole Earth Catalog*, 207.

8. Dean Fleming, 60s Communes Project interview, May 28, 1996.

9. Diamond, *What the Trees Said*, 74.

10. 60s Communes Project interview, 1996.

11. Norman Toy, 60s Communes Project interview, Aug. 4, 1996.

12. Lichtenstein, "Communal Living," 89.

13. Fairfield, *Communes USA*, 53.

14. Goodwin, "Ken Kesey Movie," 29-30.

15. Houriet, "Life and Death," in Kanter, *Communes*, 479, 481-82.

16. Joyce Gardner, "Cold Mountain," *WIN* 4, no. 1 (Jan. 1, 1969): 27-28. Reprinted from *Modern Utopian*.

17. Gordon Adams, 60s Communes Project interview, Sept. 5, 1996.

18. Jezer, "The DRV," 13.

19. Herb Goldstein, 60s Communes Project interview, July 1, 1996.

20. See Horton, *Country Commune Cooking.*

21. Jerome, *Families of Eden,* 5.

22. Zicklin, *Countercultural Communes,* 39.

23. 60s Communes Project interview, 1996.

24. See *Lewd: The Inquisition of Seth and Carolyn* (Boston: Beacon, 1972).

25. Bob Sumner, 60s Communes Project interview, Jan. 5, 1996.

26. Herb Goldstein, 60s Communes Project interview, July 17, 1996.

27. Yaswen, "Sunrise Hill Community," 7.

28. J. Gardner, *Cold Mountain Farm,* 23.

29. Marlene Heck, 60s Communes Project interview, Apr. 18, 1995.

30. Verandah Porche, 60s Communes Project interview, Dec. 6, 1995.

31. Horton, *Country Commune Cooking,* 68, 13–14, 54.

32. Lucy Horton, quoted in Raymond A. Sokolov, "The Food at the Heart of Commune Life," *New York Times,* Dec. 2, 1971, 60.

33. Horton, *Country Commune Cooking,* 59.

34. Sokolov, "Food at the Heart of Commune Life," 60.

35. 60s Communes Project interview, 1996.

36. J. Gardner, *Cold Mountain Farm,* 26–27.

37. Rico Reed, 60s Communes Project interview, Sept. 10, 1996.

38. J. Gardner, *Cold Mountain Farm,* 35ff.

39. William Wheeler, in "Home Free Home," 62.

40. Smith and Rose, "Health Problems," 536.

41. Coyote, in "Home Free Home," 113.

42. Richard Marley, 60s Communes Project interview, Sept. 13, 1996.

43. Richard B. Seymour, *Compost College: Life on a Counterculture Commune* (Walnut Creek, Calif.: Devil Mountain, 1997), 115.

44. Owens, *Assault on Eden,* 65, 66.

45. Zablocki, *Alienation and Charisma,* 115–16.

46. Yaswen, "Sunrise Hill Community," 12.

47. 25 to 6 Baking and Trucking Society, *Great Gay in the Morning! One Group's Approach to Communal Living and Sexual Politics* (Washington, N.J.: Times Change, 1972), 92.

48. Maitland Zane, "Living Together in California," *Nation* 211, no. 12 (Oct. 19, 1970): 363.

49. Richard Marley, 60s Communes Project interview, Sept. 13, 1996.

50. Charles Gruber, 60s Communes Project interview, Nov. 15, 1995.

51. Friar Tuck, quoted in "Home Free Home," 53–54.

52. For an elaboration of the idea that psychedelic use fostered communitarianism see Stanley Krippner and Don Fersh, "Mystic Communes," *Modern Utopian* 4, no. 2 (spring 1970): unpaginated.

53. For a glimpse of the activities of the Brotherhood of Eternal Love, see Leary, *Flashbacks,* 264–67.

54. Some communitarians argued that the problem with some "drugs" was that they were refined and thus had lost their native clarity; plain opium or coca leaves, for example, might be useful forms of "dope," but heroin and cocaine were destructive "drugs." See "Lou Gottlieb on Motherhood, LSD, and Revolution," 90.

55. See, for example, Levine et al., "Urban Commune," 153.

56. Susan Fisher, 60s Communes Project interview, Apr. 17, 1996.

57. Zablocki, *Alienation and Charisma,* 116–19.

58. 60s Communes Project interview, 1996.

59. 60s Communes Project interview, 1995.

60. Noelle Barton, 60s Communes Project interview, Sept. 15, 1996.

61. Huw Williams, 60s Communes Project interview, Sept. 9, 1996; Cat Yronwode, 60s Communes Project interview, May 29, 1996.

62. Glenn Lyons, 60s Communes Project interview, Mar. 20, 1996.

63. George Hurd, 60s Communes Project interview, May 31, 1996.

64. Robert Houriet, 60s Communes Project interview, Dec. 7, 1996.

65. Ayala Talpai, 60s Communes Project interview, July 19, 1995.

66. Verandah Porche, "The Making of a Culture Counter," in *Home Comfort,* 81.

67. Bruce Taub, personal communication, 1997.

68. J. Gardner, *Cold Mountain Farm,* 10.

69. Maida Tilchen, 60s Communes Project memoir, 1997.

70. Verandah Porche, "Give Me the Willies," in *Home Comfort,* 170.

71. *January Thaw,* 124–27.

72. Bruce Taub, personal communication, 1997.

73. Jerome, *Families of Eden,* 243.

74. Coyote, *Sleeping Where I Fall,* 139.

75. Richard Wizansky, "Who's in Charge," in *Home Comfort,* 72, 74.

76. 60s Communes Project interview, 1996.

77. Kenoli Oleari, 60s Communes Project interview, Sept. 16, 1996.

78. Yaswen, "Sunrise Hill Community," 23.

79. Rico Reed, lecture at Celebration of Community conference, Evergreen State College, Wash., Aug. 27, 1993.

80. Yaswen, "Sunrise Hill Community," 22.

81. "We Change the Clock," *Leaves of Twin Oaks* 4 (Jan. 1968), as reprinted in *Journal of a Walden Two Commune,* vol. 1, 33.

82. Kit Leder, "Women in Communes," *WIN* 6, no. 5 (Mar. 15, 1970): 14–16. Originally published in *Women: A Journal of Liberation.*

83. *January Thaw,* 26.

84. Ibid., 38–39.

85. Coyote, *Sleeping Where I Fall,* 132.

86. Levine et al., "Urban Commune," 156.

87. Marilyn Foster et al., "How We Live as Toads," *Women: A Journal of Liberation* 2, no. 2 (1970): 45.

88. Wagner, "Sex Roles in American Communal Utopias," *Sex Roles in Contemporary American Communes,* 36.

89. See, for example, Roger C. Palms, *The Jesus Kids* (Valley Forge, Pa.: Judson, 1971), 39.

90. Joe Roos, 60s Communes Project interview, Oct. 23, 1996.

91. Ina May Gaskin, 60s Communes Project interview, Oct. 18, 1995.

92. Richard Longstreet, 60s Communes Project interview, Sept. 7, 1996.

93. Adam Read, 60s Communes Project interview, 1996.

94. For a description of the breadth of psychic and occult practices in communes see Stanley Krippner and Don Fersh, "Psychic Happenings in Hippie Communes," *Psychic* 3, no. 2 (Sept.–Oct. 1971): 40–45.

95. Art Downing, 60s Communes Project interview, Mar. 22, 1996.

96. Yaswen, "Sunrise Hill Community," 14.

97. Bill Wheeler, 60s Communes Project interview, Mar. 24, 1996.

98. Horton, *Country Commune Cooking,* 50.

99. For a description of a festive communal wedding see Sundancer, *Celery Wine,* 130–34.

100. Houriet, "Life and Death of a Commune Called Oz," 477.

101. Martha Hanna Towle, *A History of Franklin: Past and Present, Fact or Fancy, Legend or Folksay, 1789–1989* (Franklin, Vt.: Franklin Historical Society, 1989), 167.

102. 60s Communes Project interview, 1996.

103. Art Downing, 60s Communes Project interview, Mar. 22, 1996.

104. Jim Fowler, 60s Communes Project interview, Aug. 22, 1996.

105. Maida Tilchen, 60s Communes Project memoir, 1997.

106. In a few cases residents smuggled television sets onto communal premises in violation of a general ban on the medium. For one such story see "Burgeoning of Real Goods," 8–9.

107. Smith and Sternfield, "Hippie Communal Movement," 529.

108. Rico Reed, 60s Communes Project interview, Sept. 10, 1996.

109. Glenn Lyons, 60s Communes Project interview, Mar. 20, 1996.

110. Kleps, *Millbrook,* 295–96.

111. Jon Trott, 60s Communes Project interview, Apr. 15, 1996.

112. Patsy Richardson, "Freefolk," *Modern Utopian* 4, no. 1 (winter 1969–70): unpaginated.

113. "Springtree," *Alternatives Newsmagazine* 3 (summer 1972): 41.

114. 60s Communes Project interview, 1996.

115. Lou Gottlieb, 60s Communes Project interview, Mar. 23, 1996.

116. Paul Heavens, from the internet at www.safegate.com/~heavens.

117. Gordon Adams, 60s Communes Project interview, Sept. 5, 1996.

118. Huw Williams, 60s Communes Project interview, Sept. 9, 1996.

119. Jon Trott, 60s Communes Project interview, Apr. 15, 1996.

120. Joyce Gardner, "Cold Mountain," *WIN* 4, no. 1 (Jan. 1, 1969): 26.

121. Acharya Palaniswami, 60s Communes Project interview, July 7, 1997.

122. Jezer, "The DRV," 13.

123. Diana Young, 60s Communes Project interview, Aug. 7, 1996.

124. "Hippie-Type Group Banned from Immorality in Camp," *New York Times,* Aug. 20, 1968, 83.

125. "Nantucket's Voters Adopt Rules to Discourage Influx of Youths," *New York Times,* Nov. 7, 1970, 56.

126. J. Gardner, *Cold Mountain Farm,* 40.

127. See Jonathan Shor, "All in the 'Family': Legal Problems of Communes," *Harvard Civil Rights/Civil Liberties Law Review* 7, no. 2 (Mar. 1972): 393–441; Lee Goldstein, *Communes, Law and Commonsense: A Legal Manual for Communities* (Boston: New Community Projects, 1974).

128. "Commune Thrives on Million-Dollar Income," *New York Times,* May 18, 1977, A16.

129. Steven V. Roberts, "Coast's Hippies Yearn for Simple Life," *New York Times,* Aug. 2, 1969, 52.

130. Marty Jerome, 60s Communes Project interview, Sept. 8, 1996.

131. Barry Laffan, *Communal Organization and Social Transition: A Case Study from the Counterculture of the Sixties and Seventies* (New York: Peter Lang, 1997), 210.

132. Jon Stewart, "Communes in Taos," in *Conversations with the New Reality,* 210.

133. These events and many more are recounted by Stewart, "Communes in Taos," 207–8; Hedgepeth and Stock, *The Alternative,* 72.

134. Fairfield, *Communes USA,* 323–25.

135. Stanley Krippner and Don Fersh, "Paranormal Experience Among Members of American Contra-Cultural Groups," *Journal of Psychedelic Drugs* 3, no. 1 (Sept. 1970): 112; Krippner and Fersh, "Psychic Happenings in Hippie Communes," 43.

136. "A New Mexico Road," in *Last Whole Earth Catalog,* 244.

137. "Four in New Mexico Charged in Death of Bronx Man, 25," *New York Times,* Aug.

13, 1970, 20; Dean Stillman, "Commune Murder Case," *Berkeley Barb,* Sept. 22–28, 1972, 13.

138. 60s Communes Project interview, 1996.

IO. MOVING ON

1. Richardson, "Meanwhile in Minnesota . . . ," 12.

2. Robert Houriet, 60s Communes Project interview, Dec. 7, 1995.

3. Steward Brand, "The Commune Lie," in *Last Whole Earth Catalog,* 181.

4. Charles Gruber, 60s Communes Project interview, Nov. 15, 1995.

5. Rosabeth Moss Kanter, "Getting It All Together: Some Group Issues in Communes," *American Journal of Orthopsychiatry* 42, no. 4 (July 1972): 642–43.

6. *Communities Directory* (1995), 190–209.

7. H. Gardner, *Children of Prosperity,* 244.

8. Jim Fowler, 60s Communes Project interview, Aug. 22, 1996.

9. Albert Bates, 60s Communes Project interview, Oct. 11, 1996.

10. A *Boston Globe* writer had a fairly typical experience when she decided to write about communal survival in the 1980s and had a hard time getting those who knew of ongoing communal life to tell her how to find even one commune. She hit many closed doors before she finally began to find communes that would let her visit. See Susan Trausch, "Where Have All the Flower Children Gone?" *Boston Globe Magazine,* Aug. 2, 1987, 48.

11. On the early Earth People's Park agitation see Houriet, *Getting Back Together,* 143–46.

12. For a sample appeal for funds see "Earth People's Park Statement," *WIN* 6, no. 4 (Mar. 1970): 13–14. For a description of the party on the land see Gravy, *Hog Farm and Friends,* 136–43.

13. Gravy, *Something Good for a Change,* 166.

14. John Larrabee, "Marijuana Raid Uproots Park, '60s Way of Life," *USA Today,* Nov. 23, 1990, 8A.

15. John Teare, "Incremental Nibbling in the Big Woods," *Wilderness* 57, no. 205 (summer 1994): 18.

16. Wavy Gravy, 60s Communes Project interview, Sept. 17, 1996.

17. Verandah Porche, 60s Communes Project interview, Dec. 6, 1995.

18. Ina May Gaskin, 60s Communes Project interview, Oct. 18, 1995.

19. Gravy, *Something Good for a Change,* 114.

20. Caroline Estes, 60s Communes Project interview, July 18, 1995.

21. Laird Schaub, 60s Communes Project interview, Oct. 7, 1995.

22. Shannon Perry, 60s Communes Project interview, Mar. 25, 1997.

23. Robert Houriet, 60s Communes Project interview, Dec. 7, 1995.

24. Dennis Duermeier, 60s Communes Project interview, Oct. 12, 1995.

25. Jim Fowler, 60s Communes Project interview, Aug. 22, 1996.

26. Jenny Upton, 60s Communes Project interview, July 14, 1996.

27. Marlene Heck, 60s Communes Project interview, Apr. 18, 1995.

28. Robert Houriet, 60s Communes Project interview, Dec. 7, 1995.

29. John Curl, personal communication, 1991.

30. Berger and Hackett, "On the Decline of Age Grading," 182.

31. Lucy Horton, 60s Communes Project interview, June 25, 1996.

32. Dean Fleming, quoted in David Perkins, "Commune," *Spirit: Rocky Mountain Southwest* 9, no. 1 (spring/summer 1996): 39.

33. J. Gardner, *Cold Mountain Farm,* 51–52.

34. See "Burgeoning of Real Goods."

35. Howard Lieberman, "Epilogue," in Laffan, *Communal Organization and Social Transition,* 281.

36. Rico Reed, 60s Communes Project interview, Sept. 10, 1996.

37. Gene Bernofsky, personal communication, May 1999.

38. Gottlieb, manuscript autobiography, 244.

39. Ina May Gaskin, 60s Communes Project interview, Oct. 18, 1995.

40. Robert Houriet, 60s Communes Project interview, Dec. 7, 1995.

41. Stewart Brand, "We Owe It All to the Hippies," *Time* (special issue), spring 1995, 54–56.

42. Peggy Abbott-Hathaway, quoted in Perkins, "Commune," 38.

43. Dan Questenberry, 60s Communes Project interview, July 14, 1996.

44. *Whirling Rainbow News* merged with the all-ages *FarmNet News* in 1996; the combined publication, now called *Farm Net News,* was edited by Anderson in the late 1990s.

45. Sylvia Anderson, 60s Communes Project interview, Aug. 3, 1996.

46. Verandah Porche, 60s Communes Project interview, Dec. 6, 1995.

47. Angela A. Aidala, "Communes and Changing Family Norms," *Journal of Family Issues* 10, no. 3 (Sept. 1989): 311–38.

48. On cohousing see Kathryn McCamant, Charles Durrett, and Ellen Hertzman, *Cohousing: A Contemporary Approach to Housing Ourselves,* 2nd ed. (Berkeley, Calif.: Ten Speed, 1994).

49. Huw "Piper" Williams, 60s Communes Project interview, Sept. 9, 1996.

50. Dragonwagon, *Commune Cookbook,* 186.

51. Jerry Garcia, quoted in Piper, "Some Lives and Times," 36.

Selected Bibliography

This bibliography lists only a few of the works cited in the foregoing pages. It attempts to list the important survey works on American communitarianism during the 1960s era as well as the most useful books and articles on the major communes covered in this volume. For many more citations see the endnotes.

Adams, Patch, with Maureen Mylander. *Gesundheit! Bringing Good Health to You, the Medical System, and Society through Physician Service, Complementary Therapies, Humor, and Joy.* Rochester, Vt.: Healing Arts, 1993.

Aidala, Angela A., and Benjamin D. Zablocki. "The Communes of the 1970s: Who Joined and Why?" *Marriage and Family Review* 17 (1991): 87–116.

Berger, Bennett M. *The Survival of a Counterculture: Ideological Work and Everyday Life Among Rural Communards.* Berkeley: Univ. of California Press, 1981.

Borowski, Karol. *Attempting an Alternative Society: A Sociological Study of a Selected Communal-Revitalization Movement in the United States.* Norwood, Pa.: Norwood Editions, 1984.

Conover, Patrick W. "Communes and Intentional Communities." *Journal of Voluntary Action Research* 7 (summer–fall 1978): 5–17.

Coyote, Peter. *Sleeping Where I Fall: A Chronicle.* Washington, D.C.: Counterpoint, 1998.

Davidson, Sara. "Open Land: Getting Back to the Communal Garden." *Harper's* 240 (June 1970): 91–100.

Diamond, Stephen. *What the Trees Said: Life on a New Age Farm.* New York: Dell, 1971.

Dragonwagon, Crescent. *The Commune Cookbook.* New York: Simon and Schuster, 1972.

Fairfield, Richard [Dick]. *Communes USA: A Personal Tour.* Baltimore: Penguin, 1972.

——. *The Modern Utopian: Communes, U.S.A.* San Francisco: Alternatives Foundation, 1971.

——, ed. *Modern Man in Search of Utopia.* San Francisco: Alternatives Foundation, 1971.

——, ed. *Utopia USA.* San Francisco: Alternatives Foundation, 1972.

Fike, Rupert, ed. *Voices from The Farm: Adventures in Community Living.* Summertown, Tenn.: Book Publishing Co., 1998.

Freundlich, Paul, Chris Collins, and Mikki Wenig, eds. *A Guide to Cooperative Alternatives.* New Haven, Conn., and Louisa, Va.: Community Publications Cooperative, 1979.

Gardner, Hugh. *The Children of Prosperity: Thirteen Modern American Communes.* New York: St. Martin's, 1978.

Gardner, Joyce. *Cold Mountain Farm: An Attempt at Community.* N.p., 1970.

[Gaskin], Stephen, and the Farm. *Hey Beatnik! This Is the Farm Book.* Summertown, Tenn.: Book Publishing Co., 1974.

Gravy, Wavy. *The Hog Farm and Friends.* New York: Links, 1974.

——. *Something Good for a Change: Random Notes on Peace through Living.* New York: St. Martin's, 1992.

Gustaitis, Rasa. *Turning On.* London: Weidenfeld and Nicolson, 1969.

Hall, John R. *The Ways Out: Utopian Communal Groups in an Age of Babylon.* London: Routledge and Kegan Paul, 1978.

Hedgepeth, William, and Dennis Stock. *The Alternative: Communal Life in New America.* New York: Macmillan, 1970.

Home Comfort: Stories and Scenes of Life on Total Loss Farm. Edited by Richard Wizansky. New York: Saturday Review Press, 1973.

"Home Free Home: The Story of Two Open-Door Sixties Communes, Morning Star and Wheeler's Ranch, as Told by Various Residents." Edited by Ramón Sender Barayón. Manuscript; a copy is at the library of the University of California, Riverside.

Horton, Lucy. *Country Commune Cooking.* New York: Coward, McCann and Geoghegan, 1972.

Houriet, Robert. *Getting Back Together.* New York: Avon, 1971.

Jackson, Dave and Neta. *Living Together in a World Falling Apart.* Carol Stream, Ill.: Creation House, 1974.

January Thaw: People at Blue Mt. Ranch Write About Living Together in the Mountains. New York: Times Change, 1974.

Jerome, Judson. *Families of Eden: Communes and the New Anarchism.* New York: Seabury, 1974.

Johnston, Charley M., and Robert W. Deisher. "Contemporary Communal Child Rearing: A First Analysis." *Pediatrics* 52, no. 3 (Sept. 1973): 319–26.

Kagan, Paul. *New World Utopias: A Photographic History of the Search for Community.* New York: Penguin, 1975.

Kanter, Rosabeth Moss. *Commitment and Community: Communes and Utopias in Sociological Perspective.* Cambridge, Mass.: Harvard Univ. Press, 1972.

———. "Communes in Cities." *Working Papers for a New Society* (summer 1974): 36–44.

———, ed. *Communes: Creating and Managing the Collective Life.* New York: Harper and Row, 1973.

Katz, Elia. *Armed Love.* New York: Bantam, 1971.

Kephart, William M. "Why They Fail: A Socio-Historical Analysis of Religious and Secular Communes." *Journal of Comparative Family Studies* 5 (autumn 1974): 130–41.

Kinkade, Kat. *Is It Utopia Yet? An Insider's View of Twin Oaks Community in Its 26th Year.* [Louisa, Va.]: Twin Oaks Publishing, 1994.

———. *A Walden Two Experiment: The First Five Years of Twin Oaks Community.* New York: William Morrow, 1973.

Kleps, Art. *Millbrook: The True Story of the Early Years of the Psychedelic Revolution.* Oakland, Calif.: Bench Press, 1977.

Komar, Ingrid. *Living the Dream: A Documentary Study of Twin Oaks Community.* Norwood, Pa.: Norwood Editions, 1983.

Kopkind, Andrew. "Up the Country: Five Communes in Vermont." *Working Papers for a New Society* 1 (1973): 44–49.

Krippner, Stanley, and Don Fersh. "Mystic Communes." *Modern Utopian* 4 (spring 1970): unpaginated.

Kriyananda (Donald Walters). *Cooperative Communities—How to Start Them, and Why.* Nevada City, Calif.: Ananda, 1968 (with many subsequent editions).

Laffan, Barry. *Communal Organization and Social Transition: A Case Study from the Counterculture of the Sixties and Seventies.* New York: Peter Lang, 1997.

Laurel, Alicia Bay. *Living on the Earth.* New York: Random House, 1971 [1970].

Leder, Kit. "Women in Communes." *WIN* 6 (Mar. 15, 1970): 14–16. Originally published in *Women: A Journal of Liberation.*

Lee, Martin A., and Bruce Shlain. *Acid Dreams: The CIA, LSD and the Sixties Rebellion.* New York: Grove, 1985.

Levine, Saul V., Robert P. Carr, and Wendy Horenblas. "The Urban Commune: Fact or

Fad, Promise or Pipedream?" *American Journal of Orthopsychiatry* 43 (Jan. 1973): 149–63.

Melville, Keith. *Communes in the Counter Culture: Origins, Theories, Styles of Life.* New York: Morrow, 1972.

Metcalf, Bill, ed. *Shared Visions, Shared Lives.* Forres, Scotland: Findhorn, 1996.

Mungo, Raymond. *Famous Long Ago: My Life and Hard Times with Liberation News Service.* Boston: Beacon, 1970.

———. *Total Loss Farm: A Year in the Life.* New York: Bantam, 1971 [1970].

Neusner, Jacob, ed. *Contemporary Judaic Fellowship in Theory and Practice.* New York: Ktav, 1972.

Perkins, David. "Commune." *Spirit Magazine: Rocky Mountain Southwest* 9 (spring/summer 1996): 12–15, 36–39.

Perry, Paul. *On the Bus: The Complete Guide to the Legendary Trip of Ken Kesey and the Merry Pranksters and the Birth of the Counterculture.* New York: Thunder's Mouth, 1990.

Popenoe, Cris, and Oliver Popenoe. *Seeds of Tomorrow: New Age Communities That Work.* San Francisco: Harper and Row, 1984.

Raimy, Eric. *Shared Houses, Shared Lives: The New Extended Families and How They Work.* Los Angeles: Tarcher, 1979.

Rawlinson, Andrew. *The Book of Enlightened Masters: Western Teachers in Eastern Traditions.* Chicago: Open Court, 1997.

Richard, Jerry, ed. *The Good Life.* New York: New American Library, 1973.

Roberts, Ron E. *The New Communes: Coming Together in America.* Englewood Cliffs, N.J.: Prentice-Hall, 1971.

Rothchild, John, and Susan Berns Wolf. *The Children of the Counterculture.* Garden City, N.Y.: Doubleday, 1976.

Sperber, Mae T. *Search for Utopia: A Study of Twentieth Century Communes in America.* Middleboro, Mass.: Country, 1976.

Stevens, Jay. *Storming Heaven: LSD and the American Dream.* New York: Harper and Row, 1987.

Sundancer, Elaine [Elaine Zablocki]. *Celery Wine: The Story of a Country Commune.* Yellow Springs, Ohio: Community Publications Cooperative, 1973.

Traugot, Michael. *A Short History of the Farm.* Summertown, Tenn.: The author, 1994.

Tworkov, Helen. *Zen in America.* New York: Kodansha International, 1994.

Wagner, Jon, ed. *Sex Roles in Contemporary American Communes.* Bloomington: Indiana Univ. Press, 1982.

Ward, Hiley H. *The Far-Out Saints of the Jesus Communes.* New York: Association Press, 1972.

Yaswen, Gordon. "Sunrise Hill Community: Post-Mortem." 2nd ed. 1970. Mimeographed essay, available from the author at 740 First St., Sebastopol, Calif., 95472. An abridged version is in *The Good Life,* ed. Richard, 140–72.

Zablocki, Benjamin. *Alienation and Charisma: A Study of Contemporary American Communes.* New York: Free Press/Macmillan, 1980.

Zicklin, Gilbert. *Countercultural Communes: A Sociological Perspective.* Westport, Conn.: Greenwood, 1983.

Index

The 60s Communes: Hippies and Beyond was composed in 9.7/13.5 ITC Galliard in QuarkXPress 4.04 on a Macintosh by Kachergis Book Design; printed by sheet-fed offset on 50-pound Turin Book Natural and Smyth-sewn and bound over binder boards in Arrestox B-grade cloth, and notch-bound with paper covers printed in 5 colors by Quinn-Woodbine of Woodbine, New Jersey; designed by Kachergis Book Design of Pittsboro, North Carolina; published by Syracuse University Press, Syracuse, New York 13244-5160.